🛏 Accommodation ⟩197

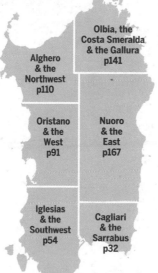

Olbia, the
Costa Smeralda
& the Gallura
p141

Alghero
& the
Northwest
p110

Oristano
& the
West
p91

Nuoro
& the
East
p167

Iglesias
& the
Southwest
p54

Cagliari
& the
Sarrabus
p32

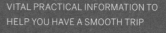

Language

THIS EDITION WRITTEN AND RESEARCHED BY

Kerry Christiani,
Vesna Maric

welcome to
Sardinia

Captivating Coastlines

Believe the hype: Sardinia has some of the most dreamy and dramatic beaches you'll find without stepping off European shores. Many think the glossy brochure images of too-blue-to-be-true seas and blindingly white sands are digitally enhanced, but when they actually arrive they realise: the pictures barely do them justice. Picture yourself dropping anchor in Costa Smeralda's scalloped bays, where film stars and supermodels frolic in emerald waters; going castaway on the Golfo di Orosei's coves, where sheer cliffs ensure seclusion; or sailing to La Maddalena's cluster of granite islands. Whether you're seeking seclusion in the dunes on the wave-lashed Costa Verde or lounging on the Costa del Sud's silky smooth bays – unroll your beach towel and you'll never want to leave, we swear.

Outdoor Adventure

Teasing you away from that same beach towel are Sardinia's mountains and forests, gorges and caves, coastal paths and downhill trails. Hike through the lush, silent interior to the twilight of Tiscali's nuraghic ruins; along vertiginous cliff tops fragrant with juniper and myrtle to the crescent-shaped Cala Luna; through holm oak forests to the boulder-strewn Gola Su Gorropu, hailed as Europe's Grand Canyon. Not enough action for you? Why not join the climbers on Cala Gonone's sea-facing limestone crags, the

This is an island where coastal drives thrill, prehistory puzzles and sheep (four million of them) rule the roads. Sardinia captivates with its wild interior, dazzling beaches and endearing eccentricities.

(left) Relaxing on the brilliant waters of Cala Mariolu (p190)
(below) Streetside dining in Bosa (p101)

horse riders cantering through pinewoods in Arborea, or the mountain bikers blazing down centuries-old mule trails in Ogliastra. The sea's allure is irresistible to windsurfers on the north coast, while divers wax lyrical about shipwrecks off Cagliari's coast, the underwater Nereo Cave and Nora's submerged Roman ruins. Whether you go slow or fast, choose coast or country, Sardinia is one of Europe's last great island adventures.

Island of Idiosyncrasies

As DH Lawrence so succinctly put it: 'Sardinia is different.' Indeed, where else but here can you go from near-alpine forests to cathedral-like grottoes, or from rolling vineyards to one-time bandit towns in the space of a day? This is the island of 7000 *nuraghi,* the puzzling Bronze Age towers and settlements where you can piece together prehistory. Only here will you find culinary curiosities like sea urchins and anemones, donkey sausages and – if you're determined – *casu marzu* (maggoty pecorino). Sardinia is also a refuge for wildlife oddities like the *asini bianchi* (albino donkeys) on Isola dell'Asinara and the wild horses that roam Giara di Gesturi plateau. And it's an island of fabulously eccentric festivals, from Barbagia's carnival parade of ghoulish *mamuthones,* said to banish winter demons, to the death-defying S'Ardia horse race in Sedilo. History and heritage, food and countryside – in every way we can think of Sardinia *is* different, and all the more loveable for it.

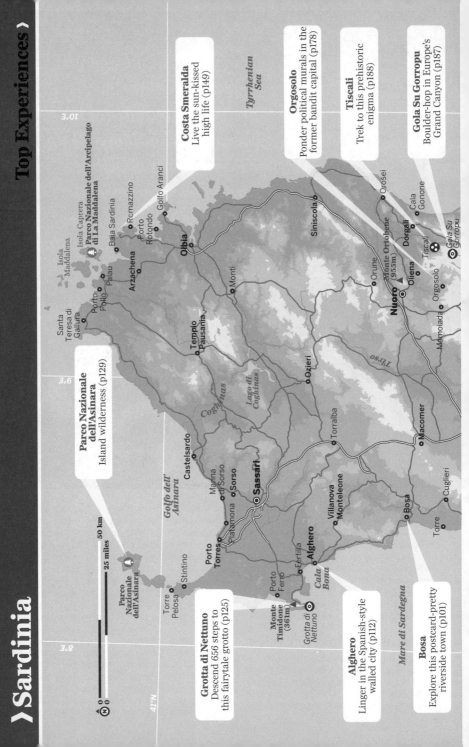

› Sardinia

Top Experiences ›

Parco Nazionale dell'Asinara
Island wilderness (p129)

Grotta di Nettuno
Descend 656 steps to this fairytale grotto (p125)

Alghero
Linger in the Spanish-style walled city (p112)

Bosa
Explore this postcard-pretty riverside town (p101)

Costa Smeralda
Live the sun-kissed high life (p149)

Orgosolo
Ponder political murals in the former bandit capital (p178)

Tiscali
Trek to this prehistoric enigma (p188)

Gola Su Gorropu
Boulder-hop in Europe's Grand Canyon (p187)

0 50 km
0 25 miles

Tyrrhenian Sea

Mare di Sardegna

Golfo dell'Asinara

Parco Nazionale dell'Asinara

Torre Pelosa
Stintino
Porto Torres
Platamona
Marina di Sorso
Castelsardo

Santa Teresa di Gallura
Porto Pollo
Palau
Porto Cervo
Isola Maddalena
Isola Caprera
Parco Nazionale dell'Arcipelago di La Maddalena
Baia Sardinia
Arzachena
Porto Rotondo
Romazzino
Golfo Aranci

Olbia

Monti

Tempio Pausania

Coghinas

Lago di Coghinas

Ozieri

Sassari
Sorso
Fertilia
Alghero
Porto Ferro
Cala Bona
Monte Timidone (361m)
Grotta di Nettuno

Villanova Monteleone

Torralba

Bosa
Torre

Cuglieri

Macomer

TIRSO

Siniscola

Orosei
Cala Gonone
Gola Su Gorropu

Dorgali
Tiscali
Oliena
Orgosolo
Monte Ortobene (955m)
Nuoro
Orune

Marnoiada

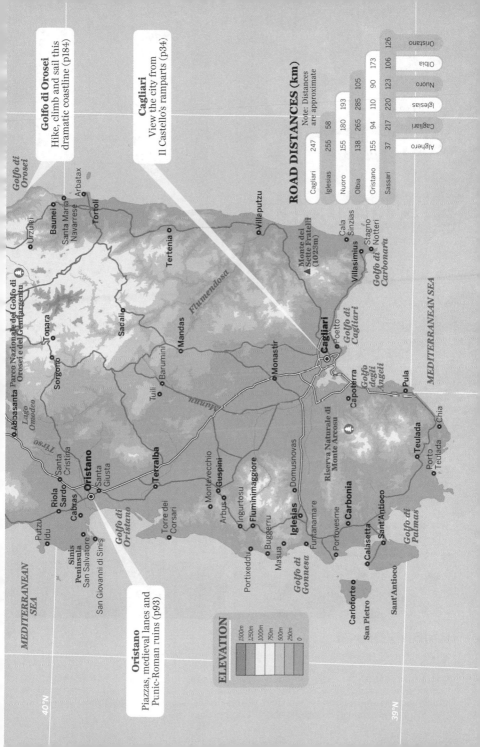

Golfo di Orosei
Hike, climb and sail this dramatic coastline (p184)

Cagliari
View the city from Il Castello's ramparts (p34)

Oristano
Piazzas, medieval lanes and Punic-Roman ruins (p93)

ROAD DISTANCES (km)
Note: Distances are approximate

	Cagliari	Iglesias	Nuoro	Olbia	Oristano	Sassari
Cagliari	247					
Iglesias	255	58				
Nuoro	155	180	193			
Olbia	138	265	285	105		
Oristano	155	94	110	90	123	
Sassari	37	217	220	106	173	126

MEDITERRANEAN SEA

Golfo di Orosei

Urzulei
Baunei
Santa Maria
Navarrese
Arbatax
Tortolì

Tertenia

Villaputzu

Tonara
Sorgono
Sacali
Mandas
Barumini
Tuili
Monastir

Parco Nazionale del Golfo di Orosei e del Gennargentu
Abbasanta
Lago Omodeo
Lago O-ru-50

Riola Sardo
Cabras
Santa Cristina
Santa Giusta
Oristano

Terralba

Torre dei Corsari

Montevecchio
Arbus
Ingurtosu
Fluminimaggiore
Buggerru
Masua
Iglesias
Domusnovas
Portixeddu

Riserva Naturale di Monte Arcosu

Carbonia

Funtanamare
Portovesme
Calasetta
Sant'Antioco
Sant'Antioco

Golfo di Gonnesa

Golfo di Palmas

Carloforte
San Pietro

Sinis Peninsula
San Salvatore
San Giovanni di Sinis
Putzu Idu

Golfo di Oristano

Monte dei
Sette Fratelli
(1023m)
Cala Sinzias
Villasimius
Stagno di Notteri
Golfo di Carbonara

Flumendosa

Flumini

Tirso

Cagliari
Poetto
Golfo di Cagliari

Capoterra
Golfo degli Angeli
Pula

Teulada
Porto Teulada
Chia

MEDITERRANEAN SEA

ELEVATION

1500m
1250m
1000m
750m
500m
250m
0

40°N

39°N

15 TOP EXPERIENCES

Golfo di Orosei

1 We can wax lyrical about sparkling aquamarine waters, sugar-white sands and sheer limestone cliffs but, trust us, seeing is believing when it comes to the Golfo di Orosei (p184). Where the mountains collide spectacularly with the sea, this huge, sweeping crescent forms the seaward section of the Parco Nazionale del Golfo di Orosei e del Gennargentu. Set your spirits soaring by hiking its cliff-top trails, exploring its sea grottoes in a kayak, or boating along the gulf to hidden coves – each more mind-blowingly beautiful than the last. Cala Goloritzè, Golfo di Orosei, above

7

Gola Su Gorropu

2 The first glimpse of Gola Su Gorropu (p187) on the scenic hike down from the Genna 'e Silana pass is mesmerising. Dubbed Europe's Grand Canyon, this mighty ravine is for explorers, with 400m-high rock walls and enormous boulders scattered like giant's marbles. At its narrowest point – just four metres wide – the gorge seems to swallow you up, blocking out the sun and silencing the world outside. Were it not for the occasional fellow trekker or climber, the chasm would have the eerie effect of seeming totally lost in time and space.

Costa Smeralda

3 Believe the hype: the Costa Smeralda (p149) is stunning. Here the Gallura's wind-whipped granite mountains tumble down to fjordlike inlets, and an emerald sea fringes a coast strung with bays like Capriccioli, Cala di Volpe and the Aga Khan's favourite, Spiaggia del Principe. Play paparazzi, eyeing up the megayachts in the millionaire's playground of Porto Cervo (p149), or eschew the high life to seek out secluded coves where the views are simply priceless. Porto Cervo, above

Il Castello, Cagliari

4 Perched on a rocky peak, Cagliari's Il Castello (p35) is never more captivating than at dusk on a warm summer's evening. As the softening light paints the sky purple-pink, the citadel's ramparts, palazzi and Pisan towers glow gold. Capture the moment by heading to the laid-back terrace of Caffè degli Spiriti (p47) or Caffè Librarium Nostrum (p47), where sundowners are served with dress-circle views of the city illuminated.

Nuraghi & Tombe dei Giganti

5 Defensive watchtowers, sacred ritual sites...the exact purpose of Sardinia's 7000 *nuraghi* is unknown. Yet the Bronze Age past is still tangible within the semicircular walls of these stone towers and fortified settlements. Most famous and best preserved is the bee-hive complex of Nuraghe Su Nuraxi (p81), a Unesco World Heritage site. Equally mysterious are the island's *tombe dei giganti* (giants' tombs), megalithic mass graves sealed off by stone stele. Coddu Ecchju (p153) is a fine example.

Orgosolo

6 Social commentary, politics, end-of-the-world prophecy – all are writ large on the shabby exteriors of houses and cafes in Orgosolo (p178). Once a byword for banditry, today Orgosolo is an enormous canvas for some of the most emotionally charged graffiti you'll ever see. Wandering along the Corso Repubblica, vivid murals recall the big events of the 20th and 21st centuries, from the creation of the atomic bomb to the fall of Baghdad; events that seem a million miles away from this small village in the heart of the tough, mountainous Barbagia.

Alghero

7 To see Alghero (p112) at its most atmospheric, come in the early evening when crowds fill its maze of dark, medieval lanes and people-watch from the grand cafe terraces on Piazza Civica. Tables are set up along the honey-coloured ramparts, softly lit by lanterns, for alfresco dining with uninterrupted views of the sea and stars. Never mind the expense, you must try Alghero's famous *aragosta alla catalana* (lobster with tomato and onion), a lingering taste of the city's past as a Catalan colony.

Bosa

8 Like many great works of art, Bosa (p101) is best admired from afar. From a distance you can take in the whole picture: the elegant houses in a fresco painter's palette of colours, the fishing boats bobbing on the Fiume Temo, the medieval castle pasted onto a steep hillside. Linger until evening to see one of Sardinia's prettiest towns without the crowds, walking its narrow alleyways and stopping to sample some of the freshest fish on the west coast at family-run restaurants.

Hilltop Villages

9 You're lost on a hairpin-bend-riddled road in the mountains that seemingly leads to nowhere, and no sat nav, map or passing flock of sheep can help you. But then, suddenly, you crest a hill and a quaint village slides into view, surrounded by titanic mountains and sweeping forests. It happens all the time in Sardinia's wild Barbagia and Ogliastra provinces. Up for an offbeat adventure? Get behind the wheel for a head-spinning drive to gloriously remote villages such as Ulassai (p196), Aritzo (p181) and Fonni (p180). The village of Ulassai, below

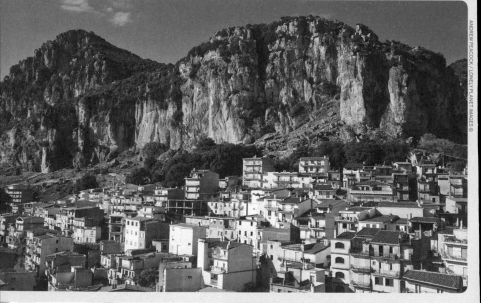

ANDREW PEACOCK / LONELY PLANET IMAGES ©

Oristano

10 One of Sardinia's great medieval cities is Oristano (p93), the capital of the 14th-century province of Arborea. History seeps through the centre's baroque lanes and piazzas, presided over by the graceful domed Duomo. Slow the pace and follow the locals' lead to the Piazza Eleonora d'Arborea to stroll and chat in front of the ornate palazzi. Or base yourself here to explore the Punic-Roman ruins of Tharros (p100) and the snow-white beaches and bird-filled lagoons of the Sinis Peninsula (p98). Statue of Eleonora d'Arborea in Oristano's Piazza Eleonora d'Arborea, left

PSF / IMAGEBROKER ©

Tiscali

11 Held hostage in the twilight of a collapsed limestone cave, the archaeological site of Tiscali (p188) is an enigma. Though only skeletal ruins remain, with a little imagination you can picture this nuraghic village as it was back in the Bronze Age. Every bit as enchanting as Tiscali itself is the trail through the lush green valley that takes you there – mighty rock faces loom above you, birds of prey wheel overhead and only the sound of your footsteps interrupts the overwhelming sense of calm that blankets this valley.

Parco Nazionale dell'Asinara

12 Dangling off the northwest tip of the island in splendid isolation, the rugged green Parco Nazionale dell'Asinara (p129) is one of Sardinia's greatest coastal wildernesses. The unique *asino bianco* (albino donkey) is at home in this outstanding national park, as are peregrine falcons, mouflon, wild boar and loggerhead turtles. For close-up wildlife encounters, hook onto one of the guided walking or cycling tours that take in the island's remote corners. Or go diving in the gin-clear waters that lap its granite cliffs and dreamy beaches. View of Cala Sant'Andrea, below

Grotta di Nettuno

13 Whether you glide in by boat from Alghero or take the vertiginous 656-step staircase that zigzags down 110m of sheer cliff, arriving at the Grotta di Nettuno (p125) is unforgettable. Enter the immense, cathedral-like grotto and it really is as though the forces of Neptune, god of the sea, have been at work. All around you are forests of curiously shaped stalactites and stalagmites, reflected in still pools of water. Nothing – not even the midday crowds – can detract from the magic of this underground fairyland.

Foodie Sardinia

14 'Organic' and 'slow food' are modern-day buzzwords for what Sardinia has been doing for centuries. Trawl the interior for farms selling their own pecorino, salami and full-bodied Cannonau red wines; buy artistic-looking loaves and almondy sweets (left) from bakeries and confectioners in Cagliari (p34) and Nuoro (p170); and tuck into a smorgasbord of seafood. Or sample the lot at a rustic *agriturismo* (farm-stay accommodation; p200), where your hosts will ply you with course after course of antipasti, ricotta-filled *culurgiones* (ravioli), slow-roasted suckling pig and honey-drenched *sebadas* (fritters).

Festive Sardinia

15 Be it the death-defying horse races of S'Ardia (p107) or *mamuthones* (costumed carnival figures) exorcising winter demons in Mamoiada (p179), Sardinians celebrate in weird and wonderful ways. Time your visit to catch standouts like the medieval tournament Sa Sartiglia (p94) in Oristano in February, Cagliari's Festa di Sant'Efisio (p45) in May or the folkloric parades of Nuoro's Sagra del Redentore (p171) in August. Hungry? Check out our line-up of seasonal food festivals (p244), where you can indulge in everything from chestnuts to sea urchins. S'Ardia, above

need to know

Currency
» Euro (€)

Language
» Sardinian (Sardo), Italian

When to Go

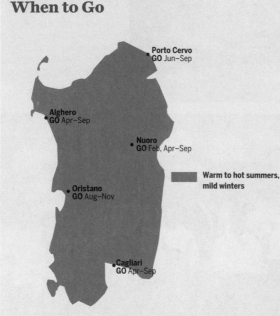

Porto Cervo
GO Jun–Sep

Alghero
GO Apr–Sep

Nuoro
GO Feb, Apr–Sep

Warm to hot summers, mild winters

Oristano
GO Aug–Nov

Cagliari
GO Apr–Sep

High Season
(Jul–Aug)

» Crowds flock to coastal resorts and room rates skyrocket.

» Prices also rise over Easter and school holidays.

» Roads are at their most congested.

» Hot days good for the beach.

Shoulder Season (Apr–Jun & mid-Sep–Oct)

» Room rates are significantly lower.

» The weather is changeable and the sea chilly.

» Excellent for hiking, cycling and climbing.

» Sights and beaches are less crowded.

Low Season
(Nov–Mar)

» Days are shorter, weather is colder and wetter.

» Many sights, hotels and restaurants are closed.

» Prices up to 50% less than high season.

» Carnevale is reason to visit in February.

Your Daily Budget

Budget less than
€150

» Dorm bed €20–25

» Double room in a budget hotel €60–100

» Avoid high season (July & August), stay in low-profile regions

» Set lunches €15–20

Midrange
€150–250

» Double room in a midrange hotel €100–200

» Dine in decent local restaurants (a good meal costs €25–45)

Top end over
€250

» Luxury doubles in well-known cities and resorts

» Relax in hotel spas

» Eat superbly in top restaurants, enjoy Sardinia's best wines

Money

» ATMs widely available in most resorts and cities. Visa, MasterCard and Cirrus often accepted in major hotels and restaurants; cash only in some smaller establishments.

Visas

» Generally not required for stays of up to 90 days (or at all for EU nationals); some nationalities need a Schengen visa (p253).

Mobile Phones

» European and Australian mobiles work, but must be set up for international roaming. US cell phones that operate on the 900 and 1800 MHz frequencies work in Sardinia.

Accommodation

» From good-value *agriturismi* (farm stays) to boutique hotels by the sea, Sardinia has accommodation to suit every pocket. Book ahead in high season. See p197.

Websites

» **Sardegna Turismo** (www.sardegnaturismo.it) The definitive portal.

» **ENIT** (www.enit.it) Italian State Tourist Board.

» **Lonely Planet** (www.lonelyplanet.com/sardinia) Destination info, bookings, traveller forum and more.

» **ARST** (www.arst.sardegna.it, in Italian) Regional transport in Sardinia.

» **Trenitalia** (www.trenitalia.com) For timetables and prices of rail journeys in Sardinia.

» **Learn a Language** (www.learnalanguage.com) Good website for Italian basics.

Exchange Rates

Australia	A$1	€0.74
Canada	C$1	€0.71
Japan	¥100	€0.86
NZ	NZ$1	€0.57
UK	UK£1	€1.14
US	US$1	€0.69

For current exchange rates see www.xe.com

Important Numbers

Country Code	39
International access code	00
Europe-wide emergency	112
Ambulance	118
Fire	115
Police	113

Arriving in Sardinia

» **Cagliari Elmas Airport**
ARST buses – to Piazza Matteotti every 30 minutes, 5.20am to 10.30pm (less frequently before 9am). Taxis – €25; 10 to 15 minutes to central Cagliari. (p50)

» **Aeroporto Olbia Costa Smeralda**
Local buses – to Olbia centre every 30 minutes between 6.15am and 11.40pm. Taxis – €15; 10 to 15 minutes to central Olbia. (p146)

Driving in Sardinia

Driving in Sardinia is generally stress-free outside of major cities like Cagliari, Sassari and Olbia, though the heat and traffic jams can fray nerves in summer. Drive on the right and heed the speed limits of 110km/h on highways, 90km/h on secondary highways and 50km/h in built-up areas. The north–south SS131 Carlo Felice highway provides speedy access between Cagliari and Sassari, and branches east to Olbia via Nuoro. Coastal and mountain roads are often narrow and riddled with hairpin bends, but drivers are generally courteous, dodgy overtaking manoeuvres aside. Flocks of sheep and, at dusk, wild animals bringing down loose rocks are the main obstacles. Some of the island's best beaches, prehistoric sites and *agriturismi* can only be accessed by dirt tracks, where you should watch out for potholes. The SS292 between Alghero and Bosa (p123) and the SS125 between Dorgali and Santa Maria Navarrese (p186) afford sensational coastal and mountain panoramas. See p261 for more details.

if you like...

Islands & Beaches

Sardinia's islands, beaches and wind-sculpted seascapes are captivating. Dive into barracuda-filled waters, drop anchor in hidden bays, or find your own patch of whiter-than-white sand on this 1800km coastline to kick back and enjoy the uplifting view.

Parco Nazionale dell'Arcipelago di La Maddalena Explore the pink granite islands and gin-clear waters of this marine national park (p159)

Spiaggia della Piscinas Visit this remote beach for dune walks and memorable sunsets (p64)

Isola dell'Asinara This wildlife-rich island is best discovered on foot or by bicycle (p129)

Cala Mariolu Be dazzled by the shimmering white pebbles and aquamarine waters of this tucked-away bay (p190)

Isola di San Pietro Look out for Eleonora's falcons on this rocky southern island (p71)

Spiaggia del Principe A gorgeous white crescent lapped by startlingly blue waters (p149)

Spiaggia della Pelosa A stunning, frost-white beach guarded by a Spanish watchtower (p129)

Is Aruttas Sparkly quartz sand, turquoise sea and peace (p99)

Archaeological Digs

Go on an archaeological dig on this island of 7000 *nuraghi* (Bronze Age fortified settlements). Roam forests of oak and olive to find nuraghic ruins, *pozzi sacri* (sacred wells) and *tombe dei giganti* (ancient mass graves, 'giant's tombs').

Nuraghe Su Nuraxi Sardinia's single Unesco-listed site, and its most famous *nuraghe* (p81)

Tiscali Ponder the meaning of this ruined *nuraghe*, hidden in a collapsed cave in the limestone Supramonte (p188)

Tharros A mighty port founded by the Phoenicians set against the blue sea – one of Sardinia's most thrilling sights (p100)

Serra Orrios Find mystery in the ruined huts and temples of this nuraghic settlement nestled in olive groves (p187)

Nuraghe di Palmavera A 3500-year-old *nuraghe* with a complex system of dwellings (p124)

Necropolis del Montessu A prehistoric cemetery set in a rocky amphitheatre (p70)

Coddu Ecchju This is a fine example of a *tombe dei giganti*, sealed off by stone stele (p153)

Nuraghe Is Paras This *nuraghe* stands out for its 11.8-metre *tholos* (conical tower; p183)

Great Outdoors

Whether you want to climb sea cliffs, breeze across the Med on a board or hike high into forest-cloaked mountains, the landscapes are exhilarating and the outdoor possibilities boundless in Sardinia.

Gola Su Gorropu Strike into the boulder-strewn wilderness of Europe's Grand Canyon, a place of primordial beauty (p187)

Golfo di Orosei Go kayaking in the gulf's sparkling waters in search of little-known bays, grottoes and sea stacks (p192)

Porto Pollo The beautiful breezes that pummel this north-coast resort are irresistible to windsurfers (p157)

Cala Gonone Have a high time of it climbing crags and overhangs above the sea (p188)

Parco Nazionale del Golfo di Orosei e del Gennargentu Hike, bike, canyon, kayak, dive, cave and climb in Sardinia's largest national park, where the mountains meet the sea (p184)

Nereo Cave Dive into the deep blue in search of Alghero's frilly red coral in the largest underwater grotto in the Mediterranean (p115)

ra

Ag
Ser
cult

Agri
Follo
fully la
garden
(p209)

Li Licci
food at thi
among oak
green hinterl

» The impressive Nuraghe Is Paras (p183)

Authentic Agriturismi

You feel like you're on the road to nowhere until – there! – you spot a stone farmstead set amid billowing oak woods and olive groves. Now all you can hear is the rustle of leaves, the bleat of sheep and your own footsteps as you approach the rural idyll the Sardinians call *agriturismo*.

Agriturismo Guthiddai This whitewashed retreat sits in one of the most beautiful spots in Sardinia, at the foot of rugged mountains, surrounded by olive and fruit trees (p211)

Agriturismo Su Pranu A genuine working farm with a restaurant serving a feast of home-grown produce (p204)

Agriturismo Rena Eat like a king and sleep like a log at this ramshackle farm (p153)

Agriturismo Su Boschettu Serene farm in Sardinia's agricultural heartland (p204)

Agriturismo Ca' La Somara Follow the donkeys to this blissfully laid-back farm, with serene gardens for relaxing moments (p209)

Li Licci Wonderful setting and food at this *agriturismo* hidden among oak trees in Gallura's green hinterland (p165)

Coastal Walks & Rides

Sardinia's soaring cliffs, wild gorges and a coast strung with crescent-shaped bays beg to be explored on foot or by bicycle. You'll appreciate that swim all the more after working up a sweat on the trail. For more on Sardinia's best beaches, see p66.

Selvaggio Blu This is the big one – an epic seven-day monster of a hike taking in Sardinia's most dramatic coastlines (p195)

Riviera del Corallo Pedal along the staggering coastal cliffs between Alghero and Bosa for widescreen panoramas (p123)

Cala Goloritzè Walk from the otherworldly highland plateau of Golgo to staggeringly beautiful Cala Goloritzè (p194)

Funtanamare to Costa Verde Cycle from Funtanamare to the remote Costa Verde, taking in glassy blue waters, sheer, rugged cliffs and sea stacks en route (p61)

Cala Luna Hike from Cala Fuili along cliff tops and through fragrant Mediterranean scrub to this captivating half-moon bay (p189)

Golgo to Cala Sisine Race down old mule trails on this technically challenging single track, stopping for a post-cycle dip in the bluest of seas (p193)

Hilltop Towns & Villages

Sardinia's quaint hill towns and villages are a great way to meet the locals, eat well, and enjoy incredible views. The hinterland is laced with winding roads and dotted with more sheep than you can count.

Castelsardo A beautiful medieval centre perched on a hilltop overlooking the sea (p129)

Ulassai A road corkscrews up to this tiny village crouching beneath jagged mountains (p196)

Monti Ferru Explore the wonderful nature of this region's villages, but most of all the magnificent beef and olive oil (p104)

Orgosolo From the creation of the atomic bomb to the destruction of the twin towers – the murals of this hill town pack a powerful political punch (p178)

San Pantaleo Tiptoe away from the Costa Smeralda's glitz to this pretty stone village surrounded by granite peaks (p152)

Laconi Peace reigns in this mountain town, where cobbled lanes twist to a verdant woodland park and the birthplace of St Ignatius (p182)

Tempio Pausania A charming grey-stone town nestled amid cork oak woods in the cool, hilly heart of the Gallura (p162)

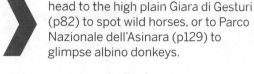

If you like... unique wildlife encounters, head to the high plain Giara di Gesturi (p82) to spot wild horses, or to Parco Nazionale dell'Asinara (p129) to glimpse albino donkeys.

Natural Wonders

Nature truly has worked wonders in Sardinia. Along wind-whipped coastlines you'll find colossal grottoes. In the mountainous interior mighty canyons. And strutting across the island, rock stars from an elephant in granite to a sugarloaf of a sea stack.

Grotta di Nettuno Feel the lure of the sea as you descend 656 steps to this cathedral-like grotto (p125)

Scoglio Pan di Zucchero Sugarloaf Rock is the largest of several *faraglioni* (sea stacks) rearing out of glassy blue waters (p61)

Grotta di Ispinigoli Find a forest of stalagmites (include the world's second tallest) in the bowels of this mammoth cave (p186)

Roccia dell'Elefante Bet you didn't think you'd find an elephant on the SS134 near Castelsardo... Novelty factor aside, this rock wonder conceals two Neolithic tombs (p130)

Il Golgo Peering down into the dark depths of this 270m abyss is enough to bring on vertigo (p194)

Roccia dell'Orso A weather-beaten lick of granite resembling a bear from certain angles, a dragon from others (p158)

Food from the Source

Sardinian food is all about simple pleasures. Ramble through the vineyards to find family-run wine cellars, stop at country farms for fresh pecorino, honey and salami, and indulge in the bounty of each season at local food festivals (see p244).

Cantine Surrau A super-slick winery near the Costa Smeralda, famous for its tangy Vermentino whites and full-bodied Cannonau reds (p151)

Cortile del Formaggio This tiny courtyard house in Orgosolo sells fresh, smoked and roasted *fiore sardo*, Sardinian pecorino matured for a minimum of three months (p179)

Cabras Try salty, flavour-packed *muggini* (mullet) and *bottarga* (mullet roe) in this fishing town (p98)

Durke A fantasy of homemade Sardinian sweets, the best made with just sugar, egg whites and almonds (p48)

Azienda Agricola Mossa Alessandro Buy tangy salami, creamy goat's-milk ricotta and *fiore sardo* pecorino at this working farm (p153)

Alghero Feast on local rock lobster and spiky *ricci* (sea urchins) from the briny blue (p112)

Historic Cities

Carthaginians, Romans, Aragonese, Pisans: all have left their stamp on Sardinia's cities. Ramble along ramparts, clamber up to citadels, relax on church-dotted piazzas and lose yourself in the pages of Sardinia's living history book.

Alghero Alghero's *centro storico* is a shady labyrinth of honey-coloured palazzi, buffered by walls that on summer evenings are crowded with diners (p112)

Cagliari Wander the twisting lanes of the medieval citadel Il Castello, lingering as the setting sun lights up its palazzi, towers and ramparts (p35)

Oristano Oristano's charming historical centre is dynamic and full of good eateries and fun bars (p93)

Iglesias The Iberian atmosphere of Iglesias and its collection of churches make it a fascinating place to explore (p55)

Olbia Be catapulted back to Roman times contemplating the mighty ships in the Museo Archeologico (p142)

Nuoro Crouched below Monte Ortobene, this mountain town had its cultural renaissance in the 19th and early 20th centuries and is the birthplace of Nobel Prize–winning author Grazia Deledda (p170)

month by month

1 **Carnevale**, February

2 **Pasqua**, March/April

3 **Festa di Sant'Efisio**, May

4 **S'Ardia**, July

5 **Festa del Redentore**, August

January

With the winter solstice passed, many villages in Nuoro province celebrate the approach of spring with bonfires. Plan ahead as many hotels close.

 Festa di Sant'Antonio Abate

Bonfires rage in Orosei, Orgosolo, Sedilo and Paulilatino at this festival from 16 to 17 January. Sinister half-human, half-animal *mamuthones* make a mad dash through Mamoiada (see p179).

February

Carnevale celebrations brighten the cool, damp days. Twitchers visit lagoons near Oristano and Cagliari to spot flamingos, herons and spoonbills.

Carnevale
Highlights include the burning of an effigy of a French soldier in Alghero, the sinister *mamuthones* in Mamoiada, costumed displays in Ottana and the townsfolk of Bosa inspecting each other's groins.

Sa Sartiglia
Medieval fun abounds at Sa Sartiglia in Oristano, with jousting, horsemen in masquerade and knightly challenges in the lead-up to Shrove Tuesday (p94).

March

The first buds of spring signal the return of warmth. Easter holidays aside, room rates are low and crowds are thin. Alghero pays tribute to the humble *ricci* (sea urchin).

Pasqua
Holy Week in Sardinia is a big deal, with solemn processions and Passion plays all over the island. The celebrations in Alghero, Castelsardo, Cagliari, Iglesias and Tempio Pausania are particularly evocative.

Sagra del Torrone
Forget eggs: Tonara in the Barbagia di Belvi gorges on the deliciously nutty local *torrone* (nougat) on Easter Monday (see www.comune tonara.org).

April

Golden mimosa trees, pink cyclamens and purple rosemary fleck the coast and countryside. The mild spring days are ideal for hiking, climbing and cycling, but the odd shower is to be expected.

Sagra degli Agrumi
Get juiced with a feast of oranges and lemons at Muravera's zesty Citrus Festival, which happens in mid-April (p53; www.sagra degliagrumi.it).

Festa di Sant'Antioco
Costumed processions, dancing, concerts and fireworks are held over four days in Sant'Antioco to celebrate the town's patron saint (p75).

May

With the Gennargentu at its greenest and temperatures rising, this is a fine month for outdoor activities. Room rates are still low and crowds minimal.

✨ Festa di Sant'Efisio

On 1 May a wooden statue of St Ephisius is paraded around Cagliari on a bullock-drawn carriage amid colourful celebrations (p45). The saint is carried to Nora, from where he returns on 4 May to yet more festivities.

✨ Cavalcata Sarda

On the second-last Sunday of May, hundreds of locals in traditional costume gather at Sassari to celebrate victory over the Saracens in AD 1000. Horsemen charge through the streets at the end of the parade (p135).

June

Sunny days and warmer seas mark the start of summer. This is a great month to beat the crowds, except for during the school holidays when rooms fill fast and accommodation is pricey.

✨ Girotonno

Cooking competitions, tastings, concerts and nautical events celebrate Carloforte's famous *mattanza* (tuna catch; p72).

July

The first peaches ripen as the mercury rises. Swing into summer with a host of outdoor festivals or join the sun-seekers on the coast. Don't turn up without a reservation.

✨ S'Ardia

In this ferocious horse race (p107) an unruly pack of horsemen race around the chapel at Sedilo.

✨ L'Isola delle Storie, Festival Letterario della Sardegna

Readings, author Q&A sessions and concerts are held in and around Gavoi during its three-day literature festival (p180).

✨ Festa della Madonna del Naufrago

This mid-July procession takes place off the coast of Villasimius, where a submerged statue of the Virgin Mary is given a wreath of flowers in honour of shipwrecked sailors (p51).

August

It's a mad dash to the coast. Temperatures soar, room rates skyrocket and the beaches heave with sun-worshippers and *bimbi* (kids).

✨ Festa di Santa Maria del Mare

Bosa's fishermen pay homage to the Virgin Mary with a river parade of boats bearing her image on the first weekend in August (p103).

✨ Matrimonio Maureddino

On the first Sunday of August, Santadi's costumed townsfolk reenact a Moorish wedding in the central piazza (p71).

✨ I Candelieri

Sassari's must-see festival takes place on 14 August (p135). The high point is the *faradda*, when the city's nine trade guilds, along with drummers and pipers, parade giant votive candles through the streets.

✨ Festa del Redentore

Horsemen and dancers accompany Sardinia's grandest costumed parade. A torch-lit procession winds through Nuoro on 28 August and an early-morning pilgrimage to the statue of Christ the Redeemer on Monte Ortobene takes place the following day (p179).

✨ Festa dell'Assunta

Processions of religious fraternities, men on horseback and women in traditional costume make this mid-August festival in Orgosolo (p179) a must.

✨ Time in Jazz

This is Berchidda's big music fest in the second week of August, with jazz jams, dance happenings and dawn concerts (p166).

September

Clear skies and still-warm days make September a golden month for low-key beach holidays, vineyard strolls and outdoor activities.

✨ Autunno in Barbagia

Rural villages in Barbagia host foodie events, craft fairs and workshops at this autumn festival (p179), held from September to December.

✨ Festa di San Salvatore

Several hundred young fellows clothed in white set off from Cabras on the Corsa degli Scalzi (Barefoot Race), an 8km dash to the hamlet and sanctuary of San Salvatore (p98).

(Above) Traditional costumes add colour to the festivities at the Festa di Sant'Efisio, Cagliari (p45)

(Below) Mysterious masked horsemen are part of the medieval fun at Sa Sartiglia, Oristano (p94)

October

Days get shorter and cooler, and some hotels and restaurants close for winter. It's a good month for hiking and for hibernating in a rustic agriturismo.

Sagra delle Castagne

The mountain town of Aritzo enlivens late October with a Chestnut Fair (p181), folk music and shows.

November

Tourism all but dries up in November. Those that do make it here will enjoy new wine from the interior's vineyards, and shellfish at the *chioschi* (beach kiosks) on Poetto beach.

Rassegna del Vino Novello

Sniff, swirl and drink new wine at this festival held in the piazzas of Milis in early November (p105).

December

Snow dusts the Gennargentu's highest peaks, but elsewhere the weather can be bleak. Christmas adds festive sparkle.

Natale

In the run-up to Christmas, processions and religious events are held. Many churches set up elaborate cribs or nativity scenes, known as *presepi*. Firework displays and concerts ring in the New Year in Alghero.

itineraries

Whether you've got 10 days or 30, these itineraries provide a starting point for the trip of a lifetime. Want more inspiration? Head online to lonelyplanet. com/thorntree to chat with other travellers.

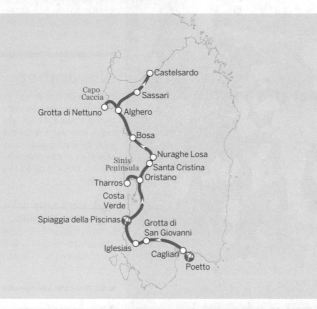

Two Weeks
West Coast

> Begin with two days in Sardinia's soulful capital, **Cagliari**, walking Il Castello's mazy lanes, lounging on **Poetto** beach and devouring shellfish in the Marina district's vibrant restaurants.

Day three takes you to **Iglesias**, Sardinia's mining heart, with a stop at the fairytale **Grotta di San Giovanni** on the way. Relax for a day or two on the **Costa Verde's** glorious beaches – hiking barefoot across the dunes at **Spiaggia della Piscinas** is a must. Devote the next few days to discovering medieval **Oristano** and the Phoenician ruins at **Tharros**, a short hop away on the wild **Sinis Peninsula**.

Meander north next for a day unravelling nuraghic mysteries at **Santa Cristina** and **Nuraghe Losa**. Day eight whisks you through the narrow alleys of pretty-in-pastels **Bosa**, and up to its castle for knockout views. Spend a couple of days exploring Spanish-flavoured **Alghero's** historic centre, the cliffs of **Capo Caccia** and the wondrous sea cave, **Grotta di Nettuno**.

Spend your last few days with the perfect mix of city and coast – contrasting the buzz of university city **Sassari** with the calm of **Castelsardo**, perched on a rocky bluff above the sea.

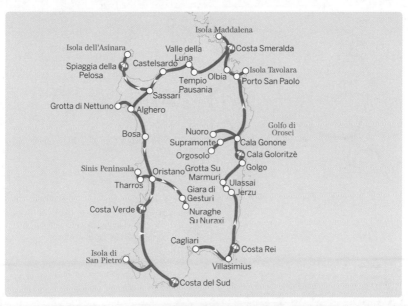

One Month
Grand Island Tour

Four weeks in Sardinia? Good choice. Kick off in **Cagliari**, strolling Il Castello's medieval lanes and dining in the seafront Marina district. On day three take the snaking SP17 east, factoring in beach time in **Villasimius** or the **Costa Rei**. Meander north on day four for wine tasting in vine strewn **Jerzu**, followed by a head-spinning drive to hilltop **Ulassai**. Linger a day to trek, climb, or explore the huge **Grotta Su Marmuri**. Swing east on day six to Baunei, detouring to the highland plateau of **Golgo** and hiking down to stunning **Cala Goloritzè**. Stay the next three days in **Cala Gonone**, a terrific base for hiking or climbing in the limestone **Supramonte** and boating to the **Golfo di Orosei's** grottoes and dazzling bays. Venture west into the rugged Barbagia on day 10, stopping for a culture fix in **Nuoro** or to marvel at **Orgosolo's** murals.

Continue north on the SS131 on day 11, overnighting in **Porto San Paolo** and rising early to catch a boat over to **Isola Tavolara**, where azure waters tempt divers. Speed north to **Olbia** on day 13 for some classic Gallurese food and a wander in the historic centre. Spend the next three days lapping up the **Costa Smeralda's** emerald waters, secluded coves and millionaire lifestyle. Time permitting, hop across to **Isola Maddalena** for some of Sardinia's most captivating seascapes.

Go west on day 17 through forests of oak and olive to the quaint hill town of **Tempio Pausania** and the surreal, boulder-strewn **Valle della Luna**, winding up on the north coast in castle-topped **Castelsardo**. Spend the next day taking in **Sassari's** medieval centre and buzzing cafe culture, before making the short trip north to the snow-white **Spiaggia della Pelosa** or the wild **Isola dell'Asinara** on day 19. Gradually move south over the next three days, stopping at Spanish-flavoured **Alghero**, the wondrous **Grotta di Nettuno** and picture-postcard **Bosa**. On days 23 and 24, **Oristano** is your charming base for exploring the Punic-Roman ruins at **Tharros** and the **Sinis Peninsula's** lagoons and deserted beaches. The next couple of days are a toss-up between lounging on the **Costa Verde's** dune-fringed beaches and spotting wild horses on the lonesome **Giara di Gesturi** plateau. If you go for the latter, allow time to see **Nuraghe Su Nuraxi**, a prehistoric marvel.

Spend your last few days in Sardinia resting and eating fresh tuna on the ravishing **Isola di San Pietro**, or relaxing on the glorious southern beaches of the **Costa del Sud**.

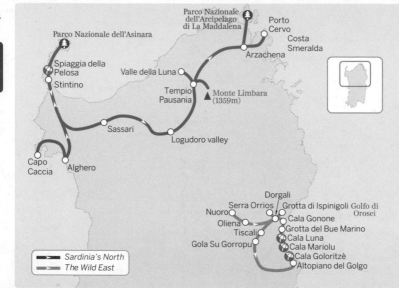

Parco Nazionale
dell'Arcipelago
di La Maddalena
Parco Nazionale dell'Asinara
Porto
Cervo
Costa
Smeralda
Arzachena
Spiaggia della
Pelosa
Valle della Luna
Stintino
Tempio
Pausania
Monte Limbara
(1359m)
Sassari
Logudoro valley
Capo
Caccia
Alghero

Dorgali
Serra Orrios
Grotta di Ispinigoli
Golfo di
Orosei
Nuoro
Cala Gonone
Oliena
Grotta del Bue Marino
Tiscali
Cala Luna
Gola Su Gorropu
Cala Mariolu
Cala Goloritzè
Altopiano del Golgo

➤➤➤ Sardinia's North
➤➤➤ The Wild East

Two Weeks
The Wild East

Be seduced by Sardinia's exhilarating landscapes on this route through the wild Parco Nazionale del Golfo di Orosei e del Gennargentu.

Get set in **Nuoro**, capital of the rugged Barbagia hill country and birthplace of Grazia Deledda, before hitting the road for **Oliena** to taste its ruby-red Cannonau wine. Swing east to **Dorgali** on days two and three, a fine base for visiting the **Grotta di Ispinigoli**, home to the world's second-tallest stalagmite, and the nuraghic village of **Serra Orrios**.

From Dorgali, it's a head-spinning drive down to the sweeping bay of **Cala Gonone**, where you can spend a full week rock climbing, diving or exploring the **Golfo di Orosei** on foot or by kayak. Boat across aquamarine waters to sublime bays, such as **Cala Luna** and **Cala Mariolu**, and the sea cave **Grotta del Bue Marino**.

Packed your walking boots? Spend your last few days striking out into the wilderness. Hike to the enigmatic nuraghic village of **Tiscali**, and to the **Gola Su Gorropu**, a vast rock chasm dubbed Europe's Grand Canyon. From the weird highland plateau of **Altopiano del Golgo**, further north, mule trails thread down to gorgeous **Cala Goloritzè**, thrashed by astonishingly blue waters.

10 Days
Sardinia's North

Feel invigorated by the sea views and piazza life in **Alghero**, a city characterised by its Spanish heritage. Daytrip to the dramatic cliffs of **Capo Caccia** and devour local rock lobster in some of the island's most stylish restaurants.

On day three, meander north to isolated **Stintino** to laze on dreamy **Spiaggia della Pelosa** nearby. Or visit the wild **Parco Nazionale dell'Asinara**, home to miniature *asini bianchi* (albino donkeys). Make time for university city **Sassari** on day four, before heading east to tour the Pisan-Romanesque churches, pink granite mountains and precipitous vineyards of the **Logudoro valley**.

Drive northeast on the SS127 on day five to the quaint hill town of **Tempio Pausania**, deep in verdant cork forests. Ramble through the otherworldly, boulder-strewn **Valle della Luna** and zigzag through cool pine woods to the peak of **Monte Limbara** (1359m).

In the northeast explore the *nuraghi* (Bronze Age fortified settlements) around **Arzachena**, and squeeze in a day's island-hopping around the pristine **Parco Nazionale dell'Arcipelago di La Maddalena**. Spend your last few days on the **Costa Smeralda**, mingling with celebs in **Porto Cervo**, and finding blissfully secluded coves.

Travel with Children

Best Regions for Kids

Alghero & the Northwest

Fantastic child-friendly beaches for all ages, nature parks, fascinating caves and wildlife watching, and an array of water sports for older kids and teens.

Cagliari

A long town beach, dizzying tower climbing in the historic centre, fun shops and the wonderful *trenino verde* train ride in the countryside.

Olbia & the Gallura

Excellent beaches with entertainment for kids, wildlife excursions, gentle hiking and dolphin-spotting boat trips.

Oristano & the West

Beautiful bird life, water-sport-heavy beaches for teens, wild, sandy beaches for toddlers.

Nuoro & the East

Cave exploring, climbing, biking and all kinds of activities for older kids and teens, family-friendly campgrounds.

Iglesias & the Northwest

Cavallini (minihorses) roaming on the mountain plateau of La Giara di Gesturi, excellent beaches on the south coast, eerie mines, wondrous caves.

Sardinia for Kids

Like all of Italy, Sardinia is wonderful for children of all ages. Babies and toddlers are cooed over everywhere, while older kids and teenagers have an array of interesting activities to join – be it horse riding, learning to dive and snorkel, spotting wildlife, or hiking up verdant hills or along coastal paths. Best of all, there's plenty of spaghetti and gelato.

Sights & Cities

The sea, sand and sun will be enough to keep children of all ages – and their parents – entertained, but there's an excellent array of family-friendly activities on the island.

Though Sardinia's main monuments – churches and cathedrals – may not prove the most entertaining places for younger children, and while museums don't have any child-friendly activities, there are ways to combine more serious sightseeing with seeing sights from a different perspective.

Schlepping around Cagliari's narrow lanes can be livened up for kids by popping into shops like the cartoon world of Bob Art, where they can watch artists create bug-eyed animal cartoons. Climbing up Cagliari's Torre d'Elefante (and learning about its gory history) and Torre di San Pancrazio and bursting out to see the city views on top will be exhilarating for older kids.

Alghero has horse-and-cart tours around the *centro storico,* and the *trenino catalano,* a tiny train, chugs around the centre.

Visiting some of the more accessible, less claustrophobic mines in the Iglesias region might prove interesting for older children – especially if they have a love of the macabre.

Teenagers will enjoy checking out the many murals around the town of San Sperate, near Cagliari, where walls are covered with drawings of skateboards, odd dogs, abstract drawings and more classic, rural scenes. Also near Cagliari, in the town of Barumini, the Parco Sardegna in Miniatura has the entire island laid out in a miniature reconstruction; there is an adjacent outdoor play area and picnic tables – perfect for the whole family.

Beaches, Natural Reserves & Wildlife

Sardinia boasts some of the Mediterranean's longest beaches and warm, limpid seas. You can take your pick from beaches that are sandy or pebbly, remote or action-packed. Older kids wanting to try water sports will find plenty of opportunities, especially around Alghero, Costa Smeralda, Olbia and the Gallura, and the Sinis Peninsula.

There's a large number of natural parks perfect for walking and wildlife spotting; you'll find natural parks in all of Sardinia's regions, from Olbia and Alghero in the north, to Oristano in the west, Olbia and the Gallura in the east and Cagliari in the south. Inspiring family excursions include boat tours to spot and learn about bottlenose dolphins in Olbia's Golfo Aranci, and gentle coastal hiking to reach an abandoned lighthouse at Capo Figaro. Costa Smeralda offers whale-watching excursions and snorkelling among the abundant sealife, while you can spot the endemic breed of *asino bianco* – albino donkey – in the northwest's Parco Nazionale Dell'Asinara.

Outdoor Activities

If your kids are into water sports, you're in luck in Sardinia, where most outfits cater for kids and teenagers. Choose your activities from snorkelling, junior level diving, kite surfing, canoeing and kayaking.

Horse riding opportunities abound in the province of Oristano, while La Giara di Gesturi in the province of La Marmilla has the unique wild *cavallini*, or minihorses. Spotting them as they descend to the lakes to quench their thirst in the morning is a fascinating sight for child and adult alike.

Visiting caves is bound to prove fascinating for older children and teenagers, from spectacular sea caves such as the Grotta di Nettuno near Alghero or the Grotta del Bue Marino at Cala Gonone (if sea-sickness isn't a problem), to the stalactite and stalagmite forests of Grotta di Santa Barbara and Grotta di Su Mannau near Iglesias.

Eating Out

Eating out with the kids is pretty stress-free in Sardinia, particularly in the coastal resorts, where kids are made to feel very welcome in hotel restaurants. There are few taboos about taking children to restaurants, even if locals with little ones in tow tend to stick to the more popular trattorias – you'll seldom see children in an expensive restaurant.

You're unlikely to come across a children's menu, but most places will cheerfully tailor a dish to appeal to young taste buds and serve a *mezzo porzione* (child's portion).

Very few restaurants have *seggioloni* (high chairs), so either bring a fabric add-on for normal chairs or stick your wiggly toddler on your knee and hope for the best.

Likewise, few places have baby-changing facilities, though the staff will almost always try and find a space for you (sometimes rolling a tray table into the toilets for you!).

Food-wise, your children are bound to find something they'll love eating in Sardinia. Spaghetti, of course, abounds, and the *spaghetti alla napolitana* (with tomato sauce) is always a wonderful option. Fish and meat are mostly prepared simply, without sauces to mask the taste, which may be perfect or awful for your child. There is always good bread at the table, and cheese is widely available. Fresh fruit is often served for desserts, and there is always a good array of ice cream and cakes too.

Children's Highlights

Beaches & Resorts

» Long sandy or tiny pebble beaches, perfect for toddlers, Sinis Peninsula.

» Family-oriented resort beaches, Cannigione and Cala Gonone.

» Stretches of sand and shallow, limpid waters along Costa del Sud, southwest coast.

» Hair-raising rides and water madness, plus long sandy beaches, Cala Battistoni, Costa Smeralda.

» Greenery and umbrellas, sun loungers and kids' play areas at Riviera del Corallo beaches, Alghero

» A pine-fringed *lungomare* (seafront promenade), a shady campground and several playgrounds, at Cala Gonone.

» Discounts are available for children on public transport and for admission to sights.

» On trains and ferries children under four generally travel for free, although without the right to a seat or cabin berth; for children between four and 12, discounts of 50% are usually applied.

» Sardinian trains are seldom very busy, but in high season it's advisable to book seats. You'll also need to book car seats if you're planning to hire a car.

» Note that coastal and mountain roads can be very curvy and travel sickness is a serious prospect, so be prepared.

» You can buy baby formula in powder or liquid form, as well as sterilising solutions such as Milton, at *farmacie*.

» Disposable nappies (diapers), *pannolini,* are widely available at *farmacie* and supermarkets, where you'll find a wider selection. Remember that shop opening hours may differ from your home country, so run out of nappies on a Saturday evening and you could be in for a messy Sunday.

» Fresh cow's milk is sold in litre and half-litre cartons in supermarkets, *alimentari* (food shops) and in some bars. If it is essential that you have milk, you should carry an emergency carton of *lungo conservazione* (UHT).

» Facilities in coastal resorts are often geared towards families, and kids are well catered for. However, those with small children will find few special amenities in less touristy areas, the major cities and mountainous areas.

» Lonely Planet's *Travel with Children* is packed with practical tips, and *Italy with Kids*, published by Open Road, has tons of useful information.

» The website www.travelwithyourkids.com provides plenty of general advice, although nothing specific to Sardinia. **Tots Too** (www.totstoo.com) is an online agency specialising in upmarket, kid-friendly properties.

Energy Burners

» Canoe expeditions and basic snorkelling, Laguna di Nora.

» Kayaking and nautical camping, Cardedu.

» Novice rock climbing at Domusnovas, Iglesias.

» Gentle half-day hike to a bay, Golfo di Orosei.

» Canoeing and beach fun at Poetto beach.

» Shallow water and sandy beaches for play and snorkelling at Villasimius and Capo Carbonara.

» Water sports around Porto Pollo and the family-oriented resorts of Cannigione and Cala Gonone.

» Horse-riding in the Oristano province.

» Canoeing, biking, caving, diving and canyoning, all great for teens, in Golfo di Orosei.

Nature & Wildlife

» Salt lakes and pink flamingos, Sinis Peninsula.

» Protected reed-fringed wetlands with abundant birdlife, Parco Naturale Regionale Molentargius.

» Flamingos, herons, coots and ospreys at the Stagno S'Ena Arrubia, outside Oristano.

» Boat trips to the islands of the Capo Carbonara marine reserve at Villasimius and Capo Carbonara.

» Half-day cruises to spot and learn about the playful bottlenose dolphins at Golfo Aranci.

» The *trenino verde,* a tiny tourist train, which chugs through some of Sardinia's most spectacular and inaccessible countryside.

» Wild boar, martens, wildcats, weasels and plenty of birds of prey at the Riserva Naturale di Monte Arcosu, a World Wildlife Fund reserve.

Rocks & Caves

» Elephant- and bear-shaped rocks – the Roccia dell'Elefante and Roccia dell'Orso outside Castelsardo and Palau.

» Grotta di Nettuno, on Capo Caccia.

» Dark-brown crystals, stalactites and stalagmites give the impression of a ghostly underground forest at the Grotta di Santa Barbara, Iglesias.

» A 50-minute walk through lake chambers, a temple for water worship, and an impressive 8m column of fused stalactite and stalagmite at the Grotta di Su Mannau, Iglesias.

regions at a glance

Sardinia may be an island, but it sure is a big one, and even with your own wheels you may be surprised how long it can take to get from A to B. Read on for inspiration and choose your region before you go.

The capital Cagliari achieves perfect balance with its blend of culture and coast. Swinging southwest brings you to the glorious Costa del Sud, the dune-dotted Costa Verde, and verdant countryside with homegrown food and must-see *nuraghi* (Bronze Age fortified settlements). The northwest seduces with Spanish soul in Alghero, shimmering white beaches, grottoes and unique wildlife. Hop over to the island's northeast for celebrity glamour and gorgeous coves on the Costa Smeralda and to tour Gallura's granite heartland. In the east, where the mountains collide with the coast, the cliffs, peaks and the bluest of seas will have you itching to climb, hike, cycle, kayak and more.

Cagliari & the Sarrabus

Culture ✓✓✓
Food ✓✓
Coast Walks ✓✓

Culture
Nothing says Cagliari like the medieval Il Castello citadel, with its grandstand views, Pisan towers and palazzi. Rococo churches, a Roman amphitheatre and a stellar archaeological museum map out the island's past.

Food
Foodies are in their element with fresh fish in Marina's buzzing restaurants, shellfish alfresco on Poetto beach, Sardinian sweets at pavement cafes and award-winning wines in Serdiana.

Coast Walks
A coastal road threads through to the 6km sands of Poetto beach, fringed with lagoons dotted with pink flamingos in winter. The fine beaches, crystal-clear waters and cape diving are draws further east.

p32

Iglesias & the Southwest

History ✓✓✓
Beaches ✓✓✓
Islands ✓✓

History
Revisit the Bronze Age at Unesco-listed Nuraghe Su Nuraxi, explore Phoenician and Roman history by diving to Nora's submerged ruins, and rewind to 3000 BC touring *domus de janas* (fairy houses) tombs at Necropolis del Montessu.

Beaches
This southwestern swathe of coastline is wildly beautiful: from the untamed Costa Verde's 30m-high dunes to the silky beaches and cobalt-blue waters of the Costa del Sud.

Islands
On Isola di San Pietro, thrill at Eleonora's falcons at Cala Fico, explore palazzi-dotted Carloforte and try Sardinia's best tuna. Sardinia's great seafaring past is evoked in Phoenician ruins studding Isola di Sant'Antioco.

p54

Oristano & the West	Alghero & the Northwest	Olbia, the Costa Smeralda & the Gallura	Nuoro & the East
Beaches ✓✓✓	History ✓✓✓	High Life ✓✓✓	Outdoors ✓✓✓
Food ✓✓	Coast ✓✓	Coast ✓✓✓	Coast ✓✓✓
Outdoors ✓✓	Wildlife ✓✓	Interior ✓✓	Mountains ✓✓

Beaches
Snow-white beaches and bluer-than-blue water: few coastlines are as compelling as the Sinis Peninsula. Escape the world on Is Aruttas' white sands or on eloquently named Isola di Mal di Ventre (Stomach Ache Island).

Food
Cabras for the island's best *bottarga* (mullet roe), Seneghe for its olive oil and *bue rosso* beef, Milis for its sweet oranges, the vineyards for crisp Vernaccia wines...this is foodie heaven.

Outdoors
On this western swathe of the island, hike volcanic Monti Ferru, surf wave-thrashed Putzu Idu and roam Arborea's flatlands and pinewoods on horseback. The lagoons teem with birdlife, from herons to flamingos.

p91

History
Long part of Catalonia, Alghero radiates a Spanish air, its honey-coloured seawalls enclosing cobbled lanes and Gothic palazzi. At sunset, take a *passeggiata* (evening stroll) along the seafront.

Coast
The coastal road weaves round to broad bays and Capo Caccia, where cliffs plunge to the fairytale Grotta di Nettuno. Go north to impossibly blue waters at Spiaggia della Pelosa.

Wildlife
Grab your binoculars and go to Isola dell'Asinara to spot *asini bianchi* (white donkeys), silky-haired mouflon and falcons; Bosco di Monte Lerno to spy Giara horses; and Le Prigionette Nature Reserve's forests for a Noah's Ark of wildlife.

p110

High Life
The Costa Smeralda is the place to daydream about a billionaire's lifestyle as you float in an emerald sea past palatial villas and super-yachts. Porto Cervo and Porto Rotondo are celebspotting central.

Coast
The Costa Smeralda is scalloped with beautiful coves and fjordlike inlets. Beach-hop south to San Teodoro's frost-white beaches, or north to the ravishing Arcipelago di La Maddalena, set in some of the Med's clearest waters.

Interior
Gallura's rugged granite interior is a staggering contrast to the coast. Weave through thick cork oak woods and vineyards to alley-woven hill towns like San Pantaleo, Tempio Pausania and Aggius.

p141

Outdoors
This is hiking and climbing paradise. Cala Gonone's cliffs are a must-climb, while hikers won't want to miss Europe's Grand Canyon, Gola Su Gorropu, and the nuraghic enigma Tiscali.

Coast
Half-moon Cala Luna, pearly Cala Mariolu, breathtaking Cala Goloritzè – everyone has their favourite Golfo di Orosei cove. The dreamiest bays nestle between cliffs and are best discovered on foot, by boat or kayak.

Mountains
In the remote interior, brooding mountains rear above deep valleys, forests and stuck-in-time villages. A helter-skelter of roads leads you to the Gennargentu's lofty peaks and Barbagia's wilds.

p167

Look out for these icons:

 TOP CHOICE Our author's recommendation

 A green or sustainable option

FREE No payment required

On the Road

Cagliari & the Sarrabus

Best Places to Eat

» Il Fantasma (p45)

» Ristorante Ammentos
(p45)

» Monica e Ahmed (p45)

» Lapola (p45)

» Ristorante Le Anforè (p52)

Best Places to Stay

» Il Cagliarese (p199)

» La Peonia (p199)

» Hostel Marina (p199)

» T Hotel (p199)

» Hotel Mariposas (p201)

Why Go?

Built high and mighty around a rocky citadel, Cagliari gazes out to the glistening Med, basks in southern sunshine and looks proudly back on almost 3000 years of history. Sardinia's cultured, open-minded capital makes a fine base if you're seeking more than the classic sun-and-sea mix, with a clutch of museums, baroque churches and fortifications begging exploration.

Still a busy, working port, Cagliari hasn't been prettified for the benefit of tourists and is all the more interesting for it. Sightseeing aside, this city is all about simple pleasures, be it fresh seafood in a Marina trattoria, crowd-watching at a pavement cafe or a stroll through Il Castello's medieval alleyways.

Slightly east of town you find yourself in a different world. The mountainous hinterland of the Sarrabus is an untamed, silent wilderness and the magnificent salt-white beaches of Villasimius and the Costa Rei are all but deserted outside of the peak summer months.

When to Go

Lent kicks off with carnival parades and rounds out with evocative Easter processions, but for true pilgrims nothing beats the saintly shenanigans at the Festa di Sant'Efisio in early May. Spring is a fine time to hike the woods and granite peaks of the Monte dei Sette Fratelli. Summer attracts a bronzed, party-loving crowd to Poetto, and sun-worshippers to the gorgeous beaches of Villasimius and the Costa Rei further east. Join the twitchers to spot the flamingos that stalk Cagliari's salt marshes in winter.

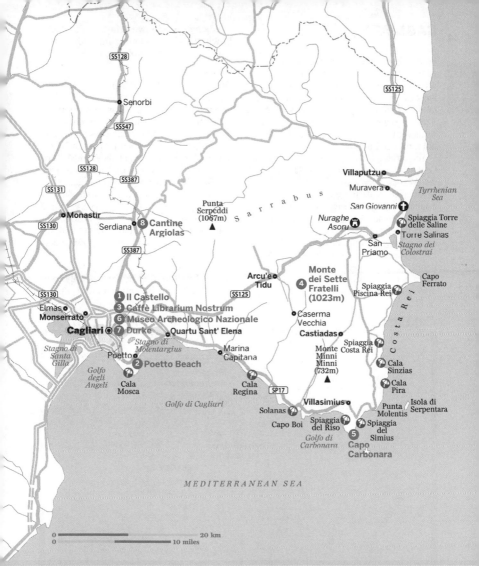

Cagliari & the Sarrabus Highlights

1 Discover the nooks and crannies of **Il Castello** (p35), Cagliari's medieval citadel

2 Sunbathe by day and party the night away at **Poetto Beach** (p43)

3 Sip a sundowner at hilltop **Caffè Librarium Nostrum** (p47) as the city is dramatically illuminated

4 Don your walking boots and head for the pine-scented hills of **Monte dei Sete Fratelli** (see boxed text, p53)

5 Dive into the lush blue waters off the **Capo Carbonara** (see boxed text, p52), a marine reserve

6 Enjoy a fascinating romp through Sardinian history at the artefact-packed **Museo Archeologico Nazionale** (p36)

7 Give in to temptation at old-world **Durke** (p48), a wonderland of traditional Sardinian sweets

8 Sample the pick of the region's wines or join a cookery class at **Cantine Argiolas** (see boxed text, p51) in Serdiana

CAGLIARI

POP 157,000

Forget flying: the best way to arrive in Cagliari is by sea, the city rising in a helter-skelter of golden-hued palazzi, domes and facades up to the rocky centrepiece, Il Castello. When DH Lawrence arrived in the 1920s, he compared the Sardinian capital to Jerusalem: '…strange and rather wonderful, not a bit like Italy.'

Yet, although Tunisia is closer than Rome, Cagliari *is* the most Italian of Sardinia's cities. Vespas buzz down tree-fringed boulevards and locals hang out at cafes tucked under the graceful arcades in the seafront Marina district. Up in Il Castello, sunset is prime-time viewing in the piazzas, when the soft evening light illuminates pastel facades and the golden fortress walls like a fresco painting. Everywhere you wander, Cagliari's rich history is spelled out in Roman ruins, museums, churches and galleries.

Edging east of town brings you to Poetto Beach, the hub of summer life with its limpid blue waters and upbeat party scene.

History

Founded by the Phoenicians in the 8th century BC, the city was first developed by the Romans, who carved a vast amphitheatre out of the rocky hillside and made the area into one of the Mediterranean's main trading ports. But it was not until the Carthaginians took control of what they called Karel or Karalis (meaning 'rocky place') around 520 BC that a town began to emerge.

Julius Caesar declared Karalis a Roman municipality in 46 BC. For centuries it remained a prosperous port, heading the grain trade with mainland Italy, but with the eclipse of Rome's power came more turbulent times.

Vandals operating out of North Africa stormed into the city in AD 455, only to be unseated by the Byzantine Empire in 533.

Cagliari

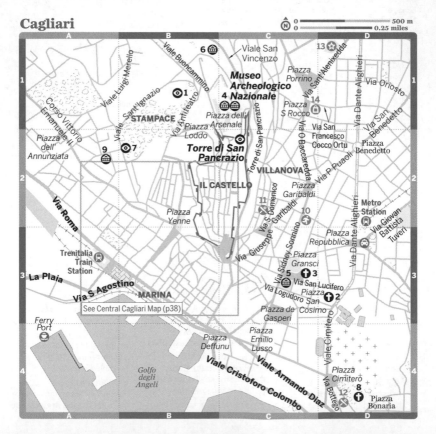

0   500 m
0   0.25 miles

See Central Cagliari Map (p38)

By the 11th century, weakening Byzantine influence (accentuated by repeated Arab raids) led Cagliari and the other districts to become virtually autonomous.

In 1258 the Pisans took the town, fortified the Castello area and replaced the local population with Pisans. A similar fate awaited them when the Catalano-Aragonese took over in 1326. The Black Death swept through in 1348, with frequent repeat outbreaks in the succeeding decades.

With Spain unified at the end of the 15th century, the Catalans were subordinated to the Spaniards. Cagliari fared better than most of the island under Spanish inertia, and in 1620 the city's university opened its doors.

The dukes of Savoy (who in 1720 became kings of Sardinia) followed the Spanish precedent in keeping Cagliari as the vice-regal seat, and it endured several anxious events (such as the 1794 anti-Savoy riots). From 1799 to 1814 the royal family, forced out of Piedmont by Napoleon, spent time in Cagliari protected by the British Royal Navy.

Cagliari continued to develop slowly throughout the 19th and 20th centuries. Parts of the city walls were destroyed and the city expanded as the population grew. Heavily bombed in WWII, Cagliari was awarded a medal for bravery in 1948.

Reconstruction commenced shortly after the end of the war and was partly complete by the time Cagliari was declared capital of the semiautonomous region of Sardinia in the new Italian republic in 1949. A good deal of Sardinia's modern industry, especially petrochemicals, has since developed around the lagoons and along the coast as far as Sarroch in the southwest.

◎ Sights

Cagliari's key sights huddle in four central districts: Il Castello, Stampace, Marina and Villanova. The obvious starting point is the hilltop Il Castello area, home to a group of fine museums at the Citadella dei Musei and affording terrific views of the cityscape.

To the west, high up the hill, is Stampace, where most of the action spirals around Piazza Yenne. Elsewhere you'll find a number of important churches, a botanical garden and Cagliari's rocky Roman amphitheatre.

Bordered by Largo Carlo Felice to the west and seafront Via Roma, the characterful Marina district is a joy to explore on foot, not so much for sights, of which there are few, but for the atmosphere of its dark, narrow lanes crammed with artisans' shops, cafes and trattorias.

In the 19th century Cagliari sprawled eastwards under the Piedmontese; their legacy, Villanova, is a showcase of wide roads and imposing piazzas. Rising above the district, a large public park covers the slopes of Monte Urpinu. On the other side of the mountain, the bird-rich Stagno di Molentargius salt marshes attract birdwatchers.

TOP CHOICE Il Castello
NEIGHBOURHOOD

(Map p38) This hilltop citadel is Cagliari's most iconic image, its domes, towers and palazzi, once home to the city's aristocracy, rising above the sturdy ramparts built by the Pisans and Aragonese. The neighbourhood is known to locals as Su Casteddu, a term also used to describe the whole city. The walls are best admired (and photographed) from afar – good spots include the Roman amphitheatre across the valley to the northwest and Bonaria to the southeast.

ROAD DISTANCES (km)

	Cagliari	Castiadas	Costa Rei	Muravera
Castiadas	47			
Costa Rei	60	13		
Muravera	56	27	30	
Villasimius	43	20	17	47

Inside the battlements, the old medieval city reveals itself like Pandora's box. The university, cathedral, museums and Pisan palaces are wedged into a jigsaw of narrow high-walled alleys. Sleepy though it may seem, life is returning to the area, with a growing crop of boutiques, bars and cafes luring students and fashionable bohemians.

The most atmospheric and attractive side of Il Castello is the **Ghetto degli Ebrei** (Jewish Ghetto), the area north of the Torre dell'Elefante, between Via Santa Croce and Via Stretta. Here the narrow streets appear little changed since medieval times. Under Spanish rule the entire Jewish community was expelled in 1492 and today nothing much remains except the name, applied to a restored former barracks, the **Centro Comunale d'Arte e Cultura Il Ghetto** (070 640 21 15; Via Santa Croce 18; adult/reduced €4/2.50; ⊙9am-1pm & 4-8pm Tue-Sun), which hosts temporary exhibitions, many with a Sardinian slant. In the wake of the Jewish expulsion, the **Chiesa di Santa Croce** (Piazzaetta Santa Croce) was built over the ghetto's former synagogue.

If you've got a moment, try to sneak a peek at the beautiful vaulted vestibule of the university's **Istituto di Architettura e Disegno** (Institute of Architecture & Design; Via Corte d'Appello 87).

FREE **Museo Archeologico Nazionale** MUSEUM
(Map p34; 070 68 40 00; Piazza dell'Arsenale; ⊙9am-8pm Tue-Sun) Of the four museums at the Citadella dei Musei, this is the undoubted star. Sardinia's premier archaeological museum, it displays artefacts spanning millennia of ancient history, including a superb collection of pint-sized nuraghic *bronzetti* (bronze figurines) on the ground floor.

In the absence of any written records, these bronzes are a vital source of information on Sardinia's mysterious nuraghic culture (approximately 1800-500 BC). In all about 400 bronzes have been discovered, many in sites of religious importance, leading scholars to conclude that they were probably used as votive offerings. Depicting tribal chiefs, warriors, hunters, mothers and animals, the figurines are stylistically crude but remarkably effective. There are even little models of the *nuraghi* (Bronze Age fortified settlements).

Sensibly, the ground floor is laid out in chronological order. You move from the prenuraghic world of stone implements and obsidian tools, rudimentary ceramics and funny round fertility goddesses to the Bronze and Iron Ages and on to the *nuraghi*. Then come the Phoenicians and Romans, a model *tophet* (sacred Phoenician or Carthaginian burial ground for children and babies), and delicate debris such as terracotta vases, glass vessels, scarabs and jewellery from ancient Karalis (Cagliari), Sulcis, Tharros and Nora.

The 1st and 2nd floors contain more of the same but are divided by region and important sites rather than by age. Among the highlights are some Roman-era mosaics, a collection of Roman statues, busts and tombstones from Cagliari, and displays of coins.

Torre dell'Elefante LOOKOUT
(Map p38; Via Università; adult/reduced €4/2.50; ⊙9am-1pm & 3.30-7.30pm Tue-Sun summer, to 4.30pm winter) One of only two Pisan towers still standing, the Torre dell'Elefante was built in 1307 as defence against the threatening Aragonese. Named after the sculpted elephant by the vicious-looking portcullis, the 42m-high tower became something of a horror show, thanks to its foul decor. The Spaniards beheaded the Marchese di Cea here and left her severed head lying around for 17 years! They also liked to adorn the portcullis with the heads of executed prisoners, strung up in cages like ghoulish fairy lights. The crenellated storey was added in 1852 and used as a prison for political detainees. Climb to the top for far-reaching views over the city's rooftops to the sea.

Torre di San Pancrazio LOOKOUT
(Map p34; Piazza Indipendenza; adult/reduced €4/2.50; ⊙9am-1pm & 3.30-7.30pm Tue-Sun summer, to 4.30pm winter) Over by the citadel's northeastern gate, this 36m-high tower is the Torre dell'Elefante's twin. Completed in 1305, it is built on the city's highest point and commands expansive views of the Golfo di Cagliari.

Cattedrale di Santa Maria   DUOMO

(Map p38; Piazza Palazzo 4; ☺7.30am-8pm Mon-Fri, 8am-1pm & 4.30-8.30pm Sat & Sun, shorter hours in winter) Cagliari's graceful 13th-century cathedral stands proud on Piazza Palazzo, once home to the city's religious authorities. Except for the square-based bell tower, little remains of the original Gothic structure: the interior is largely baroque, the result of a radical late 17th-century makeover, and the clean Pisan-Romanesque facade is a 20th-century imitation, added between 1933 and 1938.

Inside, the once-Gothic church disappears beneath a rich icing of baroque decor. Bright frescoes adorn the ceilings, and the three chapels on either side of the aisles spill over with sculptural whirls in an effect that is both impressive and appalling. The third chapel to the right, the **Cappella di San Michele**, is perhaps the pinnacle of the genre. A serene St Michael, who appears (in baroque fashion) to be in the eye of a swirling storm, casts devils into hell.

Still, there are some less gaudy bits and pieces. The two intricate stone **pulpits** on either side of the central door were sculpted by Guglielmo da Pisa between 1158 and 1162. They originally formed a single unit, which stood in Pisa's Duomo until the Pisans donated it to Cagliari in 1312. It was subsequently split into two by the meddlesome Domenico Spotorno, the architect behind the 17th-century baroque facelift, and the big stone lions that formed its base were removed to the altar where they now stand.

On the other side of the altar is the entrance to the **Aula Capitolare**, the crypt where many Savoy tombs are conserved. Carved out of rock, the barrel-vaulted chamber is an impressive sight with its mass of sculptural decoration and intricate carvings.

Museo del Duomo   MUSEUM

(Map p38; ☎070 68 02 44; Via del Fossario 5; adult/reduced €4/2.50; ☺10am-1pm & 4.30-8pm Sat & Sun) Further cathedral treasures are displayed at this compact museum. One standout is the *Trittico di Clemente VII*, which was moved here from the cathedral for safe keeping. This precious 15th-century painting in oil on timber has been attributed to the Flemish painter Rogier van der Weyden, or to one of his disciples. Another important work is the 16th-century *Retablo dei Beneficiati*, produced by the school of Pietro Cavaro.

Bastione San Remy   LOOKOUT

(Map p38) The monumental stairway that ascends from busy Piazza Costituzione to Bastione San Remy is the most impressive way

---

CAGLIARI IN...

Two Days

Begin your first day with a postcard view of Cagliari from the **Torre dell'Elefante**, or from its Pisan twin, the **Torre di San Pancrazio**. From here, wander the narrow, twisting lanes of **Il Castello**, filled with neighbourly chatter, to the ornate **Cattedrale di Santa Maria**. In the afternoon, trace the island's nuraghic past at the **Museo Archeologico Nazionale**. Toast your first day over cocktails on the panoramic terrace of **Caffè Librarium Nostrum** as the city begins to twinkle.

Wake up in style over coffee at 19th-century **Antico Caffè** on day two, followed by a languid stroll through fountain-dotted greenery at the **Orto Botanico**. Just around the corner sits Cagliari's **Roman amphitheatre**. Lunch on fresh fish in **Marina** district and spend the afternoon mooching around the boutiques and speciality shops. **Piazza Yenne** is a lively spot for an alfresco aperitif.

Four Days

Rise early on day three and head to **Mercato di San Benedetto** for picnic goodies. Take your treasures to **Poetto Beach**, where you can laze, swim or windsurf. If birdwatching is more your scene, explore the **Parco Naturale Regionale Molentargius** on foot or by bike.

Both the pristine beaches of **Villasimius** and one of Sardinia's top wineries, **Cantine Argiolas**, in Serdiana, make great day trips for day four. Or strap on your walking boots to hike the granite mountains and wildlife-rich woodlands around **Monte dei Sette Fratelli**.

Central Cagliari

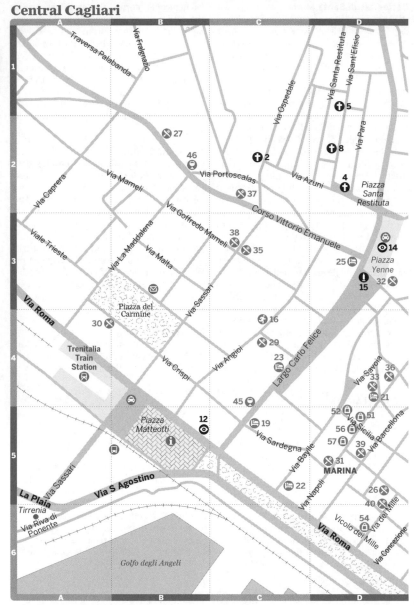

to reach Il Castello; save your legs by taking the panoramic elevator. Built between 1899 and 1902, the lookout is a mix of neoclassical and Liberty styles and affords sweeping views over Cagliari's jumbled rooftops to the Mediterranean.

FREE **Pinacoteca Nazionale** ART GALLERY
(Map p34; ☑070 68 40 00; www.pinacoteca
.cagliari.beniculturali.it, in Italian; Piazza dell' Arsenale; ◎9am-7.30pm Tue-Sun) Above and behind the archaeological museum, this gallery showcases a prized collection of 15th- to

the so-called Stampace school and arguably Sardinia's most important artist, are outstanding. They include a moving *Deposizione* (Deposition) and portraits of St Peter, St Paul and St Augustine. Also represented are the painter's father, Lorenzo, and his son Michele. Another Sardinian artist of note was Francesco Pinna, whose *Pala di Sant'Orsola* hangs here. These images tend to show the influence of Spain and Italy rather than illuminating the Sardinian condition. However, there is a brief line-up of 19th- and early-20th-century Sardinian painters, such as Giovanni Marghinotti and Giuseppe Sciuti.

Anfiteatro Romano   ARCHAEOLOGICAL SITE
(Map p34; ☎070 65 29 56; www.anfiteatroromano .it, in Italian; Viale Sant' Ignazio; adult/reduced €4.30/2.80; ⏱9.30am-1.30pm Tue-Sat, 9.30am-1.30pm & 3.30-5.30pm Sun summer, 9.30am-1.30pm Tue-Sat, 10am-1pm Sun winter) Cagliari's most impressive Roman monument is this amphitheatre. Dating back to the 2nd century AD, it is carved out of rock high up on the Buon Cammino hill, near the northern entrance to Il Castello. Although much of the original theatre has been cannibalised for building material over the centuries, enough has survived to pique the imagination. In its heyday, crowds of up to 10,000 people – practically the entire population of Cagliari – would gather to watch gladiators battle each other and the occasional wild animal. In summer, the amphitheatre occasionally hosts concerts.

Piazza Yenne   PIAZZA
(Map p38) The focal point of the Marina district, and indeed of central Cagliari, is Piazza Yenne. The small square is adorned with a statue of **King Carlo Felice** to mark the beginnings of the Carlo Felice Hwy (SS131), the project for which the monarch is best remembered. On summer nights, Piazza Yenne heaves as a young crowd flocks to its bars, gelaterias and pavement cafes.

Orto Botanico   BOTANICAL GARDEN
(Map p34; ☎070 65 29 56; Viale Sant' Ignazio; admission €3; ⏱8.30am-6pm Mon-Sat, 8.30am-1.30pm Sun) One of Italy's most famous botanical gardens, the Orto Botanico was established in 1858. Today it extends over five hectares and nurtures 3000 species of flora. Leafy arches lead to trickling fountains and gardens bristling with palm trees, cacti and *ficus* trees with huge snaking roots. Specimens from as far afield as Asia, Australia,

17th-century art. Many of the best works are *retablos* (grand altarpieces of the kind commonly found in Spain), painted by Catalan and Genoese artists for local churches.

Of those by known Sardinian painters, the four works by Pietro Cavaro, father of

Central Cagliari

Africa and the Americas sidle up to the local carob trees and oaks. Tastefully littering the gardens are ancient ruins, an old Punic cistern, and a Roman quarry and aqueduct.

Villa di Tigellio ARCHAEOLOGICAL SITE
(Map p34; ☎0331 473 13 94; Via Tigellio; adult/reduced €3/1.90; ◎9am-1pm & 4-8pm summer, 9am-5pm winter, closed Mon) Just a minute's stroll from the Orto Botanico lie the remains of three Roman houses, dating to the 1st century BC. Legend has it that Tigellio Ermogene – a famous Sardinian poet and musician, and a close a friend of Julius Caesar – lived here. Today the ruins are pretty overgrown and are surrounded by houses, so you'll need to use your imagination to picture the magnificent mosaics, columns and baths that once stood here.

Galleria Comunale d'Arte ART GALLERY
(Map p34; ☎070 49 07 27; www.galleriacomunalecagliari.it, in Italian; Viale San Vincenzo; adult/reduced €6/2.60; ◎9am-1pm & 3.30-7.30pm Wed-Mon) If you are at all interested in modern Sardinian art, you won't want to miss this

gallery and its rich collection of works by island artists, such as Tarquinio Sini (1891–1943). His humorous *contrasti* (contrasts), which show heavily dressed Sardinian girls standing frumpily beside glamorous, coiffed flappers, explore the social tension between traditional Sardinian ways and the perplexing freedoms of a rapidly modernising world. Another highlight is the work of Giuseppe Biasi (1885–1945), whose oils depict Sardinian life in a rich style that combines the bold brushstrokes of Gauguin with the moody atmosphere of Degas.

The gallery, housed in a neoclassical villa north of Il Castello, also displays an excellent selection of contemporary works, and the Collezione Ingrao, comprised of more than 650 works of Italian art from the mid-19th century to the late 20th century. Frequent temporary exhibitions are also held to showcase works by contemporary artists.

The palm-dotted **Giardino Pubblici** (Public Garden; ⊙7am-8pm winter, 6am-11pm summer) outside is a pleasant pocket of greenery with grandstand views of Cagliari.

Museo d'Arte Siamese   ART GALLERY
(Map p34; ☑070 65 18 88; Piazza dell'Arsenale; adult/reduced €2/1; ⊙9am-1pm & 3.30pm-7.30pm Tue-Sun) Cagliari's medieval heart is an unlikely place for a collection of Asian art, but that's exactly what you find here. Donated to the city by local engineer Stefano Cardu, who had spent many years in Thailand (formerly Siam), the collection is highly eclectic. Alongside Ming- and Qing-era Chinese porcelain vases, you'll find silk paintings, Japanese statuettes and some truly terrifying Thai weapons.

Museo del Tesoro e Area Archeologica di Sant'Eulalia   MUSEUM
(Map p38; ☑070 66 37 24; Vico del Collegio 2; adult/reduced €5/2.50; ⊙10am-1pm & 4-7pm Tue-Sun) In the heart of the Marina district, this museum contains a rich collection of religious art, as well as an archaeological area, which extends for up to 200 sq metres beneath the adjacent **Chiesa di Sant' Eulalia**. The main drawcard here is a 13m section of excavated Roman road (constructed between the 1st and 2nd centuries AD), which archaeologists think would have connected with the nearby port.

In the upstairs treasury you'll find all sorts of religious artefacts, ranging from exquisite priests' vestments and silverware through to medieval codices and other pre-

cious documents. Fine wooden sculptures abound, along with an *Ecce homo* painting, depicting Christ, front and back, after his flagellation. The painting has been attributed to a 17th-century Flemish artist.

Chiesa di Sant'Efisio   CHURCH
(Map p38; Via Sant'Efisio) Despite its unassuming facade, the Chiesa di Sant'Efisio is of considerable local importance. Not for any artistic or architectural reasons but rather for its ties to St Ephisius, Cagliari's patron saint. A Roman soldier who converted to Christianity and was later beheaded for refusing to recant his faith, St Ephisius is the star of the city's big 1 May festivities. An effigy of the saint that is paraded around the city on a beautifully ornate *carozza* (carriage) is kept here. The baroque interior is sadly off limits to the public.

Over the centuries, the saint has stood the city in good stead, saving the populace from the plague in 1652 – when the church got its marble makeover – and repelling Napoleon's fleet in 1793 by stirring up the storm that sent the fleet packing.

At the side of the church is the entrance to the crypt where St Ephisius was supposedly held before being executed in Nora (near Pula). It's marked in stone – *Carcer Sancti Ephysii M* (Prison of the Martyr St Ephisius) – and retains the column where Ephisius was tied during his incarceration.

FREE **Cripta di Santa Restituta**   CRYPT
(Map p38; Via Sant'Efisio; ⊙10am-1pm Tue-Sun) This crypt has been in use since pre-Christian times. It's a huge, eerie, natural cavern where the echo of leaking water drip-drips. Originally a place of pagan worship, it became the home of the martyr Restituta in the 5th century and a reference point for Cagliari's early Christians. The Orthodox

---

A BIG PUSHOVER

Stampace was Cagliari's medieval working-class district, where Sards lived huddled in the shadow of the mighty castle. In the 14th century, when the Aragonese were in charge, Sards were forbidden to enter the castle after nightfall. Those caught were mercilessly thrown off the castle walls, with the benediction *stai in pace* (rest in peace), a phrase that presumably gave rise to the name Stampace.

Christians then took it over – you can still see remnants of their frescoes – until the 13th century, when it was abandoned. In WWII it was used as an air-raid shelter, a task it wasn't up to, since many died while holed up here in February 1943. It's interesting to make out the wartime graffiti that covers the walls.

Chiesa di San Michele
CHURCH

(Map p38; Via Ospedale 2; ⊙8-11am & 6-9pm Mon-Sat, 10am-noon & 7-9pm Sun) Although consecrated in 1538, this church is best known for its lavish 18th-century decor, considered the finest example of rococo in Sardinia. The spectacle starts outside with the ebullient triple-arched baroque facade and continues through the vast colonnaded atrium and on into the sumptuous interior. Before you go inside, take a minute to admire the massive four-columned pulpit in the atrium. This was built and named in honour of the Spanish emperor Carlos V, who is said to have delivered a stirring speech from it before setting off on a fruitless campaign against Arab corsairs in Tunisia. The octagonal interior is quite magnificent, with six heavily decorated chapels radiating out from the centre, topped by a grand, brightly frescoed dome. Of particular note is the sacristy, accessible from the last chapel on the left, with its vivid frescoes and intricate inlaid wood.

Basilica di San Saturnino
CHURCH

(Map p34; Piazza San Cosimo; ⊙9am-1pm Mon-Sat) One of the oldest churches in Sardinia, the Basilica di San Saturnino is a striking example of Paleo-Christian architecture. Based on a Greek-cross pattern, the domed basilica was built over a Roman necropolis in the 5th century, on the site where Saturninus, a

much revered local martyr, was buried. According to legend, Saturninus was beheaded in 304 AD during emperor Diocletian's anti-Christian pogroms.

In the 6th century San Fulgenzio da Ruspe, a bishop in exile from Tunisia, built a monastery here. In 1098 this was reworked into the current Romanesque church by a group of Vittorini monks from Marseille. Since then the basilica has undergone various refurbishments, most notably after it was stripped in 1662 to provide building material for the Cattedrale di Santa Maria and, most recently, after it sustained severe bomb damage in WWII.

Palazzo Civico
LANDMARK

(Map p38; ☎070 677 70 49; Via Roma) Overlooking Piazza Matteotti, the neo-Gothic Palazzo Civico, also known as the Municipio, is home to Cagliari's city council. Capricious, pompous and not a little overbearing, it was built between 1899 and 1913, and faithfully reconstructed after bombing in 1943. The upstairs chambers contain works by a number of Sardinian artists, including Pietro Cavaro. Admission is by appointment only.

Santuario & Basilica di Nostra Signora di Bonaria
CHURCH, LOOKOUT

(Map p34; Piazza Bonaria 2; donations expected; ⊙6.30am-noon & 4.30-8pm daily) When the Catalano-Aragonese arrived to take Cagliari in 1323, it became clear it would be no easy task. So they sensibly set up camp on the fresh mountain slopes of Montixeddu, which came to be known as Bonaria (from *buon'aria* meaning 'good air'). In the three years of the siege, the camp became a fortress with its own church.

After ejecting the Pisans and taking the city in 1335, the Aragonese invited Mercedari monks from Barcelona to establish a monastery at the Bonaria church, where they remain to this day.

The Bonaria monks were kept well employed for centuries ransoming Christian slaves from Muslim pirates, and they are credited with saving the Genoese community of Tabarka in Tunisia and bringing them to Isola di San Pietro. But what makes this a place of international pilgrimage is a simple wooden statue of the Virgin Mary and Christ, kept in a niche behind the **altar**. Legend has it that the statue was washed up after being cast overboard by Spanish seamen caught in a storm in the 14th century, and today mariners still pray to the Madonna for

---

HAVE YOUR SAY

Found a fantastic restaurant that you're longing to share with the world? Disagree with our recommendations? Or just want to talk about your most recent trip?

Whatever your reason, head to lonelyplanet.com, where you can post a review, ask or answer a question on the Thorntree forum, comment on a blog, or share your photos and tips on Groups. Or you can simply spend time chatting with like-minded travellers. So go on, have your say.

POETTO BEACH

An easy bus ride from the city centre, Cagliari's fabulous Poetto Beach is one of the longest stretches of sand in Italy. Extending 6km beyond the green Promontorio di Sant'Elia, it's an integral part of city life, particularly in summer when much of the city's youth decamps here to sunbathe by day and party by night. The long, sandy strip is lined with funfairs, restaurants, bars and discos, many of which also act as *stabilmenti balneari* (private beach clubs). These offer various facilities, including showers and changing cabins, as well as renting out umbrellas and sunloungers – prices start at €15 for an umbrella and two sunloungers.

The southern end of the beach is the most popular, with its picturesque Marina Piccola, yacht club and outdoor cinema (July and August only). Looming over the marina, the craggy Promontorio di Sant' Elia is known to everyone as the Sella del Diavola (Devil's Saddle). According to local legend, the headland was the scene of an epic battle between Lucifer and the Archangel Michael. In the course of the struggle Satan was thrown off his horse and his saddle fell into the sea where it eventually petrified atop what was to become the headland. Although much of the headland is now owned by the military and closed to the public, there are several paths that offer great walking.

To get to Poetto hop on bus PF or PQ from Piazza Matteotti.

protection on the high seas. Above the altar hangs a tiny 15th-century ivory ship, whose movements are said to indicate the wind direction in the Golfo degli Angeli.

You'll find yet more model boats, as well as other ex-voto offerings and a golden crown from Carlo Emanuele I in the sanctuary's **museum**, accessible through the small cloister. There are also the mummified corpses of four plague-ridden Catalano-Aragonese nobles whose bodies were found miraculously preserved inside the church.

The sanctuary was originally part of a much bigger fortress complex built by the Catalano-Aragonese in 1323. Little remains of the original compound, apart from the truncated bell tower, which originally served as a watchtower, and the Gothic portal.

To the right of the sanctuary is the much larger basilica, which still acts as a landmark to returning sailors. Building began in 1704, but the money ran out and the basilica wasn't officially finished until 1926.

Castello di San Michele   CASTLE

(☑070 50 06 56; adult/reduced €5/4; ⊙4-10pm Tue-Sun) A stout three-tower Spanish fortress, Castello di San Michele stands in a commanding position northwest of the city centre. It was built in the 10th century as protection for Santa Igia, capital of the Giudicato of Cagliari, but is most famous as the luxurious residence of the 14th-century Carroz family. It is now used as a space to host art and photography exhibitions. The surrounding grounds are a peaceful green space in which to get away from the city.

To get there take city bus 5 from Via Roma to the foot of the hill on Via Bacu Abis. From there, a paved road runs for 800m up to the castle.

Exmà   ART GALLERY

(Map p34; ☑070 66 63 99; Via San Lucifero 71; exhibitions €3; ⊙9am-1pm & 4-8pm Tue-Sun) Housed in Cagliari's 18th-century *mattatoio* (abattoir), Exmà is a delightful cultural centre. A permanent exhibition details the restoration of the abattoir, but it's best known for its contemporary art shows and photography exhibitions. In summer, there are frequent open-air music concerts.

Palazzo Viceregio   PALAZZO

(Map p38; ☑070 409 20 00; ⊙8.30am-2pm & 3-8pm Mon-Fri, 10am-2pm & 4-6pm Sat) Just steps from the cathedral is this pale lime palazzo, once home to the Spanish and Savoy viceroys. Today it serves as the provincial assembly and stages regular exhibitions and summer music concerts.

Chiesa di San Lucifero   CHURCH

(Map p34; Via San Lucifero 78) Below this baroque church is a 6th-century crypt where the tomb of the early Archbishop of Cagliari, St Lucifer, rests. In earlier times the area had been part of a Roman burial ground. It's not open to the public, but its austere 17th-century facade is worth a quick look from the outside.

WORTH A TRIP

CALLING ALL BIRDWATCHERS

Slightly east of Cagliari, heading towards Quartu Sant'Elena, lie the protected reed-fringed wetlands of the **Parco Naturale Regionale Molentargius**. A housing estate forms an incongruous backdrop for these freshwater and brackish pools, which attract nesting, migrant and wintering birds in their thousands. With a little luck you may well spot pink flamingos, purple herons, little egrets, marsh harriers, sandwich terns and black-winged stilts from the observation points.

The reserve is best explored on foot or by bicycle. Get informed before you head out at the **visitor centre** (🕿070 37 91 92 01; www.parks.it/parco.molentargius; Edificio Sali Scelti, Via La Palma) on the eastern fringes of town. Dawn and dusk are prime-time viewing for twitchers.

Chiesa di Santo Sepolcro CHURCH

(Map p38; Piazza del Santo Sepolcro 5; ⊙9am-1pm & 5-8pm) The most astonishing feature of this church is an enormous 17th-century gilded wooden altarpiece housing a figure of the Virgin Mary.

Chiesa di Sant'Anna CHURCH

(Map p38; Piazza Santa Restituta; ⊙7.30-10am & 5-8pm Tue-Sun) Largely destroyed during WWII and painstakingly rebuilt afterwards, this sand-coloured church is basically baroque, but the Ionic columns give it a neoclassical edge. It was undergoing restoration at the time of research.

🏃 Activities

Not surprisingly, water sports are big at Poetto, and you can generally hire canoes at the beach clubs. The Golfo di Cagliari is littered with the wrecks of WWII ships, which makes it an excellent place for divers to explore.

Windsurfing Club Cagliari WINDSURFING

(🕿070 37 26 94; www.windsurfingclubcagliari.org; Viale Marina Piccola) From its base at Marina Piccola, this centre offers a range of water sports courses. A course of six one-hour lessons for beginner's windsurfing/catamaran/freestyle costs €150/230/200 respectively, while three hours' surfing instruction will cost you €120.

Morgan Diving SCUBA DIVING

(🕿070 80 50 59; www.morgandiving.com) This outfit arranges dives to a number of wrecks (prices range from €40 to €110) and is also authorised to conduct dives in the marine reserve of Villasimius. The company is based at Marina Capitana, 14km east of Cagliari, but you can make arrangements over the phone.

⚓ Courses

One World Language Centre LANGUAGE

(Map p34; 🕿070 67 02 34; www.italianincagliari.com; Via Sonnino 195; 20hr class €200, 40hr €400) Brush up your Italian with a course at this reputable language school, which takes an interactive approach and offers lessons for all levels. The centre can help arrange homestays (from €210 per week) and apartment rooms (from €160 per week).

L'Accademia LANGUAGE, COOKING

(Map p38; 🕿070 66 44 08; www.laccademia.com; Via Angioj 34; 15hr class €210, incl 9hr cookery classes €410) Just steps from Via Roma, this central school takes a hands-on approach to learning Italian, with trips to the market and station. You can combine an Italian course with cookery classes, where you'll learn to prepare typical dishes like *fregola* (granular pasta) and Sardinian sweets.

🧭 Tours

City Tour Cagliari CITY TOURS

(Map p38; 🕿070 66 94 09; adult/reduced €10/5; ⊙hourly tours 9.30am-6.30pm Mon-Sun) This open-topped bus does an hour's loop of the key landmarks and sights, with multilingual commentary available. The whistlestop tour takes in major landmarks and sights including Bastione San Remy, the Anfiteatro Romano and Torre di San Pancrazio. Departures are hourly from Piazza Yenne.

Sardinia Tourist Guide CITY TOURS

(🕿393 20 44 15 928; www.sardiniatouristguide.it) Based in Selargius, 12km northeast of town, these guides run a five-hour tour of Cagliari, which takes in highlights like Poetto Beach, Monte Urpinu and Il Castello. They also arrange tours to the Sella del Diavola (Devil's Saddle).

✯ Festivals & Events

Cagliari puts on a good show for Carnevale in February and Easter Holy Week, when a hooded procession takes place between the Chiesa di Sant'Efisio and the cathedral up in Il Castello.

Festa di Sant'Efisio CULTURAL
(www.festadisantefisio.it, in Italian) Pilgrims descend on the city in droves for this saintly celebration, held from 1 to 4 May. On the opening day Cagliaritani pour into the streets to greet the effigy of St Ephisius, Cagliari's patron saint, as it's paraded round the streets on a bullock-drawn carriage. As the costumed procession melts away, a hard-core retinue accompanies the statue on its 40km pilgrimage to Nora. Get the best views from the grandstand seating around Piazza Matteotti and Largo Carlo Felice. Tickets for the stands (€6 to €8) are sold at Box Office Tickets (p48).

✗ Eating

In a city where even daily staples such as bread and cheese are elevated to a near art form, *mangiare bene* (eating well) is considered a given. The Cagliaritani combine their love of food and socialising at the table, in both humble backstreet trattorias and top-end restaurants. Marina's labyrinth of narrow lanes is chock-full of restaurants, trattorias, bars and takeaways. Some places are obviously touristy but many are not and are popular with the dining locals. Other good eat streets include Via Sassari and Corso Vittorio Emanuele.

There's a certain formality to life here, so it's always best to make a reservation, especially on busy weekend evenings. Things really get going around 9.30pm, but in summer people tend to dine later. Bear in mind that many of the better restaurants close for at least part of August.

TOP CHOICE **Il Fantasma** PIZZERIA €
(Map p34; ☑070 65 67 49; Via San Domenico 94; pizzas €6.50-9; ☺Mon-Sat) This cheerful pizzeria does the best pizza in Cagliari. It's a boisterous place with wonky tables in a low barrel-vaulted interior with a splotchy red pattern on the brick walls. Amid the chaos, the friendly waiters adroitly navigate the crowds carrying platefuls of bubbling pizza hot from the wood-fired oven. Go for the Fantasma special (mozzarella, rocket and meat), or Sardinian faves with *bottarga* (mullet roe), *ricci* (sea urchins) and sea anemones. Book or expect to queue.

Ristorante Ammentos SARDINIAN €€
(Map p38; ☑070 65 10 75; Via Sassari 120; meals €15-30; ☺closed Tue) Dine on authentic Sardinian fare in rustic surrounds at this popular trattoria. *Culurgiones* (ravioli) in herby tomato sauce are a delicious lead to succulent meat dishes such as wild boar or goat stew.

Monica e Ahmed SARDINIAN €€
(Map p38; ☑070 640 20 45; Corso Vittorio Emanuele 119; meals around €30; ☺closed Sun evening) Monica welcomes you with a smile and then plies you with a tempting array of fishy delights. Start with a lavish antipasto of fresh cuttlefish, *ricci*, mussels, and lobster in vinaigrette, and follow with *spaghetti ai frutti di mare* (with mussels, clams and breadcrumbs).

Lapola SARDINIAN €€
(Map p38; ☑070 65 06 04; Vico Barcellona 10; meals around €35; ☺Tue-Sun) Seafood is the star of the menu at this bustling Marina choice, serving taste sensations such as octopus carpaccio with rocket and chicory, and sautéed clams in orange juice with *pane carasau*. The €16 lunch, including wine and coffee, is a bargain.

Trattoria Gennargentu SARDINIAN €€
(Map p38; ☑070 65 82 47; Via Sardegna 60; meals €20-30; ☺closed Sun in winter) It doesn't look much from outside, but this no-frills trattoria serves excellent food and tables fill quickly. The seafood is particularly good: try spaghetti with clams and *bottarga*, or *tonno alla carlofortina*, tuna chunks served cold in a sweet tomato and onion sauce.

DON'T MISS

SHELLFISH FEST

In summer Poetto Beach is lined with bars, snack joints and restaurants, known to locals as *chioschi* (kiosks). Things get really busy here between November and March (mollusc season), when shacks serving sea urchins and mussels are set up by fishermen along the beach road. You're charged according to the number of shells left on your table.

DON'T MISS

TOP SNACK SPOTS

Le Patate & Co
SNACKS €

(Map p38; Scalette Santo Sepulcro 1; fries €2.50; ⊘closed dinner Mon) A whiz with the frying pan and olive oil, Antonio knocks up the freshest fries in town – thin, crisp and not overly salty. Sit on the terrace when the sun's out.

Gocce di Gelato e Cioccolato
SWEETS €

(Map p38; ✆070 68 02 72; Piazza del Carmine 21; ⊘noon-9pm winter, to 1am summer) Sweet-toothed Cagliaritani come here to indulge on creamy handmade gelati, spot-on desserts (try the millefeuille), spice-infused pralines and truffles – all totally divine.

Locanda Caddeo
SNACKS €

(Map p38; ✆070 68 04 91; Via Sassari 75; snacks €2.50-8; ⊘daily) Dig into focaccia, wedges of pizza and freshly prepared salads at this cool, gallery-style haunt. Young Cagliaritani flock here for snacks, drinks and crowd-watching on the pavement terrace.

Dal Corsaro
SARDINIAN €€€

(Map p38; ✆070 66 43 18; www.dalcorsaro.com; Viale Regina Margherita 28; meals €50-55; ⊘daily) Stiff tablecloths, silver wine buckets and elegant couples set the scene at Cagliari's bastion of fine dining. Sardinian ingredients are highlighted in creative dishes such as *raviola di cipolla e pecorino semi stagionato* (onion ravioli with mature pecorino cheese) and roast octopus with lemongrass salsa. The two-course lunch is a steal at €16.

Manàmanà
CAFE €

(Map p38; ✆070 65 17 59; Via Savoia 15; meals around €20; ⊘Mon-Sat) Sitting on the prettiest square in the Marina district, this boho cafe attracts an arty crowd with its exhibitions, readings and good vibes. It's a laid-back spot for coffee, a light lunch (€10) or flavoursome mains like Sardinian swordfish with sour cream.

Crackers
TRADITIONAL ITALIAN €€

(Map p38; ✆070 65 39 12; Corso Vittorio Emanuele 193; meals around €30; ⊘Thu-Tue) A corner of Piedmont in Sardinia, Crackers specialises in northern Italian classics such as *brasato al Barolo* (meat stewed in Barolo wine) and boiled meats served with mustard. There's also a wide range of risottos, some excellent vegetable antipasti, and a thoughtful wine list.

Spinnaker
ITALIAN €€€

(✆070 37 02 95; Via Marina Piccola; meals €45-55; ⊘Tue-Sun May-Sep) At Marina Piccola on Poetto, this is the summer outpost of Dal Corsaro. Given its seafront location, it's no surprise that the onus is on high-quality seafood – think saffron-infused *fregola* with baby calamari and Carloforte tuna grilled to perfection.

Ristorante Royal
TRADITIONAL ITALIAN €€

(Map p34; ✆070 34 13 13; Via Bottego 24; meals around €30; ⊘closed Sun afternoon & Mon) On a modest residential street east of the centre, this Tuscan restaurant is where Cagliaritani come to dig into succulent Florentine steak and juicy slabs of meat. There's not much fish, but there are plenty of vegetable *contorni* (side dishes) and a range of exemplary desserts.

Enò
SARDINIAN €

(Map p38; ✆070 6 84 82 43; Vico Carlo Felice 12; www.enorestaurant.it, in Italian; meals around €20; ⊘daily) Bag a table on the terrace of this sleek bistro-cum-wine bar. Sardinian classics like *culurgiones* in herby tomato sauce and baked sea bream pair well with one of 200 different Italian wines.

Taverna Su Milese
SARDINIAN €

(Map p38; ✆338 97 73 68; Via Barcellona 32; meals €15-25; ⊘Mon-Sat) Hit-and-miss service aside, this taverna is a decent cheapie. Come midday the simple vaulted dining room buzzes with locals. Meat, fish and pasta are fixtures on the pocket-pleasing two-course lunch (€10), which includes wine and coffee.

Antica Hostaria
TRADITIONAL ITALIAN €€

(Map p38; ✆070 66 58 60; Via Cavour 60; meals around €40; ⊘Mon-Sat) Popular with local celebs and politicos, this restaurant serves traditional, seasonally inspired Italian food in an antique-strewn, picture-crowded setting. For Sardinian surf 'n' turf, start with *pennette con tonno fresco e gamberi* (pasta tubes with fresh tuna and prawns) followed by a succulent steak.

Self-catering

For a delicious packed lunch go into one of the neighbourhood *salumerie* (delicatessens) and ask for a thick cut of *pecorino sardo* (Sardinian pecorino cheese) and a slice or two of smoked ham in a freshly baked *panino* (bread roll).

Isola del Gelato ICE CREAM €

(Map p38; ☎070 65 98 24; Piazza Yenne 35; ice cream €1.50-4; ☺9am-2am Tue-Sun) Ice cream fans join the nightly crowds at this hugely popular hang-out. The Smurf-blue, mock grotto interior tempts with ice-creamy treats, including low-fat, soy, yoghurt and semifreddo, a delicious half-frozen mousse.

I Sapori dell'Isola DELI €

(Map p38; ☎070 65 23 62; Via Sardegna 50; ☺8am-1.30pm & 4.30-8.30pm Mon-Sat) Pop into this friendly deli for top quality Sardinian bread, pastries, salami, cheese, *bottarga,* olive oil, wine and more.

🍷 Drinking

Head up to Il Castello for sundowners with a dress-circle view of Cagliari. The bar scene is centred on buzzy Piazza Yenne and Corso Vittorio Emanuele, although in summer the party scene spirals around Poetto.

Antico Caffè CAFE

(Map p38; ☎070 65 82 06; www.anticocaffe1855 .it; Piazza Costituzione 10; ☺7am-2am daily) DH Lawrence and Grazia Deledda once frequented this grand old cafe, which opened its doors in 1855. Locals come to chat over leisurely coffees, frilly crêpes and salads. There's a pavement terrace or you can settle inside amidst the polished wood, marble and brass.

Caffè Librarium Nostrum BAR

(Map p38; ☎070 65 09 43; Via Santa Croce 33; ☺7.30am-2am Tue-Sun) Offering some of the best views in town, this modish Castello bar has panoramic seating on top of the city's medieval ramparts. If the weather's being difficult, make for the brick-lined interior and order yourself an Alligator cocktail, created in honour of the hero of Massimo Carlotto's novels. There's occasional live music.

Caffè degli Spiriti BAR

(Map p38; Bastione San Remy; pizzas €5-8; ☺9am-2am daily) Grab a hammock, lie back and enjoy the Il Castello views and vibe at this stylish lounge bar on the Bastione San Remy. Inside, it's all black and brick; outside, happy drinkers sit on black leather sofas drinking frozen daiquiris, listening to jazzy beats and munching pizzas at tables fashioned from studded wooden doors.

Emerson BAR

(☎070 37 51 94; Viale Poetto 4, Poetto Beach; ☺11am-5pm daily winter, 9am-1am summer) Near the fourth bus stop, and one of the most popular of the seafront *chioschi,* this swank place is a bit of everything. Part cocktail lounge, part restaurant and part beach club, it dishes up everything from pasta to *aperitivi,* live music and sunloungers.

Caffè Svizzero CAFE

(Map p38; ☎070 65 37 84; Largo Carlo Felice 6; ☺Tue-Sun) At the bottom of Largo Carlo Felice, this Liberty-style place has been a stalwart of Cagliari cafe society since the early 20th century. Anything from tea to cocktails is on offer in the frescoed interior, founded by a group of Swiss almost 100 years ago.

Ritual Caffè BAR

(Map p38; ☎070 65 20 71; Via Università 33; ☺daily) This arty cafe is hewn out of the limestone rock face. Seek out a snug alcove in the vaulted stone interior for drinks and occasional live music and DJ beats.

Il Merlo Parlante PUB

(Map p38; ☎070 65 39 81; Via Portoscalas 69; ☺7pm-3am Tue-Sun) Cagliari's nearest thing to a student pub, this is a boisterous place with lager on tap, rock on the stereo, and a young up-for-it international crowd.

Caffè dell'Elfo CAFE, BAR

(Map p38; ☎070 68 23 99; Salita Santa Chiara, 4-6 Piazza Yenne; ☺1-3pm & 8pm-2am Mon-Sat) Named after its little elves, by day this is a cafe serving tasty *piadine* (flatbread sandwiches); by night it's a warm, relaxed wine bar.

☆ Entertainment

For information on what's going on in town, ask at the tourist office or pick up a copy of the local newspaper *L'Unione Sarda.* Online, you'll find listings at www.sardegnaconcerti. com (in Italian). Most of Cagliari's big concerts are held over the summer.

Cagliari has a lively performance scene, comprising classical music, dance, opera and drama. The season generally runs from October to May, although some places also offer a summer program.

MASSIMO CARLOTTO'S ALLIGATOR

Massimo Carlotto's life reads like the plot of one of his crime novels...because it *is* the plot of one of his books.

At 19, during Italy's 'years of lead', he witnessed the murder of Margherita Magello, a 25-year-old student who was stabbed 59 times. The events that followed became the novel *Il Fuggiasco* (The Fugitive). Covered in Magello's blood, Carlotto ran to fetch the police, who accused him of the killing. He was later sentenced to 18 years' imprisonment. In 1993, after an international campaign, he was released with a full pardon from the president of Italy.

While in prison, Carlotto found the true-life material for the explicit crime novels he now writes. His most famous series is the Alligator, which is developed from real legal cases Carlotto claims to have heard of and read up on.

The protagonist is loosely modelled on Carlotto himself; he even drives the Škoda Carlotto once drove (because many people say it is the least-stopped car in Italy). The nickname comes from the character's (and Carlotto's) favourite cocktail – seven parts Calvados to three parts Drambuie, crushed ice and a slice of apple – invented by a barman in Caffè Librarium Nostrum in Cagliari, where Carlotto now lives. The cocktail's fame has since spread to bars in Rome, Milan and Naples. It's said that nobody can drink more than four.

Five of Carlotto's books have been translated into English, including *The Fugitive* (2008), *Death's Dark Abyss* (2007) and *The Goodbye Kiss* (2006). Order his books at www.massimocarlotto.it.

Box Office Tickets TICKET OUTLET
(Map p38; ☏070 65 74 28; www.boxofficesardegna .it, in Italian; Viale Regina Margherita 43) Buy major events tickets here, including those for the summer season of stand-up comedy, music and dance at the Anfiteatro Romano.

Teatro Lirico THEATRE
(Map p34; ☏070 408 22 30; www.teatroliricodica gliari.it; Via Sant'Alenixedda) This is Cagliari's premier venue for classical music, opera and ballet. The line-up is fairly traditional but quality is high and concerts are well attended.

Exmà CULTURAL CENTRE
(Map p34; ☏070 66 63 99; Via San Lucifero 71) Hosts a year-round series of small-scale concerts, mainly jazz and chamber music. In summer the action moves to the outside courtyard.

🔒 Shopping

Cagliari has a refreshing absence of overtly touristy souvenir shops, although they do exist. Style-conscious shoppers kit themselves out in designer wear on the arcaded Via Roma and boutique-studded Via Giuseppe Garibaldi. Via Giuseppe Mano is dotted with high-street stores as well as snack bars and gelaterias for relaxing between purchases.

You'll find some lovely, low-key artisans' shops tucked away in the city's nooks and crannies, particularly in the Marina district.

TOP CHOICE Durke SWEETS
(Map p38; ☏070 66 67 82; www.durke.com; Via Napoli 66) In Sardinian, *durke* means 'sweet' and they don't come sweeter than this delightful old-fashioned store. Made according to age-old recipes, the sweets here are quite special and some of the best are made with nothing more than sugar, egg whites and almonds. Indulge on fruit-and-nut *papassinos,* moist *amaretti di sardegna* biscuits and *pardulas,* delicate ricotta cheesecakes flavoured with saffron.

Sapori di Sardegna FOOD
(Map p38; ☏070 684 87 47; Vicolo dei Mille 1) Roberto, his brother and their enthusiastic team do a brisk trade in glorious Sardinian food at this breezy Marina emporium. Stop by here for the finest pecorino, salami, *bottarga,* bread, wine and pretty-packed *dolci* (sweets). If you've got no room in your luggage, staff can arrange to ship orders worldwide.

Antica Enoteca Cagliaritana WINE
(Map p38; ☏070 66 93 86; Scalette Santa Chiara 21) Wine buffs will enjoy exploring the racks at this specialist wine shop off Piazza Yenne.

You can have orders sent anywhere in the world except the US (customs difficulties, apparently).

Sorelle Piredda
FASHION

(Map p38; ✆070 65 07 72; www.sorellepiredda.com; Piazza San Giuseppe 4) For haute couture with history, visit this oh-so-stylish Castello boutique. It's graced with the imaginative designs of the Piredda sisters, whose slinky evening dresses, capes and intricate shawls are inspired by ancient Sardinian motifs and traditional costume.

Loredana Mandas
JEWELLERY

(Map p38; ✆070 66 76 48; Via Sicilia 31) For something very special, seek out this jewellery workshop. You can watch Loredana create the exquisite gold filigree for which Sardinia is so famous, and then maybe buy a piece. A pair of gold earrings will set you back anything from €220 to €2100.

Bob Art
ART

(Map p38; www.bobart.it, in Italian; Via Torino 12) *Benvenuti* to Bob's wacky cartoon world of bug-eyed sheep, owls and butterflies. Watch artists at work creating bold canvases to jazz up any kid's (or big kid's) bedroom. Opening hours vary as wildly as the colour schemes.

Succhero e Argento
ARTISANAL

(Map p38; Via Napoli 50) This hole-in-the-wall store's filigree silver jewellery, ceramics and crafts fashioned from Sardinian cork make unique gifts.

Spazio P
ART

(Map p38; Via Napoli 62; www.spaziop.it; ⊙noon-midnight Tue-Sat) A gallery showcasing contemporary works by up-and-coming artists, with a sleek bar, at the back, for talking art.

① Information

Cagliari is dotted with free wifi zones, including Piazza Amendola in the Marina district, but annoyingly you can only log in if you have an Italian SIM card (the password is sent to your mobile phone).

Banks and ATMs are widely available, particularly around the port and station, on Piazza del Carmine and Corso Vittorio Emanuele.

Guardia Medica (✆070 609 52 02; Via Talete) For an emergency call-out doctor.

Lamarù (✆070 66 84 07; Via Napoli 43; per hr €3; ⊙9am-8pm Mon-Sat) Speedy internet and wi-fi with cheap snacks and drinks on the side.

Main post office (✆070 605 41 23; Piazza del Carmine 28; ⊙8am-6.50pm Tue-Fri, 8am-1.15pm Sat)

Ospedale Brotzu (✆070 53 91; Via Peretti 21) This hospital is northwest of the city centre. Take bus 1 from Via Roma if you need to make a nonemergency visit.

Tourist office (✆070 66 92 55; www.comune.cagliari.it, in Italian; Piazza Matteotti; ⊙8.30am-1.30pm & 2-8pm) This friendly tourist office should be your first port of call for city information and maps.

Viaggi Orrù (✆070 65 98 58; www.viaggiorru.it; Via Baylle 111; ⊙9am-1pm & 4.15-7.45pm Mon-Fri, 9.30am-1pm Sat) An efficient travel agency where you can book ferries and flights and organise excursions.

① Getting There & Away
Air

Cagliari's **Elmas airport** (CAG; ✆070 211 211; www.sogaer.it) is 6km northwest of the city centre. Flights connect with mainland Italian cities: Rome, Milan, Bergamo, Bologna, Florence, Naples, Rome, Turin and Venice, as well as Palermo in Sicily. Further afield, there are flights

---

DON'T MISS

TO MARKET!

Early-risers can join locals for a mooch around one of Cagliari's bustling morning food markets from Monday to Saturday. You can pick up all sorts of Sardinian goodies – seafood, tangy salami, pecorino the size of wagon wheels, horse steaks, you name it – it's all at historic food market, **Mercato di San Benedetto** (Map p34; Via San Francesco Cocco Ortu). For a more intimate vibe, try the delightful **Mercato di Santa Chiara** (Map p38) and brush up your *Italiano* at stalls laden with fresh fish, fruit and bread.

Sundays in Cagliari are best for flea market and antique finds. On the first Sunday of the month, Cagliaritani go bargain hunting at **Piazza del Carmine** (Map p38) antique and collectors market. The following week the antiques move up the hill to **Piazza Carlo Alberto** (Map p38), where they also appear on the last Sunday of the month. In Il Castello, there's also a flea market every Sunday morning (except in August) on **Bastione an Remy** (Map p38).

to and from Barcelona, Brussels, Luton, Paris and Stuttgart. In summer, there are additional charter flights.

The main airlines serving Elmas:

Air One (AP; ☎199 207 080; www.flyairone.it)

Alitalia (AZ; ☎06 22 22; www.alitalia.it)

British Airways (BA; ☎199 712 266; www .britishairways.com)

easyJet (U2; ☎899 234 589; www.easyjet .com)

Lufthansa (LH; ☎199 400 044; www.luft hansa.com)

Meridiana (IG; ☎89 29 28; www.meridiana.it)

Ryanair (FR; ☎899 678 910; www.ryanair.com)

Boat

Cagliari's ferry port is just off Via Roma. **Tirrenia** (☎892 123; www.tirrenia.it; Via Riva di Ponente 1) is the main ferry operator, with year-round services to Civitavecchia (€61, 14½ hours, daily), Naples (€54, 16¼ hours, Monday and Wednesday), Palermo (€53, 14½ hours, Friday) and Trapani (€52, 11 hours, Saturday). Book tickets at the port or at travel agencies.

Bus

From the main bus station on Piazza Matteotti, **ARST** (Azienda Regionale Sarda Trasporti; Map p38; ☎800 865 042; www.arst.sardegna .it, in Italian) buses serve nearby Pula (€3, 50 minutes, hourly) and Villasimius (€4, 1½ hours, six daily), as well as Oristano (€7, one hour 35 minutes, two daily), Nuoro (€15.50, 2½ hours to five hours, two daily), Iglesias (€4.50, one to 1½ hours, two daily), Carbonia (€6, 1½ hours, two daily), Portovesme (€6, two hours, Friday and Sunday, one daily) and the Sulcis area, and Sassari (€18.50, 3¼ hours, three daily).

Turmo Travel (☎0789 214 87; www.gruppo turmotravel.com) runs a twice daily service to Olbia (€19, 4½ hours) and a daily bus to Santa Teresa di Gallura (€23, 5½ hours).

Car & Motorcycle

The island's main dual-carriage, the SS131 Carlo Felice Hwy, links the capital with Porto Torres via Oristano and Sassari, and Olbia via Nuoro. The SS130 leads west to Iglesias.

The coast roads approaching from the east and west get highly congested in the summer holiday season.

Train

The main **Trenitalia** (www.trenitalia.com) station is located on Piazza Matteotti. Trains from here serve Iglesias (€3.85, one hour, 14 daily), Carbonia (€4.40, one hour, seven daily), Sassari (€15.75, 3½ to four hours, four daily) and Porto Torres (€16.90, 4¼ hours, one daily) via Oristano (€5.95, one to two hours, 15 daily). A branch line also connects with Olbia (€16.90, 4¼ hours, one daily) and Golfo Aranci (€18.30, five to seven hours, five daily) via Oristano or Chilivani.

ARST (http://arst.sardegna.it, in Italian) runs a metro service from Piazza Repubblica to Monserrato, where you can connect with trains for Dolianova, Mandas and Isili.

❶ Getting Around

The centre of Cagliari is small enough to explore on foot. The walk up to Il Castello is tough, but there's an elevator at the bottom of the Scalette di Santa Chiara behind Piazza Yenne.

To/From the Airport

ARST buses run from Piazza Matteotti to Elmas airport (€4, 10 minutes, 32 daily) between 5.20am and 10.30pm. From 9am to 10.30pm departures are every hour and half-past the hour. A taxi will set you back around €25.

Bus

CTM (Consorzio Trasporti e Mobilità; ☎070 209 12 10; www.ctmcagliari.it, in Italian) bus routes cover the city and surrounding area. You might

---

TRENINO VERDE

If you're not in a rush, one of the best ways of exploring Sardinia's interior is on the **trenino verde** (☎070 58 02 46; www.treninoverde.com), a slow, narrow-gauge diesel that runs through some of the island's most inhospitable countryside, stopping at isolated rural villages en route. There are four tourist routes: Mandas to Arbatax; Isili to Sorgono; Macomer to Bosa; and Sassari to Palau.

Of the tourist routes, the twisting Mandas to Arbatax line is particularly spectacular, crossing the remote highlands of the Parco Nazionale del Golfo di Orosei e del Gennargentu.

From the metro station on Piazza Repubblica in Cagliari, a metro runs to Monserrato where you can connect with trains for Mandas. From Mandas there are two daily departures (except on Tuesday) for Arbatax (€19, five hours) on the east coast, from mid-June to mid-September.

The *trenino verde* runs between mid-June and mid-September.

SERDIANA

About 25km north of Cagliari, the pretty agricultural town of Serdiana is home to one of Sardinia's most celebrated wine producers, the award-winning **Cantine Argiolas** (☎070 74 06 06; www.argiolas.it; Via Roma 28-30; tour with tasting €13; ☉tours at 11am & 3pm Mon-Fri, 10.30am Sat). You can visit the winery by calling ahead and organising a 1½-hour guided tour; the price includes a tasting of four different wines – among them a tangy Vermentino white and a full-bodied Cannonau red. For an additional €3 the wines are matched with bread, cheese and salami.

In the winery's restaurant (meals around €52), Sardinian specialities such as *fregola* (granular pasta) are expertly paired with Argiolas wines. Or you can take a cookery class (€75) and enjoy the results with some top wines drawn from the cellar.

From Cagliari take the SS554 north and after about 10km follow the SS387 for Dolianova. After another 10km take the turn-off for Serdiana.

use the buses to reach a handful of out-of-the-way sights, and they come in handy for the Cala Mosca and Poetto beaches. A standard ticket costs €1.20 and is valid for 90 minutes; a daily ticket is €3.

The most useful lines:

BUS 7 Circular route from Piazza Matteotti up to Il Castello and back.

BUS 10 From Viale Trento to Piazza Garibaldi via Corso Vittorio Emanuele.

BUS 30 OR 31 Along the seafront and up to the sanctuary at Bonaria.

BUS PF OR PQ From Piazza Matteotti to Poetto Beach.

Car & Motorcycle

Parking in the city centre from 9am to 1pm and 4pm to 8pm Monday to Saturday means paying. On-street metered parking – within the blue lines – costs €0.50 for the first hour and €1 thereafter. Alternatively, there's a big car park next to the train station, which costs €1 per hour or €10 for 24 hours. There's no maximum stay.

Driving in the centre of Cagliari is a pain, although given the geography of the town (one big hill), you might consider renting a scooter for a day or two. **CIA Rent a Car** (☎070 65 65 03; www.ciarent.it, in Italian; Via S Agostino 13) hires out bikes/cars/scooters from €10/29/30 per day. There's also a **Hertz** (☎070 65 10 78; Piazza Matteotti 8; www.hertz.it) on Piazza Matteotti and several car-rental agencies at the airport.

Taxi

Many hotels and guesthouses arrange airport pick-ups. There are taxi ranks at Piazza Matteotti, Piazza Repubblica and on Largo Carlo Felice. Otherwise you can call the radio taxi firms **Quattro Mori** (☎070 400 101) and **Rossoblù** (☎070 66 55).

THE SARRABUS

Stretching east and north of Cagliari, the lonely Sarrabus is one of Sardinia's least-populated and least-developed areas. In its centre rise the bushy green peaks of the Monte dei Sette Fratelli, a miraculously wild hinterland where some of the island's last remaining deer wander undisturbed.

East of Poetto the SP17 hugs the coast prettily (if precariously), providing spectacular views of the azure sea scalloped by crescent-shaped coves like Cala Regina, Kal'e Moru and Solanas. A few kilometres short of Villasimius, a winding road veers south along the peninsula to Capo Carbonara, Sardinia's most southeasterly point, where you're more likely to encounter flocks of inquisitive sheep and goats than cars in the low season.

Villasimius & Capo Carbonara

POP 3600

Once a quiet fishing village surrounded by pines and *macchia* (Mediterranean scrub), Villasimius has grown into one of Sardinia's most popular southern resorts and makes a handy base for exploring the fine sandy bays and transparent waters on this stretch of coast. In summer it's a lively, cheerful place, although activity all but dies out in winter.

If you're around on the second Sunday of July, don't miss the Festa della Madonna del Naufrago, a striking seaborne procession to a spot off the coast where a statue of the Virgin Mary lies on the seabed in honour of shipwrecked sailors.

◉ Sights

Museo Archeologico　　　　MUSEUM
(☑070 793 02 90; Via Frau 5; adult/reduced €3/1.50; ⊙9am-1pm Tue-Thu, 10am-1pm & 4-7pm Fri-Sun) Villasimius' little archaeology museum harbours a collection of Roman and Phoenician artefacts, as well as various odds and ends recovered from a 15th-century Spanish shipwreck.

Fortezza Vecchia　　　　HISTORICAL SITE
(☑070 793 02 90; Via Frau 5; admission €1) Perched on cliffs close to Capo Carbonara, this ruined 14th-century fortress dates back to when the Aragonese controlled the island. The views are more extraordinary than the stronghold itself. Visits by appointment only.

🏃 Activities

In town the main activity is browsing shops and enjoying the atmosphere. Boat tours tend to operate from May to September.

Spiaggia del Riso　　　　BEACH
Just south of town lies Spiaggia del Riso. One of Villasimius' most striking beaches, this beautiful arc of pale golden sand is lapped by azure waters and scattered with granite boulders polished smooth by the sea.

Stagno Notteri　　　　LAGOON
Running all the way to Villasimius, this lagoon often hosts flamingos in winter. On its seaward side is the stunning Spiaggia del Simius beach with its Polynesian blue waters.

Fiore di Maggio　　　　BOAT TOURS
(☑070 79 73 82/340 486 28 94; www.fioredimaggio.com; Località Campulongu; per person incl lunch €45) These daily boat tours are a superb way to see the hidden bays and islands of the Capo Carbonara marine reserve. Take your bathers if you fancy a dip.

Harry Tours　　　　BOAT TOURS
(☑338 377 40 51; www.harrystours.com) At the Porto Turistico, about 3km outside of the town centre, you can arrange boat tours (€65 per person including lunch) and dives (from €36) to nearby reefs and wrecks.

🍴 Eating

Via Roma and Via del Mare are safe bets for a quick pizza, coffee or gelato, and self-caterers can find supermarkets and grocery stores in the resort centre.

Ristorante Le Anforè　　　　SARDINIAN €€
(☑070 79 20 32; Localitá Su Cordolinu; meals around €30; ⊙Tue-Sun) The chef's love of fresh local produce shines through in Sardinian dishes such as *burrida* (marinated dogfish) and spaghetti with *ricci* at this highly regarded restaurant. There's alfresco dining on the verandah overlooking gardens.

Ristorante La Lanterna　　　　SARDINIAN €€
(☑070 79 00 13; Via Roma 62; meals around €30; ⊙closed Mon lunch) With two fishmongers just down the road, it's no surprise that this cordial restaurant specialises in seafood. Specialities such as *fregola* with plump mussels and clams or baby octopus in spicy sauce go well with a litre of house white (€7.50). In summer you can dine alfresco in the small garden.

ℹ Information

Just off central Piazza Gramsci, the **tourist office** (☑070 793 02 71; www.villasimiusweb.com; Piazza Giovanni XXIII; ⊙8am-8pm Mon-Fri) can provide information on activities in the town.

ℹ Getting There & Around

Six weekday ARST buses (two on Sundays) run to and from Cagliari (€4, 1½ hours) throughout the year. Between mid-June and mid-September there are up to eight daily services.

If you want to rent your own wheels (a good idea, as most of the beaches are a few kilometres out of town), **Edilrent Simius** (☑070 792 80 37; Via Roma 77) hires out bikes (€6.50 to €10 per day), scooters (€30 to €55) and cars (€63 to €80).

DON'T MISS

DIVING OFF CAPO CARBONARA

Although the tip of the cape remains a military zone off limits to visitors, the azure waters around Capo Carbonara are a **marine reserve** (www.ampcapocarbonara.it), accessible with an authorised diving company. The reserve includes Isola dei Cavoli, Secca dei Berni and Isola di Serpentara just off the coast from Villasimius. **Morgan Diving** (☑070 80 50 59; www.morgandiving.com), based at the Porto Turistico, Quartu Sant'Elena, is a licensed operator, as is **Air Sub** (☑070 79 20 33; www.airsub.com; Via Roma 121) in Villasimius. Both outfits lead dives to a number of sites, including the Secca di Santa Caterina, an underwater mountain. Reckon on €36 to €90 for a dive, depending on location and level of difficulty.

A WALK IN THE WOODS

A world away from the urban hustle of Cagliari, Monte dei Sette Fratelli (1023m) is the highest point of the remote Sarrabus district. Its granite peaks and woodlands bristling with cork and holm oak, juniper, oleander and myrtle are a haven to wild boar, hawks and golden eagles, and it's one of only three remaining redoubts of the *cervo sardo* (Sardinian deer). Accessible by the SS125, it offers some magnificent hiking, with routes ranging from straightforward strolls to a tough 12km ascent of **Punta Sa Ceraxa** (1016m).

You can pick up a trekking map from the Caserma Forestale Campu Omu, a forestry corps station near the Burcei turn-off on the SS125. Alternatively, contact the **Coop Monte dei Sette Fratelli** (☑070 994 72 00; www.montesettefratelli.com, in Italian; Via Centrale) in Burcei, a few kilometres inland from the Costa Rei.

From Burcei, a lonely road crawls 8km up to **Punta Serpeddi** (1067m), from where you can gaze out across the whole Sarrabus to Cagliari and the sea.

Costa Rei

Stretching along Sardinia's southeastern coast, the Costa Rei boasts long strips of white sandy beach and resort-style accommodation.

From Villasimius, take the SP17 as it follows the coast north. The road actually runs a couple of hundred metres inland, but you can access the signposted beaches via the dirt tracks that branch off the main road. Crystal-clear waters and the occasional snack-cum-cocktail bar await.

About 25km out of Villasimius you hit **Cala Sinzias**, a pretty sandy strand with two campsites. Continue for a further 6km and you come to the Costa Rei resort proper, a holiday village full of villas, shops, bars, clubs and a few indifferent eateries. **Spiaggia Costa Rei** is, like the beaches to its south and north, a dazzling white strand lapped by remarkably clear blue-green water.

At the resort, **Butterfly Service** (☑070 99 10 91; www.butterflyservice.it; Via Colombo; ⊙9am-1pm & 4-7.30pm Mon-Sat, 10am-1pm & 4.30-7.30pm Sun) is an all-purpose agency offering everything from internet access (€8 per hour) to bike (€15), scooter (€35) and car hire (€75 per day) and excursions along the coast and up to the **Parco Sette Fratelli** (€20 to €90).

North of the resort, **Spiaggia Piscina Rei** is a continuation of the blinding white sand and turquoise water theme, with a camping ground fenced in just behind it. A couple more beaches fill the remaining length of coast up to **Capo Ferrato**, beyond which drivable dirt trails lead north.

The same ARST buses from Cagliari to Villasimius continue around to Costa Rei, taking about half an hour.

Nuraghe Asoru

Nuraghe Asoru is the best example of a *nuraghe* (Bronze Age fortified settlement) in southeastern Sardinia, which is largely devoid of archaeological interest. About 5km inland of San Priamo, it stands north of the SS125. Its central *tholos* (conical tower) is in reasonable shape, but it doesn't really compare to Sardinia's more important *nuraghi*.

Muravera & Torre Salinas

POP 5300

On the flood plain of the Fiume Flumendosa (Flumendosa River), Muravera is not an especially interesting place. An agricultural town, it's best known for its citrus fruit, which it celebrates on the second Sunday before Easter with the **Sagra degli Agrumi** (Citrus Fair).

South of town, the lagoons and beaches of Torre Salinas are picturesquely spread out beneath a Spanish watchtower. It's a seemingly untouched area, centred on the **Stagno dei Colostrai**, winter home to flamingos. On the seaward side of the lagoon, **Spiaggia Torre delle Saline** is the first in a line of dazzling beaches that continues north to the mouth of the Fiume Flumendosa.

In Muravera, you can get a decent bite at **Ristorante Pizzeria Su Nuraxi** (☑070 993 09 91; Via Roma 257; pizzas from €5, meals around €25) on the main road. It's a relaxed place that serves hearty meats and good pizzas.

Three weekday ARST buses run from Cagliari to Muravera (€6, three hours) via Villasimius. There are quicker inland services (€6, one hour 40 minutes, five Monday to Saturday, two Sunday).

Iglesias & the Southwest

Includes »

Best Places to Eat

» Pintadera (p59)

» Gazebo Medioevale (p59)

» L'Ancora (p62)

» La Cantina (p72)

Best Places to Stay

» La Babbajola B&B (p201)

» Agriturismo L'Aquila (p202)

» Hotel Riviera (p202)

» Hotel Luci del Faro (p203)

» B&B S'Olivariu (p203)

Why Go?

The southwest comprises diverse regions, their characters rich in history and attractions. The area's superb beaches hold the most pull, starting from the magnificent, untamed sands of the Costa Verde to the tropical waters of the Costa del Sud. Iglesiente offers photogenic coves, and the twin islands of San Pietro (Isola di San Pietro) and Sant'Antioco (Isola di Sant'Antioco) have their own distinctive charms: San Pietro with its animated and instantly likeable atmosphere, and Sant'Antioco with its earthy character and rich archaeological legacy.

Inland, Iglesias and its surrounding hills have a more melancholy quality – once the island's mining heartland, many of the abandoned mines have been resurrected as tourist attractions, resulting in some eerie sightseeing tours. Further in, at the heart of the voluptuous Marmilla region, sits Sardinia's greatest *nuraghe* (Bronze Age fortified settlement), the Unesco-listed Nuraghe Su Nuraxi, a real archaeological treat.

When to Go

Sardinia has its most impressive festivities in March and April for Easter celebrations – and Iglesias excels with its hooded processions and deathly drumming. Another wonderful time to visit the southwest is at the end of May and beginning of June, for the start of the tuna season and wonderful culinary adventures on the island of San Pietro. Don't miss the high summer; August is perfect for joining beach parties along the southern coast, but even better for getting away to the remote wilderness of the Costa Verde.

IGLESIAS

POP 27,800

Surrounded by the skeletons of Sardinia's once-thriving mining industry, Iglesias is a historic town that bubbles in the summer and slumbers in the colder months. Its historic centre is an appealing ensemble of lived-in piazzas, sun-bleached buildings and Aragonese-style wrought-iron balconies, and it's here that the townsfolk gather on warm summer evenings. The atmosphere is as much Spanish as Sardinian, as is the town's name, which is Spanish for 'churches'. Visit at Easter to experience a quasi-Seville experience during the extraordinary drum-beating processions.

History

The death of mining in the 1970s hit the area hard. Mining has been big business here since classical times. The Romans called their town Metalla, after the precious metals they mined on Monte Linas. But the Romans weren't the first to exploit the mines; when they were reopened in the 19th century, equipment belonging to the Carthaginians was discovered. Populated by slaves and immigrants, Iglesias grew, with each group establishing a church. Their buildings gave the town one of its earlier names, Villa di Chiesa (Town of Churches).

Centuries later in 1257, the Pisans grabbed the Giudicato di Cagliari (Province of Cagliari) and granted Iglesias to Ugolino della Gherardesca, a Pisan captain and member of the pro-papal Ghibelline party. He had a good business head and quickly organised the town along the lines of a Tuscan *comune* (self-governing town) with its own laws and currency. He even instituted the statute of laws known as the Breve di Villa Chiesa, a revolutionary code that granted social benefits to the miners. You can still view it on request at the city's Archivio Stòrico.

In 1323 the Catalano–Aragonese troops landed at Portovesme and took Villa Di Chiesa the following year, renaming it Iglesias. They had little interest in the mines and for the next 500 years the pits lay abandoned until private entrepreneurs, such as Quintino Sella (after whom the main piazza is named), revived their fortunes. As the nascent centre of heavy industry in a resurgent and soon-to-be-united Italy, Iglesias once again became an important town – until WWII, and then later modern economics, tolled its death knell in the 1970s.

◉ Sights

Much of modern Iglesias harks back to the 19th century. This was the period of the last big boom in the city's mining fortunes, when new laws allowed a syndicate from the Italian mainland to buy up the mines and reopen them. To herald this exciting new era, the bulk of the town's medieval walls were demolished and the spacious **Piazza Quintino Sella** was laid out in what had previously been a field just outside the city walls. The piazza became the central meeting place of the town and even today it throngs with people during the evening *passeggiata* (stroll). The **statue** in the centre commemorates Quintino Sella (of Sella e Mosca wine fame), a Sardinian statesman and vigorous promoter of the reborn mining industry.

Much of the pleasure of visiting Iglesias lies in the small medieval centre. There are no great must-see sights, but the narrow, car-free lanes and suggestive piazzas are in good nick and are much appreciated by locals who flock here throughout the day and night to browse the shops and hang out in the bars. It's also in the **centro storico** that you'll find many of the **churches** that give the city its name.

Duomo   DUOMO

(Piazza del Municipio; ⊘closed for renovation) Dominating the eastern flank of Piazza del Municipio, the Duomo retains its lovely Pisan-flavoured facade, as does the bell tower, with its chequerboard stonework. The Duomo was begun in 1337, but Catalan architects gave it a makeover in the 16th century, which accounts for the rich internal decoration. Inside, the highlight is the gilded altarpiece that once held the relics of St Antiochus. Originally this was on the Isola di Sant'Antioco, but it was bought to Iglesias in the 17th century to protect it from

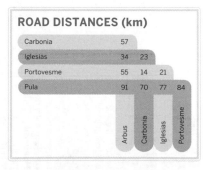

ROAD DISTANCES (km)

	Arbus	Carbonia	Iglesias	Portovesme
Carbonia	57			
Iglesias	34	23		
Portovesme	55	14	21	
Pula	91	70	77	84

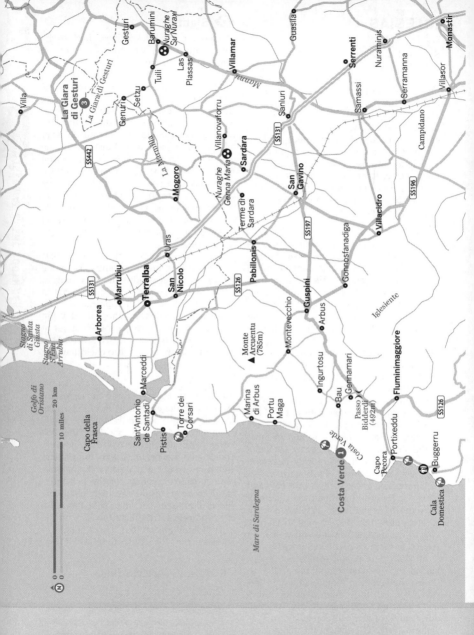

Iglesias & the Southwest Highlights

1 Indulge in some off-road driving en route to the wild, windswept beaches of the **Costa Verde** (p64)

2 Peer into the long-dead past at the **Necropolis del Montessu** (p70), a prehistoric cemetery set in a rocky amphitheatre

3 Come face to face with wild horses on Sardinia's high plain **La Giara di Gesturi** (p82)

4 Give yourself up to the sombre, spine-tingling atmosphere of Iglesias' hooded **Settimana Santa** (p59) processions in Iglesias

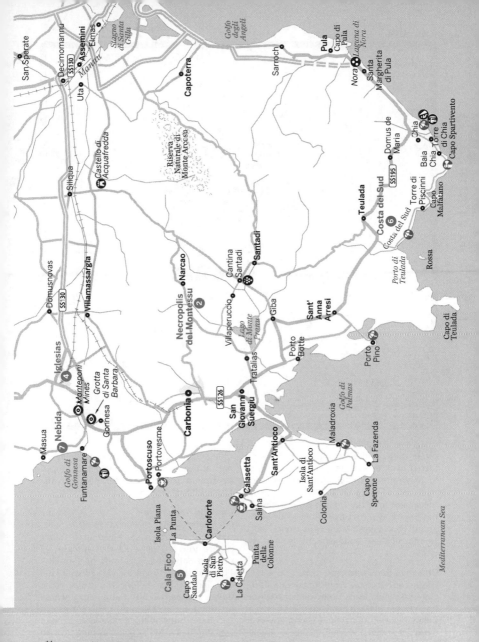

5 Thrill to the sight of an Eleonora's falcon at **Cala Fico** (p73), a photogenic cove on the ravishing Isola di San Pietro

6 Beach hop along the fantastic tropical stretches of sand on the **Costa del Sud** (p76)

7 Check out the spectacular **Scoglio Pan di Zucchero** (p61), a gigantic rugged rock dipped into the tranquil waters off the Costa Verde, viewed from the village of Nebida.

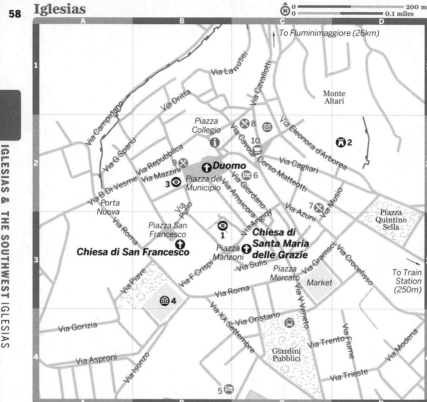

pirate raids. And although the clerics were forced to return the relics to the cathedral in Sant'Antioco in the 19th century, they managed to hang on to the altar. Across the square from the Duomo is the **bishop's residence**, while on the western side is the grand neoclassical **Municipio** (town hall). Neither of these buildings are open to the public.

Chiesa di San Francesco   CHURCH
(Piazza San Francesco) From Piazza del Municipio, Via Pullo leads to the dainty rose-red trachyte of Chiesa di San Francesco, a typical Catalan Gothic affair. Built over a 200-year period between 1300 and 1500, its single-nave interior is flanked by chapels squeezed in between the buttresses.

Chiesa di Santa Maria delle Grazie   CHURCH
(Piazza Manzoni) Outdating Chiesa di San Francesco by a century or so is the nearby

Chiesa di Santa Maria delle Grazie, the original 13th-century facade of which is topped by a pinky baroque number, dating to the 17th and 18th centuries.

Castello Salvaterra   CASTLE
(Via Montartai) Just off Piazza Quintino Sella, scruffy litter-strewn stairs lead up to a stout square tower. This is all that remains of Castello Salvaterra, Ugolino's once-mighty Pisan fortress. To get an idea of what the city looked like before the walls came down, proceed to Via Campidano, where a stretch of the 14th-century northwestern perimeter built by the Catalano-Aragonese remains defiantly in place, complete with towers.

Archivio Stòrico   HISTORICAL SITE
(☎078 12 48 50; Via delle Carceri; ☺9am-1pm & 3.45-6.15pm Mon-Fri) Records illustrating Iglesias' past are kept in the Archivio Stòrico, the city's historical archive. Of particular

Iglesias

interest is the Breve di Villa di Chiesa, the statute book of the medieval city, dating from 1327.

FREE **Museo dell'Arte Mineraria**   MUSEUM
(☏0781 35 00 37; www.museoartemineraria.it; Via Roma 47; ⊗7-9pm Fri-Sun Jul-Sep, 6-8pm Sat & Sun summer, by appointment winter) Just outside the *centro storico*, on the main road into the town centre is Iglesias' main museum. Dedicated to the town's mining heritage, it displays up to 70 extraction machines, alongside tools and a series of thought-provoking black-and-white photos. To get a real taste of the claustrophobic conditions in which the miners worked, duck down into the recreated tunnels. These were actually dug by mining students and were used to train senior workers, at least until WWII, when they were used as air-raid shelters. Upstairs you will find a collection of some 8000 carefully labelled rock and mineral specimens sourced from Sardinia and around the world.

Chiesa di Nostra Signora del Buon Cammino   CHURCH

To the northwest of the town centre, this white church is perched on a tall hill and from here commands lovely views over the city.

Chiesa di Nostra Signora di Valverde   CHURCH

(Viale Fra Ignazio) On the opposite side of town, this is another of Iglesias' historic churches. About 15 minutes' walk from Piazza Quintino Sella, it retains little of its 13th-century structure except for an elegant facade, similar to the Duomo's, with two series of blind arches in the Pisan style.

✦ Festivals & Events

Settimana Santa   EASTER FESTIVAL
(www.prolocoiglesias.it/settimanasanta.htm, in Italian) The week before Easter is a good time to visit Iglesias. During the festival the town celebrates its Spanish origins and religious traditions in a series of sinister religious processions. Every night between Holy Tuesday and Good Friday, hooded members of religious brotherhoods, bearing candles and crucifixes and accompanied by a slow, deathly drum beat, bear effigies of the Virgin Mary and Christ around town.

Estate Medioevale Iglesiente   SUMMER FESTIVAL
(www.mediatecaiglesias.it, in Italian; search under 'Feste e manifestazioni') Iglesias' Medieval Summer is a series of themed events that involve much dressing up and flag-waving. Highlights include a two-day crossbow tournament and a huge costumed procession on 13 August.

✗ Eating & Drinking

TOP CHOICE **Pintadera**   OSTERIA €€
(☏0781 251 864; Viua Mannu 22-24; meals €35-40; ⊗daily) It's a real treat to eat in Pintadera, a welcoming family-run osteria in the *centro storico*. A mother-and-son outfit, it's where you should focus on the excellent meat, from the sausage-soaked pasta, to goat, mutton or beef.

Gazebo Medioevale   TRATTORIA €€
(☏078 13 08 71; Via Musio 21; lunch set menu €13, meals around €25; ⊗Mon-Sat) Excellent value and great grilled meats. Not a bad combination, especially if you add an attractive interior – exposed brick walls lined with Sardinian masks and, for some bizarre reason, a didgeridoo – and a convenient location. Credit cards are not accepted.

Villa di Chiesa   RESTAURANT €€
(☏078 12 31 24; Piazza del Municipio 8; set menu €15, meals around €25; ⊗Tue-Sun) Grab a table on Piazza del Municipio (summer only) and

sit down to wonderful homemade pasta at this long-standing favourite. Menu stalwarts include scrumptious *culurgiones,* which sound rude but are in fact pasta pockets stuffed with ricotta, spinach and saffron, and *sebadas* (light pastry filled with cheese and covered with honey). There's also pizza in the evenings.

Caffè Lamarmora CAFE €

(Piazza Lamarmora 6; ⊘6am-1pm & 3-9.30pm) This landmark *centro storico* cafe serves deliciously strong coffee. It's not difficult to find – just look for the towering building covered in 1930s-style adverts. Confusingly, though, it shuts over lunchtime, something which doesn't make a lot of commercial sense.

❶ Information

Banco Nazionale del Lavoro (Via Roma 29) Has an ATM.

Libreria Mondadori (⌂0781 2 37 77; Piazza La Marmora; ⊘9am-1pm & 5-8.15pm) A small bookshop good for maps and guides.

Main post office (Via Mercato Vecchio; ⊘8am-1.15pm Mon-Sat)

Tourist office (⌂0781 25 25 39; Via Verdi 2; ⊘10am-1pm & 6-8pm Mon-Fri) Helpful and multilingual staff, with tons of promotional material.

❶ Getting There & Away

Bus

All intercity buses arrive at and leave from the Via Oristano side of the Giardini Pubblici. You can get timetable information and tickets from **Bar Giardini** (Via Oristano 8; ⊘5.30am-2.30pm & 3.30-9pm Mon-Sat) across the road from the stops. Buses run to Cagliari (€4.50, one to 1½ hours, two daily), Carbonia (€2, 45 minutes, eight times daily) and Funtanamare (€1, 20 minutes, 11 daily).

Car & Motorcycle

With the exception of the dual-carriageway SS130 from Cagliari (less than an hour), road approaches to Iglesias are slow. From the south, the SS195 coastal road from Cagliari connects with the SS126 from Isola di Sant'Antioco to pass via Carbonia to Iglesias. From the north, the SS126 drops south from Oristano province to Guspini and then heads through the mountains via Arbus and Fluminimaggiore.

Train

As many as 14 daily Trenitalia trains run between Iglesias and Cagliari (€3.85, one hour).

AROUND IGLESIAS

Monteponi Mines

If you're at all interested in Iglesias' industrial history, you'll be fascinated by the enormous mining centre of Monteponi. Some 2km west of Iglesias, this sprawling, now abandoned, area was the black heart of the Iglesiente mining industry – one of Sardinia's most important producers of lead, zinc and silver. Extraction dates back to 1324 and continued on and off until 1992, when the entire operation transferred to Campo Pisano across the valley.

Today it's possible to visit the Galleria Villamarina, a tunnel built in 1852 to connect the mine's two principal pits. To organise a tour, you'll need to contact the **IGEA cooperative** (⌂0781 49 13 00; adult/under 12yr €8/4.50; ⊘8.30am-5pm Mon-Fri).

If you're without wheels, you can get a local Linea B bus from Via Oristano in Iglesias eight times a day (€0.70, 20 minutes).

Grotta di Santa Barbara

A few kilometres further along the Carbonia road are the abandoned San Giovanni lead and zinc mines. Back in the 1950s, routine excavations revealed the **Grotta di Santa Barbara** (⌂0781 49 13 00; adult/reduced €12/6; ⊘8.30am-5pm Mon-Fri), a hitherto unknown cave complex. The walls of the single enormous chamber are pock-marked with dark-brown crystals and white calcite, while stalactites and stalagmites give the impression of a ghostly underground forest. Visits are by appointment only.

Funtanamare

The beach that is closest to Iglesias is at Funtanamare (also spelt Fontanamare). A long strip of golden sand backed by dunes and fertile farmland, it's a hugely popular spot, although it rarely gets too crowded, if nothing else because it's so long. Strong winds make it a surfer favourite, particularly when the *maestrale* (northwest wind) is blowing.

Up to 11 daily buses run from Iglesias down to the beach (€1, 20 minutes), and there is plenty of parking if you want to drive. Another five buses head to a point known as **Plage Mesu**, further south along the same strand.

Domusnovas

About 10km east of Iglesias just off the SS130 Cagliari road, the unremarkable town of Domusnovas sits at the centre of one of Sardinia's most exciting rock-climbing areas. The outlying countryside is peppered with limestone rocks, cliffs and caves, many of which are ideal for sports climbing. There are some 440 routes for both novice and experienced climbers, ranging from simple, single-pitch walls to tough 7c overhangs. Experts say climatic and rock conditions are at their best between early autumn and late spring. For more technical information, check out www.climb-europe.com/sardinia and www.sardiniaclimb.com.

Four kilometres north of Domusnovas, and signposted from the main road, the **Grotta di San Giovanni** (☉illuminated 9am-9pm) is well worth checking out. An 850m-long natural cave-gallery, it has only recently been closed to traffic – until 2000 you could actually drive your car straight through. If you're feeling peckish there's a bar-restaurant by the car park at the entrance.

Eight daily buses connect Iglesias and Domusnovas (€1, 15 minutes).

THE IGLESIENTE

To the north and west of Iglesias, the mountainous landscape is picturesque and strangely haunting. Wild green scrub cloaks the silent hills in a soft, verdant down, while abandoned houses serve as a poignant reminder of the mining communities that once thrived here. The coast is dramatic and offers superb seascapes.

All the towns in the region were connected with mining. You can visit the old galleries on guided tours run by the **IGEA cooperative** (☎0781 49 13 00), a locally run outfit that seeks to maintain interest in the area's history by taking visitors to places that would otherwise be abandoned. In July and August you may be able to just turn up and join a tour, but it is always advisable to book ahead as getting to these places is incredibly time-consuming.

The Coast

NEBIDA

From Funtanamare, the SP83 coastal road affords spectacular views as it dips, bends and climbs its tortuous way northwards. After 5.5km you come to the small and rather drab village of Nebida, a former mining settlement sprawled along the coastal road high above the sea. The main reason to stop here is to enjoy the mesmerising views from the **Belvedere**, a panoramic viewing point accessible by a fenced-off walkway along the cliff. Dominating the seascape is the 133m-high **Scoglio Pan di Zucchero** (Sugarloaf Rock), the largest of several *faraglioni* (sea stacks) that rise out of the glassy blue waters against a majestic backdrop of sheer, rugged cliffs. Below, the **Laveria Lamarmora** is the shell of a building used for washing and separating minerals back in Nebida's mining days. A track winds down from the main road to the site.

About 500m further north, a side road leads down to **Portu Banda**, which has a small pebble beach.

To better explore the sea, contact **Marco Salerni** (☎329 792 00 93) who organises dives out of Nebida for €25 per person plus the cost of equipment hire.

Local buses run between Iglesias and Masua, stopping off at Nebida (€1.50, 30 minutes, 11 daily).

MASUA

A few kilometres further north, Masua is another former mining centre. Seen from above, it looks a pretty ugly prospect, but it's not entirely without interest.

Descending into town, the road leads past an abandoned mining complex to a beach that, while not Sardinia's best, is pleasant enough with its stunning close-ups of the Scoglio Pan di Zucchero.

But the main drawcard here is the chance to visit the town's unique mining port. Until the 1920s, much of the ore mined around the Iglesiente was transported to sailing vessels that were hauled up onto the beaches. The boats then sailed down to Carloforte (on Isola di San Pietro) to transfer the load to cargo vessels. This system was dispensed with in 1924, when two 600m tunnels were dug into the cliffs at Masua. In the lower of the two tunnels a conveyor belt received zinc and lead ore from the underground deposits and transported it via an ingenious mobile 'arm' directly to the ships moored below. The upper tunnel was used to carry minerals to the underground deposits. Guided tours of **Porto Flavia** (☎0781 49 13 00; adult/child €8/4.50; ☉9am, 10.30am & noon Aug, rest of year by appointment only) take about one hour. To find the entrance, head down to the beach from where a road leads back uphill and then around the coast for about 2.5km. The same road leads to a shady lookout point over the Scoglio Pan di Zucchero.

CALA DOMESTICA

From Masua the road rises quickly in a series of tight turns as it works its way around Monte Guardianu to Buggerru. Beach-lovers should take the signposted turn-off for Cala Domestica, 5km short of Buggerru. Follow the road down to the car park at the end and you'll find yourself at a sandy beach wedged into a natural inlet between craggy cliffs. The water is a beautiful blue and sometimes curls up in decent sets of waves. A walk along the rocky path to the right of the beach brings you to a smaller, more sheltered side strand.

There's a car park, costing around €4 per day in summer (for most of the rest of the year it's free as there's nobody there). A snack bar behind the beach helps keep body and soul together.

BUGGERRU & PORTIXEDDU
POP 1120

A popular resort with a small harbour and a rash of holiday apartments, Buggerru is the biggest village on this stretch of coastline. Set within the natural stone walls of a steep valley, it was established in 1860 and by the early 20th century had developed into an important mining centre with a population of 12,000. For a long time it was accessible only by sea, a fact which forced it into enterprising self-sufficiency – Buggerru had its own electricity supply before Cagliari and Sassari, as well as a hospital, a mutual benefit society and a small theatre. It wasn't all roses though, and in 1904 Buggerru's miners downed tools and went on strike – the first ever recorded in Sardinia.

Information on the town and its environs is available at the **tourist office** (☑0781 5 40 93; ⊙10am-noon & 6-8pm), situated on the SP83 coastal road.

Other than hang out on the beach, a favourite with local surfers, you can hire a boat from **Società Mormora** (☑328 883 33 40) down at the Porto Turistico (Tourist Harbour) and visit Buggerru's former mine, the **Galleria Henry** (☑0781 49 13 00; adult/reduced €8/4.50; ⊙9am, 10.30am, noon, 2pm, 3.30pm, 4.30pm & 5.30pm Aug, rest of year by appointment). What makes this hour-long 1km tour a highlight are the views straight down the cliff to the sea.

A fantastic place to eat here is **L'Ancora** (☑0781 54 903; meals €25-30; ⊙closed Wed, open daily in Jul & Aug), a small trattoria that specialises in fish and seafood, prepared simply and to great effect – for a real treat, try the fish prepared *alla Vernaccia* (baked with the local sweet wine). There's a small terrace in the front, from which you can indulge in gorgeous sea views in the warmer months; wintertime seating is inside the one-room trattoria.

The road out of Buggerru climbs high along the cliff face for a couple of kilometres before you hit the long sandy stretches of **Spiaggia Portixeddu**, one of the best beaches in the area, which extends 3km up the coast to the Rio Mannu, the river marking the end of the Iglesiente coast.

Inland
FLUMINIMAGGIORE
POP 3050

A pretty but nauseatingly winding 26km stretch of the SS126 leads from Iglesias to Fluminimaggiore, an uninspiring town with a couple of museums and a few modest eateries. It's a disaffected place and, like Orgosolo in central Sardinia, it has vented its unhappy condition in murals around the town, many of which look back to the golden days of the mines with real nostalgia.

The town itself is of little interest, but in its environs you'll find the impressive Grotta di Su Mannau and the Roman Tempio di Antas.

Up to 10 daily buses link Iglesias with Fluminimaggiore (€2, 45 minutes). To get to the following two sites ask the driver to drop you off on the main road, from where you'll have to walk the last couple of kilometres.

Grotta di Su Mannau   CAVE
(☑0781 58 04 11; www.sumannau.it; adult/reduced €8/4.50; ⊙9.30am-6pm Easter-Oct, reservations essential rest of year) A few kilometres south of town, and signposted off the SS126, this is the largest cave of its sort so far discovered in the Iglesiente. The standard tour takes you on a 50-minute walk through a fraction of the cave's delights, passing through several lake chambers and the Archaeological Room, so called because there is archaeological evidence that it was used as a temple for water worship. Finally you reach the Pozzo Rodriguez (Rodriguez Well), where you see an impressive 8m column, effectively a stalactite and stalagmite fused together.

More exciting tours of the cave are possible and are open to complete beginners. These tours enable you to visit dramatic chambers like the White Room or the opalescent waters of the Pensile Lake. A six- to eight-hour tour will get you to the jewel of Su Mannau, the Virgin Room, where you can see wonderful aragonites and big snow-white slopes of solidified calcium. The latter tour is the most difficult, and requires a wetsuit to pass through the various bottlenecks and siphons.

These excursions need to be organised in advance through the cave office. Costs vary according to the duration and number of participants.

Tempio di Antas   TEMPLE

(☑0781 58 09 90; www.startuno.it; adult/reduced €3/2; ☉9.30am-6.30pm daily summer, 9.30am-3pm Fri, Sat & Sun winter) In a lovely, woody spot 9km south of Fluminimaggiore, the sand-coloured Tempio di Antas has stood in solitary isolation since the 3rd century AD. Built by the emperor Caracalla, it was constructed over a 6th-century BC Punic sanctuary, which itself was set over an earlier *nuraghe* settlement. In its Roman form the temple was dedicated to Sardus Pater, a local Sardinian deity worshipped by the nuraghic people as Babai and by the Punic faithful as Sid, god of warriors and hunters.

After centuries of disrepair, the temple was extensively restored between 1967 and 1976. Most impressively, the original Ionic columns were excavated and re-erected. At the foot of these columns you can make out remains of the temple's Carthaginian predecessor, which the Romans cannibalised to erect their version.

Between the ticket office and the temple, a narrow trail marked as *sentiero romano* (Roman way) leads after about five minutes to what little remains of the original *nuraghe* settlement. Following the trail for 1½ hours would theoretically take you to the Grotta di Su Mannau, but we haven't tried it out.

From the main road, it's about a half-hour walk to the main site.

COSTA VERDE

One of Sardinia's great untamed coastal stretches, the Costa Verde (Green Coast) extends northwards from Capo Pecora to the small resort of Torre dei Corsari. Named after the green *macchia* (Mediterranean scrub) that covers much of its mountainous hinterland, it's an area of wild, exhilarating beauty and spectacular beaches. The best of these are only accessible by dirt track, which can be tough on hire cars but means that they are largely free of unsightly development. In fact, the Costa Verde beaches are among the wildest and most unspoilt in Sardinia.

There's no road which follows the entire length of the Costa Verde, so if you're driving northwards from Portixeddu (and you really do need to drive to get the best out of the area), you'll have to head inland along the SS126 towards Arbus and Guspini.

Villacidro

POP 14,600

About 9km southeast of Arbus, a minor road leads to the Tolkienesque-sounding Gonnosfanadiga. Another 6km east on the SS196 brings you to the first of two turnoffs for Villacidro, a small agricultural town best known for its yellow, saffron-based liqueur. Follow this twisting country road and about 2.5km short of Villacidro you'll see a signpost for the **Cascata Su Spendula** waterfall. Surrounding the waterfall are imposing rock walls and a thick curtain of trees.

Arbus

POP 6780

Lounging on the slopes of Monte Linas, Arbus is home to one of Sardinia's most original museums. Up in the granite old town, just off central Piazza Mercato, the **Museo del Coltello Sardo** (☑070 975 92 20; www.museodelcoltello.it; Via Roma 15; admission free; ☉9am-noon & 4-8pm Mon-Fri) pays homage to the ancient Sardinian art of knife-making. The museum was founded by Paolo Pusceddu, whose *s'arburesi* (knives from Arbus; see the boxed text, p113) are among the most prized of Sardinian knives. Downstairs, you can contemplate Signor Pusceddu's historic knife collection and admire some of his finest creations.

At the opposite end of Arbus, **Ristorante Sa Lolla** (☑070 975 40 04; Via Libertà 225; meals around €25; ☉Thu-Tue) has a good local reputation. Hopefully you can ignore the gnomes on the tables, as it serves great lamb dishes and hearty bowls of steaming pasta.

From Capo Pecora head back via Portixeddu and northeast along the SS126 until you reach the turn-off for **Gennamari, Bau** and **Spiaggia Scivu.** If coming from the northeast, you'll see the signs on the right, 13km from Arbus. Take this narrow mountain route into the windswept, Mediterranean scrub-covered southern heights to around 450m above sea level, when the sea comes into view. Five kilometres short of the beach, Spiaggia Scivu is signposted to the left. Going straight ahead would take you to the local penitentiary, something that has helped to keep Scivu off the developers' map for many years.

You arrive at a parking area, where there's a kiosk and freshwater showers in summer only. You'll also need to bring some sort of shade (an umbrella or tent), as there are no facilities and it's very exposed. As you walk towards the beach, you find yourself atop 70m dunes from where you can view the enormous length of beach that stretches before you.

The other famous beach of the Costa Verde is the **Spiaggia della Piscinas**, some 3.7km northeast of the Spiaggia Scivu turn-off along the SS126. Take the Ingurtosu exit. This is a worthwhile exercise in its own right, as the road drops down into a valley lined with the abandoned buildings, housing and machinery of a crumbling 19th-century mining settlement.

After 9km of dirt track, you'll hit a fork. Take the left branch for Spiaggia della Piscinas, and you'll reach the beach after a further 20 minutes of off-road driving. Back from the broad strand of beach rise 30m-high dunes, known as Sardinia's desert. In summer one or two beach bars brighten the place up and offer welcome showers, umbrellas and loungers.

ARST buses reach Arbus from Cagliari (€4.50, two hours, six daily Monday to Saturday, two Sunday), although it's a pretty long haul.

Montevecchio

Surrounded by wooded hills and granite peaks, the Unesco-listed **Miniere di Montevecchio** was once Sardinia's most important zinc and lead mine. A vast, now crumbling complex, it was operative until 1991 and, although most people have since left, there's still a small town with a handful of inhabitants.

To visit the mines you'll have to arrange a visit with either **IGEA cooperative** (🕿0781 49 13 00; adult/reduced €6/3; ⏰8.30am-5pm Mon-Fri) or the **G. Fulgheri Cooperative** (🕿070 934 60 00; www.coopfulgheri.it, in Italian; tours €8; ⏰10am & 11am Sat & Sun), which also runs excursions into the heavily wooded countryside around **Monte Arcuentu** (785m), one of the last preserves of the *cervo sardo* (Sardinian deer). Six kilometres out of Montevecchio, just off the SP65 road, sits **Agriturismo Arcuentu** (🕿070 975 81 68; Localita Monte Arcuentu; meals around €25) an authentic working farm. It's a great place to stop for a royal Sardinian feast. For €25 you sit down to antipasti, a choice of two pasta dishes, two mains, vegetable side dishes, fruit, dessert, coffee and an *amaro* (a bittersweet alcoholic *digestivo*).

From Montevecchio the SP65 twists and turns its way through the great green wilderness onwards to Torre dei Corsari.

Torre dei Corsari

Marking the northernmost point of the Costa Verde, Torre dei Corsari is a small but growing resort. In itself, it's not an especially attractive place, with bland modern buildings and an ugly concrete piazza, but it does have a good beach. Stretching for about 1.5km, the broad band of golden sand is sandwiched between an emerald-green sea and a range of mountainous dunes which mushroom back into green scrubland. Overlooking the southern end of the beach is the ruined watchtower from which the town takes its name. The top end of the beach is known as **Pistis**, which is a good long walk away or an 8km drive via **Sant'Antonio di Santadi**. There is paid parking at both ends of the beach.

Torre dei Corsari is a summer town – if arriving in winter you'll find your eating and sleeping options severely limited.

continued on page 69

The Coast

Best Beaches »
Seaside Hubs »

Soaking it up at Cala Goloritzè

Best Beaches

Local lore has it that when God first came down to earth, he stepped on an island with his sandal and – hey presto! – created Sardinia. Their origins aside, the beaches on this island are nothing short of divine. Rugged and smooth, sandy and pebbly, golden and white – Sardinia has a beach to suit every mood and moment.

Spiaggia della Pelosa

1 Spiaggia della Pelosa (p129) is a died-and-gone-to-heaven vision of a beach – a frost-white strip of sand fringed by electric-blue waters. Gaze out to a craggy islet topped by a Spanish watchtower as you splash away.

Chia

2 Windsurfers, dune walkers and twitchers who come to spot flamingos in winter all rave about Chia (p77). Sheltered by junipers, its beaches are the stuff of postcards.

Cala Brandinchi

3 OK, so we thought the brochure spiel about a 'Little Tahiti' was hype until we clapped eyes on the crystalline turquoise waters and powder-soft sands of Cala Brandinchi (p148). But forget Polynesia: why imagine yourself anywhere else?

Cala Goloritzè

4 No talk of soaring limestone pinnacles, shimmering white sands and water the colour of blue Curacao quite does justice to Cala Goloritzè (p194). Descending on the old mule trail, the cliffs suddenly crack open to reveal one of the most astonishingly lovely beaches you have ever seen.

Spiaggia della Piscinas

5 Walking barefoot across the 30m-high sand dunes that rise behind the sweeping Spiaggia della Piscinas (p64) is most magical at sunset. The fact that this fantastically wild beach can only be reached by dirt track adds to its wonderful sense of remoteness.

Clockwise from top left
1. Popular Spiaggia della Pelosa 2. Bay at Chia 3. Stunning Cala Brandinchi 4. Turquoise Cala Goloritzè

DALLAS STRIBLEY / LONELY PLANET IMAGES ©

LUCA PICCIAU / CUBOIMAGES SRL / ALAMY ©

Seaside Hubs

No matter which way you point the compass, you'll find beach after glorious beach in Sardinia. But where to base yourself? Here are some of our favourite resorts, whisking you (and your towel) from the action-packed east to the windswept west, the ritzy north to the silky-sand south.

Cala Gonone

1 Cala Gonone (p188) is a terrific base for exploring the crescent-shaped bays, limestone cliffs and grottoes of the Golfo di Orosei by boat or on foot. Rock climbers wax lyrical about its crags and families love the resort's blissfully laid-back vibe.

Costa del Sud

2 Eclipsed by Sardinia's more famous coastlines, the Costa del Sud (p76) is something of an unsung beauty, with fine beaches flanked by pines and cliffs plunging into the bluest of waters. Windsurfers and surfers come for the breeze and the waves.

Costa Smeralda

3 Enjoying the emerald waters, granite seascapes and pearly-white beaches of the fabled Costa Smeralda (p149) doesn't have to cost a mint. Leave behind Porto Cervo's celeb-hungry crowds for lesser-known bays, or stay inland for the perfect coast and country mix.

Costa Verde

4 For a taste of Sardinia before the developers got here, follow dirt tracks to Costa Verde's (p64) exhilaratingly beautiful beaches backed by huge dunes and lush *macchia* (scrub). Complete the picture with a stay at an *agriturismo* (farm-stay accommodation).

Alghero

5 From the medieval city of Alghero (p112), the road swings north to an array of pine-backed bays, rocky coves and the dramatic Capo Caccia. At Sardinia's northwestern tip lies the dream beach of Spiaggia della Pelosa and the wilderness of Isola Asinara (Donkey Island).

Right
1. Beach at Cala Gonone 2. Sapphire-blue Costa del Sud

continued from page 64

Self-caterers can always stock up at the **supermarket** (🖉070 97 72 45; Piazza Stella Maris; ⊙9am-1pm & 5-8pm) on the central square near the watchtower.

During July and August, an ARST bus runs daily from Oristano bus station to Torre dei Corsari (€4, 1½ hours).

CARBONIA & AROUND

South of Iglesias, the SS126 unfolds rapidly into flatter, less-inspiring landscapes that head straight for the south's second-largest city, Carbonia. A monument to failed Fascist ambition, the city holds little of interest for visitors today, save for a couple of modest museums and an archetypal town square. Nearby Monte Sirai offers glimpses into the island's ancient past.

To the west, Portovesme is the embarkation point for ferries to Isola di San Pietro.

Carbonia

POP 30,300

Unless you're a real fan of Fascist architecture or intrigued by industrial history, you won't want to spend long in Carbonia. A modern town fallen on hard times, it was constructed by Mussolini between 1936 and 1938 to house workers from the nearby Sirai–Serbariu coalfield. The town's fortunes have always been closely tied to the coal industry – its name is even a derivation of the Italian word for coal, *carbone* – and in 1972 when mining in the area ceased, it was hit hard. The city has since trundled along in the doldrums, struggling with unemployment and managing to stay afloat, thanks to small business.

Carbonia's focal point is Piazza Roma, a typically Fascist town square, dominated by the robust **Municipio** and bleak **Chiesa di San Ponziano**, with its red trachyte bell tower believed to be a copy of Aquilea cathedral in northern Italy.

A short walk away is Carbonia's principal museum, **Museo Archeologico Villa Sulcis** (🖉0781 66 50 37; Via Napoli 1; adult/reduced €3/2, incl Museo di Paleontologia e Speleologia & Monte Siria €5/3; ⊙10am-8pm Wed-Sun summer, 9am-2pm Tue-Sun winter). Housed in the former residence of the town's mining director, it displays a modest collection of archaeological finds, most of them from Monte Sirai.

Nearby, the **Museo di Paleontologia e Speleologia** (🖉0781 69 10 06; Piazza Garibaldi; adult/reduced €3/2, incl Museo Archeologico Villa Sulcis & Monte Siria €5/3; ⊙10am-8pm Wed-Sun summer, 9am-2pm Tue-Sun winter) is Sardinia's only dedicated speleology museum. One for the specialists, it displays fossils, minerals and all sorts of geological oddities collected from caves all over Sardinia.

Of more general interest are the ruins of the Phoenician fort at **Monte Sirai** (🖉0781 66 50 37; adult/reduced incl Museo Archeologico Villa Sulcis & Monte Sirai €5/3; ⊙10am-8pm Wed-Sun summer, 9am-2pm Tue-Sun winter), about 4km northwest of Carbonia on the other side of the SS126. Built by the Phoenicians of Sulci (modern Sant'Antioco) in 650 BC, it was taken over a century later by the Carthaginians. Although not much of the fort remains, you can see the placement of the Carthaginian acropolis and defensive tower, a necropolis and a *tophet*, a sacred Phoenician and Carthaginian burial ground for children and babies. The surrounding views are magnificent.

In Carbonia, buses run to/from the porticoes on Via Manno; for tickets go to Bar Balia at Viale Gramsci 4. There are services to Iglesias (€2, 45 minutes, eight daily) and Cagliari (€6, 1½ hours, two daily), as well as to a host of local towns.

Portoscuso & Portovesme

POP 5350

It doesn't look good as you approach the coast. The enormous chimney stacks of a vast thermoelectric industrial complex rise above the flat landscape, offering a nightmarish landmark and presaging visions of foul, industrial sprawl. But when you reach the coast, you'll discover that the industrial blight is actually at Portovesme, a couple of kilometres east of Portoscuso. Portoscuso itself is an attractive fishing port capped by a Spanish-era tower and surrounded by a tiny warren of agreeable lanes. Portovesme is the main ferry port for Isola di San Pietro.

You can get information at Portoscuso's helpful **tourist office** (🖉0781 50 95 04; Via Vespucci 16; ⊙10am-noon & 6-8.30pm Mon-Sat summer, 6-8.30pm Mon-Fri winter) near the seafront.

There's not a whole lot to do in town other than stroll the pristine streets and enjoy the laid-back atmosphere, but there's a decent sandy **beach** and you can admire sweeping views from the stout 16th-century **watchtower** (admission free; ⊙6-8.30pm daily Jun-Sep).

VILLAGGIO MINERARIO ROSAS

Signposted off the main road into Narcao, the **Villaggio Minerario Rosas** is the modern reincarnation of the Rosas mine, an important source of lead, copper and zinc until it was closed in 1978. It's a striking site with its rusty minehead machinery and heavy timber structures. Strangely, though, the museum is rarely open and there's often no-one around. But this shouldn't necessarily put you off as it's a beautifully remote spot, and you can still walk around the stone buildings and along silent paths into the rocky hills.

Visit in early June, though, and you'll find the town a hive of activity as locals and visitors tuck into tuna dishes during the annual **Sagra del Tonno** (Tuna Festival). Portoscuso is one of the few places in Sardinia where tuna is still fished according to bloody, traditional methods. If you're hungry, head for **Cicittu Pizzeria** (☑0781 51 20 01; Via Amerigo Vespucci 6; pizzas €6, meals around €20; ⊙Wed-Mon), a relaxed, congenial place serving a mixed menu of pizza, pasta and seafood. The local tuna features in a number of antipasti and main courses and is always worth a try.

ARST buses run to Portoscuso and neighbouring Portovesme from Iglesias (€2, 30 minutes, hourly) and Carbonia (€1.50, 35 minutes, 14 daily). You can buy your tickets from the newsagents at the top of Largo Matteotti. **Saremar** (☑0781 50 90 65; www.saremar .it, in Italian) has up to 15 daily sailings from Portovesme to Carloforte (on Isola di San Pietro) between 5am and 9.10pm (in summer there's an additional sailing at 11.10pm). The trip takes about 30 minutes and costs €2.60 per person and €9.40 per car. Be prepared for long queues in summer.

Tratalias

Now a sleepy backwater, Tratalias was once the religious capital of the entire Sulcis area. When Sant'Antioco was abandoned in the 13th century, the Sulcis archdiocese was transferred to the village and the impressive **Chiesa di Santa Maria** (www.anticoborgo tratalias.info, in Italian; admission €1; ⊙9.30am-noon & 2.30-5.30pm Tue-Sun) was built. A curious Romanesque construction, the church presides over what little remains of the *antico borgo* (old town), abandoned after water from the nearby Lago di Monte Pranu started seeping into the subsoil in the 1950s.

The easiest way to Tratalias is by car. The old town is 4km east, off the SS195 right by the road.

Narcao

About 15km northeast of Tratalias, this small town is worth a quick detour for its *murales* (murals), depicting life in the local mines. Its other main attraction is the annual **Narcao Blues Festival** (☑800 88 11 88; www.narcaoblues.it, in Italian), one of Sardinia's top musical events. It's been going since 1989 and is held on the last weekend in July. The festival features blues, funk, soul and gospel concerts, performed by a cast of top American performers, which in previous years has included the celebrated Blind Boys of Alabama.

Necropolis del Montessu

One of Sardinia's largest and most important archaeological sites, the **Necropolis del Montessu** (adult/reduced €5/3; ⊙9am-8pm summer, to 9am-5pm winter) is hidden in verdant country near Villaperuccio. Set in a rocky natural amphitheatre, the site dates back to the Ozieri period (approximately 3000 BC) and is peppered with 35 primitive tombs, known locally as *domus de janas* (literally 'fairy houses'). Many of these appear as little more than a hole in the wall, although some harbour wonderful relief carvings. Check out the **Tomba delle Spirali**, where you can clearly make out the raised relief of spirals and symbolic bulls.

From the ticket booth it's a 500m walk up to the main site. When you first arrive up the stairs from the roadway, to your immediate right is a **Tomba Santuario**, a rectangular foyer followed by three openings into a semicircular tomb area behind. Follow the trail to its right to see a cluster of tombs and then the Tomba delle Spirali.

To get to the area from Villaperuccio, take the road for Narcao and then follow the signs off to the left. It's about 2.5km.

Santadi

Wine buffs can get to grips with the local vintage at Santadi, a busy agricultural centre a few kilometres east of Villaperuccio. The town is home to the biggest winery in the southwest, the **Cantina Santadi** (☑0781 95 01 27; www.cantinadisantadi.it; Via Cagliari 78; ⊙by appointment); its red wines include the highly rated Roccia Rubia and Grotta Rossa. Note that booking a visit can be done online.

To get an idea of how villagers lived in the early 20th century, the **Museo Etnografico 'Sa Domu Antiga'** (☑0781 95 59 55; Via Mazzini 37; admission €2.60; ⊙9am-1pm & 3-5pm Tue-Sun) recreates a typical village house.

Like many rural towns, Santadi celebrates its traditions in high style. On the first Sunday of August, townspeople gather for the **Matrimonio Maureddino** (Moorish Wedding), a costumed wedding accompanied by folk dancing, eating and drinking. At the centre of events, the blushing bride and groom are transported to the main square on a *traccas* (a cart drawn by red bulls).

Five kilometres south of Santadi, the **Grotte Is Zuddas** (☑0781 95 57 41; www .grotteiszuddas.com, in Italian; adult/child €8/5; ⊙9.30am-noon & 2.30-6pm summer, noon-4pm Mon-Sat, 9.30am-noon & 2.30-6pm Sun & holidays winter) is another of the island's spectacular cave systems. Of particular note are the helictites in the main hall. No one really knows how these weirdly shaped formations are created, although one theory suggests that wind in the cave may have acted on drops dripping off stalactites.

SOUTHWEST ISLANDS

The southwest's two islands, Isola di Sant'Antioco and Isola di San Pietro, display very different characters. The larger and more developed of the two, Isola Sant'Antioco, boasts little of the obvious beauty that one often associates with small Mediterranean islands, and is less pointedly touristy. Barely half an hour across the water, Isola di San Pietro presents a prettier picture with its pastel houses and bright bobbing fishing boats.

Isola di San Pietro

Boasting an elegant main town and some fine coastal scenery, Isola di San Pietro is a hugely popular summer destination. A mountainous trachyte island measuring about 15km long and 11km wide, it's named after St Peter who, legend has it, was marooned here during a storm on the way to Karalis (now Cagliari). The Romans had previously called it Accipitrum after the variety of falcons that nest here.

San Pietro's unique character and atmosphere come from its Genoese inhabitants, ransomed from the Tunisian bey (governor) in 1736. Coral fishermen by profession, they had been sent to the island of Tabarka to harvest the precious commodity for the Lomellini family in Genoa. But they were abandoned to their fate and fell into miserable slavery until Carlo Emanuele III granted them refuge on San Pietro. Almost out of spite, North African pirates turned up in 1798 and made off with 1000 prisoners. It took five years for the Savoys to ransom them back. Even today the inhabitants of San Pietro speak *tabarkino,* a 16th-century version of Genoese.

CARLOFORTE
POP 6430

The very image of Mediterranean chic, Carloforte offers a refined introduction to the island. Graceful palazzi, crowded cafes and palm trees line the busy waterfront while, behind, a creamy curve of stately buildings rises in a half-moon up the green hillside. There are no great sights in the town as such, but a slow wander through the quaint, cobbled streets makes for a pleasant prelude to a seaside aperitif and a fine seafood meal at one of the town's wonderful restaurants.

◎ Sights & Activities

Aside from one museum and the pretty distractions of the town, most of San Pietro's pleasures are to be had elsewhere, either out at sea or exploring the island's untamed coastline.

Museo Civico   MUSEUM
(☑0781 85 58 80; Via Cisterna del Re; adult/reduced €2/1; ⊙9am-1pm Tue & Sat, 10am-1pm & 3-6pm Wed, 3-7pm Thu & Fri, 10am-1pm Sun) Uphill from the seafront, the modest **Museo Civico** is housed in a small 18th-century fort, one of the first masonry buildings to be erected on the island. Of chief interest is the Tonnara Room, dedicated to the island's tradition of tuna fishing. Continuing the nautical theme, there's an assortment of boating bric-a-brac and a small collection of Mediterranean sea shells.

Carloforte Sail Charter SAILING
(⌐347 273 32 68; www.carlofortesailcharter.it, in Italian; Via Danero 52) If you want to take to sea yourself, this operator has a fleet of sailing boats available for charter with or without a skipper – reckon on from €1500 per week.

Isla Diving DIVING
(⌐0781 85 56 34; Viale dei Cantieri; dives from €65) On the main waterfront, this is one of several centres in Carloforte to choose from.

Carloforte Tonnare Diving Center DIVING
(⌐349 690 49 69; www.tonnaradive.it; Localita La Punta; dives from €65) This centre also offers the chance to dive with tuna fish.

☞ **Tours**

Cartur Dea BOAT
(⌐0781 85 43 31; molo Tagliafico; per person €20) Operating out of a booth on the *lungomare* (seafront), Cartur Dea is one of several outfits that offer boat tours of the island taking you round the coastal cliffs, grottoes and offshore sea stacks.

✻ **Festivals & Events**

Girotonno LOCAL CULTURE
(www.girotonno.org) The island's main annual event is this four-day festival held in late May/early June. Dedicated to the tuna catch of the *mattanza* (see the boxed text, p73), this festival features cooking competitions, tastings, seminars, concerts and various nautical-themed events. Since 2008 it has included the **Buskers Festival** (same website), where local bands play in the street.

Creuza de Má MUSIC & FILM
(www.festivalcarloforte.org) The musical theme continues with this three-day festival in July dedicated to cinema music. Check with the tourist office for details.

✗ **Eating**

Tuna is the king of *tabarkina* cuisine, as the island style of cooking is known. It's on menus throughout the year, but is only available from May to August/September. You'll also be able to sample *cuscus* (a variety of North African couscous) alongside *zuppa di pesce* (fish soup), and Genoese *farinata* (a pizza-style flatbread made from chickpea flour and olives) and Genoese (basil) pesto.

TOP CHOICE **La Cantina** TRATTORIA €€
(⌐0781 85 45 88; Via Gramsci 34; meals €25-30; ⊙Tue-Sun, daily in summer) A great place to

sample the cuisine of Carloforte, La Cantina is a simple, one-room trattoria that spreads outdoors in the summer months, with tables on the pedestrianised street. Taste the *cascá alle verdure* – the local couscous with vegetables – or any of the wonderful seafood offerings. Also try the *canestrello*, a very local dessert of hard anise biscuit dipped into sweet wine.

Osteria della Tonnara OSTERIA €€
(⌐078 185 57 34; Corso Battellieri 36; meals around €35) Located at the southern end of San Pietro's seafront, this small restaurant is run by the island's tuna cooperative. Not surprisingly, tuna dominates the menu (though it's only available during the tuna fishing season), appearing in dishes such as tuna and pesto lasagne and the ubiquitous but tasty *tonno alla carlofortina* (tuna roasted and served with a tomato sauce). Booking is recommended in the summer months and credit cards are not accepted.

Tonno di Corsa RESTAURANT €€€
(⌐0781 85 51 06; Via Marconi 47; meals around €45; ⊙Tue-Sun) This refined restaurant is the place to try tuna cooked in ways you've probably never seen before – smoked, in ragu, as tripe. Tuna tripe, known locally as *belu*, is not for everyone, but if you're tempted it's cooked in a casserole with potatoes and onions.

Da Nicolo RESTAURANT €€€
(⌐0781 85 40 48; Corso Cavour 32; meals around €55; ⊙Tue-Sun) A bastion of San Pietro cuisine, this island institution sits in elegant splendour on the seafront. Tables are laid out with starched formality in a glass pavilion, ready for diners who come from far and wide to try the magnificent tuna and light, local couscous.

🍷 **Drinking & Entertainment**

The *lungomare* is the place where it's at. Just off the seafront, **Barone Rosso** (Via XX Settembre 26; ⊙noon-3pm & 7pm-2am Tue-Sun Mar-Oct, evening only Dec-Mar) is a popular bar with a kitsch interior, lively tunes and a few street tables. Another good option in a similar vein is **L'Oblò** (⌐0781 85 70 40; Via Garibaldi 23; ⊙7.30-11pm Wed-Mon mid-May–mid-Sep).

The only disco on the island, **Disco Marlin** (⌐0781 85 01 21; ⊙10pm-4am Sat & Sun Jul, nightly Aug) is out of Carloforte, near the *tonnara* (tuna processing plant) on the way to La Punta. You'll really need a car, or a lift, to get here.

San Pietro islanders have fishing in the blood. For centuries the annual tuna slaughter, the *mattanza*, has been the island's biggest event. The *mattanza* is held in late May/early June, when schools of tuna stream between Isola Piana and San Pietro en route to their mating grounds. Waiting to entrap them is an elaborate system of nets that channel the tuna into a series of enclosures culminating in the *camera della morte* (chamber of death). Once enough tuna are imprisoned here, the fishermen close in and the *mattanza* begins (the word is derived from the Spanish for 'killing'). It's a bloody affair – up to eight or more fishermen at a time sink huge hooks into the thrashing tuna. A classic example of a *mattanza* can be seen in Rossellini's film, *Stromboli*. Even today the *mattanza* forms the centrepiece of the big annual festival, the Girotonno. But concerns about diminishing tuna stocks have placed the practice at the centre of international attention.

Driving the ever-increasing demand for bluefin tuna is Japan's insatiable appetite for sushi and sashimi (Japanese buyers snap up about 80% of the tuna caught in the Mediterranean). Tuna fishing is now a multimillion-dollar global business, and there are estimated to be around 300 tuna-fishing boats in the Med, many capable of catching up to 3000 tuna in one haul. Spotter planes have been banned by the International Commission for the Conservation of Atlantic Tunas (ICCAT), but illegal fishing remains commonplace.

Set against this context, the amount of tuna caught in Carloforte's *mattanza* is minimal – in 2008, 160 tonnes of tuna were caught against an ICCAT quota for the Med of 22,000 tonnes. But its violence and stark imagery – blue water turning red with blood – provides critics with a powerful visual tool in the campaign to preserve the Mediterranean tuna. Conservation groups and environmental organisations are deeply concerned about the effect industrial-scale fishing is having on the area's tuna stocks and are loudly calling for a lowering of fishing quotas. But with powerful business lobbies equally determined to oppose any such measures, it's not an issue that's going to go away any time soon.

The popular La Caletta beach is also the scene of dancing fun, with summer beach parties pounding on until dawn.

ℹ Information

The helpful, multilingual **tourist office** (☎0781 85 40 09; www.prolococarloforte.it, in Italian; Piazza Carlo Emanuele III 19; ☉9.30am-12.30pm & 4.30-7.30pm Mon-Sat & Sun morning May-Sep, 10am-1pm & 5-8pm Mon-Sat & Sun morning Oct-Apr) can assist with any queries. Another useful source of information is the website www.carloforte.net, although at present it's only in Italian.

You can get money from the ATM at **Banca Intesa** (Corso Cavour 1) on the waterfront.

ℹ Getting There & Away

BOAT There's a **Saremar** (☎0781 85 40 05; www.saremar.it, in Italian; Piazza Carlo Emanuele III 29) ticket office on the *lungomare*. Regular ferries depart for Portovesme (per person/car €2.60/9.40, 30 minutes, 15 daily) and Calasetta (per person/car €2.30/8, seven daily) on the neighbouring island of Sant'Antioco.

Delcomar (☎0781 85 71 23; www.delcomar .it, in Italian) runs up to 14 night services to and from Calasetta. It operates a ticket booth just in front of where the ferries dock. The crossing costs €5/15 per person/car.

BUS Between July and September, buses run from Carloforte to La Punta (12 minutes, two daily), La Caletta (15 minutes, nine daily) and Capo Sandalo (18 minutes, two daily). Single/return tickets cost €1.

AROUND THE ISLAND

A quick 5.5km drive north of Carloforte brings you to La Punta, a desolate, windswept point with views over to the offshore islet Isola Piana. In May and June it's here that you'll witness the frenzied *mattanza*, in front of the *tonnara*. A dilapidated set of stone buildings littered with rusty anchors and smelly nets, the island's old tuna processing plant is now home to the Carloforte Tonnare Diving Center (see p72), which, as well as organising dives, also runs guided tours of the old plant; contact the Diving Center to organise a time.

Most of the island's best beaches are in the south. **Spiaggia La Bobba** looks onto two great stone *colonne* (columns) that rise out of the sea, giving the island's southernmost point its name, **Punta delle Colonne.** Continue westwards and you come to the island's most popular beach, **La Caletta** (also known as Spiaggia Spalmatore), a relatively modest arc of fine sand closed off by cliffs. Further south you can detour to view the spectacular coastline of **La Conca.**

There's some wonderful walking to be had on **Capo Sandalo**, the westernmost point of the island. From the car park near the lighthouse, a series of marked trails heads through the rocky, red scrubland that carpets the cliffs. It's not exactly hard-core trekking, but you'll feel safer in a pair of walking boots.

En route to Capo Sandalo (it's only about a 20-minute drive from Carloforte), take a minute to stop off at the rocky inlet of **Cala Fico**, one of the island's most photographed spots and, along with **Isola del Corno**, home to a nesting colony of Eleonora's falcons.

If you haven't got a car, and even if you have, the ideal way to explore the island is by bike. Distances are not huge, and even if there's some hill work there's nothing too dramatic. Between June and September you can hire bikes and scooters in Carloforte, at the **newsagents** (📞0781 85 41 23) at Piazza Repubblica 4. Bank on €10 for a bike per day, and from €21 to €37 for a scooter.

Isola di Sant'Antioco

Larger and less exuberant than Isola San Pietro, Isola di Sant'Antioco is Italy's fourth-largest island (after Sicily, Sardinia and Elba). Unlike many Mediterranean islands it's not dramatically beautiful – although it's by no means ugly – and it exudes no sense of isolation. Instead it feels very much part of Sardinia, both in character and look. The animated main town (Sant'Antioco) is an authentic working port, and the green, rugged interior looks like much of southern Sardinia.

In fact, since Roman times, the island has been physically linked to the Sardinian mainland by bridge – the ruins of the Roman structure lie to the right of the modern road bridge.

There are two ways of approaching the island. The simplest is to follow the SS126 south from Iglesias and Carbonia and cross the bridge to the town of Sant'Antioco. Clunkier but more romantic is the car ferry between Calasetta and Carloforte in San Pietro.

SANT'ANTIOCO
POP 11,900

Although Isola di Sant'Antioco has been inhabited since prehistoric times, the town of Sant'Antioco was founded by the Phoenicians in the 8th century BC. Known as Sulci, it was Sardinia's industrial capital and an important port until the demise of the Roman Empire m ore than a millennium later. It owes its current name to St Antiochus, a Roman slave who brought Christianity to the island when exiled here in the 2nd century AD.

Evidence of the town's ancient past is not hard to find – the hilltop historic centre is riddled with Phoenician necropolises and fascinating archaeological litter.

CRUSADE TO SAVE THE ISLAND'S ASS

Tres cosas sunt reversas in su mundu: s'arveghe, s'ainu, e i sa femmina (There are three stubborn things in this world: sheep, donkeys and women). Sardinian proverbs tend to be cynical and blunt, evoking rural images to bludgeon home their old-fashioned messages. Central to much of this imagery is the typical stubbornness of the *asinello sardo* (Sardinian donkey), which was introduced to the island in the 3rd millennium BC from Egypt.

An affectionate and reliable worker, the diminutive *asinello* is also a regular on Sardinian menus, and with an increasing number being run over, its numbers are dwindling.

This was all the spur that Giorgio Mazzucchetti needed to jack in his work as an industrial consultant in Milan and embark on a crusade to save the loveable ass. Already enamoured with the island after numerous holidays, Giorgio bought a farm near Cala Fico on the west coast and began breeding the endangered donkeys. Starting off with 10 in 1999, he now has a healthy herd of 80.

You can visit the donkeys at the **Fattoria degli Asinelli** (📞333 144 29 93; Localita Cala Fico; ☺every afternoon 'until it gets dark'), near the Faro on Cala Fico. It can make a good day out, especially if you're travelling with children; the little ones can feed and pet the animals. Make sure you ring in advance to check opening hours.

Sights & Activities

Basilica di Sant'Antioco Martire   CHURCH
(Piazza Parrocchia 22; ⊗9am-noon & 3-6pm Mon-Sat, 10-11am & 3-6pm Sun) Hidden behind the modest baroque facade is a sublimely simple 5th-century church. To the right of the altar stands a wooden effigy of St Antiochus, his dark complexion a sign of his North African origins. Refusing to recant his faith, Antiochus was shipped off by the Romans to work as a slave in the mines of the Iglesiente. But he escaped, hidden in a tar barrel, and was taken in by an underground Christian group who hid him in the church's extensive **catacombs** (admission €2.50; ⊗same as church hours).

Accessible only by guided tour, the catacombs consist of a series of burial chambers, some dating back to Punic times, that were used by Christians between the 2nd and 7th centuries. The dead members of well-to-do families were stored in elaborate, frescoed family niches in the walls; a few fragments of fresco can still be seen. Middle-class corpses wound up in unadorned niches, and commoners' bodies were placed in ditches in the floor. A few skeletons lying *in situ* render the idea a little more vividly.

Museo Archeologico   MUSEUM
(☑0781 80 05 96; www.archeolur.it, in Italian; Via Regina Margherita 113; admission ticket for museum, tophet, ethnographic museum & Villagio Ipogeo adult/reduced €13/8, museum only €6/2; ⊗9am-7pm Wed-Sun Apr Sep, 9.30am-1pm & 3-6pm Wed-Sun Oct-Mar) This museum contains a fascinating collection of local archaeological finds, as well as a model of the town as it would have looked in the 4th century BC. Armed with a useful explanatory folder, you'll discover that the impressive pair of stone lions in the main corridor once guarded the town gates, as was customary in Phoenician towns, and that the panther mosaic at the end of the main section once adorned a Roman triclinium (dining room).

Further down the road, and spread over the hill, are the tombs of the **necropolis** (⊗closed to the public). Another 500m or so down the hill is an 8th-century BC **tophet** (adult/reduced €4/2.50, admission incl Museo Archeologico adult/reduced €7/4; ⊗9am-7pm Wed-Sun summer, 9.30am-1pm & 3-6pm Wed-Sun winter), a sanctuary where the Phoenicians and Carthaginians buried their still-born babies.

Forte Su Pisu   CASTLE
(admission €2.50; ⊗9am-8pm summer, 9.30am-1pm & 3-6pm winter) Rising uphill from the basilica, Via Castello is named after this 19th-century Piedmontese fort, which marks the highest point in town.

Museo Etnografico   MUSEUM
(Via Necropoli 24a; admission €3; ⊗9am-8pm summer, 9.30am-1pm & 3-6pm winter) Back in the town's historic centre, you can investigate age-old living habits at this museum, with its assortment of traditional farm and household implements.

Villaggio Ipogeo   TOMBS
(admission €2.50) A series of Punic tombs that once housed the poorest of the town's poor.

✦ Festivals

Festa di Sant'Antioco   TRADITIONAL FESTIVAL
(www.tuttosantantioco.it, in Italian)
Held over four days around the second Sunday after Easter, the festival celebrates the city's patron saint with processions, traditional music, dancing, fireworks and concerts. It is one of the oldest documented saint's festivities on the island, dating to 1519.

✗ Eating & Drinking

Tamarindo Blu   [TOP CHOICE]   RESTAURANT €€
(☑0781 80 20 96; Via Azuni 28; meals around €25; ⊗Thu-Tue) Don't let the over-the-top nautical paraphernalia put you off the really very good food, served in vast portions. It's all tasty, but standout options include the mixed antipasto and grilled fish.

Bar Colombo   CAFE €
(Lungomare Cristoforo Colombo 94; coffee €1, drinks from €1.50; ⊗Tue-Sun) This is where salty fishermen come for their morning coffee, which explains why it opens for business at 4am. In summer, drinkers swell onto the outside pavement.

Pizzeria Biancaneve   PIZZERIA €
(☑0781 80 04 67; Corso Vittorio Emanuele 110; pizzas €7.50; ⊗8am-midnight) On the main strip, this place does a roaring trade serving passers-by with pizza.

Pierre   BAR €
(☑078 180 04 55; Corso Vittorio Emanuele 86; drinks from €1.50; ⊗8pm-late Wed-Mon) Wooden pews and beer on tap give this popular spot an almost authentic pub feel. It can get pretty busy on summer nights and musters up a good atmosphere.

ⓘ Information

Tourist Office (☏0781 8 20 31; Piazza Repubblica 31a; ⊙10am-1pm & 5-9pm Mon-Fri)

ⓘ Getting There & Around

BOAT Ferries connect Calasetta with Carloforte on Isola di San Pietro (see p73).

BUS There are seven daily buses between Calasetta, Sant'Antioco (Piazza Repubblica) and Carbonia (€1, 50 minutes), as well as Iglesias (€4, 1¾ hours).

BIKE To get out of town and explore the island, **Euromoto** (☏0781 84 09 07; Via Nazionale 57; ⊙9am-1pm & 4-8pm) hires out bikes and scooters for €8 and €30, as well as organising guided bike rides. These are led by volunteers, so there's no fixed rate, although you're more than welcome to leave a tip.

AROUND THE ISLAND

The island's better beaches lie to the south of Sant'Antioco. About 5km south of town, **Maladroxia** is a small resort that offers a couple of hotels and a pleasant beach and port.

Back on the main road, you pass inland before hitting a big roundabout. Head left (east) to reach Spiaggia Coa Quaddus, a wild and woolly beach about 3km short of **Capo Sperone**, the southernmost point of the island; or head right for the island's windy southwest coast. The best of beaches around here is **Cala Lunga**, where the road peters out. Also check out the lovely **Spiaggia Le Saline** (Salina), another good beach in this area.

Calasetta, the island's second town, is located 10km northwest of Sant'Antioco. The town was originally founded by Ligurian families from Tabarka in 1769.

There are several beaches a few kilometres south on the northwestern coast, as well as an excellent restaurant. **Da Pasqualino** (☏0781 88 473; Via Regina Margherita 85; meals €30-35; ⊙Wed-Mon) is a real local institution that serves up local fish, caught daily. Try the *cascá* (local couscous) with fish of the day, or treat yourself to lobster, if available.

SOUTH COAST

The island's southern coast is quite magnificent. The central stretch, known as the Costa del Sud, is a dazzling 20km spectacle of twisting, turning road that winds above rugged cliffs plunging into the tantalising blue sea.

Porto Botte to Porto di Teulada

Stretching 15km along Sardinia's southwestern tip, this tract of coastline is a patchwork of pine woods, lagoons and beaches. Of the beaches, the best and busiest is the fabulous **Spiaggia Porto Pino**, at the eponymous resort near Sant'Anna Arresi. A favourite with weekending locals, this broad swath of creamy sand is lapped by lovely, shallow waters ideal for tentative toddlers and nervous swimmers. There's ample parking and a string of cheap and cheerful pizzerias near the parking lot.

A second beach, **Spiaggia Sabbie Bianche**, just south of Porto Pino and accessible on foot, is famous for its soft, silky dunes. However, as it's on military land, it's off limits to the public outside of July and August.

From Porto Pino you have no choice but to head inland to Sant'Anna Arresi. From here the SS195 swings south, bypassing a hilly triangle of land and Sardinia's southernmost point, Capo di Teulada. Like much of this area, the Capo is occupied by a controversial NATO base and so is usually inaccessible to the public. After 10km, branch south (away from the signs to Teulada) towards Porto di Teulada.

There are several beaches along this part of the coast, including **Cala Piombo** and **Porto Zafferano**, accessible only in July and August, and only by boat. You can pick up a boat at the small marina at **Porto di Teulada** near **Porto Tramatzu** beach.

Costa del Sud

One of Sardinia's most enchanting coastal drives, the Costa del Sud begins east of Porto di Teulada. The first stretch is just a prelude, passing several coves and gradually rising towards the high point of **Capo Malfatano**. As you wind your way around towards the cape, wonderful views of the coast repeatedly spring into view and just about every point is capped by a Spanish-era watchtower. Along the way, **Spiaggia Piscinni** is a great place for a dip. The sand's not amazing, but the water is an incredible colour.

Once around the bay and the next point, you could stop at **Cala Teuradda** to marvel at its vivid emerald-green water. It's a popular spot, which happens to be right by an ARST bus stop. In summer you'll find snack bars, too.

From here the road climbs inland away from the water. You can get a look at the coast here, too, if you take a narrow side road to the south at Porto Campana – it quickly turns to dust but does allow you to reach the lighthouse at **Capo Spartivento**. From here a series of beaches stretch north along the coast; watch out for signposts off the main coastal road to **Cala Cipolla**, a gorgeous spot backed by pine and juniper trees, **Spiaggia Su Giudeu** and **Porto Campana**.

At the end of this stretch you'll see another Spanish watchtower presiding over the popular summer resort of **Chia**. From the tower, you get grandstand views of the southern coast and Chia's two ravishing beaches – to the west, the long **Spiaggia Sa Colonia**; to the east, the smaller arc of **Spiaggia Su Portu**. A paradise for surfers, windsurfers and kitesurfers, these beaches play host to the annual Chia Classic **surf and windsurf competition**, usually held in early to mid-April.

From Cagliari, there are up to 10 daily ARST buses to/from Chia (€3, 1¼ hours). Then, between mid-June and mid-September, two daily buses ply the Costa del Sud, connecting Chia with Spiaggia Teulada (Porto di Teulada; €2, 35 minutes).

Chia to Santa Margherita di Pula

Unless you are staying at one of the self-contained resort hotels that hog much of this part of the coast you're unlikely to glimpse much of the sea around here. Which is a shame because the 9km of coastline between Chia and Santa Margherita di Pula is one of the most beautiful parts of the southwest of Sardinia: a string of magnificent beaches lapped by crystalline waters and backed by fragrant pine woods.

ARST buses serve Santa Margherita di Pula from Cagliari (€3, one hour, nine daily).

Pula

POP 7120

Some 27km from Cagliari, Pula is a workaday, agricultural village best known for its vicinity to the Phoenician site of Nora. Apart from a small archaeological museum, there's no compelling reason to hang around, but if you do decide to stay, you'll find that village life centres on the vibrant, cafe-clad Piazza del Popolo.

Information on the immediate area is available from the **tourist office** (☑070 924 60 57; www.prolocopula.it, in Italian; c/o Centro Culturale Casa Frau, Piazza del Popolo; ☺9.30am-12.30pm & 3-6pm Mon-Fri), situtated on the main square. You can check your email at **L'Isola del Viaggio** (☑070 920 83 73; Via Nora cnr Via Conte Corinaldi; per hr €4; ☺9am-1pm & 4.30-8pm Mon-Sat).

◉ Sights

PULA

If you're planning to visit Nora, which you probably are if you're passing through Pula, a trip to the one-room **Museo Archeologico** (☑070 920 96 10; Corso Vittorio Emanuele 67; admission €3, incl Nora €7; ☺9am-8pm Tue-Sun May-Sep, 10am-1pm & 3-6.30pm Wed-Sun Oct Apr) will help set the scene. Alongside ceramics found in Punic and Roman tombs, some gold and bone jewellery, and Roman glassware, there's a model of the Nora site and helpful explanations in both English and Italian.

NORA

Four kilometres south of Pula, the archaeological zone of Nora is the main sight in these parts. But before you get there, take a moment to stop off at the pint-sized **Chiesa di Sant'Efisio** (☑340 485 18 60; ☺4-7.30pm Sat, 10am-noon & 4-9.30pm Sun); you'll see it on the left as you drive towards Nora. This 12th-century Romanesque church was built on the prime beachside spot where the disgraced Roman commander Ephisius was executed for his Christian beliefs in AD 303. Despite its modest dimensions, it is the scene of great celebrations on 1 May as pilgrims bring the effigy of St Ephisius here as part of Cagliari's Festa di Sant'Efisio (p45).

In Ephisius' day **Nora** (adult/reduced incl Museo Archeologico in Pula €7/3; ☺9am-7.30pm) was one of the most important cities on the island and the seat of Roman government, linked to Karalis (now Cagliari) in the east and Bythia in the west. But the site was already an important trading centre long before the Romans arrived. Founded in the 11th century BC by Phoenicians from Spain, it later passed into Carthaginian hands before eventually being taken over by the Romans in the 3rd century AD. But the town's position was exposed and by the Middle Ages it had been abandoned, the temples looted by Arab pirates and the marble columns broken.

These days only a fraction of the original site remains – much of the original city is underwater – and it's only when you reach the rocky outline of the promontory that you see any remnants of the once-great imperial city.

Upon entry, you pass a single melancholy **column** from the former temple of Tanit, the Carthaginian Venus, who was once worshipped here. Much of the glass in Pula's museum was found in this area, giving rise to theories that the whole temple may have been decorated with it. Beyond this is a small but beautifully preserved Roman **theatre** facing the sea. Towards the west are the substantial remains of the **Terme al Mare** (Baths by the Sea). Four columns (a tetrastyle) stand at the heart of what was a patrician villa; the surrounding rooms retain their mosaic floor decoration. More remnants of mosaics can be seen at a temple complex towards the tip of the promontory.

Up to 16 local shuttle buses run between Pula and Nora.

LAGUNA DI NORA

Just before the entrance to the ancient site of Nora are the pleasant **Spiaggia di Nora** and, a little further around, the bigger **Spiaggia Su Guventeddu**. Note that you won't be permitted into the site in your bathing costume.

On the western side of the Nora promontory, you can often spy **pink flamingos** stalking around the Laguna di Nora. To learn more about the lagoon system and its aquatic fauna, visit the **Laguna di Nora didactic centre** (☑070 920 95 44; www.lagunadinora.it, in Italian; ☺summer), which has a small aquarium (adult/reduced €8/6) and runs summer excursions, including snorkelling tours (adult/reduced €25/15) and canoe excursions (adult/child €20/15).

✗ Eating

Su Zilleri   RESTAURANT €
(☑070 732 14 19; Piazza del Popolo 69; menus seafood/meat €16/18) A lovely place on Pula's main square, Su Zilleri has abundant fixed menus consisting of seafood or meat antipasti, such as charcuterie and smoked fish, mains – seafood risotto or a tender beef steak – wine and coffee. The service is friendly and the outside terrace a delight.

Crazy Art Gelateria   ICE CREAM €
(Corso Vittorio Emanuele 4; gelati €2.70;☺4pm-midnight Mon-Sat, noon-midnight Sun) This is

the place to grab that most Italian of accessories, an ice cream. The challenge then is to look cool while licking it on Piazza del Popolo.

Zio Dino   PIZZERIA €€
(☑070 920 91 59; Viale Segni 14; pizzas €5, meals around €30; ☺Mon-Sat) With its name graffitied high on the wall, Zio Dino serves a solid menu of pizza staples, seafood and meat dishes.

ℹ Getting There & Away

BUS There are up to 20 daily ARST buses from Cagliari (€2, 50 minutes).

CAMPIDANO

One of Sardinia's most important agricultural zones, the Campidano is a broad, flat corridor of land extending northwest from Cagliari. The dusty yellow landscape can be a little dispiriting, especially on torrid summer days when temperatures soar and the area seems enveloped in a thick grey heat haze, but it's not totally devoid of interest.

Uta, Castello di Acquafredda & San Sperate

Barely 20km northwest of Cagliari, at the eastern edge of the sprawling farm town of Uta, is one of the finest Romanesque churches in southern Sardinia. The **Chiesa di Santa Maria** (follow the brown signs for the Santuario di Santa Maria), built around 1140 by Vittorini monks from Marseille, is remarkable above all for the variegated statuary that runs around the top of its exterior.

Continuing west along the main SS131 dual carriageway, consider a quick diversion at the Siliqua crossroads, 14km west of Uta. About 5km to the south you'll see the fairytale image of castle ruins atop an extraordinary craggy mount. As you get closer, you come to realise that little more than the crumbling walls of the **Castello di Acquafredda** remain. The castle served as a temporary hiding place for Guelfo della Gherardesca when his father Ugolino, the reviled ruler of Iglesias, was imprisoned in Pisa and the family banished.

South of the *castello,* the **Riserva Naturale di Monte Arcosu** is a World Wildlife Fund reserve run by the **Cooperativa Il**

Caprifoglio (☑070 96 87 14; www.ilcaprifoglio .it, in Italian; admission €5; ⊙9am-5pm Sat & Sun) and one of the few remaining habitats of the *cervo sardo*. Covering the peak of Monte Arcosu (948m), it also harbours wild boar, martens, wildcats, weasels and plenty of birds of prey.

Some 12km northeast of Uta, San Sperate is famous for the colourful *murales* that brighten its stone walls. But, unlike those in Orgosolo, they don't represent keenly felt injustices; instead, they present a Daliesque tableau of traditional country life and some urban trends (skateboards stretching down a wall like an array of colourful tongues). Highlights include the epic *Storia di San Sperate* (Story of San Sperate) on Via Sassari. This was begun by Pinuccio Sciola (born 1942), a local sculptor who was inspired by the Mexican artist Diego Rivera.

A great place to stop and eat is Ada (☑070 96 00 972; www.ristoranteada.eu, in Italian; Via Cagliari 21; meals €25-30; ⊙Mon-Sat), named after its famed chef who hand-makes thirteen different types of ravioli – now that's seriously impressive. You should sample at least one ravioli dish, but you might also like to taste *mazzamurru* (hard bread in a meat sauce and cheese), or the interesting array of antipasti, such as baked wild asparagus or prosciutto with preserved prickly pear. For mains, the horse steak and beef *tagliata* are both divine. Finish with the fine local cheese. There is also a good wine list and some artisanal beers to choose from.

ARST buses run to Uta from Cagliari (€1.50, 45 minutes, 10 Monday to Friday, three Sunday), although the church is about a half-hour walk from the centre. For San Sperate, buses run hourly from Cagliari (€1.50, 30 minutes). To get to Castello di Acquafredda, you'll need your own transport.

Sanluri

POP 8570

One of the biggest towns in Medio Campidano province, Sanluri is a bustling agricultural centre. In the 14th century Queen Eleonora d'Arborea lived here for a period and the town was a key member of her opposition to Catalano–Aragonese expansion. In 1409 island resistance was finally crushed at the Battle of Sanluri, paving the way for centuries of Iberian domination. Unfortunately, little remains to vouch for the town's former glory apart from Eleonora's squat, brooding castle.

Just off the main thoroughfare, Via Carlo Felice, the castle today houses the **Museo Risorgimentale Duca d'Aosta** (☑070 930 71 05; Via Generale Nino Villa Santa 1; adult/reduced €6/4; ⊙4.30-9pm Tue-Mon, 10am-1pm & 4.30-9pm Sun summer, 9.45am-1pm & 3-7pm Sun winter) and its eclectic collection of assorted military paraphernalia. The garden displays a medieval catapult, torpedo and a couple of mortars, while inside you're treated to an extraordinary array of objects, from period furniture to military mementos from a number of modern conflicts.

A short walk away – cross Via Carlo Felice, follow Via San Rocco for a few hundred metres, and then take a left towards the Franciscan monastery at the top of the rise – is the **Museo Etnografico Cappuccino** (☑070 930 71 07; Via San Rocco 6; admission €3; ⊙appointment only). This houses yet another varied collection, comprising obsidian arrowheads and Roman-era coins, farm tools, clocks and works of religious art.

Sanluri is well served by ARST bus with regular connections to/from Cagliari (€3, one hour).

Sardara

POP 4270

Some 8km northwest of Sanluri along the SS131, Sardara is a sleepy village built around an attractive stone core. Rising in the centre of the village, the **Chiesa di San Gregorio** (Piazza San Gregorio) makes a fetching landmark. Built between 1300 and 1325 in a mixed Romanesque Gothic style, it boasts a sombre, soaring facade and a pretty rose window.

Further uphill is the **Civico Museo Archeologico Villa Abbas** (☑070 938 61 83; www.coopvillabbas.sardegna.it, in Italian; Piazza Liberta 7; admission €2.60, incl Chiesa di Sant'Anastasia €4.50; ⊙9am-1pm & 5-8pm Tue-Sun summer, 9am-1pm & 4-7pm winter), with a collection containing finds from local archaeological sites. Among the finest pieces are two bronze statuettes found on the edge of Sardara in 1913 and dating to the 8th century BC. Outside, excavations have been carried out on the Sa Costa site that forms the museum's back yard.

You'll find more of archaeological interest a few hundred metres away at the **Area Archeologico & Chiesa di Sant'Anastasia** (☑070 938 61 83; www.coopvillabbas.sardegna.it, in Italian; Piazza Sant'Anastasia; admission incl Civico

Museo €4.50; ⊙9am-1pm & 5-8pm Tue-Sun summer, 9am-1pm & 4-7pm winter). The small Gothic church sits in the midst of what was once a much larger nuraghic temple complex. The focus of worship was an underground well temple, known as *Sa funtana de is dolus* (Fountain of Pain), and accessible from beneath the church (enter to your left as you face the church entrance).

A few kilometres west of the town (on the other side of the SS131) is **Santa Maria de Is Acquas**, the site of thermal baths since Roman times. About 4km to the south, a dirt road leads to the empty walls of the **Castello Monreale**, built by the governor of Arborea and used as a temporary refuge by the defeated troops of Brancaleone Doria after the Battle of Sanluri. The Catalano–Aragonese garrisoned it for a time in 1478, but thereafter it soon fell into disuse. You can see some of the colourful medieval ceramics and other material dug up in the castle in Sardara's museum.

Accommodation in Sardara is not up to much, but the town is within easy striking distance of Cagliari, and regular ARST buses connect with the capital (€4, 1¼ hours, 12 Monday to Saturday, four Sunday).

LA MARMILLA

Northeast of Sardara, the landscape takes on a livelier aspect as dusty plains give way to the undulating green hills of La Marmilla. Named after these low-lying mounds – *marmilla* is derived from *mammellare,* meaning 'breast shaped' – La Marmilla is an area of bucolic scenery and quiet, rural life. It's also one of Sardinia's richest archaeological regions and it's here, in the shadow of the table-topped high plain known as La Giara di Gesturi, that you'll find the island's best-known nuraghic site, the Unesco-listed Nuraghe Su Nuraxi.

Villanovaforru & Nuraghe Genna Maria

POP 690

On the southern fringes of La Marmilla, Villanovaforru is a manicured, pretty little village that attracts coachloads of visitors to its archaeological sites. The village itself boasts a worthwhile museum, while a short hop to the west is the important *nuraghe* settlement of Genna Maria.

Housed in an attractive 19th-century palazzo in the village centre, the **Museo Archeologico** (⬛070 930 00 50; Piazza Costituzione 4; admission €3.50, incl Nuraghe €5; ⊙9.30am-1pm & 3.30-7pm Tue-Sun summer, to 6pm winter) provides a good overview of the area's prehistoric past with finds from many local sites, including Su Nuraxi and Genna Maria. Exhibits run the gamut from nuraghic times with enormous amphorae and other pots, oil lamps, jewellery and coins.

Adjacent to the museum, the **Sala delle Mostre** (admission €1.50; ⊙9.30am-1pm & 3.30-7pm Tue-Sun summer, to 6pm winter) hosts temporary exhibitions on local life and history.

The complex of **Nuraghe Genna Maria** (⬛070 930 00 50; admission €2.50, incl Museo Archeologico €5; ⊙9.30am-1pm & 3.30-7pm Tue-Sun summer, to 6pm Oct, Feb & Mar, 9.30am-1pm & 2.30-5pm winter), signposted as the Parco Archeologico, is about 1km out of the village on the road to Collinas. The *nuraghe* is a tumbledown site but, archaeologically speaking, one of the most important on the island. It consists of a central tower, around which was later raised the three-cornered bastion. Much later an encircling wall was also raised to protect an Iron Age village, but little of it remains today.

To the northeast of the village, indicated off the road to Lunamatrona, the **Museo del Territorio Sa Corona Arrùbia** (⬛070 934 10 09; www.museosacoronarrubia.it; Localita Lunamatrona; admission €8, incl chair lift €10; ⊙9am-1pm & 3-7pm Tue-Fri, 9am-7pm Sat & Sun) showcases the area's flora and fauna with recreations of four different natural habitats. Best of all, though, it has a *seggiovia* (chairlift), which whisks you up to a viewing point on the Giara di Siddi.

Two ARST buses run here from Cagliari on weekdays (€4, 1½ hours). There are also services to/from Sardara (€1, 15 minutes, five Monday to Saturday) and Sanluri (€1, 15 minutes, three Monday to Saturday).

Las Plassas

Zigzagging northeast from Villanovaforru, you find yourself heading in the direction of Barumini. Long before you hit this town, you will see the ruined walls of the 12th-century **Castello di Marmilla** atop a conical hill beside the hamlet of Las Plassas. The castle was part of the defensive line built on the frontier with Cagliari province by the medieval rulers of Arborea.

For centuries, the locals thought little about the stone towers that scattered the island and many were used as humble shepherds' shelters. Then, 70 years ago, carbon footage revealed that they were in fact Bronze Age fortified settlements, most built between 1800 and 500 BC. In the absence of any written records – a fact that has led scholars to assume that the early Sards never had a written language – the *nuraghi* (stone towers) and *tombe dei giganti* (ancient mass graves, literally 'giants' tombs') provide one of the few windows into the nuraghic civilisation.

There are said to be up to 7000 *nuraghi* across the island, probably twice that many if you count those still underground. Their exact meaning has long been debated, but it is most likely that they had a multifunctional purpose: used as watchtowers, sacred areas for religious rites, and as meeting places for celebrations and commercial exchanges. They were, some say, prehistoric community centres of sorts.

Early *nuraghi* were simple free-standing structures with internal chambers. Over time, they became bigger – the Nuraghe Santu Antine is the tallest remaining *nuraghe*, at 25m – and increasingly complex with elaborate rooms and labyrinthine passages. Walls were raised around the grand watchtowers and villagers began to cluster within the walls' protective embrace. The most spectacular example of this is the beehive complex of the Nuraghe Su Nuraxi, near Barumini.

To get there, take the left fork (for Tuili) at the beginning of Las Plassas and you will see on your left a winding footpath to the top of this hill.

Barumini

POP 1380

From Las Plassas, the road leads through the voluptuous landscape to Barumini, a village of stone houses and quiet lanes. At the crossroads in the village centre is the tiny **Chiesa di Santa Tecla**, a 17th-century church sporting a lovely, curvaceous rose window.

Nearby, the **Polo Museale Casa Zapata** (☑070 936 81 28; Piazza Giovanni XXIII; admission €7, incl Nuraghe Su Nuraxi €10; ⊗10am-1.30pm & 3-7.30pm) is an attractive museum complex housed in the 16th-century residence of the Spanish Zapata family. The whitewashed villa was originally built over a 1st-millennium BC nuraghic settlement which has been skilfully incorporated into the museum's display. Here you'll also find artefacts taken from the nearby Su Nuraxi *nuraghe,* and a section dedicated to the Zapata dynasty, La Marmilla's 16th-century rulers, plus a small collection of agricultural tools and instruments.

A kilometre west of the village, the **Parco Sardegna in Miniatura** (☑070 936 10 04; www.sardegnainminiatura.it, in Italian; adult/reduced €12/10; ⊗9am-5pm Mon-Sat, to 6pm Sun) is a miniature reconstruction of the whole island. One for the kids, it has a play area and plenty of picnic tables.

Nuraghe Su Nuraxi

Sardinia's single Unesco-listed site, and the island's most famous *nuraghe,* is **Nuraghe Su Nuraxi** (http://whc.unesco.org/en/list/833; adult/reduced €7/5, incl Polo Museale Casa Zapata €10/8; ⊗guided tours every 30min 9am-1pm & 2-7pm), about 1km west of Barumini on the road to Tuili. Note that visits are by guided tour only, usually in Italian, and that explanatory printouts are available in English. It's also worth noting that queues are the norm in summer when it can get extremely hot on the exposed site.

The focal point is the Nuraxi tower, which once had three stories and rose to a height of 20m. Dating to around 1500 BC, it originally stood in magnificent solitude, but four additional towers were later added and a connecting wall was built in 1000 BC.

The first village buildings arrived in the Iron Age, between the 8th and the 6th centuries BC, and these constitute the beehive of circular interlocking buildings that tumble down the hillside. As the village grew, a more complex defensive wall was built around the core, consisting of nine towers with arrow slits. Weapons in the form of massive stone balls have also been unearthed here.

In the 7th century BC the site was partly destroyed but not abandoned. In fact it grew and was still inhabited in Roman times. Elements of basic sewerage and canalisation have even been identified.

The site was rediscovered by Giovanni Lilliu (Sardinia's most famous archaeologist) in 1949, after torrential rains eroded the compact earth that had covered the *nuraghe* and made it look like just another Marmilla hillock. Excavations continued for six years and today the site is the only entirely excavated *nuraghe* in Sardinia. You can get an inkling of the work involved by seeing how many square bricks have been incorporated into the structure – these were deliberately made to stand out so they could be distinguished from the original basalt.

La Giara di Gesturi

Five kilometres west of Barumini, the village of Tuili is one of the main gateways to La Giara di Gesturi, a high basalt plateau that looms above the surrounding country. This remarkable 45-sq-km plain, splashed with *macchia* and small cork oaks, is home to the red long-horned bulls peculiar to Sardinia, and the unique wild *cavallini* (literally mini horses).

The best places to find the horses, in the early morning or late afternoon, are the seasonal lakes, called *paulis* (such as Pauli Maiori). In winter the lakes usually have a shallow patina of surface water, but in the warmer months most of it evaporates. At some, such as Pauli S'Ala de Mengianu, the water trapped in underground basalt sources will bubble to the surface around the *paulis,* and that is where the horses will be slaking their thirst.

The plateau also has its own microclimate, which fosters an array of unusual flora, best seen in spring, when the ground is covered in heather and the 15 species of **orchid** are in bloom. It's an interesting place to go walking; paths criss-cross the plateau, and there are a few dirt tracks that make it possible to get around in a vehicle. You can see the occasional *pinedda* (thatched shepherd's hut).

You can get information from the **tourist office** (☑070 936 30 23; www.prolocotuili.it;

Via Amsicora 3; ☺9am-7pm) in Tuili, where you'll also find a number of operators offering guided excursions, including **Jara Escursioni** (☺070 936 42 77, 3482924983; www.parcodellagiara.it, in Italian; Via Tuveri 16). Near Barumini, **Sa Jara Manna** (☑070 936 81 70; www.sajaramanna.it; SS197 km 44) offers a number of tour packages either on foot (€46 for a half day in a group of 25 or fewer) or by 4WD (€115 for a half day). It also hires out mountain bikes (€9 for a half day). A half-day or day's excursion will include a shepherd's lunch on the plateau in one of the old *pinedda.*

Before you head up into the Giara, take time to check out the **Chiesa di San Pietro** in Tuili, which harbours some fine works of art, including a grand *retablo* (altarpiece) made by the Maestro di Castelsardo in 1500. To visit, you'll need to ask at the tourist office.

You can also access the Giara from Setzu and, to the east, Gesturi. If you're coming from **Setzu,** turn right just north of the town. The road winds up 3km above the stark plains; at the 2km mark you'll see the Sa Domu de S'Orcu *tomba di gigante* (literally 'giant's tomb'; ancient mass grave) to the left. The asphalt peters out at the entrance to Parco della Giara, but you can follow the rough dirt track (slowly) in a normal car east to the Gesturi exit.

On the southeastern tip of the Giara, 5km up from Barumini, Gesturi is dominated by the big 17th-century **Chiesa di Santa Teresa d'Avila,** a centre of pilgrimage for the faithful, who flock here to celebrate Gesturi's greatest son, Fra Nicola 'Silenzio' (1882-1958), a Franciscan friar known for his religious devotion, wisdom and simplicity of life. His beatification in 1999 was a source of great pride to the good citizens of Gesturi, who have decorated the town with murals and grand portraits of the man they knew as Brother Silence.

Two weekday ARST buses run from Cagliari to Tuili (€4.50, 1½ hours), otherwise you'll need your own transport.

Sardinia Outdoors

Walking, Cycling & Riding »
Diving & Sailing »
Other Watersports »
Climbing Highs »

Rock climbing at Santa Teresa di Gallura (p154)

Walking, Cycling & Riding

Only by hitting the trail can you appreciate how big, wild and boundlessly beautiful Sardinia really is. The Parco Nazionale del Golfo di Orosei e del Gennargentu (p184) is sublime walking country, with cave-riddled coastlines and mountainous hinterland where you can trek to the primordially beautiful Gola Su Gorropu (p187) and Tiscali (p188). Peak baggers can scale Monte Limbara (p165) and volcanic Monti Ferru (p105). For a gentle coastal ramble and the chance to spot Eleonora's falcons, head to Capo Sandalo on Isola di San Pietro (p73). The seven-day Selvaggio Blu (p195) is a once-in-a-lifetime adventure.

Sardinia is combed with footpaths, many of them old mule trails, but routes are often unmarked and tricky to navigate solo. Consider hiring a guide from a local hiking cooperative; a half-day hike will cost around €40.

Big skies, sea breezes, your bum in a saddle – there's no better way to see Sardinia, say cyclists. Ogliastra (p191) is a free-ride favourite, with hurtling descents through oak forests to the glistening Med. If coastal hill cycling is more your scene, check out the spectacular road unfurling south of Alghero to Bosa (p123), and the corkscrewing SS125 between Dorgali and Santa Maria Navarrese (p186).

Bikes are available for hire in most resorts and towns for €10 to €30 per day. For cycling routes and maps, visit www. sardegnaturismo.it.

If hiking and cycling sound too strenuous, Sardinia has some fine horse-riding opportunities. The island's biggest equestrian centre is Horse Country Resort (p97), offering lessons and relaxing hacks. Or explore the coast of San Teodoro (p148) and verdant Isola Caprera (p162) on horseback. Expect to pay €30 to €35 for a 1½ hour hack.

Clockwise from top left
1. Cyclists at Cala Gonone 2. Hiking down from Tiscali, Valle di Lanaittu 3. Horse riding on Capo Carbonara

Diving & Sailing

One look at Sardinia's azure waters – among the clearest in the Mediterranean – and scuba divers are itching to take the plunge. Tuna, barracuda, groupers and even turtles, dolphins and (harmless) sharks can be spotted. Some of the best diving is off Sardinia's rocky islands, such as Isola di San Pietro (p71) in the southwest, Isola Tavolara (p147) in the northeast, and the protected waters of Arcipelago di La Maddalena (p159) in the north.

There are plenty of schools offering courses and guided dives for all levels from April to October. Expect to pay roughly €40 for a single tank dive, €420 for a PADI open water course and €20 per day for equipment hire.

Sailing in Sardinia doesn't have to mean a mega-yacht on the Costa Smeralda (p149). Sail away from the crowds to secluded bays on islands like Isola di San Pietro (p71) and La Maddalena (p159); reckon on around €1500 per week to charter a boat. For lessons, the Sporting Club Sardinia in Porto Pollo (p157) offers a range of courses, as does the Club della Vela (p124) near Alghero.

TOP FIVE DIVE SITES

» **Nereo Cave** (p115) This cathedral-like cave is the largest underwater grotto in the Mediterranean. Here Alghero's famous frilly red coral flourishes in sun-streaked waters.

» **Secca del Papa** (p147) Off Isola Tavolara, this wonderland swirls with groupers, barracudas, morays and sea bream.

» **Golfo di Cagliari** (p44) Dive more than 30m into the deep to explore this gulf's fascinating WWII wrecks.

» **Carloforte** (p71) Swim with shoals of tuna in underwater caves and gorges.

» **Nora** (p77) For a spot of underwater archaeology, dive down to submerged Punic-Roman ruins.

Clockwise from top left
1. Sailing on the Golfo di Orosei 2. Anchored in a bay at La Maddalena 3. Red coral in Nereo Cave

DALLAS STRIBLEY / LONELY PLANET IMAGES ©

ROBERTO RINALDI / BLUEGREEN PICTURES / ALAMY ©

Other Watersports

Porto Pollo (p157) on Sardinia's northeast coast is windsurf central. Beginners can experiment in sheltered waters while experts enjoy the high winds that whistle through the channel between Sardinia and Corsica. Other windsurfing hotspots include beautiful Spiaggia della Pelosa (p128) on the northwestern coast, the protected waters of Spiaggia Mugoni (p124) near Alghero, and Cagliari's huge Poetto Beach (p45). Schools charge roughly €30 for an hour's lesson and €160 for a two-day course. An excellent website for windsurfing holidays in Sardinia is www.planetwindsurfholidays.com.

Committed surfers prefer the huge rolling waves of the west coast, in particular the Sinis Peninsula where waves can reach 5m around Capo Mannu. A favourite beach is Putzu Idu at San Giovanni di Sinis (p99).

Few experiences in Sardinia beat paddling to hidden coves at your own speed. Cala Gonone (p188) is a great base for sea kayakers to explore the Golfo di Orosei. Or head to Cardedu (p192) to take in the dramatic sea stacks and coves of the Ogliastra coast. Kayak rental is around €25 per day.

TOP ADRENALINE RUSHES

» **Canyoning in the Gola Su Gorropu** Sheer drops and gigantic boulders in Europe's Grand Canyon (p187).

» **Via Ferrata del Cabirol** (p125) Flirt with mountaineering on this stunning new climbing trail above the Mediterranean.

» **Kitesurfing off Putzu Idu** Let the wind catch your kite off this dream beach (p99).

» **Caving in the Supramonte** Explore the caves and passageways burrowing through the karst (p187).

» **Waterskiing off Isola Caprera** Hold on as you're catapulted across azure waters (p162).

Clockwise from top left
1. Equipment for hire on a beach near Villasimius
2. Windsurfing at Porto Pollo **3.** Surfing at Capo Mannu

Climbing Highs

With its vertiginous coastline and craggy interior, Sardinia is climbing heaven. Bring your own rope and quick draws, a head for heights and a copy of Maurizio Oviglia's definitive *Pietra di Luna* climbing guide. The websites www.climb-eur ope.com and www.sardiniaclimb .com will give you a head start.

Cala Gonone-Dorgali

1 Cala Gonone (p188) is climbing central, with sheer limestone faces bolted with routes for beginners and advanced climbers. There's a huge variety of climbs in the surrounding countryside, including slabs, steep walls, overhangs, single-pitch and easier multipitches. See the boxed text, p189, for inspiration.

Alghero

2 Go west of Alghero to Capo Caccia (p124) for terrific rock climbing off the cliffs above the deep waters of the Mediterranean. Experienced climbers seeking a thrill can try Deep Water Soloing (DWS).

Ogliastra

3 Currently one of the hottest year-round venues is the Ogliastra province, with some 800 climbs in grades from 4 to 9b. Hotspots include Baunei (p194) for coastal climbs and Jerzu (p195), famous for its imposing limestone towers, known locally as *tacchi* (heels).

Isili

4 Isili (p183) tempts climbers with more than 250 single-pitch sports routes ranging from 5a to 8b. It's best known for its steep 'roof climbing' crags.

Domusnovus

5 Domusnovas (p61) is a renowned winter climbing centre, peppered with limestone rocks, cliffs and caves. There are some 440 routes for both novice and experienced climbers, ranging from simple, single-pitch walls to tough 7c overhangs.

Right

1. Santa Teresa di Gallura 2. Cala Gonone

PHILIP & KAREN SMITH / LONELY PLANET IMAGES ©

Oristano & the West

Best Places to Eat

» Peschiera Pontis (p98)

» Desogos (p106)

» Il Caminetto (p99)

» Trattoria Gino (p95)

» Sa Pischedda (p103)

Best Places to Stay

» Hotel Lucrezia (p204)

» Corte Fiorita (p205)

» Eleonora B&B (p204)

» Mandra Edera (p205)

Why Go?

Nature lovers will relish this part of Sardinia, with its coastal wetlands backed by windswept mountain peaks. The region is rich in wildlife – pink flamingos bob on silver lagoons and horse riding opportunities abound. This is also where you'll find some of Sardinia's loveliest beaches, from wild and deserted to popular, sporty stretches.

Gourmets will love the area; Oristano is famous for its Vernaccia wine, while the Monti Ferru massif has prized olive oil and *bue rosso* steak. Milis village is bursting with oranges, and the Sinis Peninsula boasts the island's finest *bottarga* (mullet roe). Travellers interested in history won't feel left out – Roman ruins and impressive ancient *nuraghi* are scattered across the verdant landscape.

At the heart of it all is Oristano, one of Sardinia's great medieval cities. It's an important market town with a lovely historical centre, good restaurants and an ebullient atmosphere. When you add the antique beauties of Bosa, the west can't get any better.

When to Go

Visiting in January is best for seeing pink flamingos on Sinis Peninsula. Oristano's carnival, Sa Sartiglia, the most colourful on the island, takes place in February, and it's followed closely by Bosa's *martedì grasso*, an entertaining and sometimes bizarre party. Easter festivities take over the region in April. The best time to bask in the warm sun is in May and June, while August sees Bosa's four-day Festa di Santa Maria del Mare. Witness a barefoot race from Oristano to San Salvatore at the Festa di San Salvatore in September.

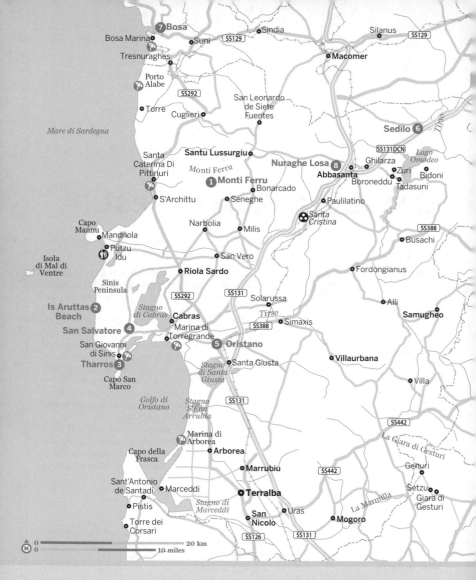

Oristano & the West Highlights

1 Revel in the sweeping views from **Monti Ferru** (p104)

2 Spend at least a day lying around on the prized quartz sand of **Is Aruttas Beach** (p99)

3 Give your imagination a workout at the windswept remains of the ancient city of **Tharros** (p100)

4 Practise your spaghetti-western swagger at **San Salvatore** (p99)

5 Throw yourself into the carnival madness of Oristano's **Sa Sartiglia** (p94)

6 Marvel at the adrenalin-charged horse race of Sedilo's **S'Ardia** (p107) festival

7 Grab yourself a canoe at **Bosa** (p101) and head upstream along the Fiume Temo, Sardinia's only inland navigable river

8 Bone up on ancient history at the impressive **Nuraghe Losa** (p109)

ORISTANO

POP 33,000

With its elegant shopping streets, ornate piazzas, popular cafes and some good restaurants, Oristano's refined and animated centre is a lovely place to hang out. Though there's not a huge amount to see beyond some churches and an interesting archaeological museum, the city makes a good base for the surrounding area.

History

The flat, fertile countryside around Oristano was an important nuraghic centre, but it was the Phoenicians who first put the area on the map. Arriving in the latter half of the 8th century BC, they established the city of Tharros, which later thrived under the Romans and became the the de facto capital of western Sardinia.

The city was eventually abandoned in 1070 when its citizens, fed up with continuous Saracen raids, decamped to a more easily defendable inland site, Aristianis (present-day Oristano). This new city became capital of the Giudicato d'Arborea, one of Sardinia's four independent provinces, and the base of operations for Eleonora of Arborea (c 1340–1404). A heroine in the Joan of Arc mould, Eleonora organised the 14th-century war against the Spanish and wrote the Carta de Logu (Code of Laws; see p225) before succumbing to the plague. With her death, anti-Spanish opposition crumbled and Oristano was incorporated into the rest of Aragonese-controlled Sardinia. It wasn't a good time for the city. Trade collapsed and the city suffered from plague and famine.

The construction of the Cagliari–Porto Torres Hwy in the 1820s and Mussolini's land reclamation programs gave Oristano a much-needed boost.

◉ Sights

Oristano's main sights are inside the *centro storico* (historic centre), a pretty area of stone houses, sunny piazzas and baroque streets.

Duomo   CATHEDRAL
(Piazza Duomo) Lording it over Oristano's skyline, the onion-domed bell tower of the Duomo is one of the few remaining elements of the original 14th-century cathedral, itself a reworking of an earlier church damaged by fire in the late 12th century. The free-standing *campanile,* topped by its conspicuous maiolica-tiled dome, adds an exotic Byzantine feel to what is otherwise a typical 18th-century baroque complex.

Inside, the look is pure baroque, although the apses and Cappella del Rimedio survive from the Gothic original. It's in the latter that you'll find the 14th-century wooden sculpture *Annunziata* or *Madonna del Rimedio,* believed to have been carved by the Tuscan sculptor Nino Pisano.

Chiesa di San Francesco   CHURCH
(Via Sant'Antonio) This neoclassical church was designed by the Cagliari architect, Gaetano Cima (1805–78). Its famous 14th-century wooden sculpture, the Crocifisso di Nicodemo, is considered one of Sardinia's most precious carvings. Also take a look at the sacristy's altarpiece by Pietro Cavaro, from the 16th century.

Piazza Eleonora d'Arborea & Around   PIAZZA
Piazza Eleonora d'Arborea, Oristano's elegant outdoor drawing room, sits at the southern end of pedestrianised Corso Umberto I. An impressive, rectangular space, it comes to life on warm summer evenings when townsfolk congregate to chew the fat and children blast footballs against the glowing palazzi. The city's central square since the 19th century, it's flanked by grand buildings, including the neoclassical **Municipio** (Town Hall). In the centre stands an ornate 19th-century **statue of Queen Eleonora**, raising a finger as if about to launch into a political speech. Bargain hunters should drop by on the first Saturday of the month when the piazza hosts an **antique market**.

Torre di Mariano II   TOWER
(Piazza Roma) Little survives of the medieval walled town except for this 13th-century tower. Known also as the Torre di Cristoforo,

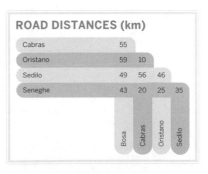

ROAD DISTANCES (km)			
Cabras	55		
Oristano	59	10	
Sedilo	49	56	46
Seneghe	43	20	25	35
	Bosa	Cabras	Oristano	Sedilo

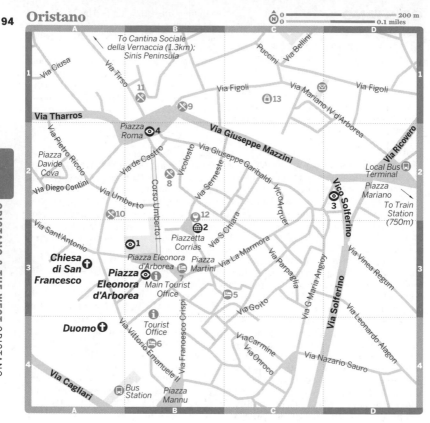

this was the town's northern gate and an important part of the city's defences. The bell was added later in the 15th century.

Portixedda TOWER
(⊘10am-noon & 4-6pm Tue-Sun) This second tower, just to the east off Via Giuseppe Mazzini, was also part of the city walls, most of which were pulled down in the 19th century. The tower is now used to stage temporary exhibitions.

Museo Antiquarium Arborense MUSEUM
(✆0783 79 12 62; www.antiquariumarborense.it; Piazzetta Corrias; adult/reduced €3/1; ⊘9am-2pm & 3-8pm) Housed in a smart palazzo, Oristano's sole museum boasts one of the island's major archaeological collections. The permanent exhibition, which includes a scale model of 4th-century Tharros, is displayed on the upper floor. There are prehistoric finds from the Sinis Peninsula, including obsidian and flint spearheads and axes, bones

and a smattering of jewellery. More interesting is the stash of finds from Carthaginian and Roman Tharros. Ceramics predominate, but also on show are glassware, oil lamps and amphorae, and a range of pots, plates and cups.

In a small side room off the main hall is a small collection of *retabli* (painted altar pieces) and a model of Oristano in its 13th-century prime. One series of panels, the *Retablo del Santo Cristo* (1533), by the workshop of Pietro Cavaro, depicts a group of apparently beatific saints. But take a closer look and you'll see they all sport the instruments of their gory tortures slicing through their heads, necks and hearts.

✦ Festivals

Sa Sartiglia CARNIVAL
(www.sartiglia.info) Oristano's carnival is the most colourful on the island. It is attended in February by hundreds of costumed par-

Oristano

ticipants and involves a medieval joust, horse racing and incredible, acrobatic riding. See the boxed text p96.

✖ Eating & Drinking

Eating in Oristano is a pleasure, especially if you like fish. There's a good range of reasonably priced restaurants, and the nearby Stagno di Cabras lagoon and Golfo di Oristano ensure a steady supply of fresh seafood. Local staples include mullet *(muggine)*, sometimes known as *pesce di Oristano* (Oristano fish), which often appears on menus as *mrecca* (boiled, wrapped in pond grass and then dried and salted). Grilled eel is popular, as are *patelle,* limpet-like dark clams.

TOP CHOICE Trattoria Gino TRATTORIA €€
(☑0783 7 14 28; Via Tirso 13; meals around €27; ☺Mon-Sat) A wonderful, simple trattoria set in one neat room, the quality of the food in Gino's explains its sustained popularity since the 1930s. Try the simple and fragrant sage and ricotta ravioli, and follow with a chargrilled *seppia* (cuttlefish) studded with fresh cherry tomatoes. Watch out for the lemon sorbetto – it's laced with vodka!

Ristorante Craf RESTAURANT €€
(☑0783 7 06 69; Via de Castro 34; meals around €35; ☺Mon-Sat) This is a place with a huge reputation among the locals. Housed in a former 17th-century granary, the brick vaulted dining rooms and folksy clutter can feel either claustrophobic or cosy. Hearty country fare dominates the menu – try the *panne frattau* (Sardinian bread soup), pastas with legumes, or grilled meat, including *asinello* (donkey), and the homemade *amaretti* (almond biscuits).

Antica Trattoria del Teatro TRATTORIA €€
(☑0783 7 16 72; Via Parpaglia 11; meals around €40; ☺Mon-Sat) This refined and intimate *centro storico* restaurant is a good place to push the boat out and try something different. Something like *panada di anguille,* a kind of rustic eel pie, served with grated *casizolu* cheese. There's also a vast choice of cheese and a comprehensive beer selection.

La Torre PIZZERIA, RESTAURANT €
(☑0783 30 14 94; Piazza Roma 52; pizzas €6.50, meals around €25; ☺Tue-Sun) This place doesn't look like much but it serves the best pizza in town. There are also pastas and grilled main courses and a jolly weekend atmosphere.

Lola Mundo BAR €
(Piazzetta Corrias 14; drinks from €1.50; ☺Mon-Sat) The historic centre is full of bars and cafes but this is one of the most popular. With its piazza seating and relaxing music, it's a great spot to hang out.

🛍 Shopping

Specialità Sarde FOOD
(☑0783 7 27 25; Via Figoli 41; ☺Mon-Sat) Stock up on Sardinian gourmet specialities at this gourmet gift shop. As well as wine and cheese, you'll find all sorts of tempting preserves in pretty jars.

Cantina Sociale della Vernaccia WINE
(☑0783 3 31 55; Via Oristano 149, Rimedio) Oristano is famous for its fortified white Vernaccia wine, and this is the place to buy it. Most of Oristano's local producers bring their grapes here to be crushed, so you can be assured of the quality.

ℹ Information

Farmacia San Carlo (☑0783 7 11 23; Piazza Eleonora d'Arborea 10/11) Central pharmacy.
Guardia Medica (☑0783 30 33 73; Via Carducci 33) For call-out medical assistance.

ORISTANO EATING & DRINKING

SA SARTIGLIA: ORISTANO'S MARDI GRAS

Sa Sartiglia is Sardinia's most colourful and carefully choreographed festival. Its origins are unknown but its godlike central figure, the Su Cumpoidori, hints at pagan ritual. The jousts and costumes are undoubtedly Spanish, probably introduced by the *giudici* (provincial governors), who were trained at the Court of Aragon. The word 'Sartiglia' comes from the Castilian *sortija*, meaning 'ring', and the central event is a medieval joust in which the Su Cumpoidori, the King of the Sartiglia, must pierce a star (ring) suspended overhead. The virgin brides who dress the Su Cumpoidori, along with his effeminate, godlike status and the throwing of grain, all suggest older fertility rites heralding spring.

The event is held over two days, Sunday and *martedi grasso* (Shrove Tuesday or Mardi Gras). At noon the Su Cumpoidori is 'born'. He sits on a table (the altar) and is reverently clothed and masked by the *sas massaieddas* (young virgins). From this point on he cannot touch the ground and is carried to his horse, which is almost as elaborately dressed as he. The Su Cumpoidori's white mask is framed by a stiff mantilla on top of which he wears a black top hat. In his hand he carries a sceptre decorated with violets and periwinkles with which he blesses the crowd. It is his task to start the Sartiglia, the race to the star, which he does with two other knights, his *segundu* (second) and *terzu* (third), who all try to pierce the star. The more times they strike it, the more luck they bring to the coming year. The last ritual the Su Cumpoidori performs is the Sa Remada, where he gallops along the course lying on his back. Then the games are open to acrobatic riders who perform feats that draw gasps from the crowd.

Ospedale San Martino (⌨0783 31 71; Piazza San Martino) Hospital south of the centre.

Post office (⌨0783 3 68 01; Via Mariano IV d'Arborea; ☺8am-6.50pm Mon-Fri, 8am-1.15pm Sat)

Main tourist office (⌨0783 3 68 31; turismo@provincia.or.it; Piazza Eleonora d'Arborea 19; ☺9am-1pm & 4-6.30pm Mon-Fri) Has plenty of printed matter on the city and province.

❶ Getting There & Away

Bus

From the main bus station on Via Cagliari ARST buses leave for Santa Giusta (€1, 15 minutes, half-hourly), Cagliari (€7, one hour 35 minutes, two daily), Sassari (€7.50, two hours, three daily) and Nuoro (€7.50, 2½ hours, six daily).

Car & Motorcycle

Oristano is just off the SS131 highway, which connects Cagliari with Sassari and Porto Torres. Branch highways head off to the northeast for Nuoro and Olbia.

Train

The main Trenitalia train station is in Piazza Ungheria, east of the town centre. Up to 15 daily trains, sometimes involving a change en route, run between Oristano and Cagliari (€5.95, one to two hours). Only a handful make the run to Sassari (€9.65, 2½ hours, four daily). For Olbia there are only two through trains (€10.95, 2¾ hours); otherwise you have to change at Ozieri-Chilivani or Macomer.

❶ Getting Around

Bus

The town centre is easily covered on foot, although you will probably want to use buses to get in from the train station. The *rossa* (red) and *verde* (green) lines stop at the station and terminate in Piazza Mariano.

The *azzurra* (blue) buses run from various stops along Via Cagliari (including the main terminal) to Marina di Torregrande (€0.70 if bought at a *tabacchi* or at the Via Cagliari bus station, or €1.10 if bought on the bus, 15 minutes).

Car & Motorcycle

Parking is not too bad if you leave your car a little out of the centre. In the centre, pay-and-display parking (per hour €0.60; 8.30am-1pm and 4-7.30pm Monday to Saturday) is available within the blue lines.

Taxi

You'll find that taxis tend to congregate at the train station and around Piazza Roma. To phone for one, call ⌨0783 7 02 80 or ⌨0783 7 43 28.

AROUND ORISTANO

Oristano's main beach is at the small resort of **Marina di Torregrande**, 7km west of the city. Behind a long, sandy strip, the village presents a familiar seaside scene with suntanned locals parading down a palm-flanked *lungomare* (promenade) and music emanating from bars. Out of season it's a different story and you'll find the holiday homes shuttered and most of the restaurants closed.

The village's one and only building of any historical note is the stout 16th-century Aragonese watchtower, after which the resort is named. Once you've seen that, there's not much to do except don your swimmers and head to the beach. You can hire sun loungers and umbrellas there – expect to pay about €16.50 per day. **Eolo** (☑329 613 64 61; www.eolowindsurf.com, in Italian; Lungomare Eleonora d'Arborea) organises sailing and windsurfing courses, as well as renting out equipment (windsurfs start at €13 per hour).

The resort's top restaurant is **Da Giovanni** (☑0783 2 20 51; Via Colombo 8; meals around €40, tourist menu €23; ☺Tue-Sun); its nondescript setting on the main road out of town belies an excellent reputation. The seafood is particularly good in dishes such as *ravioli di pesce in salsa di gamberi* (fish ravioli in prawn sauce) and *muggine locale* (local mullet).

Of the seafront eateries, the **Maestrale** (☑0783 2 21 21; Lungomare Torregrande; pizzas €8, meals around €35; ☺Tue-Sun) is a good bet for a laid-back pizza or a plate of seafood pasta.

The beach strip is lined with summertime bars. A few kilometres inland on the road to Cabras, **BNN Fashion Club** (☑338 235 75 40; SP 94, km 1.8) is a popular bar-cum-disco serving Italian tunes, house and international pop.

From Oristano, city buses on the *azzurra* line run from various stops along Via Cagliari (including the main terminal) to Marina di Torregrande (€0.70 or €1.10 if bought on bus, 20 minutes).

SOUTH OF ORISTANO

South of Oristano, flat plains extend in a patchwork of wide, open fields interspersed with canals, lagoons and the odd pocket of pine wood. Until Mussolini launched an ambitious drainage and reclamation program in 1919, the area was largely covered with malarial swampland and thick cork forests. Nowadays it's a featureless, and sometimes strange, landscape dotted with sleepy villages and agricultural towns.

Santa Giusta
POP 4750

A bustling agricultural village, Santa Giusta lies on the shores of the Stagno di Santa Giusta, Sardinia's third-largest lagoon. Once the Punic town of Othoca, it is best known for its extraordinary basilica, one of the first, and finest, examples of Pisan–Romanesque architecture in Sardinia.

Built between 1135 and 1145, the **Basilica di Santa Giusta** (☺free guided tours 9am-1pm & 2-6pm Mon-Fri) rises like a galleon aground in the lagoon. Up close it is long and low, with blind arcades, a typically Tuscan central portal, and a severe Lombard facade. Inside, three naves are separated by marble and granite columns looted from the Roman towns of Tharros and Othoca. Topping the whole austere ensemble is a fine wood-beamed ceiling.

For four days around 14 May, the basilica takes centre stage during celebrations of the town's annual **Festa di Santa Giusta**.

Six kilometres to the south of town, the **Stagno S'Ena Arrubia** is a paradise for birdwatchers – flamingos, herons, coots and ospreys are regularly sighted.

Buses from Oristano's bus station leave half-hourly to Santa Giusta (€1, 15 minutes).

Arborea
POP 3980

Founded by Mussolini in 1928, Arborea bears all the hallmarks of its Fascist inception – severe grid-patterned streets, an immaculate central piazza and an array of fantastical architectural styles.

The immediate focus is **Piazza Maria Ausiliatrice**, a beautifully tended square that wouldn't look out of place in a Swiss Alpine village. Overlooking it is the clocked facade of the Tyrolean-style **Chiesa del Cristo Redentore** (☺mass 7.30am, 9am & 7pm). Over the road, the art nouveau **Municipio** houses the town's **archaeological museum** (☑0783 8 03 31; Viale Omodeo; admission free; ☺10am-1pm Mon-Fri) with its small collection of locally found artefacts.

MARINA DI ARBOREA
Hidden behind a thick pine wood 2km northwest of Arborea, Marina di Arborea sits at the head of a long, sandy beach. It is little more than a seafront hotel and a car park, although it is being increasingly overtaken by the **Horse Country Resort**

(☎0783 80 51 73; www.horsecountry.it; Strada a Mare 24; riding lessons per person from €20), a vast hotel complex with excellent sporting facilities. The resort is the biggest equestrian centre in Sardinia and one of the most important in Italy, with a stable of Arabian, Andalucian and Sardinian horses. Nonguests can choose from a number of riding packages. Check the website for the full array. For details on staying here, see p204.

Marceddi

Looking over the mouth of the **Stagno di Marceddi**, this tiny fishing village is the embodiment of a backwater. For much of the year the only signs of modern life are a few battered cars and the ragged electricity lines flapping over dirt roads. The lagoon, which separates the Arborea plains from the Costa Verde, is an important wildlife habitat, harbouring flamingos, cormorants and herons.

If you decide to linger, you can get an excellent fish lunch at **Da Lucio** (☎0783 86 71 30; Via Sardus Pater 34; meals around €35; ☺lunch Fri-Wed Oct-May, lunch & dinner daily rest of the year) down on the waterfront. Try the octopus salad and follow with clam and *bottarga* (fish roe) spaghetti, or *fregola* (small semolina pasta) and mussel soup. For mains, try a seafood *fritto misto* with a fresh green salad.

SINIS PENINSULA

Spearing down into the Golfo di Oristano, the Sinis Peninsula feels like a world apart. Its limpid lagoons – the Stagno di Cabras, Stagno Sale Porcus and Stagno Is Benas – and snow-white beaches lend it an almost tropical air, while the low-lying green countryside appears uncontaminated by human activity. In fact, the area has been inhabited since the 5th century BC. *Nuraghi* litter the landscape and the compelling Punic–Roman site of Tharros stands testament to the area's former importance. Sports fans will enjoy great surfing, windsurfing and some fine diving.

Although summer is the obvious time to visit, early spring is a wonderful time to be here for the magnificent spectacle of flocks of migrating birds that settle on the shallow lake waters and the beautiful spring flowers that cover the landscape. The queen of the show is the gorgeous pink flamingo.

Cabras

POP 8700

Sprawled on the southern shore of the Stagno di Cabras, Cabras is an important fishing town and centre of the island's mullet fishing – the local *bottarga* is much sought-after and well worth trying. The town is rather unattractive, but you'll eat well and the archaeology museum is worth a quick once-over.

◉ Sights

The town's one site of interest is the **Museo Civico** (☎0783 29 06 36; www.penisoladelsinis .it, in Italian; Via Tharros 121; adult/reduced incl entry into Tharros €7/3; ☺9am-1pm & 4-8pm summer, 9am-1pm & 3-7pm winter), located at the southern end of town. The museum houses finds from the prehistoric site of **Cuccuru Is Arrius**, 3km to the southwest, and Tharros. Of particular interest is a series of obsidian and flint tools said to date back to the neolithic cultures of Bonu Ighinu and Ozieri.

✦✦ Festivals

Festa di San Salvatore   TRADITIONAL RACE
On the first Sunday of September every year, several hundred young fellows clothed in white mantles set off on the **Corsa degli Scalzi** (Barefoot Race), an 8km dash finishing at the sanctuary of San Salvatore. They bear with them a figure of the Saviour to commemorate an episode in 1506, when townspeople raced to San Salvatore to collect the figure and save it from Moorish sea raiders. Another race back to Oristano, in a similar fashion, takes place the following day.

✗ Eating

[TOP CHOICE] **Peschiera Pontis**   SEAFOOD €€
(☎0783 391 774; Strada Provinciale 6; fixed menus €25-30; ☺lunch & dinner daily) On the road between Cabras and Tharros, this is a fantastic place to sample fresh local fish. Fronting the Pontis fishing cooperative, it's a one-room outfit with a largish covered terrace and a loyal clientele. The fixed price menus include abundant antipasti (four per person), primo, secondo – all fish-based – desserts and wine. The fish is grilled on the terrace and is the freshest you're likely to eat on the island. Booking is essential on weekends.

The beaches on the Sinis Peninsula are well worth tracking down. One of the best is **Is Aruttas**; for years its white quartz sand was carted off to be used in aquariums and on beaches on the Costa Smeralda. But it's now illegal to take any – except the bits that get stuck between your toes. The beach is signposted and is 5km west off the main road leading north from San Salvatore.

At the north of the peninsula, the popular surfing beach of **Putzu Idu** is backed by a motley set of holiday homes, beach bars, and surfing outlets. One such, the **Capo Mannu Kite School** (☑347 007 70 35; www.capomannukiteschool.it) runs kitesurfing lessons for all levels.

Next door to the **Scuba Café** (☑Lungomare Putzu Idu; ☉9am-10pm winter, 7am-2am summer), one of the very few places that remains open in winter is **9511 Diving** (☑349 291 37 65; www.9511.it); its PADI-qualified instructors lead dives (from €50 including equipment hire), snorkelling trips (€25 per person) and excursions to the eloquently named **Isola di Mal di Ventre** (Stomach Ache Island), 10km off the coast.

There are various operators offering tours to Isola di Mal di Ventre. **Mare Mania** (☑347 191 94 80; www.mare-mania.it, in Italian; ☉8am-1pm & 3-8pm summer only) operates out of a kiosk on the main road into the village. Half-day/day tours cost €19/22, or €46 with lunch thrown in.

On the right as you approach Putzu Idu, you'll see the **Stagno Sale Porcus**, a wide, flat lagoon that hosts flamingos in winter and is baked to a shimmering white crust in summer. Horse riding around the lagoon can be arranged through **Orte e Corru Ranch** (☑0783 52 81 00; Localita Oasi di Sale Porcus).

Two weekday ARST buses run to Putzu Idu from Oristano (€2, 55 minutes). In July and August, there are an additional four services.

Il Caminetto SEAFOOD €€
(☑0783 39 11 39; Via Cesare Battisti 8; meals around €35; ☉Tue-Sun) One of the best-known restaurants in the area, this busy spot attracts hungry customers from far and wide. The main allure is the fish menu, which features Cabras classics *muggine affumicato* (smoked mullet) and *aguidda incasada* (eel with Sardinian pecorino cheese).

L'Oliveto PIZZERIA €€
(☑0783 39 26 16; Via Tirso 23; meals €30-35; ☉Wed-Mon) Tucked away in an olive grove near the northern edge of town, this is a popular restaurant-cum-pizzeria specialising in seafood and decent pizza.

❶ Getting There & Away

BUS Buses run every 20 minutes or so from Oristano (€1, 15 minutes).

San Salvatore

Used as a spaghetti-western film set during the 1960s, San Salvatore is centred on a dusty town square and surrounded by rows of minuscule terraced houses, known as *cumbessias*. For much of the year these simple shacks are deserted, as is the rest of the village, but in late August they are opened to house pilgrims for the Feast of San Salvatore. This nine-day-long celebration is focused on the 16th-century **Chiesa di San Salvatore** (☉9.30am-1pm & 3.30-6pm Mon-Sat, 9.30am-1pm Sun) in the centre of the village square.

Under the church, there is a stone *ipogeo* (underground vault), which dates back to the nuraghic period. The original sanctuary was associated with a water cult, and you can still see a well in the main chamber. It was later converted into a Roman-era church, and the dark stone walls still bear traces of 4th-century graffiti and faded frescoes.

Just beyond the turn-off for the village (blink and you've missed it) is the excellent **Agriturismo Su Pranu** (☑0783 39 25 61; www.agriturismosupranu.com; Localita San Salvatore; meals €25; ☉lunch & dinner daily), a genuine working farm with a superb restaurant. The menu depends on what's available on the day, but vegetables and fruit are home-grown and the meat, including *porceddu,* is cooked to perfection on a big outdoor barbecue. There are also guestrooms available (p204).

San Giovanni di Sinis

At the southern tip of the Sinis Peninsula, about 5km beyond San Salvatore, the road passes through the small settlement of San Giovanni di Sinis. By the roadside car park you'll see the sandstone **Chiesa di San Giovanni di Sinis** (☺9am-7pm summer, to 5pm winter), one of the two oldest churches in Sardinia (Cagliari's Basilica di San Saturnino is older – see p42). It owes its current form to an 11th-century makeover, although elements of the 6th-century Byzantine original remain, including the characteristic red dome. Inside, the bare walls lend a sombre and surprisingly spiritual atmosphere.

Tharros

From San Giovanni di Sinis, the road continues past a strip of pizzerias, bars and cafes up to **Tharros** (☐0783 39 73 06; admission incl Museo Civico in Cabras adult/reduced €7/3; ☺9am-7pm summer, to 5pm winter), the once mighty port founded by the Phoenicians in the 8th century BC. Set magnificently against the sea, these ancient ruins count among southern Sardinia's most thrilling sights. Try to visit early in the morning or just before sunset, when the site is at its most atmospheric.

History

Capo San Marco, the southernmost point of the Sinis Peninsula, was already home to a thriving nuraghic culture when the Phoenicians established a base here in about 730 BC. Tharros thrived and was eventually absorbed into the Carthaginian empire. But, as an important naval base in a strategic position, it was always vulnerable and when the Romans attacked the Carthaginians, it fell to the rampant legionnaires.

It remained a key naval town, but once the main road from Cagliari to Porto Torres was completed it was sidelined. Nevertheless, it got an overhaul in the 2nd and 3rd centuries AD. Increasingly aggressive raids from the Vandals and the North African Saracens

led to its abandonment in 1070. Much of the ancient city was subsequently stripped to build the new capital at Oristano.

◉ Sights

As you approach the site it is impossible to see the ruins until you reach the hilltop ticket office. From here follow a brief stretch of *cardo* (the main street in a Roman settlement) until you reach, on your left, the *castellum aquae*, the city's main water reserve. Two lines of pillars can be made out within the square structure. From here the **Cardo Massimo**, the city's main thoroughfare, leads to a bare rise topped by a Carthaginian acropolis and a *tophet*, a sacred burial ground for children. Also here are traces of the original nuraghic settlement.

From the bottom of the Cardo Massimo, the **Decumano** runs down to the sea passing the remains of a **Punic temple** and, beyond that, the Roman-era **Tempio Tetrastilo**, marked by its two solitary columns. These are, in fact, reconstructions, although the Corinthian capital balanced on the top of one is authentic.

Nearby is a set of **thermal baths** and, to the north, the remains of a **palaeo-Christian baptistry**. At the southernmost point of the settlement is another set of baths, dating to the 3rd century AD.

For a bird's-eye view of the site, head up to the late-16th-century **Torre di San Giovanni watchtower** (admission €5; ☺9am-7pm summer, to 5pm winter), occasionally used for exhibitions. Here you can look down on the ruins, as well as **Spiaggia di San Giovanni di Sinis**, a popular beach, which extends on both sides of the tower. There is nothing to stop you wandering down the dirt tracks to Capo San Marco and the lighthouse.

❶ Getting There & Away

BUS In July and August, there are five daily buses for San Giovanni di Sinis from Oristano (€1.50, 35 minutes).
CAR Parking near the site costs €2 for two hours, €4 per day.

GETTING AWAY FROM IT ALL

A few kilometres out of Tharros, and signposted off the main road, the **Parco Comunale Oasi di Seu** is a veritable Eden of Mediterranean flora. Once you've navigated the 3km dirt track to the entrance, you enter a silent world of sandy paths and undisturbed nature. Herby smells fill the air, rising off fragrant masses of *macchia* (scrub), rosemary, dwarf palms and pine trees.

Riola Sardo

POP 2140

Though the town itself is drab, it's worth stopping here in order to stay at the wonderful Hotel Lucrezia. For further details, see the Accommodation chapter, p197 .

NORTH OF ORISTANO

North of the beautiful Monti Ferru region the land flattens out towards Macomer, a workaday agricultural centre and important transport hub. To the northwest, Bosa is quite different, a pretty medieval town topped by a formidable hilltop castle.

Macomer

POP 10,900

You probably won't want to hang around too long in Macomer. It's not an unpleasant place, but unless you're passing through, there's really no great reason to stop off here.

If you do have some time to kill, there's the modest **Museo Etnografico** (☑0785 7 04 75; Corso Umberto 225; admission adult/reduced €3/1; ☺10am-12.30pm & 4-8pm Mon-Fri, Sat am only), which houses a motley collection of home furnishings and utensils. If it's shut, ask over the road at **Esedra Escursioni** (☑0785 74 30 44; www.esedraescursioni.it; Corso Umberto 206), where you can also arrange excursions and trips on the *trenino verde* (p50).

Those with a car can visit the 15m-high **Nuraghe di Santa Barbara**, off the SS131 about 2km north of Macomer, or, near the town hospital, the dilapidated **Nuraghe Ruiu**. A third *nuraghe,* the **Nuraghe di Santa Sabina** is south of Silanus, 15km east of Macomer, positioned next to a sweet Byzantine chapel.

For a bite to eat, **Ristorante Su Talleri** (☑0785 7 16 99; Corso Umberto I 228; pizza €6, meals €25-30; ☺Mon-Sat) offers all the ambience of a 1980s roller-disco but does pretty good food, including takeaway pizza.

Macomer is a major rail hub. Trenitalia trains connect with Oristano (€3.30, 45 minutes, nine daily), Cagliari (€8.75, 1¾ hours, 10 daily) and Sassari (€6.35, 1¾ hours, four daily). A handful of buses head eastwards to Nuoro (€4, 1¼ hours, four daily).

The train and bus stations are at the western edge of town along Corso Umberto.

Bosa

POP 8050

Bosa is one of Sardinia's most attractive towns. Seen from a distance, its rainbow townscape resembles a vibrant Paul Klee canvas, with pastel houses stacked on a steep hillside, tapering up to a stark, grey castle. In front, moored fishing boats bob on a glassy river and palm trees line the elegant riverfront.

Bosa was established by the Phoenicians and thrived under the Romans. During the early Middle Ages it suffered repeat raids by Arab pirates, but in the early 12th century the Malaspina family (a branch of the Tuscan clan of the same name) moved in and built their huge castle. In the 19th century, the Savoys established lucrative tanneries here, but these have since fallen by the wayside.

◉ Sights & Activities

Most of Bosa lies on the north bank of the Fiume Temo. The main strip, Corso Vittorio Emanuele, is one block north of the riverfront and leads down to the two central piazzas: Piazza Costituzione and Piazza IV Novembre. West of here, the modern town is laid out on a simple grid pattern. South of the river, Via Nazionale runs 3km west to Bosa Marina, the town's seaside satellite.

Castello Malaspina   CASTLE
(☑333 544 56 75; admission adult/reduced €3/1; ☺10am-1pm & 4-7pm Jul & Aug, 10am-1pm & 3.30-6pm Apr-Jun, Sep & Oct) Commanding huge panoramic views, the hilltop castle was built in 1112 by the Tuscan Malaspina family. Little remains of the original structure except for the skeleton – the imposing walls and a series of tough brick towers – and, inside, a humble 4th-century chapel, the **Chiesa di Nostra Signora di Regnos Altos**. This houses an extraordinary 14th-century fresco cycle depicting saints, ranging from a giant St Christopher through a party of Franciscans to St Lawrence in the middle of his martyrdom on the grill.

You can get to the castle by any route that goes up through the maze of lanes in Sa Costa, the medieval town. You're bound to get lost at some point but, unless you're in a rush, it's quite enjoyable just meandering through the lanes. If you want to visit between November and April, it's best to phone ahead.

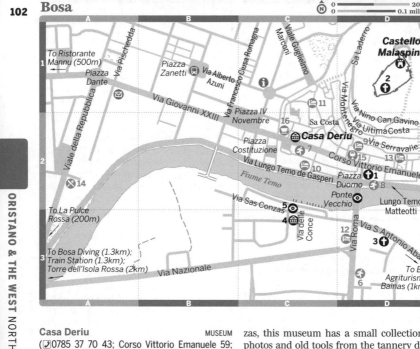

Casa Deriu
MUSEUM

(☏0785 37 70 43; Corso Vittorio Emanuele 59; adult/reduced €4.50/2; ⊙10.30am-1pm & 8.30-11pm Tue-Sun Jul & Aug, 11am-1pm & 5.30-8.30pm Tue-Sun Jun, 10am-1pm & 4-6pm Tue Sun rest of yr) Each of the three floors in this museum has a different theme that relates to the city and its past: the 1st floor features a display on the old tanning business and typical products from the surrounding region; the 2nd floor has been decorated as a typical 19th-century interior; and the top floor is dedicated to Melkiorre Melis (1889–1982), one of Sardinia's most important modern artists.

Cattedrale dell'Immacolata
CATHEDRAL

(Piazza Duomo; ⊙10am-noon & 4-7pm) This is a rare if not overly riveting example of rococo (officially called Piedmontese baroque).

Sas Conzas
STREET

(Via Sas Conzas) Located over the river, Sas Conzas is where former 19th-century tanneries line up along the southern bank. Many of the tanneries were still in business until after WWII.

Museo La Vecchie Concerie
MUSEUM

(☏329 414 49 21; Via delle Conce 13; admission €2; ⊙11am-1pm & 6-11pm) Adjacent to Sas Con-zas, this museum has a small collection of photos and old tools from the tannery days. Panels (in English and Italian) explain the whole smelly business.

Chiesa di Sant'Antonio Abate
CHURCH

A short walk from Sas Conzas, over Via Roma, is the little Chiesa di Sant'Antonio Abate. It's usually closed to the public but is the focus of a town festival dedicated to the saint on 16 and 17 January and again at Carnevale.

Cattedrale di San Pietro Extramuros
CATHEDRAL

(admission €1) Two kilometres upstream from the Chiesa di Sant' Antonio Abate is the 11th-century cathedral with its Gothic facade and largely Romanesque interior.

Cuccu
BIKE HIRE

(☏0785 37 54 16; Via Roma 5; bike hire per day €8; scooters €40) You can hire bikes and scooters at this mechanic's shop on the southern side of the river.

Pischedda Noleggio
CYCLING, BOATING

(☏339 489 01 05; Lungo Temo Matteotti) On the other side of the river, this operator can set you up with bikes (€10 per day), canoes (€25 for half a day) and *gommone* (dinghies, €35 per half day).

Bosa

⌖ Tours

Bosa is also an important **wine centre**, renowned for its dessert wine, Malvasia. To tour local producers ask at the tourist office for information on the local wine route, the Strada della Malvasia.

Esedra   WALKING & BOAT TOURS
(☎0785 37 42 58; www.esedrasardegna.it; Corso Vittorio Emanuele 64; ◷9.30am-1pm & 4.30-8pm Mon-Sat, 10.30am-1pm Sun) If you're interested in joining an organised tour, this place offers a wide range of packages, including river cruises, birdwatching excursions and boat tours, as well as trips on the *trenino verde*. Prices depend on the activity and size of the group but are usually between €25 and €35 per person. The company operates out of a shop on the town's main strip where you can also pick up ISOLA certified craftwork.

✸ Festivals & Events

Carnevale   CARNIVAL
(www.bosaonline.com, in Italian) Carnevale kicks off with a burning pyre outside the Chiesa di Sant'Antonio Abate and follows with days of parades. The last day, *martedi grasso*, is the most intriguing. In the morning townsfolk dress in black to lament the passing of Carnevale, while in the evening groups of boisterous locals dress in white to hunt the *giolzi*, a manifestation of the carnival that is said to hide in people's groins. To find it locals hold lanterns up to each other's nether regions shouting '*Giolzi! Giolzi! Ciappadu! Ciappadu!*' [*Giolzi! Giolzi!* Gotcha! Gotcha!].

Festa di Santa Maria del Mare   RELIGIOUS
(www.bosasardinia.com) For four days around the first Sunday of August, Bosa celebrates the Festa di Santa Maria del Mare. Fishermen form a colourful procession of boats to accompany a figure of the Virgin Mary along the river from Bosa Marina to the cathedral.

Festa di Nostra Signora di Regnos Altos   RELIGIOUS
(www.bosaonline.com, in Italian) In the second week of September, streets in the old town are bedecked with huge palm fronds, flowers and *altarittos* (votive altars) to celebrate the Festa di Nostra Signora di Regnos Altos.

✸ Eating

⎁ Sa Pischedda   SEAFOOD €€
(☎0785 37 30 65; Via Roma 8; meals around €30; ◷Wed-Mon, daily summer) Located at the hotel of the same name, Sa Picchedda is one of Bosa's best restaurants. Specialising in fish, both freshwater and saltwater, it has tables laid out on a romantic riverside verandah and in a stylish back garden. The menu features classics such as mullet *bottarga* (salted roe) and *fregola alla arselle* (rice-shaped pasta with clams and cherry tomatoes).

Ristorante Barracuda   TRATTORIA €€
(☎0785 37 45 10; Viale della Repubblica; meals around €28; ◷Wed-Mon, daily summer) This big, bustling restaurant is on a residential street 10 minutes' walk from the centre. The atmosphere is laid-back and the food is similarly unpretentious with the emphasis on hearty, home-cooked pastas and simple seafood dishes.

ORISTANO & THE WEST BOSA

Ristorante Mannu OSTERIA €€
(☑0785 37 53 06; Viale Alghero 28; meals around €30) Despite its unenticing location – next to a busy petrol station – this restaurant serves fine island food. A novel dish to try is the *agliata di razze*, an unusual combination of fish rays served in a sweet garlic sauce. If you want to stick to safer terrain, the homemade *panadinas* (like ravioli) are a reliable bet.

La Pulce Rossa PIZZERIA €
(☑0785 37 56 57; Via Lungo Temo Amendola 1; pizzas €6, meals around €25; ☺daily) Located down in the modern town, this friendly, family-run restaurant serves up filling fare for workers at decidedly untouristy prices.

🍷 Drinking

A good people-watching spot, **Caffè Chelo** (☑0785 37 30 92; Corso Vittorio Emanuele 71; ☺8am-10pm, later in summer) is an original Liberty-style cafe with street-side tables overlooking Piazza Costituzione.

For a more publike atmosphere, get down to **Birreria Alla Corte del Malaspina** (Corso Vittorio Emanuele 39; ☺8pm-2am Mon-Sat), a cosy drinking den on the central strip.

❶ Information

Banco di Sardegna (Piazza IV Novembre) Has an ATM.

Farmacia Passino (☑0785 37 60 47; Corso Vittorio Emanuele 51) Central pharmacy.

Post office (Via Pischedda; ☺8am-6.50pm Mon-Fri, 8am-1.15pm Sat) In the modern town.

Tourist office (☑079 37 61 07; www.infobosa .com; Via Alberto Azuni 5; ☺10am-1pm Thu-Sat) If it's shut, as it usually is, staff at the Casa Deriu museum are very helpful.

❶ Getting There & Away
Bus

Buses terminate at Piazza Zanetti. There are services to/from Alghero (€3-4.50, 55 minutes, four daily), Macomer (€2.50, 50 minutes, nine daily), Sassari (€5.50, 2¼ hours, two daily) and Oristano (€5.50, two hours, four daily Monday to Saturday). Buy tickets at **Bar Mouse** (Piazza Zanetti).

Car & Motorcycle

Bosa is connected to Macomer by the SS129 and to Alghero by the scenic coastal road, the SP105. In central Bosa it is easy to find street-side parking in the modern town, west of the centre.

❶ Getting Around
Bus

Up to 20 daily buses run from central Bosa (Piazza Zanetti) to Bosa Marina (€1, 10 minutes).

Bosa Marina & the Coast

At the mouth of the Fiume Temo, about 3km from Bosa proper, Bosa Marina is a busy summer resort set on a wide, kilometre-long beach. Overlooking the beach, the Catalano–Aragonese **Torre dell'Isola Rossa** (admission €2.50; ☺11am-1pm & 2.30-6.30pm Sat & Sun Apr-Jun, 10.30am-7.30pm daily Jul-Aug) is used to host temporary exhibitions.

Bosa Diving (☑335 818 97 48; www.bosa diving.it, in Italian; Via Cristoforo Colombo 2) offers dives (from €35) and snorkelling excursions (€25), as well as hiring out canoes (from €7) and dinghies (from €25). It also runs biweekly tours to beaches on the Capo Marargiu (€18 per person), just north of Bosa Marina.

If you have your own transport, you can search out a number of other beaches. Stretching south are the **Spiaggia Turas**, **Spiaggia Porto Alabe** and **Cala Torre Columbargia**. The first two are respectively a 1.5km and 8km drive from Bosa Marina and can get busy in high season. Cala Torre Columbargia is reached via the town of Tresnuraghes and involves some dusty trail driving. It's about an 18km drive from Bosa Marina.

For a different take on the area, the **trenino verde** (www.treninoverde.com) runs, slowly, between Bosa Marina, Tresnuraghes and Macomer. Every Saturday in July and August it leaves Macomer at 9.30am and arrives at Bosa Marina at 11.17am (the return journey is by bus). From Bosa Marina there's a Saturday and Sunday return service to Tresnuraghes (45 minutes), where you can connect with a bus for Macomer. Fares are: Macomer to Bosa Marina (single/return €9.50/13); Bosa Marina to Tresnuraghes (single/return €8/11).

MONTI FERRU

Rising to a height of 1050m (Monte Urtigu), the volcanic Monti Ferru massif is a beautiful and largely uncontaminated area of ancient forests, natural springs and small market towns. Seneghe produces some of Sardinia's best olive oil, and the island's finest beef, and Milis is famous for its sweet succulent oranges. But more than the towns, it's the glorious verdant countryside that is the main draw. Lonely roads snake over rocky peaks covered in a green down of cork,

The best way of exploring Monti Ferru is to ditch the car and walk. This scenic route leads up to the summit of Monte Entu, at 1024m one of the highest peaks in western Sardinia. It's not especially demanding, although you should allow about four hours.

You'll need a car to get to the start, which is by the Nuraghe Ruju, outside of Seneghe. From Seneghe, head towards Bonarcado and after a few hundred metres follow the sign for S'iscala. Leave your car at the Nuraghe Ruju and join the path a few metres down from the car park, in the wood to the left of the stone wall. Heading upwards you'll arrive at an opening, marked by a holm-oak tree, where you should go left. Carry on past the wooden gate until you reach a second metal gate. Go through it and continue until you reach a fork in the trail. Head left for some marvellous views of the coast, as far as Alghero on a clear day. From here you can continue onwards to the foot of the volcanic cone that marks the summit of Monte Entu.

chestnut, oak and yew trees while falcons and buzzards float on warm air currents overhead. Mouflon and Sardinian deer are slowly being introduced back to their forest habitats after coming close to extinction.

Milis

POP 1660

A one-time Roman military outpost (its name is a derivation of the Latin word *miles,* meaning soldier), Milis is a small and prosperous village, surrounded by the orange orchards that have brought it wealth.

The manicured village centre is dominated by the 18th-century **Palazzo Boyl**, a fine example of Piedmontese neoclassicism. In the late 19th and early 20th centuries, it became something of a literary meeting place, and Gabriele D'Annunzio, Grazia Deledda and Honoré de Balzac all spent time here. Now, the palazzo houses Milis' small **museum** (☑0783 5 16 65; Piazza Martiri; admission free; ⊙by appointment only) dedicated to traditional costumes and jewellery.

There are also a couple of churches worth a passing glance. Opposite Palazzo Boyl, the 14th-century **Chiesa di San Sebastiano** features an impressive rose window in its Gothic-Catalan facade and, near the eastern entrance to town, the Tuscan-Romanesque **Chiesa di San Paolo** harbours some interesting paintings by 16th-century Catalan artists.

In early November, Milis holds the **Rassegna del Vino Novello** (Festival of Young Wine), a chance for Sardinia's wine producers to show off their best products. You can do the rounds sampling the wines and grazing the food stalls that line the streets.

Seneghe

POP 1920

Seneghe is an essential stop on any gastronomic tour of central Sardinia. A dark stone village with little obvious appeal, it is famous for its extra-virgin olive oil, a one-time winner of the prestigious Premio Nazionale Ercole Olivario award (the Oscars of the Italian olive-oil industry). Beef is another speciality. Russet-red *bue rosso* cows are bred only here and in Modica in Sicily, and gourmets consider the meat to be among the finest in Italy.

The village also provides food for the soul, hosting an annual poetry festival in late August or early September. The **Settembre dei Poeti** (www.settembredeipoeti.it, in Italian) is a four-day celebration of local and international poetry with readings, Q&A sessions and a poetry slam competition – a thoroughly entertaining, dramatic performance in which adversaries improvise rhyming responses to each other, much like a freestyle rap battle.

You can stock up on olive oil at the **Oleificio Sociale Cooperativo di Seneghe** (☑0785 5 46 65; www.oleificiodiseneghe.it, in Italian; Corso Umberto I; ⊙9am-12.30pm & 5-7.30pm Mon-Fri) on the Bonarcado road into town. You'll pay around €7 for 0.5L; €39 for 5L.

To feast on the local beef, head for the **Osteria Al Bue Rosso** (☑0783 5 43 84; Piazzale Montiferru 3/4; meals €30-35; ⊙lunch & dinner Fri & Sat, dinner by reservation Sun & Tue-Thu), an unprepossessing restaurant in a 1920s dairy by the exit to Narbolia. Here you can try a number of beefy dishes, including *insalata di bue rosso* (beef salad) and delicious grilled *filetto* (filet steak). The organically produced house wine is pretty good too. Management can advise on B&Bs in the area.

Bonarcado

POP 1650

About 5km northeast of Seneghe, the sleepy village of Bonarcado is home to one of Sardinia's most unlikely pilgrimage sites. According to an edict issued by Pope Pius VII in 1821, anyone who confesses at the tiny **Santuario della Madonna di Bonacattu** between 14 and 28 September will receive full plenary indulgence. Constructed in the 7th century, and modified some 800 years later, the sanctuary is little more than a chapel with a dome on top. There are no official opening hours, but you'll usually find it open.

A short walk away, the modest Romanesque **Chiesa di Santa Maria**, once part of a medieval monastery, stands in the centre of a sombre grey square.

Santu Lussurgiu

POP 2560 / ELEV 503M

On the eastern slopes of Monti Ferru, Santu Lussurgiu lies inside an ancient volcanic crater. The main point of interest is the small *centro storico,* a tight-knit huddle of stone houses banked up around a natural amphitheatre. Further information is available from the small **tourist office** (⌨0783 55 10 34; Via Santa Maria 40; ◷9.30-11am Mon-Fri summer, 9.30am-1pm Mon-Fri winter) just off the main through road.

Santu Lussurgiu has long been known for its crafts and is still today a production centre for ironwork, woodwork and leatherwork. Investigate the town's rural traditions at the **Museo della Tecnologia Contadina** (Museum of Rural Technology; ⌨0783 55 06 17; Via Deodato Meloni), which has a comprehensive collection of rural tools, utensils and machines.

A great place to eat in this town is **Sas Benas** (⌨0783 55 08 70; Via Cambosu 4; meals €35-40; ◷Tue-Sun), a veritable gastronomic treat if you want to sample the juicy *bue rosso* beef. It's a relatively formal place, set in an old mansion, with attentive service. For antipasti, try the *insalatina di bue rosso,* a salad with beef, followed by the *pennette al bue rosso* – or if you want to have a break from the beef, opt for the cheese tagliatelle. For mains, you guessed it, there's more *bue rosso* – both the *tagliata,* with vegetables, and the *casadinas* (focaccia bread pieces) with *bue rosso* are excellent. Alternatively, if you're a bit overwhelmed by the ubiquitous beef, go for the tender wild boar.

San Leonardo de Siete Fuentes

From Santu Lussurgiu, the road to Cuglieri twists steeply up the eastern flank of Monti Ferru. Before you've gone far, a minor road heads off right (towards Macomer) for San Leonardo de Siete Fuentes, a tiny woodland hamlet famous for its gurgling spring waters. Its grandiose name is a reference to the seven fountains (*siete fuentes*) through which the water gushes.

In the village centre, a path leads up to the charming 12th-century **Chiesa di San Leonardo,** a Romanesque church that once belonged to the Knights of St John of Jerusalem. Beyond this, trails continue uphill, through the oak and elm woods. It's pretty easygoing walking, ideal for parents with little 'uns.

Cuglieri

POP 3010 / ELEV 483M

Perched high on the western face of Monti Ferru, the farming village of Cuglieri makes an excellent lunch stop. You'll build a growling appetite by climbing up to the town's landmark **Basilica di Santa Maria della Neve,** a hulking church whose silvery dome is visible for miles around. The views down to the sea are quite something.

You might also want to stock up on olive oil at the **Azienda Agricola Peddio** (⌨0785 36 92 54; Corso Umberto 95; ◷8.30am-1pm & 3-8pm Mon-Fri) on the main road through the village. A litre of oil costs between €7 and €9.

And now for lunch. Hidden among the grey stone houses of the *centro storico* is the **Desogos** (⌨/fax 0785 3 96 60; Via Cugia 6; meals €15-20), a fabulous *trattoria* specialising in mountain fare. There is a menu, but it's best to surrender into the hands of the maternal owner who will ply you with a lip-smacking array of cured hams, marinated vegetables and tangy cheeses, mostly homemade. And that's just for the antipasti. If you've got room, the pastas and meat courses are similarly huge – go for the wild boar or rabbit, and end with a shot or two of homemade wild fennel liqueur or the ubiquitous (also homemade) *limoncello.*

There are five buses between Cuglieri and Oristano (€3, one hour) between Monday and Saturday. In July and August, there are an additional two buses on Sunday.

Santa Caterina di Pittinuri & Around

The northern Oristano coast features some superb beaches around the popular resort of Santa Caterina di Pittinuri. The town's beach, capped by white cliffs, is fairly small but its shallow, protected waters are ideal for small kids.

A few kilometres to the south, the **Spiaggia dell'Arco** at **S'Archittu** features a dramatic stone arch which rises 6m above the emerald green waters. Inland from S'Archittu, and accessible by a signposted dirt track off the SS292, are the scanty remains of the Punic-Roman town of **Cornus**, scene of a historic battle in 215 BC. The isolated site is open to free exploration.

About 3km south of **Torre del Pozzo** (also known as Torre Su Putzu), tracks lead off the main road to **Is Arenas** beach, which at 6km is one of the longest in the area.

From Oristano, ARST buses run to Santa Caterina (€2, 40 minutes, five Monday to Saturday, plus two on Sunday in July and August) and S'Archittu (€2, 40 minutes, five

daily Monday to Saturday, plus two on Sunday in July and August). They will stop on request at the camping grounds.

LAGO OMODEO CIRCUIT

Surrounded by the green hills of the Barigadu, Lago Omodeo is Sardinia's largest manmade lake. Some 22km long and up to 3km wide, it was created between 1919 and 1924 to supply water and electricity to the agricultural lands around Oristano and Arborea. The countryside around it is sparsely populated and rich in archaeological interest with two of central Sardinia's most important nuraghic sites.

Bidoni

On the eastern side of Lago Omodeo, the hamlet of Bidoni hides one of Sardinia's strangest museums. The creepy **Museo S'Omo 'e sa Majarza** (The Witch's House; ☎0783 69 0 44; Via Monte 9; adult/reduced €3/2; ☉on request), signposted as the Museo del

---

THE ARDENT GUARD

On 6 and 7 July Sedilo hosts Oristano's most exciting festival, **S'Ardia**, when nearly 50,000 people pack themselves into the tiny village to see Sardinia's most reckless and dangerous horse race.

It celebrates the Roman Emperor Constantine, who defeated the vastly superior forces of Maxentius at Rome's Ponte Milvio in AD 312. But since then the festival has received a Christian gloss. Tales say Constantine received a vision before the battle, in which he saw a cross inscribed with the words 'In Hoc Signo Vinces' ('in this sign you will conquer'). He took the sign as the insignia for his forces, and the following year he passed an edict granting the Christians religious freedom. So, locally, although not officially, he was promoted to St Constantine (Santu Antine in the local dialect).

The race circles his sanctuary and the stone cross bearing his insignia. One man – the Prima Pandela (First Flag) – is chosen to bear Constantine's yellow-brocade standard. He selects two of the best horsemen to ride with him, and they choose three cohorts each. These men will be the Prima Pandela's guard and, armed with huge sticks, they will strive to prevent the hundred other horsemen from passing him. To be chosen as the Prima Pandela is the highest honour of the village. Only a man who has proven his courage and horsemanship and substantiated his faith can carry the flag.

On 6 July the procession prays in front of the stone cross and the riders are blessed by the parish priest. In theory the priest should start the race, but in practice it is the Prima Pandela who chooses his moment and flies off at a gallop down the hill. The other horsemen are after him in seconds, aiming to pass the Prima Pandela before he reaches the victory arch. Hundreds of riflemen shoot off blanks, exciting the horses. The stampede towards the narrow entrance of the victory arch is the most dangerous moment, as any mistake would mean running into the stone columns at top speed. In 2002 one rider died. If all goes well, the Prima Pandela passes through the arch and races on to circle the sanctuary, to deafening cheers from the crowd.

Sedilo sits 40km northwest of Oristano, on the SS131.

ANTONIO GRAMSCI

A giant of 20th-century political thought, Antonio Gramsci (1891-1937) was one of the founding fathers of Italian communism. Born to a poor family in Ales, he later moved to Ghilarza and then on to Cagliari and Turin.

It was in Turin that his political thoughts came to fruition. A vociferous advocate of trade unionism – at the time Turin was at the forefront of Italian industrialisation – he joined the Socialist Party in 1913 and six years later co-founded the Marxist newspaper *L'Ordine Nuovo*. Internal rifts within the Socialist Party led to division and, in 1921, Gramsci and a group of fellow activists broke away to form the Italian Communist Party. Much influenced by events in Russia – he visited Moscow in 1922 and married a Russian violinist – Gramsci was arrested by the Fascist police in 1926 and sentenced to 25 years in prison. He died in 1937 at the age of 46.

Of Gramsci's ideas, the best known is his theory of hegemony, which holds that to challenge the cultural homogenisation through which the ruling classes maintain control it's necessary for the working class to arm themselves with alternative cultural and aspirational beliefs.

In **Ghilarza** you can visit the **Gramsci House** (☎0785 54 1 64; www.casagramsci ghilarza.org; Corso Umberto I 36; admission free; ☉10am-1pm & 4-7pm Fri-Sun winter, 10am-1pm & 4.30-7.30pm Wed-Mon summer), which is where the great man lived between 1898 and 1914.

Territorio, is dedicated to witches and local folklore and features the reconstruction of a 16th-century witch's cave. Visits are by guided tour only.

Bidoni is signposted from Ghilarza, the main town on the western side of Lago Omodeo.

Santa Cristina & Paulilatino

The main feature of the nuraghic complex of Santa Cristina is the central well temple, one of the most important and best preserved in Sardinia. The worship of water was a fundamental part of nuraghic religious practice, and there are reckoned to be about 40 sacred wells spread across the island.

Just off the SS131, the **Nuraghe Santa Cristina** (☎0785 5 54 38; admission incl Museo Archeologico-Etnografico in Paulilatino adult/reduced €7/3; ☉8.30am-9.30pm summer, to 9pm winter) sits on the high Abasanta plateau a few kilometres south of Paulilatino. Before you get to the remains you'll pass the **Chiesa di Santa Cristina**, an early Christian church dedicated to Santa Cristina. The church and the terraced *muristenes* (pilgrims' huts) that surround it are opened for only nine days a year – for the feast days of Santa Cristina, around the second Sunday in May, and San Raffaele Arcangelo, on the fourth Sunday in October.

From the church, follow a path east for 100m to reach the nuraghic village, which is set in a peaceful olive grove. Inhabited up until the early Middle Ages, the village is focused on the extraordinary *tempio a pozzo* (well temple), which dates back as far as the late Bronze Age (11th to 9th century BC).

To get down into the well, you go through a finely cut keyhole entrance and descend a flight of 24 superbly preserved steps. When you reach the bottom you can gaze up at the perfectly constructed *tholos* (conical tower), through which light enters the dark well shaft. Every 18 years, one month and two days, the full moon shines directly through the aperture into the well. Otherwise you can catch the yearly equinoxes on 21 March and 23 September, when the sun lights up the stairway down to the well.

Continuing 5km up the SS131 brings you to **Paulilatino**, an agricultural town with grey stone houses that lend it a somewhat severe demeanour. Finds from the Santa Cristina archaeological site are displayed in the **Museo Archeologico-Etnografico** (☎0785 5 54 38; Via Nazionale 127; admission incl Santa Cristina adult/reduced €7/3; ☉9am-1pm & 4.30-7.30pm Tue-Sun summer, 9am-1pm & 3-5.30pm Tue-Sun winter) alongside farm and domestic implements from tougher rural days.

Nuraghe Losa & Around

A few kilometres north of Paulilatino and just off the SS131, the **Nuraghe Losa** (☎0785 5 23 02; www.nuraghelosa.net; adult/reduced €3.50/2; ☉9am-1hr before sunset) is one of Sardinia's most impressive *nuraghi*.

The site's centrepiece is a three-sided keep, around which are three circular towers, two joined by a wall, and one standing alone. The central tower has lost its top floor but still rises to almost 13m. It has been dated to the Middle Bronze Age, about 1500 BC.

Entrance is by way of one of the side towers, which is connected to the main keep by an internal corridor. Passages lead left and right from the corridor to two towers, one fully enclosed, the other open.

Fordongianus

Southwest of Lago Omodeo, almost at the confluence of the Tirso and Mannu Rivers, sits the spa town of Fordongianus, most easily reached along the SS388 from Oristano.

The spa waters around here were known to Ptolemy, and the Romans established a health spa here, naming it Forum Traiani. Their 1st century AD baths, the **Terme Romane** (☎0783 6 01 57; www.forumtraiani.it, in Italian; admission incl Casa Aragonese €4; ☉9.30am-1pm & 3.30-8pm Tue-Sun summer, 9.30am-1pm & 2.30-5.30pm winter), are still in operation today. In the centre of the complex you'll see a rectangular pool that was once surrounded by a portico, some of which still stands today (although only one side).

The red trachyte stone that is part of every building imparts a rosy glow to the village. As red as the rest is the lovely late-16th-century **Casa Aragonese** (admission incl Terme Romane €4; ☉same hr as above), a typical aristocratic Catalan house. The strange statues outside, also fashioned from the ubiquitous trachyte, are the result of an annual sculpture competition held here.

Seven weekday buses connect with Oristano (€2, 40 minutes).

Alghero & the Northwest

Best Places to Eat

» La Botteghina (p119)

» Mabrouk (p119)

» Agriturismo Sa Mandra (p123)

» La Guardiola (p130)

Best Places to Stay

» Hotel El Faro (p206)

» Angedras Hotel (p205)

» Camping La Mariposa (p205)

» Villa Las Tronas (p206)

Why Go?

Sardinia's northwestern corner is a fine example of how popular resorts can fit seamlessly alongside quiet beaches and remote national parks – visitors can flit between historical and coastal beauties, dip into urbanity, and rest in remote national parks and deserted beaches, all the while tapping into the region's unique character.

The coast is this region's belle of the ball, with brilliant stretches of sand, heady cliffs and rocky coves that dip into the sea. But head inland, and surprises await – architectural and archaeological gems litter the sun-bleached countryside, a string of Pisan-Romanesque churches stand testimony to glories past, while tumbledown ruins tell of prehistoric times.

The two cities – the petite, attractive Alghero and cosmopolitan Sassari – speak of their historical heritage: one with an Iberian sensibility, the other Genoese graces. This entire area seems less Sardinian than other parts, less rural and less reserved, but enchanting all the way.

When to Go

Join the masses to munch a mountain of sea urchins in January, at Alghero's Sagra del Bogamari food festival. April sees the start of the wonderful carnival season, best witnessed in Alghero's *centro storico* (historic centre). One of Sardinia's most prestigious festivals, Cavalcata Sarda, takes place in Sassari during the month of May – thousands gather to sing and dance while watching acrobatic horse riding. The summer and autumn months of July, August and September are made for hitting the busy beaches of Riviera del Corallo or seeking out hidden swimming spots.

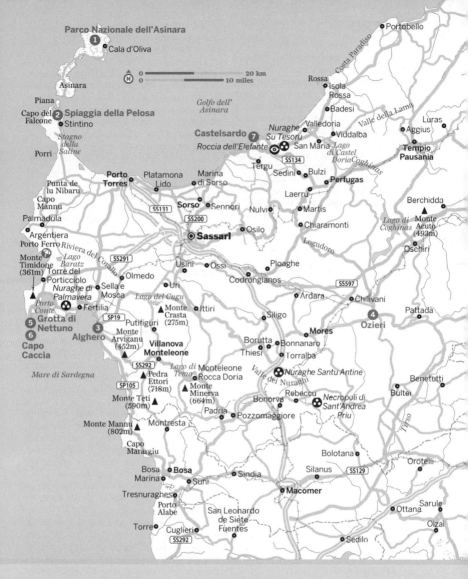

Alghero & the Northwest Highlights

1 Spy on albino donkeys and birds of prey in the **Parco Nazionale dell'Asinara** (p129)

2 Have a swim at the northwest's most stunning beach, the **Spiaggia della Pelosa** (p128)

3 Weave through the medieval lanes and robust ramparts in **Alghero** (p112)

4 See how prehistoric cavemen lived in the Grotta di San Michele in **Ozieri** (p138), then check out their tools in the town's Museo Archeologico

5 Dive into the Mediterranean's largest underwater lake and explore the fairy-tale **Grotta di Nettuno** (p124)

6 Take in the marvellous sea views from the windswept and rugged **Capo Caccia** (p124) headland

7 Wander through the old town's medieval lanes in **Castelsardo** (p130) and look over to Corsica from the impregnable hilltop *castello* (castle)

ALGHERO

POP 40,600

For many people a trip to Sardinia means a trip to Alghero, the main resort in the northwest and an easy flight from many European cities. Although largely given over to tourism, the town has managed to avoid many of its worst excesses, and it retains a proud and independent-minded spirit. It has long been an important fishing port, and still today fishing provides a vital contribution to the local economy. In gastronomic terms, Alghero's lobster is one of the island's great treats.

The main focus is the picturesque *centro storico*, one of the best preserved in Sardinia. Enclosed by robust, honey-coloured seawalls, this is a tightly knit enclave of shady cobbled lanes, Spanish Gothic palazzi and cafe-lined squares. Below, yachts crowd the marina and long, sandy beaches curve away to the north. Hanging over everything is a palpable Spanish atmosphere, a hangover of the city's past as a Catalan colony. Even today, more than three centuries after the Iberians left, the Catalan tongue is still spoken and street signs and menus are often in both languages.

History

A modern city by Sardinian standards, L'Alguerium (named after algae that washed up on the coast) started life as an 11th-century fishing village. Thanks to its strategic position, it was jealously guarded by its Genoese founders who, despite a brief Pisan interregnum in the 1280s, managed to retain control until the mid-14th century.

Alghero forcibly resisted the Catalano-Aragonese invasion of Sardinia in 1323, but after 30 years of struggle it fell to the Spanish invaders in 1353. Catalan colonists were encouraged to settle here, and after a revolt in 1372 the remaining Sardinians were expelled and relocated inland. From then on Alghero became resolutely Catalan and called itself Alguer.

The settlement remained a principal port of call in Sardinia for its Catalano-Aragonese and subsequently Spanish masters. Raised to the status of city in 1501, it experienced a frisson of excitement when the Holy Roman Emperor (and king of Spain) Charles V arrived in 1541 to lead a campaign against North African corsairs. Unhappily, the discovery of the Americas was bad news for Alghero, whose importance as a trading port quickly ebbed.

In 1720 the town passed to the House of Savoy. By the 1920s the population was scarcely more than 10,000. Both heavy bomb damage suffered in 1943 and the onset of tourism in the late 1960s led to frenetic building, the result being the modern new town that mushrooms out of the *centro storico*.

◉ Sights

Centro Storico NEIGHBOURHOOD

A leisurely stroll around Alghero's animated *centro storico* is a good way of tuning in to the city's laid-back rhythms. The dark, medieval lanes come to life in the early evening when crowds swell the alleyways to parade their tans and browse the shop windows.

The entire city centre was originally enclosed, but in the 19th century the landward walls were torn down and partially replaced by the **Giardini Pubblici** (Map p116), a green space that now effectively separates the old town from the new.

Near the Giardini, the 14th-century **Torre Porta a Terra** (Map p116; ☑079 973 40 45; Piazza Porta Terra; adult/reduced €2.50/1.50; ☉9am-1pm & 6-11pm Mon-Sat Jul & Aug, 9.30am-1pm & 4.30-8pm Mon-Sat mid-May-Jun & Sep, 10am-1pm & 5-7pm Mon-Sat Oct-Mar) is all that remains of Porta a Terra, one of the two main gates into the medieval city. A stumpy 23m-high tower known originally as Porta Reial, it now houses a small multimedia museum dedicated to the city's past and, on the 2nd floor, a terrace with sweeping, 360-degree views.

To the south, another impressive tower, the **Torre di San Giovanni** (Map p116; ☑339 468 77 54; Largo San Francesco; ☉depends on exhibition) hosts temporary art exhibitions.

Guarding the sea by busy Piazza Sulis, **Torre Sulis** (Map p116) closes off the defensive line of towers to the south of the

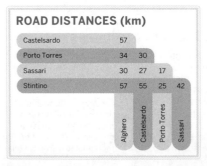

ROAD DISTANCES (km)

	Alghero	Castelsardo	Porto Torres	Sassari
Castelsardo	57			
Porto Torres	34	30		
Sassari	30	27	17	
Stintino	57	55	25	42

Of all the fine knives made in Sardinia, the most prized is *sa pattadesa* (the Pattada knife), and these days they are only made by a handful of artisans. The classic Pattada knife, first made in the mid-19th century, is the *resolza*, with its so-called myrtle-leaf-shaped blade that folds into a horn handle. Only the finest knives have their blades protected in such a way. To a Sardinian a *sa pattadesa* is the ultimate in Sardinian craftsmanship, more impressive than any valuable piece of jewellery.

Most of the best craftsmen only work to order and take at least two days to fashion such a knife, folding and tempering the steel for strength and sharpness. The handle is then carved from a single piece of mouflon (silky-haired wild sheep) horn. If you're looking at a handle that is two parts screwed together, you're not looking at a quality piece. A good knife will cost at least €10 a centimetre.

In the past such knives were made all over the island, but now only a few towns follow the traditional methods. **Pattada** is the most famous, although quality knives are also made in Arbus, Santu Lussurgiu and Tempio Pausania. The classic *s'arburesa* (from Arbus) has a fat, rounded blade and is used for skinning animals, while the *lametta* of Tempio Pausania is a rectangular job good for stripping the bark from cork oaks. Of the *pattadesa* knives the best known is the *fogarizzu*. The best *s'arburesa* to look for is the *pusceddu*.

Note that it is illegal in Italy to carry a blade longer than 4cm.

old town. To the north the **Bastione della Maddalena** (Map p116), with its eponymous tower, forms the only remnant of the city's former land battlements.

Just west of the bastion, and overlooking the crowded marina, is **Porta a Mare** (Map p116), the second of Alghero's medieval gateways. Steps by the gate lead up to the portside bastions, which stretch around to **Torre della Polveriera** (Map p116) at the northernmost tip of the *centro storico*. The Mediterranean crashes up against the seaward walls of the **Bastioni Marco Polo** (Map p116) and **Bastioni Cristoforo Colombo**, the city's western wall. Along these seaward bulwarks are some inviting restaurants and bars where you can watch the sunset over a cocktail.

Cattedrale di Santa Maria   DUOMO
(Map p116) Overlooking Piazza Duomo, Alghero's oversized Cattedrale di Santa Maria appears out of place with its pompous neoclassical facade and fat Doric columns. An unfortunate 19th-century addition, the facade was the last in a long line of modifications that the hybrid cathedral has endured since it was built, orginially on Catalan Gothic lines in the 16th century. Inside it's largely Renaissance, with some late-baroque baubles added in the 18th century. Free guided tours (in Italian) of the cathedral are available between 10am and 1pm Monday to Friday between February and September.

Of greater interest is the Catalan **campanile** (Map p116; adult/child €2/free; ⊙7-9.30pm Tue, Thu & Sat Jul & Aug, 5-8pm Tue, Thu & Sat Sep, on request rest of yr) around the back in Via Principe Umberto. A fine example of Catalan-Gothic architecture, this is the tall octagonal tower that you see towering over Alghero's rooftops.

Museo Diocesano d'Arte Sacra   MUSEUM
(Map p116; ☑079 973 30 41; Piazza Duomo; adult/reduced €3/2; ⊙10am-12.30pm Thu-Tue year-round & 5-8pm Apr, May, late Sep & Oct, 6-9pm Jun & early Sep, 6.30-9.30pm Jul & Aug) In the former Oratorio del Rosario, the Museo Diocesano d'Arte Sacra houses the cathedral's collection of religious artefacts, including silverware, statuary, paintings and woodcarving. A ghoulish touch is the reliquary of what is claimed to be one of the *innocenti* (newborn babies slaughtered by Herod in his search for the Christ child). The tiny skull is chilling, but apparently it appealed to Alghero artist Francesco Pinna, who received it from a Roman cardinal in the 16th century.

Piazza Civica   PIAZZA
(Map p116) Just inside Porta a Mare (Sea Gate) at the northeastern tip of the *centro storico*, Piazza Civica is Alghero's showcase square. In a former life it was the administrative heart of the medieval city, but where Spanish aristocrats once met to debate affairs of empire, tourists now converge to browse jewellery displays in elegant shop windows,

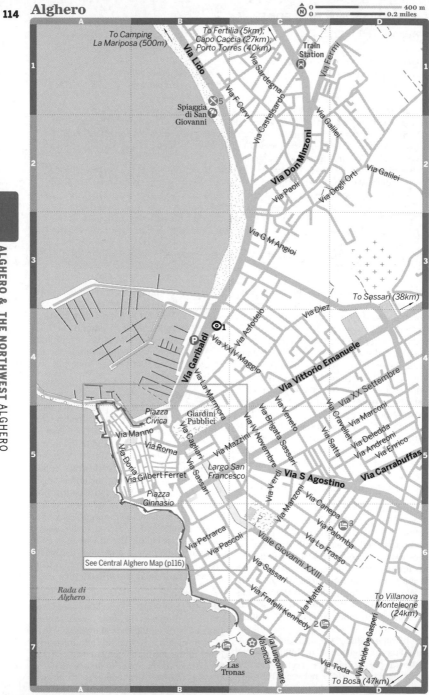

0   400 m
0   0.2 miles

To Camping
La Mariposa (500m)

To Fertilia (5km);
Capo Caccia (27km);
Porto Torres (40km)

Train
Station

Via Lido

Via Sardegna

Via Castelsardo

Via F Cervi

Via Ferni

Via Galilei

Via Don Minzoni

Spiaggia
di San
Giovanni

5

Via Paoli

Via Degli Orti

Via Galilei

Via G M Angioi

To Sassari (38km)

Via Diez

1

Via Asfodelo

Via XXIV Maggio

Via Vittorio Emanuele

Via XX Settembre

Via Garibaldi

P

Via La Marmora

Piazza
Civica

Giardini
Pubblici

Via Cagliari

Via IV Novembre

Via Brigata Sassari

Via Veneto

Via Satta

Via Cravellet

Via Marconi

Via Deledda

Via Andreoni

Via Enrico

Via Manno

Via Roma

Via Mazzini

Via S Agostino

Via Carrabuffas

Via Doria

Via Gilbert Ferret

Via Sassari

Largo San
Francesco

Via Verdi

Via Manzoni

Via Canepa

Via Palomba

3

Piazza
Ginnasio

Via Lo Frasso

See Central Alghero Map (p116)

Via Petrarca

Via Pascoli

Viale Giovanni XXIII

Via Sassari

Rada di
Alghero

Via Fratelli Kennedy

Via Mattei

To Villanova
Monteleone
(24km)

2

Via Lungomare

Via Valencia

4

6

Via Toda

Via Alcide De Gasperi

Las
Tronas

To Bosa (47km)

Alghero

◉ Sights

eat ice cream and drink at the city's grandest cafe. Caffè Costantino occupies the ground floor of the Gothic **Palazzo d'Albis** (Map p116), where the Spanish emperor Charles V stayed in 1541.

Chiesa di San Francesco   CHURCH

(Map p116) In contrast to the self-aggrandising cathedral, the Chiesa di San Francesco is a model of architectural harmony. Sitting behind an austere stone facade, the church was originally built to a Catalan-Gothic design in the 14th century but was later given a successful Renaissance facelift after it partially collapsed in 1593. Of interest here is the 18th-century polychrome marble altar and a strange 17th-century wooden sculpture of a haggard Christ tied to a column.

Through the sacristy you can enter the beautiful 14th-century cloisters, the 22 columns of which connect a series of round arches. The buttery sandstone used in the arcades and columns lends it special warmth and makes it a wonderful setting for summer concerts.

Chiesa di San Michele   CHURCH

(Map p116) Further along Via Carlo Alberto, the *carrer major* (main street) of the medieval town, the Chiesa di San Michele is best known for its maiolica dome, typical of churches in Valencia, another former Catalan territory. The present tiles were laid in the 1960s, but this doesn't detract from its beauty.

Just before you reach the church you cross Via Gilbert Ferret. The intersection is known as the *quatre cantonades* (four sides), and for centuries labourers would gather here in the hope of finding work.

Beaches   BEACH

Alghero's beaches extend along Via Garibaldi, north of the port. **Spiaggia di San Giovanni** (Map p114) and the adjacent **Spiaggia di Maria Pia** (Map p114) are long and sandy, although they're not the best beaches in the area. Nicer by far are Spiaggia Bombarde and Spiaggia del Lazzaretto, both located beyond the airport at Fertilia, and both accessible by local bus (see p123). In Alghero you can hire umbrellas and sunloungers at the beach for about €8 per day, as well as windsurfers (€10) and canoes (€10). Bus line AO covers the length of the beachfront.

🏃 Activities

Sea Excursions   BOAT TOURS

From the port you can take a boat trip along the impressive northern coast to Capo Caccia (p124) and the grandiose Grotta di Nettuno (p124) cave complex. There are a number of operators offering day tours with fishing and swimming stops (prices range from about €40 to €100 per person), but if you just want to go to the caves and back it makes sense to use the **Navisarda ferry** (Map p116; ☑079 95 06 03; www.navisarda.it; adult/child return €14/7, not incl cave entrance fee), which departs hourly between 9am and 5pm from June to September, and four times daily the rest of the year.

Nautisub Centro Immersioni
Alghero   DIVE CENTRE

(Map p114; ☑079 95 24 33; www.nautisub.com; Via Garibaldi 45) This organisation offers diving (from €38), snorkelling (€25) and kit hire (€25 for air tank, regulator, jacket and lead belt), as well as a number of boat tours.

Diving Centre Capo Galera   DIVE CENTRE

(off Map p114; ☑079 94 21 10; www.capogalera. com; Localita Capo Galera) A few kilometres from Alghero, signposted off the main road to Capo Caccia, this place operates out of a big white villa on a panoramic promontory. Dives and courses are available for all levels, but more advanced swimmers will enjoy some superlative cave diving, including exploration of the Nereo Cave, the biggest underwater grotto in the Mediterranean. Dives start at €20 and full kit hire costs €20. It also offers accommodation for divers (doubles €65 to €100, six-person apartments €110 to €180) and serves splendid barbecue dinners.

Central Alghero

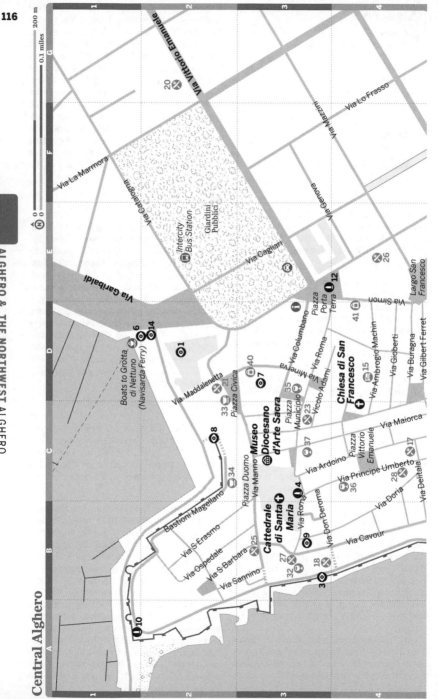

200 m
0.1 miles

Via Vittorio Emanuele

20

Via La Marmora

Via Catalogna

Via Garibaldi

Intercity
Bus Station

Giardini
Pubblici

Via Cagliari

Via Mazzini

Via Lo Frasso

Via Genova

Largo San
Francesco

Via Simon

26

41

Piazza
Porta
Terra

12

Boats to Grotta
di Nettuno
(Navisarda Ferry)

6
14

1

Via Maddalenetta

21
33

Piazza Civica

40

7

35

Via Columbano

Via Minerva

Via Roma

Piazza
Municipio

23

Vicolo Adami

Chiesa di San
Francesco

15

Via Ambrogio Machin

Via Gioberti

Via Buragna

Via Gilbert Ferret

Via Maiorca

Museo
Diocesano
d'Arte Sacra

37

Piazza
Vittorio
Emanuele

36

Via Ardoino

Via Principe Umberto

17

28

Via Delitala

8

34

Piazza Duomo

Via Manno

Bastioni Magellano

Via S Erasmo

Via Ospedale

Via S Barbara

Cattedrale
di Santa
Maria

4

Via Roma

Via Don Deroma

Via Doria

Via Cavour

9

25

27

32

18

Via Sannino

3

10

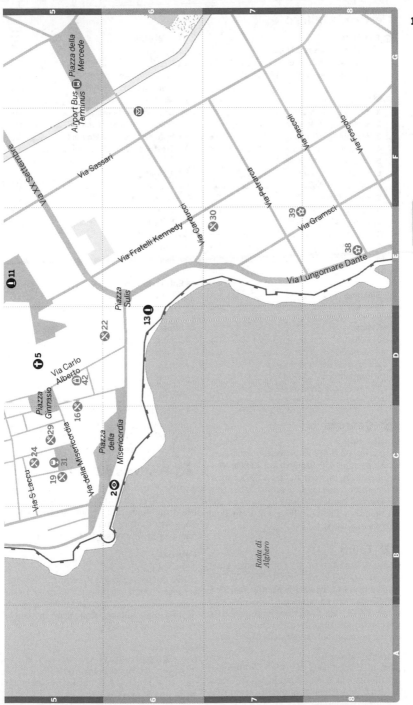

Central Alghero

🎓 Courses

Stroll & Speak　　　　　　　LANGUAGE
(Map p116; ☎339 489 93 14; www.strollandspeak.com; Via Cavour 4; ⊙9am-1pm & 2.30-8pm Mon-Sat) Brush up on your Italian with a course at an established language school in the *centro storico*. Bank on €200 (10 hours), €285 (15 hours) or €360 (20 hours) of individual lessons in a week.

🚗 Tours

Horse & Cart Tours　　　HORSE & CART
(Map p116; ☎079 97 69 27; adult/2-10yr €5/3.50; ⊙10am-11pm Jul & Aug, 10am-8.30pm Apr-Jun, Sep & Oct) Parents can entertain the little ones with a tour of the old town. The 25-minute trot tickets are available from the starting point on the port side of Bastione della Maddalena.

Trenino Catalano　　　　　　TRAIN
(Map p116; adult/under 8yr €5/3; ⊙10am-1pm & 4.30-11pm Jul & Aug, 10am-1pm & 3.30-9pm Apr-Jun & Sep) This is a miniature train that chugs around the *centro storico*. Departures are half hourly from the port; buy tickets on board.

🎉 Festivals & Events

Alghero has a full calendar of festivals and events, although spring and summer are the best times to catch an event. To check what's on, go to Culture and then Feasts, festivals and events at www.sardegnaturismo.it.

February

Sagra del Bogamarì　　　FOOD FESTIVAL
(www.comune.alghero.ss.it/eventi/2011/sagra_bogamari/) Alghero locals pay homage to the humble sea urchin by eating mountainloads of the spiky molluscs. Runs from the end of January into February.

Carnevale　　　　　　　　　CARNIVAL
(www.sardegnaturismo.it) On *martedì grasso* (Shrove Tuesday) an effigy of a French soldier (the *pupazzo*) is burned at the stake amid much merry-making.

March/April
Easter Holy Week RELIGIOUS FESTIVAL
Figures of Christ and the Virgin Mary are borne through town in enactments of the *Misteri* (Passion of Christ) and *Incontru* (Meeting of the Virgin with Christ).

July/August
Ferragosto
(Feast of the Assumption) RELIGIOUS FESTIVAL
Alghero puts on a show on 15 August with fireworks, boat races and music.

✖ Eating

Seafood rules in Alghero, a fishing town famous for its sardines and rock lobsters. However, lobster doesn't come cheap so always get it weighed before you order – on the menu its price is usually listed as per gram.

TOP CHOICE La Botteghina MEDITERRANEAN €€
(☑079 97 38 375; www.labotteghina.biz; Via Principe Umberto 63; meals €25-30) A crisp new place in the *centro storico*, La Botteghina only deals in local food bought from small producers, which means the ingredients are simple and tastes intense. Try the *fregola* (small pasta made from semolina, similar to couscous) with seafood, or one of the pizzas. The decor is white wood and vaulted ceilings and the atmosphere and clientele relaxed.

Mabrouk SEAFOOD €€
(Map p116; ☑079 97 00 00; Via Santa Barbara 4; menu €40; ☉dinner only, closed Nov) A fish-only restaurant close to the cathedral, the Mabrouk is the kind of place where you pay your money but the cook, Marie Antonetta, makes your choice – for the €40 charge you are plied with the day's fish offerings, several antipasti, three types of pasta with fish as *primi piatti* (first courses), and three types of fish for the mains (or *secondo*), plus dessert and wine. It's an excellent place to sample locally caught, fresh fish, in simple and friendly surroundings.

Angedras Restaurant MEDITERRANEAN €€
(Map p116; ☑079 973 50 78; www.angedrasrestaurant.it; Bastioni Marco Polo 41; lunch menu €16; meals around €35; ☉Wed-Mon) Dining on Alghero's honey-coloured stone ramparts is a memorable experience. This is one of the better restaurants on the walls, serving a largely traditional menu, including the king of all Sardinian meat dishes, *porceddu* (roast suckling pig). Part of the Angedras Hotel (p205).

Il Refettorio MEDITERRANEAN/WINE BAR €€
(Map p116; ☑079 973 11 26; Vicolo Adami 47; meals around €30; ☉closed Tue in winter) Il Refettorio is a good-looking place with tables outdoors under a low stone arch and inside, in a vaulted interior. There's a strong emphasis on wine, so take the opportunity to taste the local reds and whites, while sampling the tuna steaks drizzled with balsamic vinegar.

Osteria Machiavello OSTERIA €€
(Map p116; ☑079 98 06 28; Bastioni Marco Polo 57; land/sea menus €16/18, meals around €35; ☉dinner Wed-Mon) Recently taken over by the owners of Angedras Restaurant, this is a panoramic spot for a memorable dinner on the city ramparts. The menu covers most tastes with grilled meats, including horse, and a number of classic fish dishes. Try the *zuppa di cozze e vongole* (mussel and clam soup).

Spaghetteria Al Solito Posto MEDITERRANEAN €
(Map p116; ☑328 913 37 45; Piazza della Misericordia; meals €15-20; ☉Fri-Wed) This small barrel-vaulted place is one of the most popular eateries in town. The workaday atmosphere is TV-on-in-the-corner, but the food – pasta with a range of sauces – is good and the bustling vibe is fun. Booking is recommended.

Borgo Antico SEAFOOD €€
(Map p116; ☑079 98 26 49; Via Zaccaria 12; meals around €35; ☉closed Sun dinner) Housed in an ex-convent, this is a formal restaurant with outdoor seating on an atmospheric piazza. It's known for its excellent seafood, which appears in dishes like *spaghetti all'aragosta* (lobster spaghetti; €40 for two people) and *triglie al cartoccio* (red mullet roasted in tin foil).

Al Tuguri OSTERIA €€
(Map p116; ☑079 97 67 72; www.altuguri.it; Via Maiorca 113; tasting menus veg/sea/land/€36/40/40; ☉Mon-Sat) Serious vegetarian food is something of a novelty in Sardinia, and this is the place to find it. A discreet restaurant decorated in traditional rustic style, it serves a dedicated vegetarian menu alongside more traditional seafood and meat dishes. Booking is advisable.

Andreini GASTRONOMIC €€€
(Map p116; ☑079 98 20 98; www.ristoranteandreini.it; Via Ardoino 45; meals around €55; ☉Tue-Sun) In recent years this elegant restaurant has become a point of reference for creative, modern cuisine in Alghero, and in 2010, it

was awarded a single, shiny Michelin star. Tables are set beneath a huge fig tree where you can dine on beautifully presented food, served in adventurous combinations of fruit, fresh fish, meat and herbs.

Osteria Taverna Paradiso OSTERIA €€
(Map p116; ☑079 97 80 07; Via Principe Umberto 29; meals around €30; ☺Tue-Sun) Cheese is king at this convivial, unpretentious trattoria. Owner and 'Cheese Master' Pasquale Nocella adores the stuff and takes great delight in introducing it to his guests in its many myriad forms – a cheese platter costs €16. If cheese isn't your thing, there are excellent grilled meats and hearty pastas.

Trattoria Maristella TRATTORIA €€
(Map p116;☑079 97 81 72; Via Fratelli Kennedy 9; meals around €27) Visitors and locals flock to this bustling little trattoria for reliable seafood – the *insalata di mare* (seafood salad) is excellent – and Sardinian specialities such as *culurgiones* (ravioli stuffed with potato, pecorino cheese and mint). All at very honest prices.

Il Pavone TRATTORIA €€€
(Map p116; ☑079 97 95 84; www.ristoranteilpavone.com; Piazza Sulis 3/4; meals around €45; ☺closed lunch Sun) The granddaddy of Alghero dining, Il Pavone can still cut it. Defiantly retro in look, it serves a mix of innovative Sardinian fare and old-fashioned classics.

Santa Cruz MEDITERRANEAN €€
(Map p114; Via Lido 2; pizza €6.50-8, meals around €30; ☺Tue-Sun) This brash Spanish joint is good for pizza, paella (€18) and grilled meats. More than the food, though, it's the beachside location that's the real draw.

Il Ghiotto ITALIAN €
(Map p116; ☑079 97 48 20; Piazza Civica 23; meals €10-15; ☺Tue-Sun) One of the few truly budget places in Alghero. At lunchtime choose from the tantalising spread of *panini,* pastas, salads and main courses.

Self-Catering
You can stock up on picnic supplies, fresh meat and fish at Alghero's fresh produce market (Map p116; entrance Via Sassari 23; ☺6.30am-1.30pm & 4.30-8.30pm Mon-Sat) between Via Sassari and Via Cagliari. Otherwise, there's a Euro Spin supermarket (Map p116; Via La Marmora 28; ☺8.30am-9.30pm Mon-Sat, 9am-1.30pm & 5-9pm Sun) near the Giardini Pubblici.

🍸 Drinking

There's no shortage of drinking options in Alghero. Popular areas include the beaches, the city ramparts and the seafront south of the *centro storico*. In summer many places stay open late, typically to around 2am.

Baraonda WINE BAR
(Map p116; ☑079 97 59 22; Piazza della Misericordia; ☺10am-2am) Burgundy walls and black-and-white jazz photos set the tone at this moody wine bar. In summer sit out on the piazza and watch the world parade by.

Diva Caffè CAFE, BAR
(Map p116; ☑079 98 23 06; Piazza Municipio 1; cocktails €7; ☺10am-midnight Mon-Sat) A favourite lunch venue (pastas €6) for passing tourists, the Diva shows her true colours at night when the suntanned sophisticates drop by for a cocktail on the square. It stays open late on Friday and Saturday nights in summer.

Caffè Latino BAR
(Map p116; ☑079 97 65 41; Bastioni Magellano 10; cocktails from €4.80; ☺9am-11pm Wed-Mon, to 2am daily in summer) Up on the ramparts overlooking the port, this chic bar is a summer classic. Kick back on the grey rattan chairs, order from the ample menu and listen to the breeze rattle the masts of the boats below you.

Caffè Costantino CAFE
(Map p116; ☑079 97 61 54; Piazza Civica 31; ☺7.30am-midnight Thu-Tue) On Alghero's showpiece piazza, Caffè Costantino is the classiest cafe in town. It's also one of the busiest, attracting a constant stream of tourists to its tables on the edge of the square. There's a full food menu alongside the drinks list, although if you just want to eat, you'll get better value for money almost everywhere else.

Buena Vista BAR
(Map p116; Bastioni Marco Polo 47; cocktails €6.50-8; ☺3.30pm-3am) Fabulous mojitos, fresh fruit cocktails, stunning sea sunsets – what more could you want of a seafront bar? Upbeat tunes and a cavernous interior add to the vibe at this popular bar on the western walls.

Jamaica Inn PUB
(Map p116; Via Principe Umberto 57; cocktails €6; ☺Tue-Sun) This is a cheerful pub, good for wine, beer and bar snacks (€6), including bruschetta.

Mill Inn   LIVE MUSIC
(Map p116; Via Maiorca 37; ☺Thu-Tue) A cosy drinking den beneath stone vaults. Occasional live music.

☆ Entertainment

As the bars begin to quieten from around 1am, the action shifts to the waterfront clubs south of the old town. Alghero's clubs attract punters from all over northern Sardinia. The scene is at its hottest in summer, but you can usually catch some action on winter weekends. The biggest clubs tend to be out of town, making transport a problem unless you can bag a lift or have around €35 for a taxi. Clubs open late, usually around midnight, and admission costs around €15, which might or might not include a drink.

Poco Loco   LIVE MUSIC
(Map p116; ☎079 973 10 34; Via Gramsci 8; ☺7pm-1am) A popular all-purpose venue with internet, beer on tap, pizza, live music and an upstairs bowling alley (closed on Mondays). Concerts cater to most tastes, although jazz and blues headline more than most.

L'Arca   LIVE MUSIC
(Map p116; ☎079 97 79 72; Lungomare Dante 6; ☺8am-2am) A rocking bar on the southern *lungomare* (seafront promenade). Inside, DJs conduct the mayhem between Thursdays and Saturdays, while outside, drinkers add to the festive atmosphere on the crowded seafront.

El Trò   CLUB
(Map p114; ☎079 973 30 00; Via Lungomare Valencia 3; ☺9pm-late Tue-Sun) A disco pub on the rocks, El Trò becomes a steamy mosh pit on hot summer weekends as hyped-up holidaymakers dance till dawn on the seafront dance floor.

Il Ruscello   CLUB
(off Map p114; ☎339 235 07 55; SS Alghero-Olmedeo; ☺nightly Jul & Aug, Fri & Sat Jun & Sep, Sat rest of yr) One of Alghero's historic clubs, Il Ruscello attracts top Sardinian DJs and a clued-up crowd. It's about 2km northeast of Alghero on the road to Olmedo.

La Siesta   CLUB
(off Map p114; ☎079 98 01 37; Localita Scala Piccada; ☺from 1am nightly Jul & Aug, Sat Jun) About 10km out of town to the south, this is a big, open-air affair with four dance floors,

mainstream tunes and a regular program of live music. For big nights, there is sometimes a shuttle bus (€1.50) from central Alghero.

🛍 Shopping

Browsing past the elegant shop windows along Via Carlo Alberto, the main shopping strip, is integral to a trip to Alghero. Throughout the *centro storico*, the streets are lined with shops selling foodie souvenirs, designer threads and jewellery made from Alghero's famous coral (see the boxed text, p125).

Enodolciaria   FOOD
(Map p116; ☎079 97 97 41; Via Simon 24) A fantastic place to get bottles of island wine, olive oil, packets of *fregola* and *bottarga* (mullet roe), and tins of local tuna.

Antonio Marras   FASHION
(Map p116; ☎079 97 32 085; Piazza Civica) Antonio Marras is Alghero's most famous son in the fashion world – he is the director of Kenzo for women and the designer of some fine upmarket clothing. Check out this lovely boutique, if only to admire the colourful textiles and tasteful styling.

Il Labirinto   BOOKS
(116; ✆079 98 04 96; Via Carlo Alberto 119) A small store with a good range of books (mostly in Italian) on all things Sardinian. Also a small selection of English books.

❶ Information

Airport tourist office (off Map p114; ☎079 93 51 50; ☺8.30am-1pm & 3.30-10pm)

Banca Carige (Map p116; Via Sassari 13) Has an ATM.

Bar Miramare (Map p116; ☎079 973 10 27; Via Gramsci 2; internet per hr €5; ☺8.30am-1pm & 4.30pm-2am)

Farmacia Cabras (Map p116; ☎079 97 92 60; Lungomare Dante 20) English-speaking service.

Main post office (Map p116; Via Carducci 35; ☺8am-6.50pm Mon-Fri, to 1.15pm Sat)

Ospedale Civile (Map p114; ☎079 99 62 00; Via Don Minzoni) The main hospital.

Police station (Map p116; ☎079 972 00 00; Piazza della Mercede 4)

Tourist office (Map p116; ☎079 97 90 54; www.comune.alghero.ss.it, in Italian; Piazza Porta Terra 9; ☺8am-8pm Mon-Sat year-round, plus 10am-1pm Sun summer) The best tourist office in Sardinia with helpful English-speaking staff and tonnes of practical information.

ⓘ Getting There & Away

Air

Alghero's **Fertilia airport** (AHO; off Map p114; ☑079 93 52 82; www.algheroairport.it) is about 9km northwest of Alghero. It's served by a number of low-cost carriers, including Ryanair and Air One, with connections to mainland Italy and destinations across Europe, including Barcelona, Birmingham, Dublin, Frankfurt, Liverpool and London.

For more flight information, see p255.

Bus

Intercity buses stop at and leave from Via Catalogna, by the Giardini Pubblici. Buy tickets at the booth (Map p116) in the gardens.

Up to 11 buses daily (15 on weekdays) run to/from Sassari (€2.50 to €3, one hour). There are also buses to Porto Torres (€2.50, one hour, eight daily Monday to Friday, five daily Saturday and Sunday) and Bosa (€4.50, one hour 35 minutes, two daily). The Bosa buses travel inland via Villanova Monteleone, but there's also a daily bus that follows the scenic coastal route (€3, one hour 10 minutes).

There are no direct links with Olbia. Instead you have to travel to Sassari, from where you can pick up the Turmo Travel link (see p136).

Car & Motorcycle

From Sassari, the easiest route is via the SS291, which connects with the SP19 into Alghero. Approaching from Bosa, there are two routes: one along the inland SS292, and the other, one of Sardinia's great coastal drives, along the SP105 (see the boxed text, p123).

Train

The train station (Map p114) is 1.5km north of the old town on Via Don Minzoni. ARST runs up to 11 trains daily to/from Sassari (€2.20, 35 minutes).

ⓘ Getting Around

Your own feet will be enough to get you around the old town and most other places, but you may want to jump on a bus to get to the beaches.

ⓘ **CENTRO STORICO DRIVING ALERT!**

Note that it is illegal for nonresidents to drive into the old town of Alghero – travellers with hire cars face a fine each time they enter the old town and these fines can mount up to hundreds of Euros, payable to your car-hire company.

To/From the Airport

Up to 11 buses daily (€0.70, 20 minutes) connect the airport with Piazza della Mercede in the town centre. Two daily **Logudoro Tours** (☑079 28 17 28) buses run to Cagliari (€20, 3½ hours), Oristano (€15, 2½ hours) and Macomer (€10, 1½ hours). To/from Nuoro, **Redentours** (☑0784 3 14 58; www.redentours.com) has three daily buses (€20, 2¼ hours) for which bookings are required.

A taxi to the airport costs around €25.

Bus

Bus line AO runs from Via Cagliari (via the Giardini Pubblici) to the beaches. Urban buses also operate to Fertilia as well as several places beyond. You can pick up these buses at stops around the Giardini Pubblici. Tickets (€0.70) are available at florist **Floridea** (Map p116; Via Cagliari 4) in the park and most *tabacchi* (tobacconists).

Car & Motorcycle

The best place to park in Alghero is at the large free car park along the *lungomare* (seafront promenade) on Via Garibaldi; it's always free and never gets so crowded that there's no space.

Local and international car-hire companies have booths at Fertilia airport. **Avis** (Map p116; ☑079 93 50 64; Piazza Sulis 9) also has a handy office in town.

Operating out of a hut on the seaward side of Via Garibaldi, **Cicloexpress** (Map p114; ☑079 98 69 50; www.cicloexpress.com; Via Garibaldi) hires out cars (€65 per day), scooters (€55) and bikes (€6).

Taxi

There's a **taxi rank** (Map p116) on Via Vittorio Emanuele near the tourist office. Otherwise you can call for one by phoning ☑079 989 20 28.

RIVIERA DEL CORALLO

Heading northwards from Alghero the coastal road sweeps scenically around to the west, passing through Fertilia, a low-key resort, and Porto Conte, a broad bay sprinkled with hotels and discreet villas. The end of the road, quite literally, is Capo Caccia, a rocky headland famous for its thrilling cave complex, the Grotta di Nettuno. Along the way there are a couple of great beaches and some interesting archaeological sites. Inland, the landscape flattens out and you'll find one of the island's top wine producers as well as a number of hospitable and peaceful *agriturismi* (farmstay accommodation).

One of Sardinia's great scenic roads unfurls along the coast south of Alghero to Bosa, 46km away. The corniche dips and curves through the coastal cliffs, offering sensational panoramas and taking in the best of *il mare* (the sea) and *il monte* (the mountains). It can be done as either a full-day road trip or a two-day 108km cycling tour (detailed in the following paragraphs). It's best to travel south via the inland road (SS292) through Villanova Monteleone and return via the coastal corniche to enjoy the spectacular views of the Riviera del Corallo and Capo Caccia.

For the cyclist, day one (62km) is the hardest, a classic up-and-over day gaining ground to 600m. The road winds up into the hills, revealing views across the water to Capo Caccia, before dipping over a ridge into deep woods that take you out of sight of the coast. After 23km you reach **Villanova Monteleone** (567m), perched like a natural balcony on the slopes of the Colle di Santa Maria. The centre of town is just off the main route and every morning except Sunday you'll find a produce market here (follow the signs to *mercato*).

On the high road beyond Villanova you will enjoy some great coastal views as the road bobs and weaves through shady woods. The final 5km climb is far outweighed by the sizzling 10km descent to Bosa.

The return journey via the corniche road takes you along a truly spectacular stretch of deserted coastline (bring sandwiches and water). There's only one significant climb of 6.2km to 350m, but the effort is offset by the commanding views. The brilliant white cliffs of Capo Caccia (after 16km) can often be seen on the northern horizon. Other than the jangle of goats' bells from the rugged, high slopes or a bird of prey winging on the thermals, there's little to disturb you.

There are two swimming spots along the way: a path to the beach after about 5.4km (look for cars parked by the roadside) just south of Torre Argentina, and **Spiaggia La Speranza** at 35.4km. Here you can lunch on fresh seafood at **Ristorante La Speranza** (☎079 91 70 10; meals around €35; ☺closed Wed winter) before the final 10.8km run into Alghero.

Fertilia

Sandy, pine-backed beaches fringe the coast round to Fertilia, about 4km northwest of Alghero. A rather soulless little town with ruler-straight streets and robust rationalist palazzi, its atmosphere comes as something of a surprise to visitors after Alghero's medieval hustle. It was built by Mussolini, who intended it to be the centre of a grand agricultural reclamation project, and who brought in farmers from northeastern Italy. Later postwar refugees arrived from Friuli-Venezia Giulia, bringing with them an allegiance to the lion of St Mark, symbol of Venice, which adorns the statue at the waterfront.

There's not a great deal to see or do once you've pottered around the seafront, but there are a couple of excellent beaches nearby. A few kilometres west of town, the **Spiaggia delle Bombarde** is a local favourite, set amid greenery and well equipped with umbrellas, sun-loungers and a kids play area. If it's too crowded, and it does get extremely busy in summer, you could try the next beach along, the **Spiaggia del Lazzaretto**. Both beaches are signposted off the main road, but if you don't have your own car, the Capo Caccia bus from Alghero passes nearby.

From Alghero, take local bus AF for Fertilia (€0.70, 15 minutes); it runs hourly between 7am and 9.40pm.

North of Fertilia

About 7km north of Alghero, just to the left (west) of the road to Porto Torres, lie scattered the ancient burial chambers of the **Necropoli di Anghelu Ruju** (admission €3, with guided tour €5, with audio guide €6, incl Nuraghe di Palmavera €5, with guided tour €8, with audio guide €10; ☺9am-7pm May-Oct, to 6pm Apr, 9.30am-4pm Mar, 10am-2pm Nov-Feb). The 38 tombs carved into the rock, known as *domus de janas*, date from between 2700 BC and 3300 BC. Most of the sculptural decor has been stripped off and removed to museums, but in some of the chambers you can make out lightly sculpted bull's horns, perhaps the symbol of a funeral deity.

Continue north up the road, and after a further 2km or so you come to the 650-hectare estate of Sardinia's top wine producer, **Sella e Mosca** (☑079 99 77 00; www.sellae mosca.com). Here you can join a free guided tour of the estate's lovingly tended **museum** (☻5.30pm Mon-Sat end May-Oct, by request rest of yr) and learn how the company grew to become the island's best-known vintner. The museum also has a small archaeological section dedicated to the Necropoli di Anghelu Ruiu. Afterwards sample some wines at the beautiful **enoteca** (wine shop; ☻8.30am-1pm & 3-6.30pm Mon-Sat year-round, plus 8.30am-8pm Sun mid-Jun–end Sep). From Alghero, there are two daily buses that pass by the turn-off for Sella e Mosca (€1.50, 25 minutes).

With your wine you'll want food and fortunately there are a number of delicious eating stops dotted around the countryside. Start at the wonderful **Agriturismo Barbagia** (☑079 93 51 41; www.agriturismobarbagia.it; Localita Fighera, Podere 26; meals around €30), offering simple accommodation (rooms €30 to €40) and abundant farmhouse food. Kids will enjoy the swings while Mum and Dad enjoy their meal on the shaded terrace overlooking the lawn. Alternatively, feast like royalty at **Agriturismo Sa Mandra** (☑079 99 91 50; www.aziendasamandra.it; Localita Fighera, Podere 21; meals around €35) a beautiful place 2km north of the airport. The daily menu is fixed, but you're not exactly short of choice with antipasti of cured ham, salami, herbed cheese and marinated vegetables. Then there's pasta followed by a choice of roast lamb or suckling pig. Book early and come hungry.

Nuraghe di Palmavera

Back on the coast, a few kilometres west of Fertilia on the road to Porto Conte, is the **Nuraghe di Palmavera** (admission €3, with guided tour €5, with audio guide €6, incl Necropoli di Anghelu Ruiu €5, with guided tour €8, with audio guide €10; ☻9am-7pm May-Oct, to 6pm Apr, 9.30am-4pm Mar, 10am-2pm Nov-Feb), a 3500-year-old *nuraghe* (Bronze Age fortified settlement) village. At its centre stands a limestone tower and an elliptical building with a secondary sandstone tower that was added later. The ruins of smaller towers and bastion walls surround the central edifice,

and beyond the walls are the packed remnants of circular dwellings, of which there may have been about 50 originally.

The circular **Capanna delle Riunioni** (Meeting Hut) is the subject of considerable speculation. Its foundation wall is lined by a low stone bench, perhaps for a council of elders, and encloses a pedestal topped by a model *nuraghe*. One theory suggests there was actually a cult to the *nuraghi* themselves.

You'll need your own transport to get here. The AF local bus (€0.70, 15 to 20 minutes) from Alghero passes through here but returns via an inland route, which will leave you stranded.

Porto Conte

Known more poetically as the Baia delle Ninfe (Bay of Nymphs), Porto Conte is a lovely unspoilt bay, its blue waters home to an armada of bobbing yachts and its green shores thick with mimosa and eucalyptus trees. The main focus is Spiaggia Mugoni, a hugely popular **beach** that arcs round the bay's northeastern flank. With its fine white sand and protected waters, it makes an excellent venue for beginners to try their hand at water sports. The **Club della Vela** (☑338 148 95 83) offers windsurfing, canoeing, kayaking and sailing courses, and also rents out boats.

Just west of Ponte Conte, and signposted off the main road, **Le Prigionette Nature Reserve** (☑079 94 90 60; admission free; ☻8am-4pm Mon-Fri, to 5pm Sat & Sun) sits at the base of Monte Timidone (361m). Encompassing some 12 sq km, and nicknamed the Arca di Noé (Noah's Ark) because of the variety of animals introduced here since the 1970s, it has well-marked forest paths and tracks, suitable for walkers and cyclists. You're unlikely to spot many animals, but the park is home to deer, unique white donkeys from the Isola Asinara, Giara horses and wild boar. Griffon vultures and falcons fly its skies. There's no admission charge, but you'll need to show ID to get in.

Regular buses run between Porto Conte and Alghero (€1, 30 minutes, up to 10 daily between June and September, six daily rest of year).

Capo Caccia

The road running down the eastern flank of the nature reserve skirts the waters of Porto Conte on its way to Capo Caccia, a dramatic

Since ancient times the red coral of the Mediterranean has beguiled and bewitched people. Many believed it to be the petrified blood of the Medusa, attributing to it aphrodisiac and other secret qualities, and fashioning amulets out of it.

Alghero's coast south of Capo Caccia is justifiably called the Riviera del Corallo (Coral Riviera). The coral fished here is of the highest quality and glows a dark orangey-red. The strong currents around the headland mean the little coral polyps have to work super hard to build their small coral trees, making them short and very dense to withstand the drag of the sea. Technically speaking, this is great news for Alghero's jewellers, as it means the coral trees have few air pockets – the sign of top-quality coral.

The coral is a precious commodity and its fishing is tightly regulated – in fact, coral fishing is currently on hold. It's difficult work, requiring sophisticated equipment and decompression chambers, as the coral is fished at a depth of 135m. It's then sold to Alghero's jewellers in chunks, prices varying according to colour, quality and size.

Agostino Marogna has been working in the business for years and now owns the finest coral shop in Alghero. Its signature necklaces composed of big, round coral beads often take years to create. To make one smooth red ball results in nearly 60% wastage. As there is only a certain amount of coral for sale each year, staff often have to put these necklaces aside until the new season, when they have to hunt for exactly the same shade and quality of coral. Such necklaces can cost as much as €30,000. Most items in the shop go for less, though, with prices starting at around €100. You'll find **Marogna** (Map p116; ☑079 98 48 14; Piazza Civica 34) at Palazzo d'Albis.

cape jutting out high above the Mediterranean. White cliffs sheer up from impossibly blue waters affording wonderful seascapes; just before the road ends, there's a signposted viewing point from where from you get a dramatic view of the cape and the wave-buffeted offshore island, Isola Foradada.

A few hundred metres further on brings you to a car park at the entrance to the **Escala del Cabirol**, a vertiginous 656-step staircase that descends 110m of sheer cliff to the **Grotta di Nettuno** (☑079 94 65 40; adult/child €10/5; ☺guided tours 9am-7pm summer, to 5pm Oct, to 4pm Jan, Mar, Nov & Dec), an underground fairyland of stalactites and stalagmites. Note that if you're going to walk the steps – and it's a pretty exhilarating experience – it takes about 15 minutes to get down them. Tours of the caves, which depart on the hour, last around 45 minutes and take you through narrow walkways flanked by forests of curiously shaped stalactites and stalagmites, nicknamed the organ, the church dome (or warrior's head) and so on. At its furthest point the cave extends back for 1km, but a lot is not open to the public, including several freshwater lakes deep inside grotto. In bad weather the grotto is closed.

If you don't fancy the staircase, you can visit the cave via boat trips from Alghero (see p115).

Rock climbers can enjoy exclusive views of the sea at the **Via Ferrata del Cabirol** (www.ferratacabirol.it), a stunning climbing site of medium difficulty; it's best visited in spring and autumn, though it stays in the shade until 2pm on summer days. To get here, turn off the Capo Caccia road after 10km, towards the spot that offers views of the island of Foradada. Check the website for technical information.

To get to the cape by public transport from Alghero, a bus departs from Via Catalogna (€3.50 return, 50 minutes) daily at 9.15am and returns at noon. It runs right to the cape and stops in the car park, where you'll find the staircase down to the grotto. From June to September, there are two extra daily runs, departing at 3.10pm and 5.10pm and returning at 4.05pm and 6.05pm.

Alternatively, the 27km makes for a scenic and relatively easy-going bike ride.

North of Capo Caccia

The road north of Porto Conte leads through the flat, green land known as the Nurra. As you head north, the first turn-off takes you to the coast at **Torre del Porticciolo**, a tiny natural harbour, backed by a small arc of beach and overlooked by a watchtower on the northern promontory. High cliffs mount

GETTING AWAY FROM IT ALL

About 11km north of Lago Baratz, the tiny inlet of Argentiera is dominated by the ghostly ruins of its silver mine, once the most important on the island. *Argento* (silver) was first extracted here by the Romans and continued right up to the 1960s when the mine was finally abandoned. The dark-brick mine buildings, now held together by wooden scaffolding, rise in an untidy jumble from a small grey-sand beach. You can't actually go into them, but they make for a stark and melancholy sight.

If you fancy overnighting, the **Hostel Argentiera** (☎079 53 02 19; www.hostelargen tiera.it; d per person €30-35) is a brand-new hostel with beds in sunny doubles, with an on-site restaurant. A few metres back from the beach, the **Bar Il Veliero** (☎079 53 03 61; Via Carbonia 1; panini €3.50) sells snacks, pastas and main courses.

Argentiera is at the end of the SP18, signposted from Palmadula.

guard on the southern side, and you can explore adjacent coves along narrow walking trails.

Six kilometres to the north, and hidden behind thick tracts of pine woods, is one of the island's longest stretches of wild sandy beach, **Porto Ferro**. To get there, take the Porto Ferro turn-off and, before reaching the end of the road (which is where the bus from Alghero stops), take a right (follow the Bar Porto Ferro signs). Buses run from Alghero (€1.50, 35 to 65 minutes depending on route and traffic) twice daily and three times in high summer.

From Porto Ferro a series of back roads lead 6km inland to **Lago Baratz**, Sardinia's only natural lake. Surrounded by low hills, the lake attracts some bird life, although the winged fellows tend to hang about the less accessible northern side. Paths circle the lake's marshy banks and there's a 3km dirt track connecting with the northern tip of Porto Ferro beach.

South of the lake, the workaday village of Santa Maria la Palma is home to the **Cantina Sociale di Santa Maria la Palma** (☎079 99 90 08; www.santamarialapalma.it; ◎8am-1pm & 2.30-6.30pm Mon-Fri, 8am-1pm Sun, longer hr in summer), the area's second winery after the grand Sella e Mosca spread. You can mosey around the *enoteca* and fill up with wine straight from the barrel. If you want to have a bite to eat, head for **Agriturismo Porticciolo** (☎079 91 80 00; www.agriturismoporticciolo.it; Località Porticciolo; B&B per person €30-45, 4-person apt per week €600-1000; P❀), a welcoming 24-hectare working farm with 100 pigs, along with pleasant accommodation (see p206). The restaurant, housed in a grand barn with a heavy timber ceiling and huge fireplace, serves delicious homemade food.

THE NORTH COAST

Extending 70km from Sardinia's northwestern tip round to Castelsardo, this stretch of coast encompasses the sublime and the distinctly unsightly. The industrial sprawl around Porto Torres, the north coast's busiest port, is far from inviting, but you don't have to go far to find some superb beaches. A few kilometres to the west, the Spiaggia della Pelosa is one of Sardinia's most famous beachside haunts.

Porto Torres
POP 22,100

Not one of Sardinia's most alluring towns, Porto Torres is a busy working port surrounded by a fuming petrochemical plant. There's no compelling reason to hang around, but if you find yourself passing through – and you might, especially if heading to or from Corsica – there are a couple of worthwhile sights, most notably the Basilica di San Gavino, one of Sardinia's most important Romanesque churches.

Porto Torres had its heyday under the Romans, who founded it as their main port on Sardinia's north coast. It remained one of the island's key ports until the Middle Ages and was capital of the Giudicato di Torres.

◎ Sights & Activities

Basilica di San Gavino   CHURCH
(crypt €1.50, guided tour €2.50) The limestone basilica is Sardinia's largest Romanesque church. Built between 1030 and 1080, it is notable for the apses on either end – there is no facade – and its two dozen marble columns, pilfered by the Pisan builders from

the nearby Roman site. Underneath the main church, a crypt is lined with religious statuary and various stone tombs.

The church is built over an ancient pagan burial ground and takes its name from one of the great Sardinian saints, the Roman soldier Gavino, who commanded the garrison at Torres in Diocletian's reign. Ordered to put to death two Christian priests, Protus and Januarius, he was converted by them and he himself shared their martyrdom. All three were beheaded on 25 October 304. Evidence for these events is scanty, but the legend of the *martiri turritani* (martyrs of Torres) flourishes.

To get here follow Corso Vittorio Emanuele south from the port for about 1km. The basilica is one block west of the street.

Parco Archeologico & Antiquarium   ARCHAEOLOGICAL PARK, MUSEUM

(Antiquarium 079 514 433; www.archeologia.be niculturali.it; Via Ponte Romano 92, adult/reduced €2/1; 9am-8pm Tue-Sun) Most of Roman Turris Libisonis lies beneath the modern port, but some vestiges have been uncovered. Known collectively as the 'archaeological park', the area is made up of the remains of public baths, an overgrown Roman bridge and the so-called Palazzo del Re Barbaro. The latter is the centrepiece and constitutes the main public bathing complex of the Roman city. Parts of the town's main roads, some *tabernae* (shops) and some good floor mosaics can also be seen on the site, which is entered via the **Antiquarium**. Almost all the items in this museum were found in Roman Turris, and they include a range of ceramics, busts, oil lamps and glassware. The site is near the train station, about a five-minute walk from the town centre.

Le Ginestre   BOAT TOURS

(079 51 34 93; day trip adult/4-10yr €42/27; 10am-noon & 6-8pm) Operating out of a kiosk on the seafront is one of several outfits offering excursions to the Parco Nazionale dell'Asinara (p129). A day trip includes a tour of the island on a dinky train.

Eating

Cristallo   MEDITERRANEAN €€

(079 51 49 09; Piazza XX Settembre 11; meals €35-40; Tue-Sun) Above a popular *pasticceria* (pastry shop)-bar on street level, this modern restaurant serves great seafood and a selection of favourites, including several tasty lamb concoctions.

Information

Banca Nazionale del Lavoro (Corso Vittorio Emanuele 20) One of several banks with ATMs along the main drag.

Post office (Via Ponte Romano; 8am-1.15pm Mon-Fri) Three blocks right of Corso Vittorio Emanuele.

Tourist office (079 51 50 00; Piazza Garibaldi 17; 8am-2pm) A couple of streets back from the port, just off Corso Vittorio Emanuele.

Getting There & Away

Boat

Tirrenia (89 21 23; www.tirrenia.it), **Grandi Navi Veloci** (GNV; 010 209 45 91; www.gnv.it) and **Moby Lines** (199 30 30 40; www.moby lines.it) all run ferries between Porto Torres and Genoa. Tirrenia and GNV ferries sail year round, while Moby Lines operates between mid-May and September. Fares for the 11-hour crossing cost €86 to €105.

SNCM (France 0825 88 80 88; www.sncm .fr) and **CMN La Méridionale** (France 0810 20 13 20; www.cmn.fr) together operate ferries to/from Marseille (€78, 15 to 17 hours) via Corsica. Note, however, that in July and August some of these ferries sail from Toulon instead. You can purchase tickets at **Agenzia Paglietti** (079 51 44 77; fax 079 51 40 63; Corso Vittorio Emanuele 19). For more details on ferry routes, see p258.

Bus

Most buses leave from Piazza Colombo, virtually at the port. There are services to Sassari (€1.50, 30 to 40 minutes, six daily), Alghero (€2.50, one hour, six daily Monday to Friday, five daily Saturday and Sunday) and Stintino (€2.50, 45 minutes, four Monday to Saturday, two Sunday). Get tickets at **Bar Acciaro** (Corso Vittorio Emanuele 38) or from newsstands.

Train

Trains run to Sassari (€1.55, 20 minutes, four daily), Cagliari (€16.05, 4½ hours, two daily) and Olbia (€8.35, 2¼ hours, one daily).

West of Porto Torres

West of Porto Torres, the flat land has a desolate feel, especially when the *maestrale* (northwesterly wind) blows in, whipping the *macchia* (Mediterranean scrub) and bleak rocks. But follow the road to the northwestern tip and you'll find laid-back Stintino, approached via its shimmering *saline* (saltpans), and the fabulous Spiaggia della Pelosa, one of Sardinia's most celebrated beaches.

STINTINO
POP 1240

Until not very long ago Stintino was a remote and forgotten fishing village. But in recent years tourism has replaced tuna as its main source of income, and it's now a sunny little resort, wedged tidily between two ports – one full of bobbing blue fishing boats (Porto Mannu), the other given over to yachts (Porto Minori). Its pastel-painted houses add charm, while its location near the much-feted Spiaggia della Pelosa and Isola Asinara make it a useful summer base.

Many of Stintino's residents are descended from the 45 families who established the village in 1885. They settled here after being forcibly removed from Isola Asinara to make way for a new prison and quarantine station. The villagers turned to the sea for their livelihood and developed a reputation for tuna fishing, culminating in the annual *mattanza* (slaughter).

⊙ Sights & Activities

Museo della Tonnara MUSEUM

(☑079 52 00 81; Porto Mannu; adult/child €2/1; ☺6-11.30pm daily Jun–mid-Sep) Stintino's tuna-fishing heritage is documented at this small museum at Porto Mannu. Six rooms are ordered as the six chambers of the *tonnara* (the net in which the fish are caught), and filled with documents, seafaring memorabilia, photos and film, recalling this centuries-old trade. The *tonnara* here was shut down in 1974, although locals attempted to revive it briefly in the late 1990s for scientific purposes. The *mattanza* still takes place in Carloforte and Portoscuso, in the south, as well as a couple of spots in Sicily. For more on the tuna hunt, see the boxed text, p73).

Beaches BEACH

Just south of Stintino a signpost left directs you to the abandoned *tonnara* and the **Spiaggia delle Saline**, once the site of a busy saltworks, now a beautiful white beach. The marshes extend inland to form the **Stagno di Casaraccio**, a big lagoon where you might just see flamingos at rest.

In late August you can also catch Stintino's **regatta**, a race of 'Latin' sailing boats, the triangular sails of which fill the narrow causeway between Stintino and the Isola Asinara.

Excursions BOAT TOURS

Stintino is the main gateway to the Parco Nazionale dell'Asinara, and during summer a regular fleet of ferries operates out of Porto Mannu; see p129 for details.

Windsurfing & Diving WATER SPORTS

Windsurfers and divers are well catered for in these parts with various operators hiring out equipment and organising lessons/dives. You'll find most of these at Spiaggia della Pelosa (p129).

✗ Eating

Skipper MEDITERRANEAN €

(☑079 52 34 60; Lungomare Cristoforo Colombo 57; lunchtime menu €12; ☺6am-11pm Tue-Sun) A longstanding favourite, this casual bar is a jack of all trades. You can sit down on the sea-view terrace and order anything from coffee and cocktails to seafood pastas, lasagne, hamburgers, salads and *panini*. It's all good and none of it is expensive.

Ristorante Da Antonio SEAFOOD €€

(☑079 52 30 77; Via Marco Polo 16; meals around €40; ☺closed Thu Oct-Apr) Setting its sights higher than most, this elegant restaurant dishes up classic fish dishes with some style. Menu stalwarts include *polpo marinato* (marinated octopus) and an abundant *fritto misto* (mixed fry). On the flip side, the service can be very slow.

Lu Fanali PIZZERIA €

(☑079 52 30 54; Lungomare Cristoforo Colombo 89; pizzas €7) A good spot for a cheap and cheerful pizza down on the seafront, Lu Fanali is a friendly, unbuttoned kinda place with a wide terrace and a solid selection of pizzas, pasta and ice cream.

❶ Information

Your best bet for information is the private **Agenzia La Nassa** (☑079 52 00 60; www .escursioniasinara.it; Via Tonnara 35; ☺8.30am-1pm & 5-8pm daily Mar-Oct, rest of yr by appointment), which can advise on local accommodation and excursions. It also offers internet (€4 per hour), and car and bike hire (bikes per day €10, cars from €60).

For online information, www.infostintino.it is a useful resource.

❶ Getting There & Away

Between June and mid-September, there are three daily buses between Stintino and Alghero's Fertilia airport (€7, 50 minutes).

There are four weekday buses (two on Sundays) to Stintino from Porto Torres (€2.50, 45 minutes) and Sassari (€4, one hour 10 minutes). Services increase between June and September.

CAPO DEL FALCONE
Holiday complexes, residences and holiday homes fill in the gaps between Stintino and

Capo del Falcone. The main draw here is the **Spiaggia della Pelosa**, a dreamy image of near beach perfection: a salt-white strip of sand lapped by shallow, turquoise waters and fronted by strange, almost lunar, licks of land. A craggy islet capped by a Catalano-Aragonese watchtower completes the picture. In high summer you will, of course, have to share the scene with tens of thousands of fellow admirers, but visit in the low season and you'll find the crowds far more manageable.

Two kilometres north of Stintino, just before Pelosa beach, you'll find the **Asinara Diving Centre** (☑079 52 70 00; www.asinara divingcenter.it; Porto dell'Ancora) at the Ancora hotel. It offers a range of dives around Capo del Falcone and the Parco Nazionale dell'Asinara, including night and enriched-air dives. Further north, on the Spiaggia della Pelosa, the **Windsurfing Centre Stintino** (☑079 52 70 06; www.windsurfingcenter.it) rents out windsurfers (€17 per hour) and canoes (from €10 per hour), as well as offering windsurfing lessons (€45 per lesson) and courses (€155).

Year-round buses run to the beach from Stintino (€1, five minutes, four Monday to Saturday, three Sunday). In summer bus services are considerably increased.

To park within the blue lines by the side of the road you'll be looking at around €5 for half a day.

PARCO NAZIONALE DELL'ASINARA

Sardinia's second-largest offshore island (the largest is Isola Sant'Antioco), **Isola dell'Asinara** (Donkey Island) is named after the island's most famous resident – its unique *asino bianco* (albino donkey). There are estimated to be about 120 examples on the island, along with 80 other animal species, including mouflon (silky-haired wild sheep) and peregrine falcons.

Ironically, though, until it was designated a national park in 1997, Isola dell'Asinara was home to one of the most notorious maximum-security prisons in Italy. Now closed, the prison was built, along with a quarantine station for cholera victims, in 1885.

Tours of the island are only possible with licensed operators, setting out from Stintino (see p128) or Porto Torres (see p127).

From May through to late October, **Linea Parco** (☑079 52 31 18; Porto Mannu; ☺ticket office 9.30am-12.30pm & 4-7pm) sells tours from a kiosk near the ferry port. There are a number of options available, but the standard tour costs €36 per person (excluding lunch) and departs at 9am.

Agenzia La Nassa (☑079 52 00 60; www .escursioniasinara.it; Via Tonnara 35; ☺8.30am-1pm & 5-8pm daily summer, rest of yr by appointment) also has a number of packages from €18 to €65 per person. The cheapest, available between June and September, covers your ferry passage only, leaving you free to walk or cycle within designated areas on the island. The more expensive options provide 4WD or bus transport.

Although much of the island is off limits to visitors, including the beach of **Cala Sant'Andrea** (a breeding ground for turtles), most tours provide a good overview. Swimming breaks are usually programmed for **Cala d'Oliva** or **Punta Sabina** beaches, both in the north of the island.

Note that many tours do not include lunch, so either take a picnic or head to Cala D'Oliva where there's a restaurant.

East of Porto Torres

East of Porto Torres, the SP81 and its continuation the SS200 follow the coast as it gradually rises up to Castelsardo. For much of the way the road is flanked by pine woods, behind which you'll find various isolated beaches. Inland, the flat-topped tablelands of the Anglona, a struggling farm district, lie sandwiched between the Gallura to the east, Logudoro to the south and the small Romangia district to the west.

CASTELSARDO
POP 5700

An attractive and popular day-trip destination, Castelsardo huddles around the high cone of a promontory jutting into the Mediterranean. Towering over everything is a dramatic *centro storico,* a hilltop ensemble of dark alleyways and medieval buildings seemingly melded onto the grey rock peak.

The town was originally designed as a defensive fort by a 12th-century Genoese family. Named Castel Genoese, it was the subject of much fighting and in 1326 fell to the Spanish, who changed its name to Castel Aragonese. It became Castel Sardo (Sardinian Castle) in 1767 under the Piedmontese. By then this outpost, once an independent *citta demaniali* (royal city), had lost its defensive raison d'être. Now the fortress is a museum, and locals linger as reluctant custodians.

☉ Sights

Centro Storico NEIGHBOURHOOD

The most interesting part of town is the hilltop *centro storico*, lorded over by the medieval **Castello**, around which the original town was established. Built by the Doria family and home to Eleonora d'Arborea for a period, it commands superb views over the Golfo dell' Asinara to Corsica. It also houses a museum, the **Museo dell'Intreccio** (🖉079 47 13 80; Via Marconi; admission €2; ☉9.30am-1pm & 3-5.30pm Tue-Sun Nov-Mar, to 6.30pm Tue-Sun Mar, to 7.30pm daily Apr, to 8.30pm daily May, to 9pm daily Sep, 9am-midnight daily Jul & Aug), dedicated to the basket-weaving for which the town is famous.

Just below the castle is the **Chiesa di Santa Maria**, largely a 16th-century structure, famous for its 13th-century crucifix, known as the Critu Nieddu (Black Christ).

Cattedrale di Sant'Antonio Abate CATHEDRAL

A town landmark, the slender bell tower of the cathedral is topped by a brightly tiled cupola. In a setting worthy of a Grimm Brothers' fairy tale, the cathedral almost appears suspended in midair atop the craggy cliffs. Inside, the main altar is dominated by the *Madonna con gli angeli,* a painting by the mysterious Maestro di Castelsardo. More of his works can be seen in the **crypts** (admission €2) below the cathedral. A series of small rooms chiselled out of the living rock, these are what remain of the Romanesque church that once stood here. The crypt exit takes you past neat lawns that separate you from the Spanish-era seaward battlements.

A couple of fairly small **beaches** flank the promontory.

🎎 Festivals

Lunissanti RELIGIOUS

On the Monday of Holy Week, the people of Castelsardo celebrate a series of Masses and processions as part of the festival, ending with a solemn evening torchlight parade through the old town to the Chiesa di Santa Maria.

✗ Eating

TOP CHOICE La Guardiola SEAFOOD €€

(🖉079 47 07 55; Piazza Bastione 4; lunchtime set menus €18 & €22, meals around €35; ☉closed Mon Oct-May) Dine on quality seafood while admiring wonderful views from La Guardiola's panoramic pavilion at the top of the old town. The lunch menus – pasta, main course and side dish – are a good way of saving a euro or two.

Il Piccolo Borgo MEDITERRANEAN €

(🖉079 47 05 16; Via Seminario 4; plates €10; ☉Tue-Sun) A handy place for a light lunch, this small *centro storico* bar serves various snacks including a delicious platter of cured hams, olives and cheeses.

Cormorano SEAFOOD €€€

(🖉079 47 06 28; Via Colombo 5; meals up to €55; ☉closed Tue Oct-May) Just round the corner from Piazza Pianedda, this is a good option for high-end seafood. There's a creative edge to many of the dishes, which include an excellent *linguine con sarde* (thin pasta with sardines) and grilled fish served with crayfish and prawns.

🛍 Shopping

You can't fail to notice the handicrafts shopping emporia in Castelsardo. As you wander through the old town you'll see women on their doorsteps, creating intricate baskets and other objects of all shapes and sizes.

❶ Information

Tourist office (🖉079 47 15 06; Piazzetta del Popolo; ☉10am-12.30pm & 5-7.30pm) Note that these opening hours are flexible and the office is often closed. An alternative, and more reliable, source of information is the *comune*'s website: www.comune.castelsardo.ss.it.

❶ Getting There & Away

Buses stop just off Piazza Pianedda. They run each way between Sassari (€2.50, one hour, 10 Monday to Saturday, four Sunday), Santa Teresa di Gallura (€5.50, 1½ hours, three daily) and Lu Bagnu (€1, five minutes, six Monday to Saturday, four Sunday). Buy tickets from the nameless *edicola* (newsstand) on the square.

ROCCIA DELL'ELEFANTE: A WONDER ROCK

As you approach Castelsardo from Sedini, along the SS134, you'll notice a curious shape arching on the side of the road – a rock that looks like an elephant, its trunk in the air. Believe it or not, the rock was weathered into this shape entirely by the elements. And that's not the least of it – inside you'll find two neolithic tombs. The upper tomb is partially gone through erosion, but the lower is still in good shape, with four small rooms and a rock carving of a bull's horns and head.

AROUND CASTELSARDO

With your own vehicle you could comfortably take in the following places in a one-day circuit from Castelsardo. If you're relying on public transport it becomes substantially more difficult.

TERGU

Barely 10km south of Castelsardo lies a fine Romanesque church, the **Nostra Signora di Tergu**. The church is set in a pleasant garden, partly made up of the few visible remains of a monastery that once housed up to 100 Benedictine monks. Built in the 12th century of dark wine-red trachyte and white limestone, the facade is a particularly pretty arrangement of arches, columns, geometric patterns and a simple rose window.

SEDINI

From Castelsardo, the SS134 Sedini road leads to one of the area's most lovable landmarks, the **Roccia dell'Elefante** (Elephant Rock), a bizarre trachyte rock by the junction with the SS200. Its uncanny resemblance to an elephant has been the source of local interest for millennia, as witnessed by the presence of some *domus de janas* (literally 'fairy houses'; tombs cut into rock) in the hollow interior.

Eleven kilometres south of the elephant is Sedini, a small, sleepy town with a well-known *domus de janas*. Gouged out of a huge calcareous rock by the town's main through-road, Via Nazionale, the prehistoric tomb was lived in by farmers in the Middle Ages, and used as a prison until the 19th century. It now houses a small **museum** (☏349 844 04 36; http://web.tiscali.it/sedini; admission €2; ☉10am-1pm & 3-8pm May-Sep, rest of yr on request) displaying traditional farming and household implements.

Buses run from Castelsardo (€1.50, 25 minutes, three daily).

NURAGHE SU TESORU & VALLEDORIA

Backtracking to the Roccia dell'Elefante, you can pick up the SS200 towards Valledoria. Just beyond the elephantine rock, you'll see the Nuraghe Su Tesoru on the left-hand side of the road. One of the last *nuraghi* to be built, it's best admired from the comfort of your own car as stopping on the main road is not very convenient.

Seven kilometres on and you arrive at the sprawling town of Valledoria, fronted by beaches that stretch more than 10km east to the small fishing village of Isola Rossa. A couple of buses running from Castelsardo stop in Valledoria (€1, 25 minutes), although if you can't convince the bus driver to stop at the camping ground turn-off, you'll have to hitch or walk.

SASSARI

POP 121,700

With Sassari, what you see is the real thing – it doesn't boast prettiness, it's not a big tourist destination and it's slightly ragged round the edges, but the atmosphere is unpretentious and genuine. This is Sardinia's second city, a proud and cultured centre and a vibrant university town, with a medieval heart and a modern outlook.

Like many Italian towns it hides its charms behind an outer shell of drab apartment blocks and confusing, traffic-choked roads. But once through to the inner sanctum it opens up, revealing a grand centre of wide boulevards, impressive piazzas and stately palazzi. In the evocative and rundown *centro storico*, medieval alleyways hum with Dickensian activity as residents run about their daily business amid grimy facades and hidden churches.

History

Sassari (Tatari in the local dialect) owes its medieval rise to prominence to the decline of its coastal counterparts. As the ancient Roman colony of Turris Libisonis (modern Porto Torres) succumbed to malaria and repeated pirate raids, people gradually retreated to Sassari. Porto Torres (and at one point the town of Ardara) remained capital of the Giudicato di Torres (or Logudoro), but Sassari's increasing importance led it to break away from the province and, with support from Genoa, declare itself an autonomous city state in 1294.

But the Sassaresi soon tired of Genoese meddling and in 1321 called on the Crown of Aragon to help rid them of the northern Italians. The Catalano-Aragonese arrived in 1323, but Sassari soon discovered it had leapt from the frying pan into the fire. The first of many revolts against the city's new masters came two years later. It took another century for the Iberians to fully control Sassari.

For a time the city prospered, but waves of plague and the growing menace from Ottoman Turkey sidelined Sardinia, leaving Sassari to slide into decline in the 16th century. A century later the founding of the city's university, Sardinia's first, was a rare highlight in this otherwise grim period.

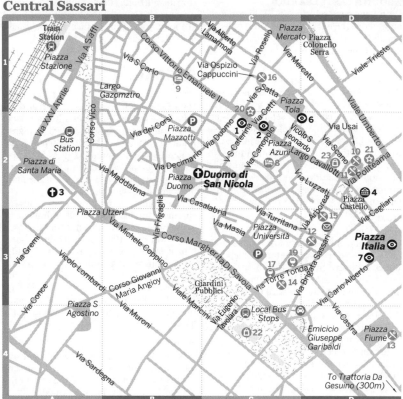

It wasn't until the middle of the 19th century that Sassari began to take off again, following the modernisation of Porto Torres and the laying of the Carlo Felice highway between the port, Sassari and Cagliari. Since 1945 the city has maintained a slow pace of economic growth. It has also been an industrious producer of national politicians, including former presidents Antonio Segni (1891–1972) and Francesco Cossiga (b 1928), the charismatic communist leader Enrico Berlinguer (1922–84), and Beppe Pisanu, interior minister in Silvio Berlusconi's second government (2001–06) and Senate member since 2006.

◎ Sights

Museo Nazionale
Sanna   ARCHAEOLOGICAL MUSEUM
(☏079 27 22 03; Via Roma 64; admission €3.10; ◌9am-8pm Tue-Sun) In a grand Palladian villa, Museo Nazionale Sanna houses a comprehensive archaeological collection, a small painting gallery and an ethnographical section dedicated to Sardinian folk art. The archaeological section is the real draw.

Exhibits are displayed in seven chronologically ordered rooms, starting with the Sala Preistorica, which showcases the island's very earliest Stone Age and neolithic finds. In this and the next room you'll find an array of fossils, pottery fragments and finds from the 3rd-century BC temple of Monte d'Accoddi (p137).

Beyond these two rooms, the museum opens up in a series of displays dedicated to megalithic tombs and *domus de janas*. The highlight is the sophisticated bronzeware, including axe heads and similar tools, weapons, bracelets, votive boats and *bronzetti* (bronze figurines depicting humans and animals).

Room X is dedicated to Phoenician and Carthaginian objects. Some exquisite pot-

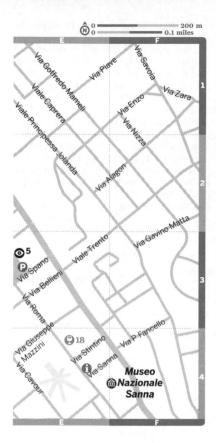

tery is mixed in with gold jewellery and masks. Rooms XI and XII contain Roman finds, mostly ceramics and oil burners but also some statuary and a sprinkling of coins, jewellery and household objects. Off to one side lies a stash of heavy Roman anchors.

The museum's *pinacoteca* (picture gallery) displays works from the collection of Giovanni Sanna, a mining engineer whose family built the museum and after whom it is named. The works are mostly ponderous 18th-century paintings, although the fine 14th-century Pisan triptych *Madonna con Bambino* (1473), by Bartolomeo Vivarini, is worth seeking out.

There is also a small collection of Sardinian folk art in the separate ethnographic section (currently closed for refurbishment) with an eclectic array of carpets, saddlebags, embroidered clothes and curious terracotta hot-water bottles.

Piazza Italia   PIAZZA

Sassari's largest piazza, Piazza Italia, is one of Sardinia's most impressive public spaces. Covering about a hectare, it is surrounded by imposing 19th-century buildings, including the neoclassical **Palazzo della Provincia**, seat of the provincial government. Opposite, the red neo-Gothic **Palazzo Giordano** provides a palatial home for the Banca San Paolo. Presiding over everything, the statue of King Vittorio Emanuele II was unveiled in 1899 to much pomp and costumed celebration, in anticipation of the grand folk celebration that would become the city's main festival, the Cavalcata Sarda. The piazza also marks the starting point for Sassari's other big jamboree, I Candelieri (see p135).

Museo della Brigata Sassari   MUSEUM
(Piazza Castello; admission free; ☺8.30am-4pm Mon-Thu, to noon Sat) Sassari is home to one of Italy's most revered army regiments. The Sassari Brigade was established in 1915 and during WWI established a reputation for bravery in the face of appalling conditions. You can glean something of the suffering they endured in the tiny Museo della Brigata Sassari in the regiment's city-centre barracks. Uniforms, photos, documents and other memorabilia testify to the ferocious bravery of the Sardinian soldiers, who were thrown into battle against the Austrians in northern Italy. There are old guns and grenades on show, and a recreation of a wartime trench. Most touching, however, are the proud poses of the men in the old black-and-white photographs.

Centro Storico   NEIGHBOURHOOD
Sassari's small medieval centre is not in great nick, but it retains enough of its 13th-century character to reward a leisurely look. Unlike many Italian towns, Sassari did not simply expand beyond its historic walls; instead, it regenerated itself over the centuries by eliminating the old to make way for the new. Fortunately, some jewels survived the revamps, and Sassari's two grand churches – the Duomo and Chiesa di Santa Maria di Betlem – are impressive.

The main strip in the *centro storico,* Corso Vittorio Emanuele II, follows the path of the original Roman road from Porto Torres to Cagliari. Little has survived to suggest its 13th-century heyday (it was at the time the top address in town), but if you look above the shop windows, you'll find a few faint signs of past grandeur among the chipped and scarred stonework. A case in point is **Casa Farris** (Corso Vittorio Emanuele II 25), whose high Gothic windows has withstood centuries of neglect. A few metres on, on the other side of the road, **Casa di Re Enzo** (Corso Vittorio Emanuele II 42) provides a remarkable 15th-century Catalan Gothic setting for an undies shop. Wander inside for a closer look at the vibrant frescoes and frilly knickers.

Opposite, the **Teatro Civico** was a 19th-century addition, built in the Liberty style in 1826, and modelled on Turin's Teatro Carignano.

North of Corso Vittorio Emanuele II, **Piazza Tola** was medieval Sassari's main market, and you'll still find a market here on weekday mornings. It is also where condemned heretics were burned in front of spectators on the balcony of the 16th-century **Palazzo d'Usini**, now the city's public library.

From the piazza, take Via Alberto Lamarmora and Via Rosello for Piazza Mercato, a busy and unsightly traffic junction outside the city walls. Here, in a sunken patch of grass, you'll find the Renaissance **Fontana di Rosello** (☺9am-1pm & 5.30-8.30pm Tue-Sat, 5.30-8.30pm Sun May-Sep, 9am-1pm & 4-7pm Tue-Sat, 9am-1pm Sun Oct-Apr), Sassari's most famous fountain. A monumental marble box ringed by eight lion-head spouts and topped by two fine marble arches, it was for a long time the focus of city life.

A short walk away, down Corso Trinita, you can admire the only substantial remnant of the city's **medieval walls**.

Duomo di San Nicola & Around   DUOMO
Sassari's baroque **Duomo** (Piazza Duomo) rises like an exotic beast over the otherwise sober streets of the medieval centre. What hits you first is the 18th-century baroque facade, a giddy free-for-all of sculptural joie de vivre, with statues, reliefs, friezes and busts. It's all just a front, though, because inside the cathedral reverts to its true Gothic character. The facade covers a 15th-century Catalan Gothic body, which was itself built over an earlier Romanesque church. Nothing remains of this except for the 13th-century *campanile* (bell tower). Of note inside are the frescoes in the left transept and the Gothic fresco in the first chapel on the right. In the neighbouring chapel, check out the fine painting of the *Martirio dei SS Cosma e Damiano* (Martyrdom of Saints Cosimo and Damien).

The narrow streets around here are full of life. At some point you'll almost certainly arrive in Piazza Mazzotti, locally dubbed Piazza di Demolizione (Demolition Piazza) and arguably one of Sardinia's ugliest squares. It was once a warren of old streets like the rest of the quarter, but hard-to-control prostitution plagued its narrow lanes, so the authorities decided to knock it all down and create a car park instead.

Chiesa di Santa Maria di Betlem   CHURCH
(Piazza di Santa Maria) With its distinctive dome and proud Romanesque facade, the

Chiesa di Santa Maria di Betlem reveals a curious blend of architectural styles. The exterior betrays Gothic and even vaguely Oriental admixtures. Inside, the Catalan Gothic vaulting has been preserved, but much baroque silliness has crept in to obscure the original lines of the building. Lining each aisle in the chapels stands some of the giant 'candles' that the city guilds parade about town for the 14 August festivities.

✪ Festivals & Events

Cavalcata Sarda   SARDINIAN RIDING
One of Sardinia's most high-profile festivals is held in Sassari on the second-last Sunday of May. Thousands of people converge on the city to participate in costumed processions, to sing and dance, and to watch fearless horse-riders exhibit their acrobatic skills.

I Candelieri   HISTORICAL
A second big festival, held every 14 August. Teams wearing medieval costume and representing various 16th-century guilds bear nine wooden columns (the 'candlesticks') through the town. The celebrations have their origins in 13th-century Pisan worship of the Madonna of the Assumption.

🍴 Eating

Eating in Sassari is a real pleasure. Eateries range from cheap student cafes to smart, refined restaurants, and standards are universally high. A local curiosity is *fainè*, a cross between a crêpe and a pizza with a base made from chickpea flour.

TOP CHOICE Trattoria Da Gesuino   TRATTORIA €€
(☎079 27 33 92; Via Torres 17g; meals around €30; ☺Mon-Sat) Halfway between an earthy neighbourhood trattoria and an upmarket restaurant, Da Gesuino hits exactly the right tone. It's relaxed, the service is efficient, the interior inviting and the food excellent. The menu covers all the usual bases with pasta, risottos, fresh fish and grilled meats. A standout choice is the *risotto con scampi e verdura* (risotto with scampi and vegetables).

Fainè alla Genovese Sassu   FAST FOOD €
(Via Usai 17; meals €3.50-6; ☺Mon-Sat) A no-frills spot for a cheap fill-up, this is Sassari's original purveyor of *fainè*. There's nothing else on the menu, but with a wide range of toppings you should find something to suit your tastes.

Trattoria L'Assassino   TRATTORIA €
(☎079 23 50 41; Via Ospizio Cappuccini 1a; set lunch €8-12; ☺Mon-Sat) A model trattoria in a tiny back alley, L'Assassino – The Assassin – is popular with local workmen who come here to lunch on simple pastas and chunks of roast meat. You can also order a selection of eight starters for €18 (minimum two people).

L'Antica Hostaria   OSTERIA €€€
(☎079 20 00 60; Via Giuseppe Mazzini 27; meals around €45; ☺Mon-Sat) Hidden behind a discreet exterior, L'Antica Hostaria is one of the top restaurants in town. In intimate surroundings you are treated to inventive cuisine that is rooted in local culinary tradition, such as fricassee of lamb with white beans and red peppers. Desserts are similarly impressive, and there's a decent wine list.

Trattoria Da Antonio   TRATTORIA €€
(☎079 23 42 97; Via Arborea 2b; meals around €25; ☺Tue-Sun) Affectionately known as *Lu Panzone* (the Big Belly), this boisterous, unpretentious trattoria does a great line in homespun, no-nonsense food. The focus here is on meat (and lots of it) – start with pasta and sausage, and then choose between a tender horse steak, lamb with olives and herbs, or pork with tomato and chickpeas, all the while sipping the local red wine.

Ristorante Enoteca Antica Posta   MEDITERRANEAN €€
(☎079 200 61 21; Via Torre Tonda 26; meals around €30; ☺Mon-Sat) Traditional cuisine is given a modern makeover at this designer wine-bar-cum-restaurant. There's also a decent wine list comprised of Italian and Sardinian labels.

Il Castello   MEDITERRANEAN €€
(☎079 23 20 41; Piazza Cavallino de Honestis 6; meals around €35; ☺Thu-Tue Oct-May, daily Jun-Sep) A favourite with the theatre crowd, this formal restaurant has tables laid out in a glass pavilion overlooking Piazza Castello and offers a seasonal menu.

La Vela Latina   TRATTORIA €€
(☎079 23 37 37; Largo Sisini 8; meals around €30; ☺Mon-Sat) If you're a carnivore with a yen for culinary adventure you'll find plenty of hard-core meat dishes here, including *trippa* (tripe), *cervella* (brain) and *lingua di vitello* (ox tongue).

♀ Drinking

With its big student population and busy business community, Sassari has a vibrant cafe culture. You'll find a number of popular spots on Via Roma and further south on Via Torre Tonda, a lively student strip. Many places stay open late and some offer occasional live music.

Caffè Italiano   CAFE
(Via Roma 38/40; ⊙Mon-Sat) One of the best places on Via Roma is this big, bustling bar with pavement tables and a stylish interior. Business folk like to lunch here, and young locals come most afternoons to chat over an aperitif.

Accademia   BAR
(Via Torre Tonda 11; ⊙Mon-Sat) In the university district, this place has tables in an attractive wrought-iron pavilion. It gets very busy at lunchtime and on Friday and Saturday nights, when it stays open until 2am. If you're lucky, you might also catch a gig here.

Caliente Caffè   WINE BAR
(Via Torre Tonda 1b) A cool wine bar with outdoor tables beneath a stretch of 13th-century city wall, this place is great for a relaxed evening out.

☆ Entertainment

Meccano   CLUB
(☎079 27 04 05; Via Carlo Felice 33; ⊙11pm-late Thu-Sat) If you want to dance late, jump in a taxi and head out to this mainstream disco on the eastern edge of town.

Teatro Civico   THEATRE
(☎079 23 21 82; Corso Vittorio Emanuele II 39) This is Sassari's main theatre, staging plays and classical musical concerts.

Teatro Verdi   THEATRE, CINEMA
(☎079 23 94 79; Via Politeama) Teatro Verdi doubles as a cinema when it's not hosting dance performances or opera, usually between October and January.

ⓘ THEATRE TIP

The town's theatres don't tend to move into gear until September or October, after the sting has gone out of the summer heat. For show information, check the local newspaper *La Nuova Sardegna* or contact the theatres directly.

🛍 Shopping

Isola   CRAFTS
(☎079 23 01 01; ⊙9.30am-1pm & 5-8pm Mon-Fri, 9.30am-1pm Sat) Located in the town's green Giardini Pubblici, this is the place to find the best in Sardinian craftwork, including nice ceramic ware, traditional rugs and some extremely impressive wrought-iron work.

Mondadori   BOOKS
(☎079 201 20 98; Largo Cavallotti 17) Has an excellent choice of maps and a small selection of English-language books.

ⓘ Information

Banca Intesa (Piazza Italia 23) Has an ATM.
Farmacia Simon (☎079 23 11 44; Piazza Castello 5; ⊙8pm-9.10am) Pharmacy that does the night shift.
Guardia Medica (☎079 206 22 22; Via Maurizio Zanfarino 23) For nonemergency medical assistance.
Lavalandia (Corso Vittorio Emanuele II; 6kg wash €4; ⊙9am-9pm) One of Sardinia's few self-service laundrettes.
Net Gate Internet (☎079 23 78 94; Piazza Universita 4; per hr €3; ⊙9am-1.15pm & 3.30-7.30pm Mon-Fri, 9am-1pm Sat)
Nuovo Ospedale Civile (☎079 206 10 00; Via de Nicola) Hospital south of the city centre.
Police station (Questura; ☎079 249 50 00; Via Ariosto 3) The main police headquarters.
Post office (Via Brigata Sassari 13; ⊙8am-6.50pm Mon-Fri, to 1.15pm Sat)
Tourist office (☎079 23 17 77; aastss@tiscali.it; Via Roma 62; ⊙9am-1.30pm & 4-6pm Mon-Thu, 9am-1.30pm Fri) Has information on Sassari and the surrounding area.

ⓘ Getting There & Away

Air

Sassari shares Alghero's **Fertilia airport** (☎079 93 52 82; www.algheroairport.it), about 28km west of the city centre. For information on flights, see p122.

Bus

Sassari's **bus station** (Via XXV Aprile) is near the train station. You can buy tickets at the bus station, where there's also a small left-luggage office (per bag €1.50).

ARST (☎800 865 042; www.arst.sardegna.it, in Italian) buses serve Alghero (€3, one hour, hourly), Oristano (€9.50, 2¼ hours, seven daily), Porto Torres (€1.50, 35 minutes, hourly) and Castelsardo (€2.50, one hour, 11 Monday to Saturday).

For Olbia port, **Turmo Travel** (☎0789 214 87; www.gruppoturmotravel.com) has two daily buses (€6.50, 1½ hours).

Car & Motorcycle

Sassari is located on the SS131 highway linking Porto Torres to Cagliari. From Alghero, take the road north towards Porto Torres and then the SS291 east to Sassari. You take the same route from Fertilia airport.

A host of car-hire outlets is based at Fertilia airport. In Sassari itself, you can pick up wheels at **Eurorent** (☎079 23 23 35; www.rent.it; Via Roma 56) and **Maggiore** (☎079 23 55 07; Piazza Santa Maria 6).

Train

The main train station is just beyond the western end of the old town on Piazza Stazione. Direct trains run to Cagliari (€13.75, 4¼ hours, four daily), Oristano (€8.75, 2½ hours, five daily) and Olbia (€6.35, one hour 50 minutes, four daily).

Once a week, between the end of June and early September, the **Trenino Verde** (www.tren inoverde.com) departs from Sassari for the slow panoramic ride to Tempio Pausania (€12.50, two hours 35 minutes).

ℹ Getting Around

To/From the Airport

Up to five daily buses run from the bus station on Via XXV Aprile to Fertilia airport (€3.50, 30 minutes). A further three depart from the stop on Via Turati.

For the Aeroporto Olbia Costa Smeralda you'll need to catch the train/bus to Olbia and then the city bus to the airport.

Bus

ATP (☎079 263 80 00; www.aptsassari.it, in Italian) orange buses run along most city routes, although you're unlikely to need one in the small city centre. In summer they also run to beaches north of Sassari from the terminus on Via Eugenio Tavolara. Tickets cost €0.80 on city routes and €1.10 for the Buddi Buddi beach line.

Car & Motorcycle

Parking in Sassari is generally a nightmare. Within blue lines, hourly rates cost up to €2 for the first two hours and €1 for each hour thereafter. Get tickets from traffic wardens or newsagents.

Taxi

You can catch a taxi from ranks on Emiciclo Giuseppe Garibaldi or along Viale Italia and Via Matteotti. To phone for one, call **Taxi Sassari** (☎079 25 39 39).

AROUND SASSARI

The most scenic route from Sassari to the coast is the SS200, lined with umbrella pines standing sentry as it passes through the twin market towns of **Sennori** and **Sorso**. These towns are famous for their wine and together produce the sweet Moscato di Sorso-Sennori. A good place to try some is the well-known restaurant Da Vito (☎079 36 02 45; Via Napoli 14; meals around €40) in Sennori, which serves delicious seasonal food.

On weekends the Sassaresi abandon the city for the long sandy beaches at **Platamona Lido**. This is a cheerful and, on summer weekends, crowded spot known optimistically as the Sassari Riviera.

Regular summer buses run from Sassari up to a point just east of Platamona and then the length of coast as far as Marina di Sorso. Take the Buddi Buddi bus (line MP) from Via Eugenio Tavolara.

Midway between Sassari and Porto Torres, 11km along the SS131, you'll find a signpost for the temple of **Monte d'Accoddi** (admission €3.10; ⊙9am-8pm Apr-Sep, to 4.30pm Oct-Mar), built in the 3rd millennium BC. Nowhere else in the Mediterranean has such a structure been unearthed – the closest comparable buildings are the fabled ziggurats of the Euphrates and Tigris River valleys in the Middle East. Excavations have revealed there was a Neolithic village here as early as 4500 BC. The temple went through several phases and appears to have been abandoned around 1800 BC. Soon after, the first *nuraghe* began to be raised.

Unfortunately, you don't actually see anything like the Mayan temple you might be imagining. Instead you can just make out a rectangular-based structure (30m by 38m), tapering to a platform and preceded by a long ramp. On either side of the ramp are a menhir and a stone altar believed to be for sacrifices.

THE LOGUDORO & MONTE ACUTO

Extending south and east of Sassari, this fertile area has been inhabited since nuraghic times and is rich in archaeological interest. It was an important granary for the Roman Empire and still today the landscape is a patchwork of rugged slopes and golden wheat fields – the name Logudoro means 'place of gold'. As the medieval Giudicato del Logudoro, it enjoyed a medieval heyday, and it's to this period that many of the area's impressive churches date. In the heart of the region is the *comune* of Monte Acuto, a collection of village communities sharing a common mountain heritage. You'll find www.monteacuto.it (in Italian) a useful website.

It's not an immediately alluring area, but if you've got a car, you'll find it rewards a little exploration.

Ozieri

POP 11,100

A prosperous agricultural town, Ozieri sits in a natural hollow, its 19th-century centre sloping upwards from a striking central piazza. The surrounding hills were once home to a number of thriving Neolithic settlements and the town has lent its name to a period in prehistory – the Ozieri (or San Michele) culture, which spanned the millennium between 3500 and 2700 BC.

You can investigate the town's rich archaeological legacy at the wonderful **Museo Archeologico** (079 785 10 52; Piazza Micca; admission €3.50, incl Grotta di San Michele €5; 9am-1pm & 4-7pm Tue-Sat, 9.30am-12.30pm Sun), one of Sardinia's best small museums. Housed in the Convento di Clarisse, an 18th-century convent, it has a small but rich collection, including a couple of copper ingots (nuraghic settlements were trading copper as far back as the neolithic age), some surprisingly modern-looking tools, and a selection of fine ceramic fragments found in the **Grotta di San Michele** (079 785 10 52; admission €3.50, incl Museo Archeologico €5; 9am-1pm Fri & Sat, 9.30am-12.30pm Sun), itself well worth a visit. The *grotta,* signposted from

---

THE CHURCHES OF THE LOGUDORO

The **Basilica della Santissima Trinità di Saccargia** (Comune di Codrongianus; admission €1.50; 9am-8pm Jun-Aug, to 6.30pm Sep, to 6pm May, to 5.30pm Oct, to 5pm Apr, to 4.30pm Mar) lies in the centre of a fertile valley, just 15km southeast of Sassari along the SS597 Olbia road. You can't miss its stripy limestone and basalt *campanile,* which dominates the horizon as you approach. Legend has it that it was built by the Giudice Constantino di Mariano in 1116, after he and his wife camped the night here and received a revelation that they were to have their first longed-for child. The delighted Giudice built the church and a neighbouring monastery, which the pope gave to the Camaldolite monks. Little remains of the monastery, although the dramatically simple church with its blind basalt walls is still in use.

A further 3km down the road you'll see the abandoned **Chiesa di San Michele e Sant'Antonio di Salvènero** at the road junction to Ploaghe, but continue to Ardara, 10km further on. It was once the capital of the Giudicato di Torres, and a quick turn to the left as you enter the town will bring you face to face with the brooding mass of the **Chiesa di Santa Maria del Regno**, made of greying basalt. One of its oddest features is the squat *campanile,* finished in a rough-and-ready manner after the church was completed and not at all typical of the style.

Further east along the SS597 you'll see a turn-off for the majestically ruined 11th- to 12th-century **Chiesa di Sant'Antioco di Bisarcio** (079 78 02 57; admission €1.50; 9am-4pm Sat & Sun, other days on request), 2km north of the highway. The *campanile* was decapitated by a burst of lightning, and much of the facade's decoration has been lost, but the uniquely French-inspired porch and interior convey the impression of its one-time grandeur.

From here continue along the SS597 and see the tiny **Chiesa di Nostra Signora di Castro** on the banks of the Lago di Coghinas, or head north along the winding SS132 to **Chiesa di San Pietro di Simbranos** (or delle Immagini) at Bulzi and the **Chiesa di San Giorgio** at Perfugas.

If you're planning this tour, the hotel **Funtanarena** (079 43 50 48; www.funtanarena .it; Via S'Istradoneddu 8/10; s €63-70, d €94-105; P) is a convenient, and delightful, place to stay. In the small village of Codrongianos, 14km from Sassari, it's housed in a refurbished manor house surrounded by fragrant fruit trees and olive groves. The nine country-style rooms are furnished with framed prints of flowers, wrought-iron beds and parquet floors.

MONTE LERNO

About 8km east of Ozieri, **Lago Lerno** presents a bucolic picture. Although an artificial lake – it was created in 1984 by damming the Rio Mannu – it fits perfectly into the surrounding scenery with grassy slopes gently rising from the still waters and rocky **Monte Lerno** (1094m) looming in the near distance. Nearby, deer, mouflon and wild horses roam in the **Bosco di Monte Lerno** (Monte Lerno Wood). To get to the wood, pass Ozieri, enter Pattada, some 4km east, and once out of Pattada, follow the road for Oschiri. After about 11km, turn right and continue over the Rio Mannu into the northwest reaches of the forest.

the top of town, was used as a habitation as well as a tomb and place of cult worship.

Not far from the museum, Ozieri's bombastic **Cattedrale dell'Immacolata** (Piazza Duomo) harbours an important work of art, the *Deposizione di Cristo dalla Croce* (Deposition of Christ from the Cross), by the enigmatic Maestro di Ozieri.

During December Ozieri hosts one of the island's major poetry competitions, the **Premio di Ozieri**. It started in 1956, inspired by the *gare poetiche* (poetry wars) that took place informally at local festivals, and now showcases the work of Italian and Sardinian poets.

For a bite to eat, **Ristorante Pizzeria L'Opera** (☎079 78 70 26; Piazza Garibaldi; meals €30) serves pizzas and excellent lamb chops in a strange concert-hall setting.

By public transport the easiest way to get to Ozieri is by bus from Sassari (€4, one hour, five Monday to Saturday). These drop you off near Piazza Garibaldi.

Nuraghe Santu Antine & Around

Heading west from Ozieri, you pass through **Mores**, to the south of which lies the majestic **Dolmen Sa Coveccada**, said to be the largest dolmen (a megalithic chambered tomb) in the Mediterranean. Dating to the end of the 3rd millennium BC, the rectangular construction consists of three massive stone slabs, roofed by a fourth, weighing around 18 tonnes. As it stands, it reaches a height of 2.7m, is 5m long and 2.5m wide. To find it, take the exit just before you enter Mores from the east and follow the road for a further 10km or so.

From Mores follow the road for **Torralba**, an unremarkable village at the head of the Valle dei Nuraghi (Valley of the Nuraghi). The land around here is scattered with prehistoric *nuraghi*, but pride of place goes to the **Nuraghe Santu Antine** (☎079 84 72 96; www.nuraghesantuantine.it; admission €3; ☉9am-sunset), 4km south of the village. One of the largest nuraghic sites in Sardinia, it is focused on a central tower, now standing at 17.5m but which originally rose to a height of 25m. Around this, walls link three bastions and enclose a triangular compound. Its oldest parts date to around 1600 BC, but much of it was built over successive centuries.

You enter the compound from the southern side and can walk through the three towers, connected by rough parabolic archways. The entrance to the main tower is separate. Inside, four openings lead into the chamber from an internal hall. Stairs lead up from the hall to the next floor, where a similar but smaller pattern is reproduced. Apart from tiny vents there is no light, and the presence of the dark stone is overwhelming. You ascend another set of steps to reach the floor of what was the final, third chamber, now open to the elements.

Back in Torralba, the **Museo Archeologico** (☎079 84 72 96; Via Carlo Felice 143; admission incl Nuraghe Santu Antine €3; ☉9am-8pm summer, to 5pm winter) has a scale model of the *nuraghe* and a modest collection of finds lifted from the site.

On weekdays there are up to nine buses from Sassari to Torralba (€2.50, 1½ hours). To get to the *nuraghe* from there you'll have to walk (about 4km).

BORUTTA

On the map it' a fairly straightforward drive up to the village of Borutta, but in practice it can be confusing – signs point you in the right direction and then abandon you to your navigational instincts. It's worth persevering, as Borutta boasts a fine example of Romanesque architecture, the **Chiesa di San Pietro Sorres** (☎334 853 77 51;

admission €2.50; ⊘guided visits 8.30am-noon & 3.30-6.30pm Mon-Sat, 9.30-10.30am & 3.30-6.30pm Sun).

The original 12th-century Pisan church and adjacent abbey had long been abandoned when a community of Benedictine monks moved here in 1955. They soon got busy, rebuilding the abbey and scrubbing the church into shape. The white-and-grey banded facade has three levels of blind arches and is decorated with some lovely elaborate stonework. Of note inside is an intriguing stone Gothic pulpit set on four legs.

NECROPOLI DI SANT'ANDREA PRIU & AROUND

About 7km east of Bonorva, a ridge-top farming town just off the main SS131, the Necropoli di Sant'Andrea Priu (☑348 564 26 11; admission €3.50; ⊘10am-1pm & 3-5.30pm, to 7.30pm summer) lies in the thick of lush, verdant countryside. An isolated site, acces-sible by a narrow potholed road, it is made up of around 20 small grottoes carved into the trachyte and dating as far back as 4000 BC. The **Tomba del Capo**, accessible only with a guide, is by far the most interesting. In the early Christian period three of the main rooms were transformed into a place of worship, and partly restored frescoes from the 5th century survive in two of them. Most striking is the fresco of a woman in the *aula* (hall) where the faithful heard Mass.

On the road back up to Bonorva, it's worth taking an hour or so to stop off at **Rebeccu**, a windswept and largely abandoned medieval hamlet carved into calcareous rock. The village, signposted off to the left, is the unlikely setting for a film festival in mid-August.

Getting around this area without your own transport is well-nigh impossible, although a few buses run from Sassari to Bonorva (€4, 70 minutes, five on weekdays).

Olbia, the Costa Smeralda & the Gallura

Best Places to Eat

» Ristorante Gallura (p143)

» Spinnaker (p150)

» Trattoria Gallurese (p163)

» La Vecchia Costa (p150)

Best Places to Stay

» B&B Lu Pastruccialeddu (p209)

» Hotel Panorama (p207)

» B&B Petite Maison (p210)

» La Villa Giulia (p208)

» Agriturismo Ca' La Somara (p209)

Why Go?

Costa Smeralda evokes Sardinia's classic images: pearly-white beaches and weird, wind-whipped licks of rock tapering into emerald seas. The stretch of dazzling coast that the Aga Khan bought for a pittance in the 1960s is today the playground of millionaires and A-listers. Come summer, the scandal-hungry paparazzi haunt the marinas, zooming in on oligarchs cavorting with bikini-clad beauties on yachts so big they eclipse the sun.

A few kilometres' drive inland and you could be on another island entirely: here vine-striped hills roll to deeply traditional villages and mysterious *nuraghe* (Bronze Age fortified settlements), silent cork-oak woods and granite mountains. Immune to time and trends, the hinterland is a refreshing contrast to the coast. Hide away in a country *agriturismo* (farm stay) for a few days to appreciate a very different version of the good life.

Further north the Gallura coast becomes wilder, the preserve of the dolphins, divers and windsurfers who splash around in the startlingly blue waters of La Maddalena marine reserve.

When to Go

Room rates and temperatures soar in summer, when beach-goers, yachties and families flock to the coast, particularly the Costa Smeralda. Spring is a great time to visit: days are mild, wildflowers cloak Gallura's granite interior and the coast is quiet. Taste top-notch Vermentino whites at the wine festivals in Porto Cervo in May and Monti in August. Tempio Pausania hosts pre-Lenten carnival parades and Aggius solemn Easter processions. Surfers come for winter waves and sailors for summertime regattas.

OLBIA

POP 54,900

Often ignored in the mad dash to the Costa Smeralda, Olbia has more to offer than first meets the eye. Look beyond its industrial outskirts and you'll find a fetching city with a *centro storico* (historic centre) crammed with boutiques, wine bars and cafe-rimmed piazzas. Olbia is a refreshingly authentic and affordable alternative to the purpose-built resorts stretching to the north and south.

History

Archaeological evidence has revealed the existence of human settlement in Sardinia's

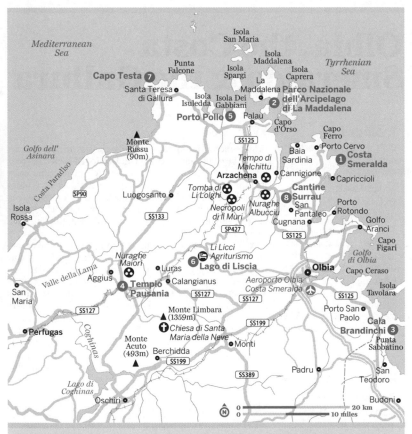

Olbia, the Costa Smeralda & the Gallura Highlights

① Hang out with the bronzed, beautiful and superfamous on the **Costa Smeralda** (p149)

② Island-hop around the **Parco Nazionale dell'Arcipelago di La Maddalena** (p159) and dive into its jewel-coloured waters

③ Lounge on the frosty white sands of **Cala**

Brandinchi (see boxed text, p148), nicknamed 'Little Tahiti'

④ Explore the endless cork forests around **Tempio Pausania** (p162)

⑤ Go with the wind and take to the wild waters off **Porto Pollo** (p157)

⑥ Swap the glamour of the coast for the

haunting silence of **Lago di Liscia** (p154)

⑦ Clamber the weirdly sculptured boulders of **Capo Testa** (p157)

⑧ Taste crisp Vermentino whites and rich Cannonau reds in contemporary winery **Cantine Surrau** (see boxed text, p151)

northeast in the mid-neolithic period (about 4000 BC), but Olbia was almost certainly founded by the Carthaginians in the 4th or 5th century BC. Certainly Carthaginians had been present in the area since the mid-6th century BC as proved by their participation in the Battle of Mare Sardo (a naval battle between Greek colonists from Corsica and a combined Etruscan and Carthaginian fleet in 538 BC, considered by some to be the first ever naval battle in Western waters).

Under the Romans, Olbia became an important military and commercial port – a dozen or so relics of Roman vessels were unearthed in the 1990s. Known as Civita, it went on to become the capital of the Giudicato di Gallura, one of the four independent kingdoms that encompassed Sardinia in the 12th and 13th centuries. But when the Catalano-Aragonese took control, decline set in. Not until the arrival of the highways and railway in the 19th century did the town show signs of life again. The surrounding area was slowly drained and turned over to agriculture and some light industry, and the port was cranked back into operation. Now as a working industrial centre and joint capital of the recently formed Olbia-Tempio province, Olbia is thriving.

◉ Sights

To the south of Corso Umberto, the tightly packed warren of streets that represents the original fishing village has a certain charm, particularly in the evening when the cafes and trattorias fill with groups of hungry locals. A stroll along the *corso,* culminating in a drink on Piazza Margherita, is an agreeable way to spend the evening.

Museo Archeologico MUSEUM
(Isolotto di Peddone; admission free; ⊙10am-1pm Mon-Fri, also 4-6pm Mon & Wed) Architect Vanni Macciocco designed Olbia's striking new museum near the port. The museum spells out local history in artefacts, from Roman amulets and pottery to nuraghic finds. The highlight is the relic of a Roman vessel discovered in the old port. A multimedia display recreates the scene of the Vandals burning and sinking such ships in AD 450.

Chiesa di San Simplicio CHURCH
(Via San Simplicio; ⊙7.30am-1pm & 3.30-6pm) Considered to be Gallura's most important medieval monument, this Romanesque granite church was built in the late 11th and early 12th centuries on what was then the

	Arzachena	Olbia	Porto Cervo	Santa Teresa di Gallura
Olbia	22			
Porto Cervo	18	25		
Santa Teresa di Gallura	27	49	45	
San Teodoro	49	27	52	76

edge of town. It is a curious mix of Tuscan and Lombard styles with little overt decoration other than a couple of 13th-century frescoes depicting medieval bishops.

Chiesa di San Paolo CHURCH
(Via Cagliari) Another granite church worth a look is the 18th-century Chiesa di San Paolo, spectacularly topped by a Valencian-style multicoloured tiled dome (added after WWII).

🎊 Festivals & Events

During July and August, outdoor concerts are staged in the city centre as part of the **L'Estate Olbiese**, a cultural festival that includes concerts, performances, readings and cabarets.

✕ Eating

The bulk of the hotels, restaurants and bars are crowded into the web of narrow streets to either side of Corso Umberto. Cafe life centres on Piazza Margherita and Piazza Matteotti.

Ristorante Gallura SARDINIAN €€€
(☎0789 2 46 48; Corso Umberto 145; meals €40-60; ⊙Tue-Sun) Rita runs a tight ship at the homely Gallura, one of northern Sardinia's best restaurants. Fresh, seasonal and local ingredients go into specialities like sea anemones fried in yoghurt, pasta with cuttlefish ink and wild oysters, and suckling pig perfumed with myrtle – all perfectly cooked and utterly delicious. Reservations are essential.

Officina del Gusto MODERN ITALIAN €€
(☎0789 2 87 01; Piazza Matteotti 1; meals €40-50; ⊙lunch & dinner winter, dinner only summer) Housed in a 19th-century palazzo, this monochrome restaurant is a classy little number. Flavours are clean and bright, with an emphasis on fresh fish and homemade pasta. Eat alfresco by the olive tree on the square in summer.

Olbia

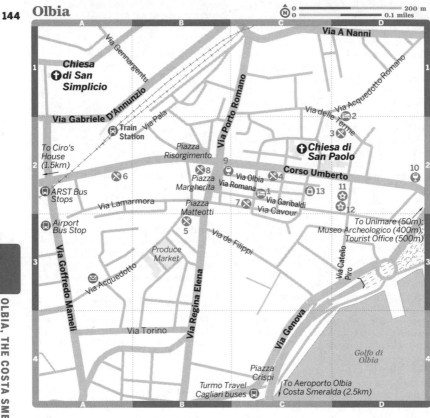

La Lanterna
TRADITIONAL ITALIAN €€

(☏0789 2 30 82; Via Olbia 13; pizzas €6-10, meals around €30; ☺Thu-Tue winter, daily summer) The Lanterna distinguishes itself with its cosy subterranean setting and beautifully fresh food. Start off with sweet and sour sardines and move on to almond-crusted bream served with handmade *gnochetti*.

Ristorante da Paolo
SARDINIAN €€

(☏0789 2 16 75; enter from Via Garibaldi 18 or Via Cavour 22; meals around €30; ☺Mon-Sat) Stone walls, timber ceilings and coastal paintings set the scene at this cheerful restaurant. Take a seat for soul food like Gallurese soups, *risotto ai funghi* (mushroom risotto) and handmade gnocchi.

Pizzeria del Corso
SNACKS €

(Corso Umberto 181; snacks €1.50-3; ☺Mon-Sat) A cheerful pizza and focaccia pit stop near the station, with smiley staff and rock-bottom prices.

Antica Trattoria
ITALIAN €€

(☏0789 2 40 53; Via delle Terme 1; meals €25-30; ☺Tue-Sun) Tucked behind Chiesa di San Paolo, this place has an appetising antipasti buffet, pizza, pasta and fail-safe meat dishes.

🍷 Drinking & Entertainment

Enoteca Vignando
WINE BAR

(www.enotecavignando.com, in Italian; Corso Umberto 2; ☺closed Sun winter) Bottles line the walls at this inviting wine bar. Snag a barrel table to taste Sardinian wines from Vermentinos to Cannonaus, together with a tasting plate of local cheese and salami.

Enoteca Cosimino
WINE BAR

(Piazza Margherita 3; ☺daily) This popular cafe serves coffee and *cornetti* (croissants) by day, but in the evening it morphs into an elegant wine bar with cocktails and *vino* on the menu.

Olbia

Pepe Bianco   LIVE MUSIC
(☑338 706 3027; Via Catello Piro 8) Olbia's beautiful people flock to this oh-so-chic lounge barcum-restaurant for dinner (meals around €25), DJs and occasional live Latin music.

Pascia   CLUB
(Via Catello Piro) Sidling up to Pepe Bianco, this is the go-to club for house-driven fun and a dressy lounge scene.

🛍 Shopping

Corso Umberto is a catwalk to designer labels and stylish Italian fashion. Explore its side streets for arts, crafts and Sardinian specialities.

Anticas Licanzias   SWEETS & PASTRY
(Via Olbia 42; ⊘closed Sun morning) Stop by this fabulous patisserie for bread fresh from a wood oven, *pane carasau* (Sardinian flatbread), and delectable Sardinian sweets laced with almonds and honey. There's also a first-class selection of wine, handmade pasta and olive oil.

❶ Information

You'll find banks with ATMs on Corso Umberto.
Inter Smeraldo (☑0789 2 53 66; Via Porto

Romano 8b; per hr €5; ⊘9.45am-1.15pm & 4-8.30pm Mon-Sat) A busy internet cafe with 10 terminals.
Post office (Via Aquedotto 5)
Tourist office (☑0789 55 77 32; www.olbia tempioturismo.it; Via Alessandro Nanni 39; ⊘8am-8pm Mon-Sat & 8am-2pm Sun summer, 8am-6pm Mon-Fri, 8am-2pm Sat winter) This helpful tourist office has stacks of info and brochures on Olbia and the surrounding region.
Unimare (☑070 2 35 24; www.unimare.it; Via Principe Umberto 1; ⊘8.30am-12.30pm & 3.30-7.30pm Mon-Fri, 8.30am-12.30pm Sat) A central travel agent where you can book ferries and flights.

❶ Getting There & Away

Air

Olbia's **Aeroporto Olbia Costa Smeralda** (OLB; ☑0789 56 34 44; www.geasar.it) is about 5km southeast of the centre. At the time of research, 60 airlines were operating flights into the airport, including Alitalia, Iberia, Lufthansa, Meridiana and the low-cost operators Air Berlin, easyJet and Niki. Destinations served include most mainland Italian airports as well as London, Paris, Madrid, Barcelona, Hamburg, Amsterdam, Vienna and Prague.

Boat

Olbia's ferry terminal, Stazione Marittima, is on Isola Bianca, an island connected to the town centre by the 1km causeway, Banchina Isola Bianca. All the major ferry companies have counters here, including **Grandi Navi Veloci** (☑010 209 45 91; www.gnv.it), **Moby Lines** (☑199 30 30 40; www.mobylines.it), **SNAV** (☑081 428 55 55; www.snav.it) and **Tirrenia** (☑892 123; www.tirrenia.it). There are frequent services – especially during the summer months – to Civitavecchia, Genoa, Livorno and Piombino.

You can book tickets at any travel agent in town, or directly at the port. For timetable information and fare details see boxed text, p258.

Bus

Azienda Regionale Sarda Trasporti (ARST; ☑800 865 042; www.arst.sardegna.it, in Italian) buses run from Olbia to destinations across the island. Get tickets from **Café Adela** (Corso Vittorio Veneto 2; ⊘5am-10pm), just over the road from the main bus stops. Destinations include Arzachena (€2.50, 45 minutes, 12 daily) and Porto Cervo (€3.50, 1½ hours, five daily). Further afield you can get to Nuoro (€9, 2½ hours, eight daily), Santa Teresa di Gallura (€5, 1½ hours, seven daily) and Sassari (€7, 1½ hours, two daily) via Tempio Pausania (€3.50, 1¼ hours, seven daily). There are fewer connections on Sunday.

Turmo Travel (☎0789 2 14 87; www.gruppo turmotravel.com) runs two buses each weekday from Cagliari (€19, 4½ hours), arriving in Piazza Crispi; one continues to Santa Teresa di Gallura. Another daily bus runs from the port to Sassari (€12, 1½ hours). Get tickets at Stazione Marittima or on the bus.

Car & Motorcycle

Car hire is available at the airport, where all the big international outfits are represented, and at the Stazione Marittima ferry terminal. Bank on about €50 per day for a Fiat Punto.

Train

The station is off Corso Umberto. One train a day runs directly to Cagliari (€16.90, four hours). Otherwise you change at Chilivani, 70 minutes, eight daily) and sometimes Macomer as well. Up to three trains run to Sassari (€7.35, two hours) and up to six to Golfo Aranci (€2.35, 25 minutes).

❶ Getting Around

You are unlikely to need local buses, except for getting to the airport and Stazione Marittima. You can buy tickets at tobacconists and some bars.

To/From the Airport

Local bus 2 (€1 or €1.50 if ticket is bought on board) runs half hourly between 6.15am and 11.40pm from the airport to Via Goffredo Mameli in the centre. A **taxi** (☎0789 6 91 50) costs €15.

Several buses for destinations around the island depart from the airport, including a service for Nuoro run by **Deplano** (☎0784 29 50 30; www.deplanobus.it), which operates five times a day from June to September. Tickets cost €12 and journey time is 1¾ hours.

Bus

Local buses are run by **ASPO** (☎0789 55 38 56; www.aspo.it). Bus 9 (€1) runs every half hour between Stazione Marittima and the town centre (Via San Simplicio).

Car & Motorcycle

Driving in Olbia is no fun thanks to a confusing one-way system and almost permanent roadworks. The main strip, Corso Umberto, is closed to traffic between Piazza Margherita and Via Goffredi Mameli. Metered parking (€1 per hour from 8am to 8pm) is available around Olbia, and there is limited free parking by the port – follow the signs.

Taxi

You can sometimes find taxis on Corso Umberto near Piazza Margherita. Otherwise call ☎0789 6 91 50 or ☎0789 2 27 18.

AROUND OLBIA

Olbia's main beach is the busy **Lido del Sole** (catch bus 5), which is about 6km east of the airport off the main southbound road, the SS125. It's fine for a swim, but far preferable is the swath of white sand at **Pittulongu** or **Sos Aranzos** to the north of town.

Golfo Aranci

POP 2400

Perched on the northern tip of the Golfo di Olbia, Golfo Aranci is a port, low-key resort and fishing village rolled into one. Most people blaze through without a second glance, but it's worth considering as a cheaper alternative to the Costa Smeralda, especially if activities like diving, speargun fishing and dolphin-spotting rock your boat.

◉ Sights & Activities

There are three sandy white beaches in town – **Spiaggia Primo**, **Secondo** and the best of the three, **Terzo** (they're translated to First Beach, Second and Third), and with your own transport you can easily get to others. It's also well equipped for families, with a number of public parks and well maintained playgrounds.

Capo Figaro   NATURE RESERVE
Rising up behind the port are the craggy heights of Capo Figaro (340m), which is now a minor nature reserve. Trails crisscross the *macchia* (Mediterranean scrub), and they lead up to an abandoned lighthouse on the summit, known as *il vecchio semaforo* (old traffic light). It was from here that Guglielmo Marconi sent the first radio signal to the Italian mainland in 1928.

Alpha Diving   DIVE CENTRE
(☎0789 4 60 12; www.alphadiving.it; Piazzetta dei Pescatori 4) Operating out of the port, this ESA-accredited diving outfit will set you up for dives around Cape Figaro and Tavolara. A single dive will set you back around €40, a new-diver course €230.

✖ Eating

Seafood features heavily in the restaurants lined up on and around Via della Liberta. Nearly everywhere closes from November to March.

FLIPPER & CO

For a truly memorable experience, join the **Bottlenose Diving Research Institute** (⏱0789 183 11 97; www.thebdri.com; Via Diaz 4, Golfo Aranci) on one of its half-day cruises to spot (and learn about) the playful bottlenose dolphins that splash around in these waters. While sightings aren't guaranteed, the odds are excellent. Budget around €70/50 per adult/child for the four- to five-hour expedition.

La Cortice SEAFOOD €
(⏱338 6214685; www.lacortice.it; Piazza del Porto; meals €15-28; ⊙closed Mon-Wed winter) Aquatic murals jazz up this *ittiturismo* by the port, dishing up good-value fish and shellfish. As it's run by a fishing cooperative, everything is incredibly fresh. If you fancy hooking your own, ask about their fishing trips in the gulf.

La Spigola SEAFOOD €€
(⏱0789 4 62 86; Via Colombo 19; meals around €30; ⊙daily) Skip the rest and go straight for the grilled fish and seafood at this friendly beachside restaurant. Bag a table on the terrace for breezy sea views.

❶ Getting There & Away

Between June and September six daily ARST buses link Golfo Aranci with Olbia (€2, 25 minutes). Trains (€2.35, 25 minutes) also cover the same route, running six times daily year-round.

Sardinia Ferries (⏱199 400 500; www.sardiniaferries.com) operate frequent daily ferries between Livorno (€53 to €76, six to 10 hours) and Civitavecchia (€54 to €79, 3½ to 6¾ hours) to Golfo Aranci.

SOUTH COAST

The coast reaching south of Olbia is peppered with resorts that heave in summer and slumber in winter. Typical of the type is Porto San Paolo, the main embarkation point for Isola Tavolara, and 11km further south, party-loving San Teodoro.

Porto San Paolo & Isola Tavolara

POP 3200

Porto San Paolo's major attraction lies offshore. Unless you've booked a holiday apartment here, the one real reason to stop off is to catch a boat for Isola Tavolara. Rising from the sapphire sea like some kind of giant sea creature, the rocky island is a sight to behold.

At Easter time, and from mid-July to September, **boat excursions** depart from the port. Outward-bound boats leave half hourly between 9am and 3pm, and return trips set off on the hour between 12.30pm and 6.30pm. The return trip (25 minutes each way) costs €12.50 per person, but longer cruises taking in the smaller Isola Molara and Isola Piana will set you back €25 a head.

The Isola used to be known as the Island of Hermes, perhaps because you need wings to reach the plateau (565m), which is inhabited only by sea birds and falcons, as well as a few nimble-footed wild goats. The few people who live here reside on the western side on the **Spalmatore di Terra**, where the boats land.

Aside from snacking at a couple of beachside eateries, there is nothing much to do but splash about in the translucent water of the white-sand **Spiaggia Spalmatore**, and admire the incredible views of Tavolara's heights and mainland Sardinia. You could wander down to the little cemetery to see the graves of Tavolara's kings (the title was bestowed by Carlo Alberto in 1848 after a successful goat-hunting trip), each marked with a crown.

Tavolara's craggy coves and crystal-clear waters present some wonderful diving opportunities around the underwater mountain of Secca del Papa. If you're interested, you can arrange dives with **Centro Sub Tavolara** (⏱0789 4 03 60; www.centrosubtavolara.com; Via Molara 4). Reckon on €45 for a single dive.

Back on the mainland, there's not much to hold you in San Paolo, but if you're hungry you can grab a wood-fired pizza at **Cala di Junco** (⏱0789 4 02 60; Via Nenni 8/10; pizza €4-12; ⊙Wed-Mon) before heading off. Or for dreamy sunset views of Isola Tavolara, book a table at **Il Portolano** (Via Molara 11; meals around €40; ⊙closed Wed), a chic waterfront place serving up great antipasti and fresh fish.

San Teodoro

POP 4300

Fun-loving San Teodoro lives to party in summer, its glam beach bars and clubs providing an affordable alternative to the megabucks Costa Smeralda. The model resort is perfect, almost to the point of characterlessness, but its pristine white-sand beaches are glorious. Watersports and boat excursions race you out to sea, while back on dry land trekking, mountain biking and horse riding entice you away from the beach towel.

◉ Sights & Activities

Stagno San Teodoro   NATURE RESERVE
Nestled amid fragrant *macchia* (Mediterranean scrub) and wind-eroded granite formations, and backing onto La Cinta beach, this lagoon attracts ramblers and birdwatchers. Keep an eye out for bird life including pink flamingos, herons, cormorants, little egrets and kingfishers.

Wetdreams   WATER SPORTS
(☑0784 85 20 15; www.wetdreams.it; Via Sardegna) A surf shop on the beach, Wetdreams offers three-hour introductory kitesurfing sessions for €190.

Maneggio La Cinta   HORSE RIDING
(☑0784 85 10 07; Località La Cinta; ⋒) You can saddle up here for a scenic 1½-hour hack (€30) along La Cinta beach.

✕ Eating

Bear in mind that nearly everywhere closes from mid-October to March.

Bal Harbour   ITALIAN €€
(☑0784 85 10 52; www.balharbour.it; Via Stintino; meals €30-40; ☷11am-3am) This supertrendy beachside lounge-restaurant attracts gym-fit guys and girls, who come to pose by the palm-fringed pool by day and sip mojitos to DJ beats by night. The food is surprisingly good, whether you go for a sizzling steak from the Brazilian grill or lighter Italian dishes such as seafood risotto.

La Taverna degli Artisti   ITALIAN €€
(☑0784 86 60 60; Via del Tirreno 17; pizzas €5-9, meals around €30) Great seafood and service are on the menu here. Follow garlicky mussels with handmade tagliatelle with scampi and pesto or salt-crusted sea bass. There's also pizza to take away.

🍷 Drinking & Entertainment

San Teodoro is the south coast's party central, its lounge bars and clubs attracting the young, bronzed and beautiful in summer.

Buddha del Mar   BAR
(Piazza Gallura 2) Summer evenings at this Asian-inspired lounge can resemble an MTV beach party, with the fun fuelled by dancing, cocktails and good vibes.

L'Ambra Night   CLUB
(www.ambranight.it, in Italian; Via Cala d'Ambra) Down by the beach, opposite Hotel L'Esagono, this smart disco with an outdoor dance floor rocks to a mainly commercial beat.

Luna Glam Club   CLUB
(www.lalunadisco.com, in Italian; Località Stirritoggiu) Dress to impress the eagle-eyed bouncers and fit in with the glossy 30-plus crowd at this ubertrendy club. It's just south of town, off the exit road from the SS125.

ℹ Information

The efficient **tourist office** (☑0784 86 57 67; www.santeodoroturismo.it; Piazza Mediterraneo 1; ☷9am-1pm & 4pm-midnight summer, 9am-1pm & 3-6pm winter) can provide information on local operators and tour guides. Another useful website is **www.visitsanteodoro.com**.

DON'T MISS

SAN TEODORO BEACHES

San Teodoro has some wonderful beaches, many of which can easily compete with the Costa Smeralda in the beauty stakes. Central **Cala d'Ambra** is pretty, but more striking still is **Spiaggia La Cinta**, a ribbon of frosty-white sand strung between the topaz sea and the Stagno San Teodoro. It's a popular sports beach, particularly for kitesurfing. Or take your beach towel further north to the stunning crescent-shaped bays of **Lu Impostu** and 'Little Tahiti' **Cala Brandinchi**, separated by a wooded spit of land. Commanding fine views of the limestone hump of Isola Tavolara, **Capo Coda Cavallo** is a marine reserve and its transparent waters bubble with snorkellers and divers.

OASI NATURALISTICA USINAVA

The **Oasi Naturalistica Usinava** (☑328 648 60 63; www.usinava.it, in Italian) is a cool escape from the summer crowds. Encompassing forests, conical peaks, water torrents and Mediterranean scrub, the nature reserve is a refuge for mouflon, wild boar, coots, grouse and hares. For a back-to-nature stay in the oasis, book a berth in one of the three *pinettos*, typical stone huts with thatched roofs. A night costs €25 per person.

To get to the oasis from Budoni, 10km south of San Teodoro, follow the road for Brunella, Talava, Su Cossu and Sos Rios. About 1.5km beyond Sos Rios you'll find the station of the forestry guard.

❶ Getting There & Away

ARST buses make the run up the coast to Olbia (€2.50, 40 minutes, six daily, up to nine on weekdays) and inland to Nuoro (€8, one hour 50 minutes, five daily). Deplano buses also run to/from Olbia airport (€4, 30 minutes, five daily) and Nuoro (€10, 1¼ hours, five daily).

COSTA SMERALDA & AROUND

Back in 1962 flamboyant millionaire Karim Aga Khan and some pals set up a consortium to buy a strip of beautiful, unspoilt coastline in northeastern Sardinia from struggling farmers. Each paid roughly US$25,000 for their little piece of paradise, and the coast was christened Costa Smeralda (Emerald Coast) for the brilliant green-blue hue of its waters.

What a difference 50 years makes. Today US$25,000 would get you (at a push) a night in the Presidential Suite at Hotel Cala di Volpe. Today billionaire jet-setters cruise into Costa Smeralda's marinas in mega-yachts like floating mansions, and models, royals, Russian oligarchs and balding media moguls come to frolic in its waters. Bill Gates and the Sultan of Brunei, Rooney and George Clooney have all been spotted here.

Starting at Porto Rotondo on the Golfo di Cugnana, about 17km north of Olbia, the Costa stretches for 55km northwards up to the Golfo di Arzachena. The 'capital' is the yachtie haven of Porto Cervo, although Porto Rotondo attracts its fair share of paparazzi attention as base of Silvio Berlusconi's island operations.

South of Porto Cervo

Despite its superficial fluff, the Costa Smeralda is quite stunning: the Gallura's granite mountains plunge into emerald waters in a succession of dramatic fjordlike inlets.

The Costa starts at the Golfo di Cugnana, the drive beginning with a spectacular view of **Porto Rotondo**, a second marina developed in 1963 following the success of Porto Cervo. Resembling an upmarket harbourside suburb of Sydney or San Francisco, Porto Rotondo is where Berlusconi maintains his main Sardinian residence, the pharaonic Villa Certosa. The resort's attractive seafront promenade is dotted with cafes, pizzerias and chichi lounge bars for sundown celeb-spotting.

Travelling north, look out for a turn-off to dreamy **Spiaggia Liscia Ruia**, shortly before reaching the grand Moorish fantasy that is the Hotel Cala di Volpe. Next along is **Capriccioli**, another splendid beach with crystalline waters and soft sand.

Beyond that you reach the curving **Spiaggia Romazzino**, named after the rosemary bushes that grow in such abundance. Nearby is one of the best beaches on the Costa, the hard-to-find **Spiaggia del Principe** (also called Portu Li Coggi). Apparently the Aga Khan's favourite, a magnificent crescent of white sand is bound by unspoilt green *macchia* (Mediterranean scrub) and Caribbean-blue waters. To find it, follow the signs for Hotel Romazzino, but before reaching the hotel, turn right at Via degli Asfodeli. Park your car at the barrier and then walk for the last half a kilometre or so.

Porto Cervo

POP 2100

Porto Cervo is a curious, artificial vision of Mediterranean beauty. The utopian village combines Greek, North African, Spanish and Italian architectural elements, and the overall effect is pseudo-Moorish with a touch of the Flintstones. Its perfectly manicured streets are strangely sterile and characterless. For apart from the magnificent coastal scenery that surrounds it, there's nothing remotely Sardinian about Porto Cervo. Instead, it resembles exactly what it is: a purpose-built leisure centre for the super-rich; a kind of Disneyland for Gucci-clad grown-ups.

◎ Sights & Activities

As nearly everyone in Porto Cervo has a boat (it has the best marine facilities on the island), most of the action takes place elsewhere during the day, in the paradisal inlets and on the silky beaches. Things begin to heat up in the early evening when the playboys and -girls come out to browse the boutiques and pose in the piazzas.

The place to be seen is the **Piazzetta**, a small square at the centre of a web of discreet shopping alleys. From the piazza, stairs lead to the **Sottopiazza** and **La Passeggiata**, both lined with fancy boutiques – Cartier, Gucci, Versace, Prada, Valentino, Moschino – you name it, they're all here.

Chiesa di Stella Maris   CHURCH
(Piazza Stella Maris) Perched above Porto Cervo is Michele Busiri Vici's surreal white church with a funnel-shaped bell tower. The church hosts classical-music concerts in the summer. Unsurprisingly, it's also done rather well in the donations department, receiving El Greco's impressive *Mater Dolorosa* as a Dutch aristocrat's bequest.

Louise Alexander Gallery   ART GALLERY
(www.louise-alexander.com; Via del Porto Vecchio 1; ☺May-Sep) Visit this gallery for temporary exhibitions showcasing works by contemporary artists. It also sells modern art, so if you're in the market for a Warhol or Lichtenstein drop them a line.

✖ Eating

Porto Cervo's best restaurants are a quick drive or taxi hop out of town.

TOP CHOICE La Vecchia Costa   SARDINIAN €
(☎0789 9 86 88; meals around €20; ☺daily) This big open-plan restaurant keeps it fresh, seasonal and affordable. Authentic fare such as *lorighittas* (twisted, ring-shaped pasta) in *porcini*-lamb sauce and *malloreddus* (Sardinian gnocchi) with crab and mullet roe make this place popular with the locals, so book ahead. It's a five-minute drive from town, on the SP59 between Arzachena and Porto Cervo.

Spinnaker   MODERN ITALIAN €€
(☎0789 9 12 26; www.ristorantespinnaker.com; Liscia di Vacca; meals €40-50; ☺closed Wed in low season) This fashionable restaurant buzzes with beautiful people, who come for the stylish ambience and fabulous seafood. Pair dishes like calamari with fresh artichokes or rock lobster with a local Vermentino white. The restaurant is on the road between Porto Cervo and Baia Sardinia.

I Frati Rossi   MODERN ITALIAN €€
(☎0789 9 43 95; www.fratirossi.it; Località Pantogia; meals around €45; ☺lunch & dinner Tue-Sun, Jan-Oct) This rustic-chic restaurant has sublime sea views from its hilltop perch, 3.5km south of Porto Cervo. Local ingredients shine in beautifully cooked and presented dishes such as black tagliatelle with squid and ripe cherry tomatoes. Follow the signs up a narrow country lane off the SP59.

La Petronilla   SARDINIAN €€
(☎0789 9 21 37; Via Sa Conca 42; meals around €40; ☺daily) Massimo's convivial restaurant feels a million miles away from the glamour of the Piazzetta. Take a seat amid the still lifes and model ships for fine marina views and great home cooking – try the house special, *spaghetti al granseola* (spider crab).

▼ Drinking & Entertainment

Porto Cervo's nightlife is a strictly summer-only scene. People-watching is one of the few affordable options, although the moment you sit down at a bar on the Piazzetta you'll be looking at around €10 for a drink. To get in on the real clubbing action, however, dress to impress and head a couple of kilometres south of town.

Lord Nelson   PUB
(Porto Cervo Marina; ☺5pm-3am daily) Strangely, for such a swish resort, one of the favourite drinking hang-outs is this nautically themed English-style pub.

Cafe Mediterraneo   CAFE, BAR
(Porto Cervo Marina; ☺8.30am-late daily) Overlooking the marina, this slick little cafe-bar is a relaxed spot to begin an evening with a frozen cocktail. Or come during the day for bruschetta, creative salads (around €8) and homemade gelati.

Sottovento   CLUB
(www.sottoventoclub.it,inItalian;LocalitàSottovento) Bono, Craig David and Denzel Washington

CANTINE SURRAU

Surrounded by vineyards and mountains, contemporary **Cantine Surrau** (☑0789 8 29 33; www.vignesurrau.it, in Italian; Località Chilvagghja; ⊕9am-11pm summer, 9am-8.30pm winter) takes a holistic approach to winemaking. You can take a spin around the cellar and admire Sardinian art in the gallery before tasting some of the region's crispest Vermentino white and beefiest Cannonau red wines. The standard tasting (€8) gets you three different wines served with *pane carasau* (Sardinian flatbread), while the €30 tasting consists of five different wines accompanied by local cheese, salami, *bottarga* (mullet roe) and Sardinian sweets. You'll find the winery on the road between Arzachena and Porto Cervo.

have all been spotted at this exclusive club. Getting in is no party and depends entirely on the whim of the stony-faced bouncers.

Billionaire　　　　　　　　　CLUB
(www.billionaireclub.it; Via Rocce sul Pevero) Opened by former Formula One boss Flavio Briatore in 1998, Billionaire's dance floor is like a who's who of the absurdly rich and famous. It's almost impossible to get in unless you happen to know someone or book dinner at the swank restaurant.

❶ Getting There & Away

ARST has up to five bus connections between Porto Cervo and Olbia (€3.50, 1½ hours).

Between June and September, **Sun Lines** (☑348 260 98 81) buses run at 7.30am, 12.30pm, 3.30pm and 6.30pm from Olbia airport to the Costa Smeralda, stopping at Porto Cervo and various other points along the coast. Tickets cost between €3 and €4.

Poltu Quatu

From Porto Cervo the coast road swings north and west around Capo Ferro headland to Poltu Quatu, a fjordlike inlet flanked by rugged granite cliffs. A jumble of whitewashed, terracotta-roofed villas centred on a picture-perfect marina, the resort is easier on the eye than many nearby resorts.

Shopping in the boutiques and galleries, dining alfresco and soaking up the views are the main activities. Or head to **Aqua Centre** (☑0789 9 90 01, www.orsodiving.com; ⊕Easter-Oct) to dive in the marine parks of La Maddalena and Tavolara (single dives from €45), snorkel in the fish-filled waters around Isola Caprera, or join a half-day whale-watching excursion (€100). The centre also offers the whole shebang of PADI courses.

Baia Sardinia

POP 200

Follow the meandering road 4km north of Poltu Quatu and you reach Baia Sardinia, just outside the Costa Smeralda but for all intents and purposes a Costa resort like its more famous neighbours. The main attraction here is the beach, **Cala Battistoni**, a sweep of fine sand lapped by remarkable blue waters. If you can't find any room on the sand but still fancy a swim – not to mention hair-raising rides and slides – the nearby **Aquadream** (☑0789 9 95 11; www .aquadream.it, in Italian; Località la Crucitta; adult/ child €18/12; ⊕10.30am-7pm mid-Jun–mid-Sep) fits the bill.

🍴 Eating & Drinking

Most places close from November to Easter.

Locanda del Tre Botti　　　SEAFOOD €€
(☑0789 99 1 50; Località Baia Sardinia; meals around €30; ⊕daily) On the road into town, this is a friendly, family-run affair. Opt for the terrace or the countrified dining room overlooking the Gulf of Arzachena. The seafood risotto and the mixed fish grill are spot-on.

News Café　　　　　　　　　CAFE €
(Piazza Centrale; ⊕8am-2am) In the seafront arcade, this central cafe is a popular meeting point and good for a quick bruschetta at lunchtime and live music and drinks by night.

☆ Entertainment

Phi Beach　　　　　　　　　BAR, CLUB
(www.phibeach.com; Forte Capellini) One of the coast's hottest venues, this is a great place to hang out and watch the sunset. By day it's a regular bathing club with sun-loungers and umbrellas to hire, but as the sun goes down

it transforms into a cool lounge bar and restaurant. All the while DJs spin chilled sounds in the background.

Ritual   CLUB
(www.ritual.it; Località La Crucitta) Just out of town on the road for Porto Cervo, this club is an old favourite. Even if you're not going to dance it's worth a look for the sexy cavernous interior gouged out of the rockside.

❶ Getting There & Away

From Olbia, the Sun Lines bus service to Porto Cervo continues on for 15 minutes to Baia Sardinia (see p151).

Cannigione

Some 12km southwest of Baia Sardinia, Cannigione sits on the western side of the Golfo di Arzachena, the largest *ria* (inlet) along this coast. Originally a fishing village established in 1800 to supply the Maddalena islands with food, it grew bigger when coal and cattle ships began to dock at its harbour in the 1900s and is now a prosperous, and reasonably priced, tourist town.

The helpful Ascor **tourist office** (✆0789 8 85 10; Via Nazionale 47; ◷9.30am-12.30pm & 5.30-7.30pm daily summer) has bags of information on Cannigione and the surrounding area.

Down at the port, there are various operators offering excursions to the Arcipelago di La Maddalena, including **Consorzio del Golfo** (✆0789 8 84 18; www.consorziodelgolfo.it). Bank on €25 to €40 per person. Diving, snorkelling and boat hire are available from **Anthias** (✆0789 8 63 11; www.anthiasdiving.com; Tanca Manna), on the seafront between Cannigione and Palau. Dives start at €50, while snorkelling excursions cost €50/30 per adult/child. Boat hire comes in at a whacking €800 for half a day, although that also gets you lunch, fuel and a skipper. You'll find the best beaches north of Cannigione, including **Tanca Manna**, a good bet for families with its soft sand and shallow water.

❶ Getting There & Away

Regular **ARST** (✆0789 2 11 97) buses make the run to Arzachena (€1.20, 10 minutes, four Monday to Saturday), Baia Sardinia (€1.50, 30 minutes, three Monday to Saturday), Palau (€1.50, 20 minutes, two Monday to Saturday) and Olbia (€2.50, one hour, four Monday to Saturday).

INLAND FROM THE COSTA SMERALDA

San Pantaleo

Although only about 16km from Porto Cervo, the rural village of San Pantaleo provides a welcome dose of authenticity after the sterile resorts on the coast.

The village sits high up behind the coast, surrounded by gap-toothed granite peaks, and has become something of an artists' haven. It is also one of the few Sardinian villages set around a piazza, a sturdy little church at one end. In summer you'll often find a bustling market here, and in spring the blossoms make it picture-perfect.

Browsing the shops is a favourite pastime here. Find paintings and sculpture by local artists at the small gallery **Arte in Piazza** (✆338 165 45 21; Piazza Vittorio Emanuele; ◷9am-1pm Mon-Sat, also 3-6pm Tue & Thu).

After that, take a pew at cosy, stone-walled **Caffè Nina** (Piazza Vittorio Emanuele 3; cheese platters €10; ◷daily summer, Thu-Sun winter) and enjoy a glass of Vermentino with some pecorino and olives.

Between 27 July and 30 July San Pantaleo holds its annual knees-up, a weekend of general jollity with traditional Sardinian dancing.

Near the entrance to the village is the highly regarded **Ristorante Giagoni** (✆0789 6 52 05; Via Zara 43; meals €40-50; ◷Tue-Sun Apr-Oct), the menu of which features meat classics such as *porceddu* (suckling pig) and rabbit loin in myrtle sauce. Bookings are recommended.

ARST runs five daily buses to San Pantaleo from Olbia (€2, 35 minutes) and Arzachena (€1.50, 20 minutes).

Arzachena
POP 13,200
Were it not for its position a few kilometres inland from the Costa Smeralda, Arzachena would be overlooked as just another workaday town with a mildly interesting historical centre. Which is pretty much what it is. But with the Mediterranean's most exclusive resorts an easy drive away, it has gone from being a humble shepherds' village in the 1960s to something of a tourist centre.

Most people use it as a base for exploring the Costa, but if you want to hang around,

DON'T MISS

FARM FRESH

Keep an eye out for the *'formaggi e salumi'* sign on the SP59 Arzachena-Porto Cervo road to find **Azienda Agricola Mossa Alessandro** (☑380 366 13 25; Località La Punga; ⊙8am-12.30pm & 4-7pm daily), a working farm where you can buy creamy goats-milk ricotta, mature *fiore sardo* pecorino and salami. Alessandro might let you take a peek at the huge wheels of cheese and racks of salami and pancetta out the back. It's a great place to pick up picnic supplies.

action is focused on **Piazza del Risorgimento**, a small piazza with a couple of cafes, and a stone church, the **Chiesa di Santa Maria delle Neve**. A short stroll away is the bizarre **Mont'Incappiddatu**, a mushroom-shaped granite rock at the end of Via Limbara. Archaeologists believe the overarching rock may have been used as a shelter for Neolithic tribespeople as long ago as 3500 BC.

☆ Eating

TOP CHOICE **Agriturismo Rena**   AGRITURISMO €€
(☑0789 8 25 32; www.agriturismorena.it; Località Rena; meals €25-30; ⊙Mar-Oct; ⓐ) Luigi welcomes you like one of the family at this hilltop *agriturismo*. Take a seat at a communal table in the rustic dining room for a hearty feast of home-produced cheese, meat and wine – think antipasti followed by ricotta-filled *culurgiones* (ravioli), succulent roast kid or lamb and Sardinian sweets. To reach the *agriturismo*, turn right (if exiting Arzachena) just after the Bar del Ponte at the northern edge of town.

Il Fungo   PIZZERIA €
(☑0789 8 33 40; Via Lamarmora 21; pizzas from €5, meals around €30; ⊙daily summer, closed Wed winter) Wood-fired pizza and cracking seafood are the hallmarks of this popular eatery. Locals come here to grab a takeaway and chat with the *pizzaiola* (pizza-maker) while out-of-towners sit down to huge helpings of fresh fish and grilled meat.

❶ Getting There & Away

Arzachena has good bus connections. ARST services run to/from Olbia (€2.50, 45 minutes, 12 daily), Santa Teresa di Gallura (€3, one hour, five daily) and Palau (€1.50, 25 minutes, five daily). Regular buses also link with the Costa Smeralda resorts, namely Porto Cervo and Baia Sardinia.

Between mid-June and mid-September you can pick up the **trenino verde** (☑070 58 02 46; www.treninoverde.com) to Tempio Pausania (€11, 1½ hours, one daily Wednesday to Saturday).

Around Arzachena

Arzachena serves as a springboard to some inland treasures: a series of mysterious *nuraghi* ruins and two *tombe dei giganti* (literally 'giants' tombs'); ancient mass graves.

NURAGHIC SITES

What makes Arzachena interesting is the mysterious countryside around it, littered with *nuraghi* and *tombe dei giganti*. These are managed by the local cooperatives **Anemos** (☑340 820 9749; www.anemos-arzachena.it, in Italian) and **Lithos** (☑0789 8 15 37). The following sites are open from 9am to 7pm daily from Easter to October and in winter on request. Entry costs €3 for a single site, €5 for two and €7.50 to €10 for three. Guided tours in English, German, Spanish and French are available by arrangement.

Nuraghe di Albucciu   ARCHAEOLOGICAL SITE
This is the nearest *nuraghe* to town, and certainly the easiest to find, on the main Olbia road, about 3km south of Arzachena. It's one of Gallura's finest prehistoric relics and unusual for several reasons, not least for its flat granite roof instead of the usual *tholos* (conical shape) and its warren of what appear to be emergency escape routes.

Tempio di Malchittu   ARCHAEOLOGICAL SITE
Accessible via a 2km track from the Nuraghe di Albucciu ticket office, this temple dating back to 1500 BC is one of a few of its kind in Sardinia. The experts can only guess at its original purpose, but it appears it had a timber roof and was closed with a wooden door, as was Nuraghe di Albucciu. From this vantage point you have views over the surrounding countryside, strewn with granite boulders.

Coddu Ecchju   ARCHAEOLOGICAL SITE
Taking the Arzachena–Luogosanto road south, you can follow signs to one of the most important *tombe dei giganti* in Sardinia. The

most visible part of it is the oval-shaped central stele (standing stone). Both slabs of granite, one balanced on top of the other, show an engraved frame that apparently symbolises a door to the hereafter, closed to the living. On either side of the stele stand further tall slabs of granite that form a kind of semicircular guard of honour around the tomb.

Li Muri
ARCHAEOLOGICAL SITE

This necropolis is a curious site made up of four interlocking megalithic burial grounds, possibly dating to 3500 BC. Archaeologists believe that VIPs were buried in the rectangular stone tombs. At the rim of each circle was a menhir or betyl, an erect stone upon which a divinity may have been represented. To reach Li Muri, turn left (west) for Luogosanto on the Arzachena–Luogosanto road. After about 3km turn right and follow the signs to Li Muri along a dirt track.

Li Longhi
ARCHAEOLOGICAL SITE

Just a short signposted drive from Li Muri, this *tomba di gigante* is similar to that of Coddu Ecchju. The central east-facing stele, part of which was snapped off and later restored, dominates the surrounding countryside from its hilltop location.

LAGO DI LISCIA & AROUND

From Arzachena, the SP427 heads inland into the undeveloped and utterly transfixing heart of Gallura. The road bobs and weaves through lush green fields and wood-crested hills as it twists its way up to the agricultural town of **Sant'Antonio di Gallura** en route to Lago di Liscia, one of Sardinia's unspoilt secrets. An 8km-long artificial lake, the main source of water for Gallura's east coast, it is set beautifully amid granite-scarred hills and woods of billowing cork and oak trees. The best place to admire it is a picnic spot at a tiny nature reserve, signposted as *olivastri millenari,* above the southern shores. The **olivastri** are a group of wild olive trees that have been growing for thousands of years. Scientists from the University of Sassari have calculated that the biggest, measuring 20m in circumference and reaching a height of 14.5m, is about 3800 years old. Certainly, it's quite a specimen, its gnarled and twisted trunk writhing upwards like something out of *Lord of the Rings.* To get to the site from Sant'Antonio di Gallura follow the road for Luras and Tempio Pausania, then take the turning marked *olivastri millenari.* After a further 10km or so, there's a short, steep dirt track up to the left – the *olivastri* are at the top.

NORTH COAST

North of Palau the wind-whipped coast rises and falls like a rocky sculpture, culminating in the lunarlike headland of Capo Testa. Fine beaches stretch out towards Vignola in the west and sunny Santa Teresa di Gallura in the east, the fashionable heart of the summer scene. The windy waters are a magnet for wind- and kitesurfers; competitions are often held here, some of which dash across the windy straits to Bonifacio in Corsica.

Santa Teresa di Gallura
POP 5300

Bright and breezy Santa Teresa di Gallura occupies a prime seafront position on Gallura's north coast. The resort gets extremely busy during high season yet somehow manages to retain a distinct local character, making it an agreeable alternative to the more soulless resorts on the Costa Smeralda.

The town was established by the Savoy rulers in 1808 to help combat smugglers, but the modern town grew up as a result of the tourism boom since the early 1960s. Santa Teresa's history is caught up with Corsica as much as it is with Sardinia. Over the centuries plenty of Corsicans have settled here, and the local dialect is similar to that of southern Corsica.

◉ Sights & Activities

When they're not on the beach, most people hang out in the centre, lounging on the cafe-lined piazza and admiring the pastel-coloured houses. Otherwise, you can wander up to the 16th-century **Torre di Longonsardo**, which overlooks a natural deep port on one side and the entrance to the town's idyllic (but crowded) **Spiaggia Rena Bianca** on the other. If you tire of the beach head down to the **Porto Turistico**, a small enclave of whitewashed villas set round a cloistered courtyard and crowded marina.

At the bottom of Via del Porto you'll find operators running excursions to the Maddalena archipelago. If you want a boat to yourself, you'll have to dig deep into your wallet; prices start at around €1800 per week. There's also excellent diving around Santa Teresa and the islands in the Bocche di Bonifacio.

Consorzio delle Bocche BOAT TOURS
(☎0789 75 51 12; www.consorziobocche.com, in Italian; Piazza Vittorio Emanuele 16; ☺9am-1pm & 5pm-12.30am May-Sep) This outfit runs various excursions, including trips to the Maddalena islands and down the Costa Smeralda (summer only). These cost between €40 and €45 per person and include lunch.

Centro Sub Marina di Longone DIVE CENTRE
(☎0789 74 10 59; www.marinadilongone.it, in Italian; Viale Tibula 11) For an adventure in the deep blue, check out the offer at this PADI accredited dive centre. Single dives start at €35.

✕ Eating

Santa Teresa's restaurants open daily in summer and then close completely in winter.

Agriturismo Saltara AGRITURISMO €€
(☎0789 75 55 97; Località Saltara; meals €35-40; ☺dinner daily; ⚑) Natalia and Gian Mario welcome you warmly at this *agriturismo*, 10km south of town off the SP90. Tables are scenically positioned under the trees for a home-cooked feast. Bread from a wood-fired oven is a delicious lead to dishes such as ricotta-filled *culurgiones* (ravioli) and myrtle-infused suckling pig. It's a challenge to find (follow the signs up a dirt track), but well worth it.

Il Chiostro SEAFOOD €€
(☎0789 74 10 56; www.ilchiostrodelporto.it, in Italian; Porto Turistico; meals €25-45; ☺daily) Sunset is prime-time viewing at this welcoming restaurant overlooking the marina, which prides itself on the freshness of its local produce. Try to snag a table on the terrace to eat fish caught that morning – the tuna is superb – or melt-in-the-mouth *porceddu*.

Il Grottino ITALIAN €€
(☎0789 75 42 32; Via del Mare 14; pizzas €6-11, meals around €30; ☺daily) Il Grottino sets a rustic picture with bare, grey stone walls and warm, low lighting. In keeping with the look, the food is wholesome and hearty with no-nonsense pastas, fresh seafood and juicy grilled meats.

Ristorante Papè Satan PIZZERIA €
(☎0789 75 50 48; Via La Marmora 20; pizzas €8; ☺daily) Great wood-fired pizza is the main draw here. The internal courtyard is a pleasant place to linger, and the service is smiley and quick. It's popular so book ahead or arrive early.

MUST-TRY GALLURESE DISHES 155

» **Zuppa gallurese** Layers of bread and cheese drenched in broth and baked to a crispy crust

» **Ortidas** Fried sea anemones

» **Capretto al mirto** Roast kid infused with myrtle

» **Fregola con cozze e vongole** Sardinian granular pasta with mussels and clams

» **Mazzafrissa** Creamy fried semolina

♪ Drinking & Entertainment

Hang out with the locals at the cafe-bars on Piazza Vittorio Emanuele. Between May and October regular concerts are staged at the Porto Turistico among the boutiques and expensive cafes.

Caffè Mediterraneo CAFE
(Via Amsicora 7; ☺8am-midnight Mon-Thu, 7am-3.30am Fri-Sun) With its arched windows, polished-wood bar and jazzy beats, this stylish cafe attracts a young, good-looking crowd. Join them for a lunchtime *panino* (sandwich; €3.50) or a cool evening cocktail.

Bar Central 80 BAR
(☎0789 75 41 15; Piazza Vittorio Emanuele; ☺6am-2am) Right on the main square, this central hub swells with happy holidaymakers until the early hours. Grab an outside table and enjoy ringside views of the piazza with your drink.

Estasi's CLUB
(www.estasisdisco.com, in Italian) Towards Palau, 3km south of town, is Santa Teresa's night-life hub, centred on this outdoor club, where DJs and the occasional band crank up the party vibe in summer.

⌂ Shopping

Coral, some of it found locally, is the big item here, and you'll find plenty of boutiques and jewellery shops. The pedestrianised Via Umberto and Via Carlo Alberto, leading south from Piazza Vittorio Emanuele, host a nightly market in summer.

Mascheras ARTISANAL
(Via Maria Teresa 54) Watch Signor Maura at work, skilfully carving traditional Sardinian carnival masks, at this tiny shop. His

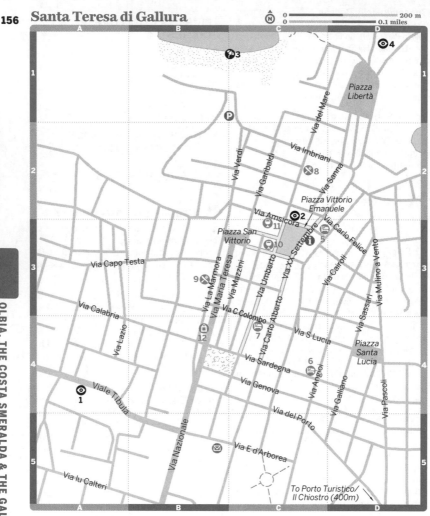

intricate masks include the wooden *boes* and *merdules* (from €130) typical of Ottana. There's also a range of cheaper wooden knick-knacks.

ⓘ Information

Banca di Sassari (Via XX Settembre 21) Has an ATM.

Bar Sport (Via Mazzini 7; per hr €5; ☺6am-midnight) For internet access.

Post office (Via Eleonora d'Arborea; ☺8am-1.15pm Mon-Sat)

Tourist office (☎0789 75 41 27; www.comune santateresagallura.it; Piazza Vittorio Emanuele 24; ☺9am-1pm & 5-9pm daily summer, 9am-1pm & 4-6pm Mon-Fri winter) Very helpful, with loads of information.

ⓘ Getting There & Around

Boat

Santa Teresa is the main jumping-off point for Corsica. Two companies run car ferries on this 50-minute crossing to Bonifacio, although between November and March services are drastically reduced.

Saremar (☎0789 75 41 56; www.saremar.it, in Italian) has three daily departures each way (two at weekends between October and mid-March).

Santa Teresa di Gallura

A one-way adult fare in high season is €10 and a small car costs up to €37. Taxes add another €8 to the price.

Between the end of March and late September **Moby Lines** (☑199 30 30 40; www.mobylines .it) operates four daily crossings. Adult tickets cost around €19, a car around €31.

Bus

Departing from the bus terminus on Via Eleonora d'Arborea, ARST buses run to/from Arzachena (€3, one hour, five daily), Olbia (€5, 1½ hours, seven daily), Castelsardo (€5, 1¼ hours, two daily) and Sassari (€7, 2½ hours, three daily).

Turmo Travel (☑0789 2 14 87; www.grup poturmotravel.com) operates a daily service to/from Cagliari (€23, 5½ hours), as well as a summer service to Olbia airport (€8, 1½ hours, six daily June to September) via Arzachena and Palau.

Other summer services are provided by **Caramelli** (☑079 67 06 13), which runs a daily bus to/from Porto Cervo (€5, 1¼ hours) via Palau (€2, 30 minutes) and Baia Sardinia (€4.50, one hour).

Car & Motorcycle

Santa Teresa di Gallura is at the northernmost end of the SS133b and on the SP90, which runs southwest to Castelsardo.

There are numerous rental agencies in Santa Teresa di Gallura, including **Just Sardinia** (☑0789 75 43 43; Via Maria Teresa 26), which has bikes (from €10 per day), scooters (€25) and cars (€65).

Around Santa Teresa di Gallura

If you've got transport it's worth exploring the long sandy beaches around Santa Teresa. East of town is the Conca Verde, a wild stretch of coastline covered with bushy umbrella pines. Along here you can try **La Marmorata** (8km) or **La Licciola** (11km).

Head 10km in the other direction (west) and you'll arrive at the long, sandy **Rena Maiore**, backed by appealing, soft dunes. ARST buses to Castelsardo can drop you at the turn-off. Further on are the beaches of **Montirussu**, **Lu Littaroni** and **Naracu Nieddu**, none of them very busy even in high summer. Finally, you'll come to the little seaside resort of **Vignola Mare**, the heart of kitesurfing territory.

CAPO TESTA

Four kilometres from Santa Teresa, this extraordinary granite headland seems more like a sculptural garden. Giant boulders lie strewn about the grassy slopes, their weird and wonderful forms the result of centuries of wind erosion. The Romans quarried granite here, as did the Pisans centuries later.

The place also has a couple of beaches. **Rena di Levante** and **Rena di Ponente** lie either side of the narrow isthmus that leads out to the headland itself.

Right on Rena di Ponente you can rent surfing gear, beach umbrellas and sunloungers at **Nautica Rena di Ponente** (☑347 321 52 14; www.nauticarenadiponente.com).

Porto Pollo & Isola Dei Gabbiani

Seven kilometres west of Palau, windsurfers and kitesurfers converge on Porto Pollo (also known as Portu Puddu) and Isola Dei Gabbiani, where stiff breezes and crystalline waters create the best conditions on the island.

Along the beachfront you'll find various outfits hiring out kit and offering lessons. **Sporting Club Sardinia** (☑0789 70 40 01; www.portopollo.it) takes you windsurfing, kitesurfing and sailing, and has a chilled bar for post-watersport drinks and gigs. Expect to pay €90 for two 90-minute windsurfing lessons, €260 for a block of five kitesurfing lessons, and €6/18/25/30 for an hour's kayak/windsurf/boat/kite rental. Four 30-minute kids' windsurfing lessons cost €100.

Another reputable choice is **Pro Center MB** (☎0789 70 42 06; www.procenter.it; Baia dei Delfini), where two-hour windsurfing taster sessions cost €59 and two-day courses including equipment hire and lessons cost €160.

Buses on the Palau–Santa Teresa di Gallura route stop off at the signposted road junction, from where you have to walk about 2km.

Palau

POP 4500

Palau is a lively summer resort, its streets lined with surf shops, boutiques, bars and restaurants. It's also the main gateway to Arcipelago di La Maddalena's granite islands and jewel-coloured waters. Out of town, the coast is famous for its bizarre weather-beaten rocks, like the Roccia dell'Orso, 6km east of Palau.

◎ Sights & Activities

Fortezza di Monte Altura FORTRESS
(adult/reduced €2.50/2; ◎guided tours hourly 10.15am-12.25pm & 3.15-7.15pm summer, closed winter) Standing sentinel on a rocky crag, this sturdy 19th-century bastion was built to help defend the north coast and Arcipelago di La Maddalena from invasion – something it was never called on to do. A guided 45-minute tour leads you to watchtowers and battlements with panoramic views out to sea. The fortress is signposted off the SS125, 3km west of town.

Roccia dell'Orso LOOKOUT
(adult/reduced €2/1; ◎9am-7.30pm daily, to 9pm in summer; ♿) This weather-beaten granite sculpture sits on a high point 6km east of Palau. The Roccia dell'Orso (Bear Rock) looks considerably less bearlike up close, resembling more – dare we say it? – a dragon. Analogies aside, the granite formations are extraordinary, as are the far-reaching views of the coast from up here.

Petag BOAT TOURS
(☎0789 70 86 81; www.petag.it) Down at the port, this is one of several outfits offering boat excursions around the Maddalena islands. Trips cost around €35 per person and include lunch and time to swim on well-known beaches.

Nautilus DIVE CENTRE
(☎0789 70 90 58; www.divesardegna.com; Piazza G Fresi 8; ♿) There's some excellent diving in

the marine park. This PADI-accredited centre runs dives to 40 sites, with single dives starting at around €50. Kids' Bubblemaker courses are available.

✖ Eating

As elsewhere along the coast, most restaurants close their doors in winter.

San Giorgio SARDINIAN €€
(☎0789 70 80 07; Via La Maddalena 4; pizzas €6-9, meals around €30; ◎Wed-Mon) The open-plan kitchen and friendly welcome tell you all you need to know about this buzzy pizzeria-cum-restaurant. The spaghetti *allo scoglio* (with mixed seafood) is an excellent bet, as is the grilled fish. Reservations are recommended.

Il Porticciolo SARDINIAN €
(☎0789 70 70 51; Piazza del Comune 7; pizzas €3-7, meals around €20; ◎closed Fri) Locals swear by the authentic antipasti, pasta and fresh fish at this no-frills harbourside restaurant. Stop by for a good-value lunch, or in the evening when chefs fire up the pizza ovens.

La Gritta MODERN ITALIAN €€€
(☎0789 70 80 45; www.ristorantelagritta.it, in Italian; Località Porto Faro; meals €70-80; ◎Thu-Tue) One for a special occasion, La Gritta is a memorable place to dine. Floor-to-ceiling windows allow you to take in the wondrous coastal scenery while the superbly presented seafood combines modern techniques with Italian ingredients. Cheese buffs will enjoy a selection of up to 20 different cheeses, while everyone will appreciate the classic Sardinian desserts.

❶ Information

The multilingual staff at the **tourist office** (☎0789 70 70 25; www.palauturismo.com; Palazzo Fresi; ◎9am-1pm & 4-8pm daily summer, 9am-1pm & 3-5.30pm Mon-Fri winter) can provide information about the surrounding area, including the Arcipelago di La Maddalena.

❶ Getting There & Away

Boat
Car ferries to Isola Maddalena are operated by **Saremar** (☎892 123; www.saremar.it, in Italian) and **Delcomar** (☎0781 85 71 23; www.delcomar.it, in Italian). Saremar runs crossings every half hour between 7.30am and 7.30pm. Delcomar runs six night crossings between 12.30am and 5.30am and then has crossings roughly hourly from 8.15am to 11.15pm. The 15-minute crossing costs €5.30 per passenger, €7.90 for a small car. For ferries to Genoa, see boxed text, p258.

Bus

There are ARST buses connecting Palau with Olbia (€3, 1¼ hours, eight daily), Santa Teresa di Gallura (€2, one hour, five daily) and Arzachena (€1.50, 25 minutes, five daily).

In summer, **Nicos-Caramelli** (☑0789 67 06 13) buses run frequently to nearby destinations like Isola dei Gabbiani (€2, 40 minutes), Porto Pollo (€1.50, 35 minutes), Capo d'Orso (€1.20, 20 minutes), Baia Sardinia (€3, 35 minutes) and Porto Cervo (€3, 50 minutes).

In the same summer period, **Turmo Travel** (☑0789 2 14 87) buses connect Palau with Olbia airport (€6, 50 minutes, six daily).

All buses leave from the port, and you can purchase tickets on board or at **Stefy's Bar** (Via Razzoli 12), right at the top of town.

Train

The *trenino verde* runs from Palau port to Tempio Pausania (€11, 1¾ hours, one daily Wednesday to Saturday) from mid-June to mid-September. It's a slow ride along a narrow-gauge line through some great countryside.

PARCO NAZIONALE DELL'ARCIPELAGO DI LA MADDALENA

One of Sardinia's most ravishing beauty spots, the Arcipelago di La Maddalena provides some spectacular, windswept seascapes. Nelson and Napoleon knew the archipelago well, as did that old warhorse Giuseppe Garibaldi, who bought Isola Caprera for his retirement.

A national park since 1996, **Parco Nazionale dell'Arcipelago di La Maddalena** (www.lamaddalenapark.it, in Italian) consists of seven main islands and 40 granite islets, as well as several small islands to the south. The seven principal islands are the high points of a valley, now underwater, that once joined Sardinia and Corsica. When the two split into separate islands, waters filled the strait now called the Bocche di Bonifacio. Over the centuries the prevailing wind, the *maestrale* (northwesterly wind), has helped to mould the granite into the bizarre natural sculptures that festoon the archipelago.

The area is an important natural habitat, and although national-park status has imposed protection, the ecosystem remains fragile. For this reason, developments are underway to create a joint Italian-French marine park, the **Parco Marino Internazionale delle Bocche di Bonifacio** (www.pmibb.com)

by 2013. Parco Nazionale dell'Arcipelago di La Maddalena has been on the tentative list of Unesco World Heritage Sites since 2006.

Isola Maddalena

POP 11,900

Just over the water from Palau, the pink-granite island of Maddalena lies at the heart of the archipelago. From the moment you dock, you'll be taken by the urbane character of the place, its cobbled piazzas and infectious holiday atmosphere.

Until the end of the 17th century the island's small population lived mainly in the interior, farming a meagre living out of the poor soil. But when the Baron des Geneys arrived with the Sardo-Piedmontese navy in 1767 to establish a naval base they gladly gave up their hilltops and relocated to the growing village around Cala Gavetta, now La Maddalena's main port.

◉ Sights & Activities

Beyond the harbour, the island's drawcard is its startlingly lovely seascapes. Divers sing the praises of the sapphire waters here, which are among the cleanest in the Med and teem with marine life. A 20km panoramic road circles the island, allowing easy access to several attractive bays such as **Giardinelli, Monti della Rena, Lo Strangolato** and **Cala Spalmatore**.

Museo Diocesano   MUSEUM
(☑0789 73 74 00; Via Baron Manno; admission €1; ☻10am-12.30pm & 3.30-8pm Tue-Sun summer, 10am-noon, 3-7pm Tue-Sun winter) You could pass half an hour or so inspecting the religious bits and bobs at this museum in the back of the modern Chiesa di Santa Maria Maddalena.

Museo Archeologico Navale   MUSEUM
(☑0789 79 06 33; Località Mongiardino; admission €4; ☻by appointment 9.30am-12.30pm & 3.30-6.30pm) About a kilometre out of town, on the road to Cala Spalmatore, this museum exhibits finds from a 1st-century shipwreck. The two modest rooms are presided over by an impressive reconstructed cross-section of the Roman vessel containing more than 200 amphorae.

Sea World Scuba Centre   DIVE CENTRE
(☑0789 73 73 31; www.seaworldscuba.com; Piazza XXIII Febbraio) There's some excellent diving in the marine park and this centre can

organise dives from about €40. Opening hours can be irregular, so phone ahead or email via the website.

Oasis Charter
BOAT TOURS

(⏹333 590 9750; www.oasischarter.it) Oasis runs cruises of the island in a beautiful 20m schooner. A day trip, with a lobster lunch thrown in, costs between €80 and €100 per person. You can arrange excursions around the islands with operators at Cala Mangiavolpe (east of the Cala Gavetta).

Saint Tropez
WATER SPORTS

(⏹0789 72 77 68, 335 654 5214; Via Giuseppe Mari 15) If larking around on water skis, a wake board or canoe in the calm waters of the Passo della Moneta appeals, try Saint Tropez, located near the bridge over to Isola Caprera.

✕ Eating & Drinking

Most of the best eating options are in La Maddalena town. Strolling around its lively centre is the main evening activity, perhaps stopping for a coffee along Via Vittorio Emanuele or a cold beer in Piazza Garibaldi, hub of the evening *passeggiata* (stroll). Nearly every place closes from November to March.

Trattoria Pizzeria L'Olimpo
PIZZERIA €

(⏹0789 73 77 95; Via Principe Amedeo 45-47; pizzas €6, meals €25; ☉daily) It's worth hunting down this popular trattoria in the bland streets east of the centre. The food is excellent – pizzas and the usual array of pastas, grilled meats and seafood – and the friendly service a pleasure.

Sottovento
SEAFOOD €€

(⏹0789 73 77 49; www.ristorantilamaddalena.it, in Italian; Via E Dandolo 9, La Maddalena; meals €40; ☉Tue-Sun) Sardinian home cooking is on the menu at bistro-style Sottovento, a short stroll north of the harbour. Go for seafood antipasti, handmade pasta and fresh fish and you won't be disappointed.

Parco Nazionale Dell'Arcipelago di la Maddalena

MILITARY CHIC

When the US Navy withdrew from La Maddalena in 2008 after a controversial 35-year sojourn, the question on everyone's lips was this: 'What now?' It looked set to be the G8 summit in 2009, but the venue was switched to Abruzzo in the wake of the L'Aquila earthquake. By then preparations were already underway to totally revamp the former military bases. The result? The strikingly contemporary **La Maddalena Hotel & Yacht Club** (☑0789 79 42 73; www.lamaddalenahyc.com; Piazza Faravelli, Località Moneta; d €200-500, ste €450-1100; ✱🛜✸). Where once derelict garrisons stood, today you can wander in vast, light-filled spaces, marvel at Zaha Hadid's sci-fi chandelier illuminating the lobby and gaze up at the geometric Murano-glass conference centre designed by Stefano Boeri. Besides rooms that are the epitome of minimalist chic, the hotel boasts a rooftop pool with panoramic sea views, immaculately landscaped gardens, a top-notch restaurant and a spa. And yes, there is space to dock your megayacht or land your helicopter (just in case you were wondering). If your budget doesn't quite stretch to the five-star price tag, you can sneak a peek at the hotel by booking a treatment in the spa, enjoying a drink at the bar or booking a table in the restaurant.

❶ Information

The **tourist office** (☑0789 73 63 21; www.comune.lamaddalena.ot.it, in Italian; Cala Gavetta; ☺8.30am-1pm & 3.30-5.30pm Mon-Fri, 9am-1pm Sat summer, shorter hr winter), to the right of the port as you face seawards, has limited information on the archipelago; opening hours should be taken with a pinch of salt as they change frequently.

❶ Getting There & Away

See p158 for information on ferries to La Maddalena from the mainland. They arrive (and leave) at separate points along the waterfront.

❶ Getting Around

Turmo Travel operates two island bus services, both departing from Via Amendola on the waterfront. One goes to the Compendio Garibaldi complex on Isola Caprera, and the other heads around the island, passing the Museo Archeologico Navale and several beaches, including Cala Spalmatore and Spiaggia Bassa Trinita.

To go it alone you can hire bikes and scooters from **Noleggio Vacanze** (☑0789 73 52 00, 339 265 5837; Via Mazzini 1; ☺9am-1pm & 3-8pm), just off the waterfront. Budget for about €15 per day for a bike and from €30 for a scooter.

Isola Caprera

Giuseppe Garibaldi's 'Eden', Isola Caprera is a wild, wonderfully serene island, covered in green pines which look stunning against the ever-present seascape and ragged granite cliffs. The road east out of La Maddalena town takes you through desolate urban relics to the narrow causeway that spans the Passo della Moneta between Isola Maddalena and Isola Caprera.

◉ Sights

Giuseppe Garibaldi, professional revolutionary and all-round Italian hero, bought half of Caprera in 1855 (he got the rest 10 years later). He made it his home and refuge, the place he would return to after yet another daring campaign in the pursuit of liberty. You can visit his home, the **Compendio Garibaldino** (☑0789 72 71 62; adult/reduced €5/2.50; ☺9am-7.15pm Tue-Sun), an object of pilgrimage for many Italians. Entry is by guided visit (in Italian) only.

The red-shirted revolutionary first lived in a hut that still stands in the courtyard while building his main residence, the Casa Bianca. You enter the house proper by an atrium adorned with his portrait, a flag from the days of Peru's war of independence and a reclining wheelchair donated to him by the city of Milan when he became infirm a couple of years before his death. You then proceed through a series of bedrooms where he and family members slept. The kitchen had its own freshwater pump, a feat of high technology in such a place in the 1870s. In what was the main dining room are now displayed all sorts of odds and ends, from binoculars to the general's own red shirt. The last room contains his death bed, facing the window and the sea, across which he would look longingly, dreaming until the end that he might return to his native Nice.

Outside in the gardens are his rough-hewn granite tomb and those of several family members (he had seven children by his three wives and one by a governess).

🏃 Activities

Green, shady Caprera is ideal for walking, and there are plenty of trails weaving through the pine forests. There's a stairway right up to the top of the island (212m) where you'll find the **Teialone** lookout tower. As you wander, keep an eye out for seabirds like royal seagulls, cormorants and peregrine falcons.

The island's rugged coast is indented with several tempting coves. Many people head south for fine sands and turquoise-blue waters at **Due Mari** bays. You could, however, head north of the Compendio Garibaldino for about 1.5km and look for the walking trail that drops down to beautifully secluded **Cala Coticcio**. Marginally easier is **Cala Brigantina** (signposted), southeast of the Garibaldi complex.

Cavalla Marsala   HORSE RIDING
(☑347 235 9064; Località Stagnali, Isola di Caprera)
Cavalla Marsala's hacks along the beach and through the fragrant *macchia* are particularly atmospheric in the early evening. Reckon on on €35 for a 1½-hour trek.

🍴 Eating

TOP CHOICE **Agriturismo Garibaldi** AGRITURISMO €€
(☑0789 72 74 49; meals €30; ⊘daily summer)
Housed in the buildings where Garibaldi's farmers used to live, this *agriturismo* is a top spot to feast on traditional Sardinian food. The farm produces all its own honey, vegetables, lamb and pork, all of which appear on the delicious fixed menu. Reservations are essential. To get here follow the signs left after crossing the bridge over from Isola Maddalena.

Other Islands

The five other main islands can only be reached by boat. Numerous excursions leave from Isola Maddalena, Palau and Santa Teresa di Gallura and approach the islands in various combinations. Alternatively, you can hire motorised dinghies and do it yourself.

Since NATO bid the **Isola Santo Stefano** farewell in 2008, it is once again a green, tranquil escape. **Isola Spargi**, west of Isola Maddalena, is necklaced by sandy coves and inlets. One of best is **Cala Corsara**, where the sea is topaz blue. To the north lies a trio of islands: **Isola Budelli**, **Isola Razzoli** and **Isola Santa Maria**. With your boat and time to paddle about you could explore all sorts of little coves and beaches. On tours it's likely you'll sail past the gorgeous **Spiaggia Rosa** (Pink Beach) on Isola Budelli, so-called because of the sand's unique pink tinge; it's now protected and access to its environmentally threatened sands and waters is forbidden. Other popular stops include fjordlike **Cala Lunga** on Isola Razzoli and the often-crowded **Cala Santa Maria** on the island of the same name. The beautiful stretch of water between the three islets is known as the **Porto della Madonna** and is on most waterborne itineraries through the archipelago.

THE INTERIOR

Away from the preening millionaires on the beach, Gallura's granite interior is remote and resolutely rural. In fact, it was this fertile hinterland that attracted the waves of Corsican migrants who settled here to farm the cork forests and plant the extensive Vermentino vineyards. Cork has long been a mainstay of the local economy.

Tempio Pausania
POP 14,300

Elevated above the hot Gallurese plain and surrounded by dense cork woods, Tempio Pausania stays cool and calm even in the height of summer. Joint capital of the Olbia-Tempio province, it's an unpretentious spot with a rustic *historic centra* and a laid-back pace of life.

The town was founded by the Romans in the 2nd century BC, and was developed to become an administrative centre of the medieval Giudicato di Gallura. Tempio Pausania's heyday came under the Spanish and then the Savoys, when many of the churches that adorn the town's grey stone centre were constructed. These days it's a relaxed place to hang out and the surrounding countryside is perfect for touring. Nearby Monte Limbara provides numerous trekking opportunities.

⊙ Sights

Tempio is replete with churches, and an indication of the town's former importance lies in the presence of the 17th-century

Do your bit for the Sardinian environment and buy wine with a natural cork. Cork has long been a mainstay of the local economy, but the spread of synthetic bottle stoppers is threatening the industry.

According to a 2006 World Wildlife Fund report, the increased use of plastic corks could lead to the loss of up to three-quarters of the western Mediterranean's cork forests within 10 years.

The impact in Sardinia would be devastating. The island accounts for 80% of Italy's cork production and the industry is a major employer in the northern towns of Calangianus and Tempio Pausania. Each year about 120 quintals of cork bark are harvested, most of it then sold to wine bottlers.

As well as the economic aspect, there are also environmental concerns. Cork harvesting doesn't actually harm the trees – harvesters simply shave the bark off the trunk – but a lack of care might. And if the cork companies don't protect the island's cork forests (and they're unlikely to do so without a vested interest), who will?

Convento degli Scolopi (Piazza Mazzini). It's now a college, but you can peer through the gates to the leafy cloister from Piazza del Carmine.

Cattedrale di San Pietro DUOMO
(Piazza San Pietro; ⊗8am-12.30pm & 3-8pm) This granite cathedral is the town's imposing centrepiece. All that remains of the 15th-century original is the bell tower and main entrance. Across the square, the **Oratorio del Rosario** dates to the time of Spanish domination of the island.

Chiesa del Purgatorio CHURCH
(Piazza del Purgatorio) This modest 17th-century church, presiding over Piazza del Purgatorio, has an intriguing history. The story goes that a member of the noble Misorro family was found guilty of carrying out a massacre on this very spot. To expiate his sins, the pope ordered the man to fund the building of this church, where to this day it is the custom of townspeople to come and pray after a funeral.

Fonti di Rinaggiu SPA
Since Roman days Tempio has been known for its springs; the Fonti di Rinaggiu is a pleasant 1km walk southwest from the centre (take the shady Via San Lorenzo and follow the 'Alle Terme' signs).

Cantina Gallura WINERY
(☑079 63 12 41; www.cantinagallura.com; Via Val di Cossu 9; ⊗9am-noon & 3.30-7pm) For liquid sustenance of a more alcoholic nature, head 1.5km east of town to this cantina, where you can stock up on the local DOCG Vermentino di Gallura.

★☆ Festivals & Events

Tempio has a whole host of festivals and events, from music concerts to folklore parades and key religious festivals.

Carnevale (in February) is big here, as is **Easter**. On Good Friday members of *confraternita* (religious brotherhoods) dress up in sinister-looking robes and hoods for the **Via Crucis** night procession. The musical **Festival d'Estate** runs from July to mid-August.

✗ Eating

On tree-shaded Piazza d'Italia and Piazza Gallura you'll find a couple of cafes with alfresco seating where you can grab an espresso, *panino* or pizza.

TOP
CHOICE **Trattoria Gallurese** SARDINIAN €
(☑079 63 93 012; Via Novara 2; set menu €15, meals €20-25; ⊗closed dinner Mon) Venture upstairs to the simple homespun dining area for a warm welcome and some genuine Gallurese soul food. Dig into *lumache piccante* (spicy snails) or *pecora alla gallurese* (Gallurese-style lamb) to experience some local traditions. Round out with delicious tiramisu and homemade wild-mint liqueur.

Ristorante Il Purgatorio SARDINIAN €€
(☑079 63 43 94; Piazza del Purgatorio 9; meals around €45; ⊗Wed-Mon) One of the best restaurants in town, this stone-walled restaurant serves earthy seasonal fare and fresh seafood. Menu stalwarts include *cinghiale in umido* (wild-boar stew) and *ravioli carciofi e bottarga* (ravioli with artichokes and mullet roe).

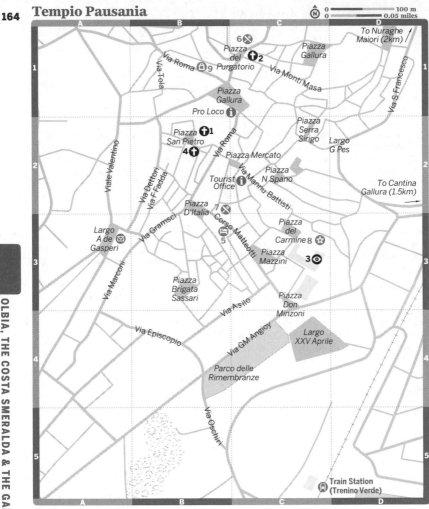

☆ Entertainment

Teatro del Carmine   THEATRE
(☎079 67 15 80; Piazza del Carmine) A variety
of performances, ranging from operetta
to classical concerts, can be enjoyed here,
especially during the summer Festival
d'Estate.

🛍 Shopping

Casa Mundula   ARTISANAL
(www.casamundula.com, in Italian; Via Roma 102)
This atmospheric store is a one-stop shop
for cork-based knick-knacks, ceramics, filigree jewellery and hand-crafted knives, as

well as Sardinian specialities such as *pane
carasau*, local honey and wine, Carloforte
tuna and the like.

ℹ Information

Post office (Largo A de Gasperi)

Pro Loco (☎079 63 12 73; Piazza Gallura 2;
⊙10am-1pm & 4-7pm Mon-Fri, 10am-1pm Sat)
An extremely friendly information office.

Tourist office   (☎079 639 00 80; www.
comune.tempiopausania.ss.it, in Italian; Piazza
Mercato 3; ⊙9am-1pm & 4-8pm Mon-Sat,
10am-1pm Sun) Run by helpful, multilingual
staff.

Tempio Pausania

❶ Getting There & Away

From Olbia (€3.50, 1¼ hours) there are seven daily ARST buses on weekdays to Tempio and three on Sunday.

The train station, a downhill walk from the centre, comes to life for the summertime **trenino verde** (☑070 58 02 46; www.treninoverde .com) to/from Sassari (€14.50, 2½ hours, one Thursday), Arzachena (€11, 70 minutes, two Wednesday, one daily Thursday to Saturday) and Palau (€13, 1¾ hours, two Wednesday, one daily Thursday to Saturday).

Around Tempio Pausania

NURAGHE MAIORI

Two kilometres north of town on the SS133 road to Palau is the **Nuraghe Maiori** (admission €3; ☺9am-8pm), signposted off to the right and immersed in billowing cork woods. As the name suggests (*maiori* means 'major'), it is a good deal bigger than many of the simple ruined towers that dot the countryside around here.

A trail leads through fragrant herb gardens to the tower, which has a chamber on each side, and a ramp to a third, open room at the back. Stairs to the left allow you to walk to the top. It's pitch black inside the chambers, so bring a headlight – or ask to borrow a torch – to spot clusters of rare and tiny lesser horseshoe bats.

MONTE LIMBARA

Some 17km southeast of Tempio, the jagged summit of Monte Limbara (1359m) dominates the gritty landscape. The easiest

way to reach it is to drive. From Tempio, head south out of town past the train station and follow the SS392 road for Oschiri. After 8km you will hit the left turn-off for the mountain.

The initial stretch takes you through thick pine woods. As you emerge above the treeline, a couple of *punto panoramico* (viewing spots) are indicated, from where you have terrific views across all of northern Sardinia. One is marked by a statue of the Virgin Mary and child, near the simple **Chiesa di Santa Maria della Neve**.

The road then flattens out to reach the viewing point of Punta Balistreri (1359m), where the RAI national TV network has stacked its relay and communication towers. The air is cool and refreshing, even on a midsummer's day, and the views west towards Sassari and beyond and north to Corsica are breathtaking.

Monte Limbara is also a popular trekking spot. If you want a guide, contact **Gallura Viaggio Avventura** (☑079 63 36 80), which organises trekking and mountain-biking excursions on the mountain.

CALANGIANUS & AROUND

Archaeology devotees might want to make the short drive to Calangianus, Sardinia's cork capital, situated about 10km east of Tempio. Its **Tomba dei Giganti di Pascaredda** is among the best preserved in the area.

Nearby, the small town of Luras is worth a quick stopover for a look at its **Dolmen de Ladas** and small museum. The **Museo Etnografico Galluras** (☑368 33 76 321; www .galluras.it, in Italian; Via Nazionale 35a; adult/reduced €5/2.50; ☺by appointment) celebrates the area's rural traditions with a collection of agrarian tools and a reconstructed village house. Among the displays, look out for Sa Femina Accabadora, a gruesome hammer traditionally used to put the terminally sick out of their misery in a practice of rural euthanasia.

It's worth sticking around for dinner at **Li Licci** (☑079 66 51 14; www.lilicci.com; Località Valentino; meals €44; ☺dinner), a delightful country retreat (see p210) hidden among cork oaks. There's a verandah for summer dining, while an open fire warms the beamed dining room on winter evenings. The fixed menu is a feast of local goodies: fresh pasta and gooey *zuppa cuata* (casserole of bread, cheese and broth) are followed by crispy suckling pig and

WORTH A TRIP

LUNAR LANDSCAPES

A few kilometres northwest of Aggius towards Trinita d'Agultu you reach the **Valle della Luna**. It's a surreal and evocative landscape, where huge granite boulders spill across rolling hills and farmland like giants' marbles. The lookout point on the SP74 commands fantastic views of the surrounding countryside, honeycombed with bizarrely sculpted rocks. The valley is a fantastic place for a cycle ride, and the road through here down to the coast is tremendously scenic.

honey-drenched *sebadas* (fritters). Reservations are essential. The *agriturismo* is signposted off the SP38 between Olbia and Sant'Antonio di Gallura.

AGGIUS & LUOGOSANTO

Cowering at the foot of granite peaks, Aggius is a deeply traditional village, clustered around a historic centre of twisting lanes and squat stone houses. It's famous for its choral music and carpets, the latter tradition dating back to the 1900s, when 4000 looms were busy in the area. You can see the looms, and the richly brocaded costumes worn for festive occasions, alongside displays on cork and granite, at the **Museo Etnografico 'Olivia Carta Cannas'** (☑079 62 10 29; www .museomeoc.com; Via Monti di Lizu 6; adult/reduced €4/3; ☉10am-1pm & 4-7pm).

For a more sinister peek at Aggius' past, stop by the new **Museo del Banditismo** (☑079 62 10 29; Via Pretura; adult/reduced €4/3; ☉10am-1pm & 4-6pm). Housed in the former magistrate's court, the museum zooms in on banditry in Gallura (still a problem until the 1990s), with a collection of arms, police reports and snapshots of the island's most wanted outlaws.

From Aggius it's possible to loop round northwest onto the SS133 towards remote **Luogosanto** (Holy Place). It's a pretty place that's peppered with churches, the grandest of which is the **Basilica di Nostra Signora di Luogosanto**, built in 1227. Pope Onorio III gave it the title of basilica when he sanctioned its Holy Door which, like the one at St Peter's in Rome, is walled up and only opened every seven years. There's an even older church here, the **Chiesa di San Trano**, which was built to honour the 6th-century St Trano and is moulded into the granite rock.

Lago di Coghinas, Oschiri & Berchidda

Those with wheels could make another excursion south of Monte Limbara. Once down from the mountain, turn left on the SS392 and head south for Oschiri. The road skirts the western side of the Limbara massif, passing through cork oak and pine woods, crests the Passo del Limbara (646m) and then begins its descent. After about 12km the green gives way to scorched straw-coloured fields and the blue mirror of the artificial Lago di Coghinas comes into view.

Just before the bridge over the lake, a narrow asphalted road breaks off east towards Berchidda around the northern flank of **Monte Acuto** (493m), the woody hill where Eleonora d'Arborea hid out for a period in the 14th century. Berchidda is a fairly nondescript farming town with a strong wine tradition. You can find out about local winemaking and taste some of the area's Vermentino at the modern **Museo del Vino** (☑079 70 45 87; adult/reduced €3/2.50; ☉9am-1pm & 3-6pm Tue-Fri, to 7pm Sat & Sun) right at the top of town. The best time to visit is August, when Berchidda holds its weeklong **Time in Jazz** (www.timeinjazz.it, in Italian) festival, a multicultural event showcasing anything from string quartets to piano soloists and saxophonists.

At the **Cantina del Vermentino** (☑0789 4 40 12; www.vermentinomonti.it, in Italian; Via San Paolo 2, Monti; ☉8.30am-6pm Mon-Fri, 8.30am-noon Sat) in Monti, just over 15km east of Berchidda, taste and buy some of the region's finest wines, including the crisp Vermentino di Gallura, Sardinia's only DOCG-rated wine.

A daily ARST bus passes through Berchidda en route from Nuoro (€7, 1¼ hours) to Olbia (€3, two hours).

Nuoro & the East

Best Places to Eat

» La Locanda (p173)

» Su Gologone (p177)

» Ristorante Ispinigoli (p186)

» Agriturismo Nuraghe Mannu (p190)

Best Places to Stay

» Agriturismo Guthiddai (p211)

» The Lemon House (p213)

» Hotel L'Oasi (p213)

» Silvia e Paolo (p211)

» Albergo Diffuso Mannois (p212)

Why Go?

Nowhere is nature such an overwhelming force as in the wild, wild east, where the Supramonte's imperious limestone mountains roll down to the Golfo di Orosei's cliffs and startling aquamarine waters. Who knows where that winding country road might lead you? Perhaps to deep valleys concealing prehistoric caves and *nuraghi* (Bronze Age fortified settlements), to the lonesome villages of the Barbagia steeped in bandit legends, or to forests where wild pigs snuffle amid centuries-old holm oaks. Neither time nor trend obsessed, this region is refreshingly authentic.

Outdoor action is everywhere: along the coast where you can drop anchor in a string of pearly white bays, up in the cliffs where you can multi pitch climb above the sea, on old mule trails best explored by mountain bike, and at peaks and ravines only reachable on foot. True, the Costa Smeralda attracts more celebrities, but we think you'll agree that the real rock stars and rolling stones are right here.

When to Go

Mamuthones wearing shaggy sheepskins and beastly wooden masks run riot in Mamoiada during February's carnival festivities. For seasonal colour, visit in spring for wildflowers or autumn for foliage. Room rates nose-dive in low season, the best time for hiking, cycling and climbing without the heat and crowds. Come in summer for lazy beach days and water sports.

August is festival time, with pilgrims flocking to the exuberantly folkloric Sagra del Redentore in Nuoro and Festa dell'Assunta in Orgosolo.

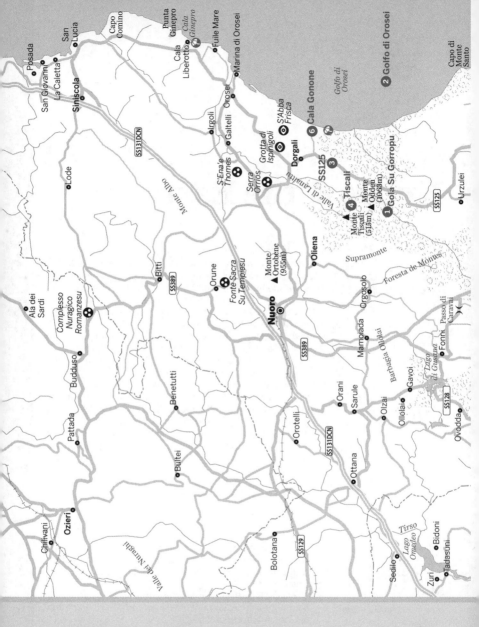

Nuoro & the East Highlights

1. Walk on the wild side in the **Gola Su Gorropu** (p187), Europe's Grand Canyon

2. Drop anchor at the hidden coves and secluded beaches of the **Golfo di Orosei** (p184), lapped by brilliant aquamarine waters

3. Take a scenic drive along the serpentine **SS125** (p186) for captivating views of the mountains and Med

4. Marvel at the mysterious nuraghic ruins of **Tiscali** (p188) high in the limestone Supramonte

5. Leave the world behind as you explore the weird highland plain of the **Altopiano del Golgo** (p194)

6 Enjoy exhilarating coastal climbing in **Cala Gonone** (p188), cooling off with a dip in the bluest of seas

7 Scale the hidden heights in the hills around **Ulassai** (p196)

NUORO

POP 36,500

Once an isolated hilltop village and a byword for banditry, Nuoro had its cultural renaissance in the 19th and early 20th centuries when it became a hotbed of artistic talent. Today museums in the historic centre pay homage to local legends like Nobel Prize–winning author Grazia Deledda, acclaimed poet Sebastiano Satta, novelist Salvatore Satta and sculptor Francesco Ciusa.

The city's spectacular backdrop is the granite peak of Monte Ortobene (955m), capped by a 7m-high bronze statue of the Redentore (Christ the Redeemer). The thickly wooded summit commands dress-circle views of the valley below and the limestone mountains enshrouding Oliena opposite.

History

Archaeologists have unearthed evidence of prehistoric nuraghic settlements in the Nuoro area. A popular theory maintains that the city was established when locals opposed to Roman rule grouped together around Monte Ortobene. But little is known of the city before the Middle Ages, when it was passed from one feudal family to another under the Aragonese and, later, Spain.

By the 18th century the town, by now under Piedmontese control, had a population of around 3000, mostly farmers and shepherds. A tough, often violent, place, it rose in rebellion in 1868 when citizens burned down the town hall to protest attempts to privatise public land (and thus hand it to the rich landowners). This action, known as Su Connuttu, no doubt confirmed the new Italian nation's view of the whole Nuoro district as a 'crime zone', an attitude reflected in its treatment of the area, which only served to further alienate the Nuoresi and cement their mistrust of authority.

ROAD DISTANCES (km)

	Aritzo	Cala Gonone	Nuoro	Orosei
Cala Gonone	85			
Nuoro	53	32		
Orosei	88	20	35	
Tortoli	65	54	72	69

Nuoro was appointed a provincial capital in 1927. It quickly developed into a bustling administrative centre. Although the traditional problem of banditry has subsided and the town presents a cheerful enough visage, Nuoro remains troubled, as high unemployment forces many young people to leave in search of work.

Sights & Activities

TOP CHOICE Museo della Vita e delle Tradizioni Sarde MUSEUM

(☎0784 25 70 35; Via Antonio Mereu 56; adult/reduced €3/1; ⏱9am-8pm daily summer, 9am-1pm & 3-6pm Tue-Sun winter) Zooming in on Sardinian folklore, this museum harbours a peerless collection of filigree jewellery, carpets, tapestries, rich embroidery, musical instruments, weapons and masks. The highlight is the display of traditional costumes – the styles, colours and patterns speaking volumes about the people and their villages. Look out for fiery red skirts belonging to the fiercely independent mountain villages, the Armenian-influenced dresses of Orgosolo and Desulo finished with a blue-and-yellow silk border, and the burkalike headdresses of the ladies of Ittiri and Osilo.

Other rooms display life-size exhibits from the region's more unusual festivals. These include Mamoiada's sinister *mamuthones,* with their shaggy sheepskins and scowling masks, and Ottana's *boes,* with their tiny antelopelike masks, huge capes and furry boots.

A short wander up from the museum brings you to the quiet **Parco Colle Sant'Onofrio**. From the highest point you can see across to Monte Ortobene and, further south, to Oliena and Orgosolo.

Museo d'Arte (MAN) ART GALLERY

(☎0784 25 21 10; www.museoman.it; Via Satta 15; adult/reduced €3/2; ⏱10am-1pm & 4.30-8.30pm Tue-Sun) Housed in a restored 19th-century townhouse, the MAN is the only serious contemporary art gallery in Sardinia. Its permanent collection boasts more than 400 works by the island's top 20th-century painters, including Antonio Ballero, Giovanni Ciusa-Romagna, Mario Delitalia and abstract artist Mauro Manca. Local sculptors Francesco Ciusa and Costantino Nivola are also represented. To see a bronze copy of Francesco Ciusa's *La Madre dell'Ucciso* (Mother of the Killed), which won a prize at the Venice Biennale in 1907, you should visit the pink chapel **Chiesa di San Carlo** (Piazza San Carlo; ⏱hr vary).

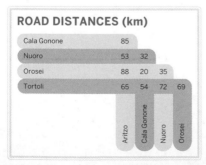

MONTE ORTOBENE

About 7km northeast of Nuoro is the granite peak of **Monte Ortobene** (955m), capped by a 7m-high bronze statue of the Redentore (Christ the Redeemer), strewn with weird and wonderful granite boulders, and covered in thick woods of ilex, pine, fir and poplar. A favourite picnic spot, the mountain is the focus of Nuoro's annual festival, the **Sagra del Redentore**. On 29 August, the brightly clothed faithful make a pilgrimage here from the cathedral, stopping off for mass at the **Chiesa di Nostra Signora del Monte**, and then again under the statue.

The statue was raised in 1901 in response to a call by Pope Leo XIII to raise 19 statues of Christ around Italy to represent the 19 centuries of Christianity. Since then the statue, which shows Christ trampling the devil underfoot, has been an object of devotion to pilgrims who attribute all manner of cures and interventions to it.

The views across the valley to Oliena and Monte Corrasi are at their most breathtaking from the viewpoint near the summit, particularly at dusk when the last light makes the limestone peaks blush pink. To get to the summit by public transport take local bus 8 from Via A Manzoni in Nuoro.

The gallery also hosts more wide-ranging temporary exhibits, usually held on the ground and top floors.

Museo Deleddiano · MUSEUM
(☏0784 25 80 88; Via Grazia Deledda 53; adult/reduced €3/1; ☻9am-7pm daily summer, 10am-1pm & 3-5pm Tue-Sun winter) Up in the oldest part of town, the birthplace of Grazia Deledda (1871–1936) has been converted into this lovely little museum. The rooms, full of Deledda memorabilia, have been carefully restored to show what a well-to-do 19th-century Nuorese house actually looked like. There's a storeroom piled with sacks of wheat and legumes, an internal courtyard, and a large kitchen crammed with pots and pans. Best of all is the material relating to her Nobel prize – a congratulatory telegram from the king of Italy and prize-giving ceremony photos which show her, proud and tiny, surrounded by a group of stiffly suited men.

Although she lived 36 of her 65 years in Rome, Deledda's life was consumed by Nuoro and its essential dramas. Fittingly, she was brought home to be buried in the plain granite church of the **Chiesa della Solitudine** (Viale della Solitudine). You will find her granite sarcophagus to the right of the altar.

Piazza Satta · PIAZZA
From the MAN, a brief walk up Via Satta leads to Piazza Satta, a small square dedicated to the great poet Sebastiano Satta (1867–1914), who was born in a house here. To celebrate the centenary of his birth, sculptor Costantino Nivola gave the square a complete makeover in 1967. Nivola whitewashed the surrounding houses to provide a blank backdrop for his curious work – a series of granite sculptures planted in the piazzalike menhirs. Each sculpture has a carved niche containing a small bronze figurine (a clear wink at the prehistoric *bronzetti*) depicting a character from Satta's poems.

Museo Archeologico Nazionale · MUSEUM
(☏0784 3 16 88; Via Mannu 1; www.museoarcheologiconuoro.it; adult/reduced €2/1; ☻9am-1pm Tue-Sat, plus 3 5.30pm Tue-Thu) This museum presents a romp through the region's archaeological sites. Finds from the surrounding province range from ancient ceramics and fine *bronzetti* to a drilled skull from 1600 BC and Roman and early-medieval artefacts. Anyone with more than a passing interest in nuraghic culture will enjoy the reconstruction of a prehistoric temple and ancient bronze laboratory.

Cattedrale di Santa Maria della Neve · CATHEDRAL
(Piazza Santa Maria Della Neve) A big, pink wedding cake of a church, the 19th-century Cattedrale di Santa Maria della Neve is one of 300 or so Italian churches dedicated to the Madonna della Neve. The so-called Mary of the Snow earned her name after she supposedly appeared to Pope Liberius in a dream and told him to build a church on the site where it would snow the next morning. It promptly snowed the next day and the Pope commissioned what was to become the Basilica di Santa Maria Maggiore in Rome. The cathedral's facade is a big flouncing neoclassical

Nuoro

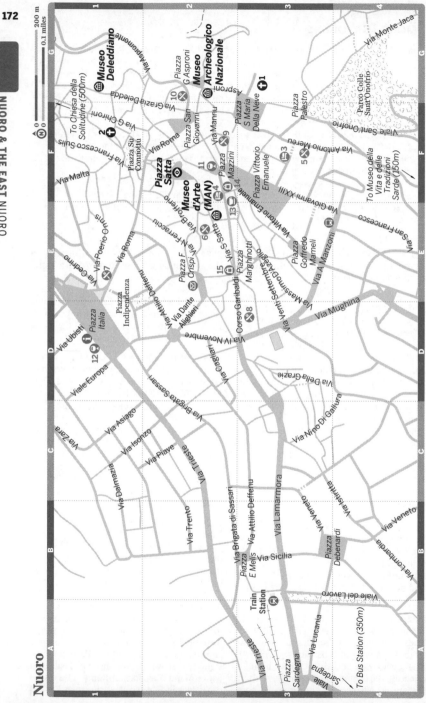

Nuoro

spread, giving onto a single-nave interior. Of note inside is *Disputa de Gesù Fra i Dottori* (Jesus Arguing with the Doctors), a canvas attributed to the school of Luca Giordano and located between the first and second chapels on the right.

🎊 Festivals & Events

The **Sagra del Redentore** (Feast of Christ the Redeemer) in the last week of August is the main event in Nuoro. It's one of Sardinia's most exuberant folkloric festivals, attracting costumed participants from across the island and involves much parading, music-making and dancing. On the evening of 28 August a torchlit procession, starting at the Chiesa della Solitudine, winds its way through the city.

🍴 Eating

The main street is Corso Garibaldi, which bisects a warren of tidy lanes, where you'll find several restaurants and popular cafes.

TOP CHOICE La Locanda SARDINIAN €
(📞0784 3 10 32; Via Brofferio 31; meals €15-20; ☺Mon-Sat) It's all about the food at this friendly, down-to-earth trattoria, and the €9.20 set lunch is a bargain. Bag a table and you're in for a treat – think antipasti, fresh pasta and grilled steaks, washed down with a litre (€6) of highly quaffable house wine.

Ristorante Il Portico SARDINIAN €€
(📞0784 21 76 41; Via Monsignor Bua 13; meals €35; ☺Thu-Tue) You'll receive a heartfelt welcome at this restaurant, where abstract paintings grace the walls and jazzy music plays. Behind the scenes, a talented husband-and-wife team rustle up a feast of local fare like *spaghetti ai ricci* (spaghetti with sea urchins) and fresh gnocchi with lamb *ragù*. Save room for the delectable caramel-nougat semifreddo.

Il Rifugio SARDINIAN €€
(📞0784 23 23 55; Via Antonio Mereu 28-36; meals €30; ☺Thu-Tue) One of Nuoro's most popular eateries, this jovial restaurant has won a faithful following for its creative brand of local cooking. Typical dishes include risotto with vegetables, prawns and saffron and *pecora alla nuorese con cipolline* (Nuoro lamb with onions). And all at very reasonable prices.

Premiata Pasticceria Il Golosastro PASTRY & SWEETS
(Corso Garibaldi 173-5) As fine as lace, the intricately crafted local cakes here are *almost* too pretty to eat. Award-winning cake-baking duo Felicina and Antonietta Mele create edible bouquets laced with almond, dainty pastries and nutty *torrone* (nougat) – all totally divine.

Monti Blu SARDINIAN €€
(📞0784 23 14 43; Via Roma 22; meals €25-40; ☺Tue-Sun) Clean, bright Mediterranean flavours shine through in regional dishes such as *tagliata di tonno* (sliced tuna steak with rocket and pecorino) at this stylish little restaurant. You can round out a meal in the tea room and stock up on pecorino, salami and preserves in the deli.

Ristorante Tascusì TRATTORIA €
(📞0784 3 72 87; Via Aspromonte 15; meals €10-25; ☺Mon-Sat) This trattoria is a good spot for a hearty meal of no-nonsense grub. Tables are set out in a sunny white dining room where you can tuck into bowls of tasty pasta, pizza and simply cooked meat dishes.

Drinking

Nuoro has a lively cafe scene. Take your pick of the pavement terraces in the historic centre for drinks and light bites.

Caffè Tettamanzi Bar Mayore CAFE
(Corso Garbaldi 71; ☺6am-3am, closed Sun morning) Going strong since 1875, Nuoro's oldest cafe is something of a local institution. The interior recalls a more glamorous age, with frescoes, marble tables and deep velvet armchairs where you can read works by Grazia Deledda and poet Sebastiano Satta. Snag a chair outside for crowd-watching and *panini*.

Bar Nuovo BAR, CAFE
(Piazza Mazzini 6; ☺7am-midnight) Right on Piazza Mazzini, this is an excellent place to park yourself with a cool beer and watch the world go by. It's equally good for the morning paper, midday gelato and evening aperitif.

Café America BAR, CAFE
(Piazza Italia 5; ☺7am-midnight, to 2am Sat) A busy coffee bar during the day, by night this cafe attracts young locals who come to sip drinks in the wooden alcoves and chill to a soft jazz soundtrack. It hosts occasional gigs and party nights.

Shopping

Corso Garibaldi is studded with Italian fashion boutiques, and springs to life with an antiques market on the second Saturday of the month.

Galleria Il Portico ART
(Piazza del Popolo 3) This art gallery showcases works by contemporary artists such as Antonio Corriga, Vittorio Calvi and Franco Carenti. Oils and watercolours predominate here, and prices generally range from a few hundred euros up to several thousand.

Coltelli Sardi ACCESSORIES
(Corso Garibaldi 53) True to Nuoro's pastoral heritage (not to mention those dastardly bandits), Francesco Piredda crafts exquisite Sardinian knives, including the famous Pattada jackknife with a myrtle-leaf-shaped blade that is carved from mouflon or ram horn.

Information

The train and bus stations are down Via Lamarmora, the extension of Corso Garibaldi.

For banks with ATMs and bookshops, head to Corso Garibaldi. The **main post office** is on Piazza F Crispi.

The **tourist office** (☏0784 23 88 78; www.provincia.nuoro.it, in Italian; Piazza Italia 19; ☺8.30am-2pm & 3.30-7pm daily summer, same hr Mon-Fri winter) has plenty of useful information on Nuoro and environs.

Getting There & Away

Bus

ARST (☏0784 29 08 00; www.arst.sardegna.it, in Italian) buses run from the **bus station** on Viale Sardegna to destinations throughout the province and beyond. These include Dorgali (€3, 45 minutes, six daily), Orosei (€3, one hour, 10 daily), La Caletta (€4.50, one hour, seven daily), San Teodoro (€8, one hour 50 minutes, five daily), Baunei (€6, two hours, four daily), Santa Maria Navarrese (€7, two hours 25 minutes, five daily) and Tortolì (€6, two hours 40 minutes, five daily). There are also regular buses to Oliena (€1.50, 20 minutes) and Orgosolo (€2, 35 minutes). Two daily nonstop buses connect with Cagliari (€15.50, 2½ to five hours).

For Olbia, there's an ARST bus (€8.50), and **Deplano** (☏0784 29 50 30; www.deplanobus.it, in Italian) also runs up to five daily buses to Olbia airport (€12, 1¾ hours) via Budoni (€6, one hour) and San Teodoro (€6, 1¼ hours).

For Alghero, **Redentours** (☏0784 3 03 25; www.redentours.com, in Italian) has two daily buses (€18, 2¼ hours), for which bookings are required.

Car & Motorcycle

The SS131DCN cross-country, dual-carriage highway between Olbia and Abbasanta (where it runs into the north-south SS131 Carlo Felice highway) skirts Nuoro to the north. Otherwise, the SS129 is the quickest road east to Orosei and Dorgali. Several roads head south for Oliena, Orgosolo and Mamoiada.

Train

The **train station** is west of the town centre on the corner of Via Lamarmora and Via G Ciusa Romagna. Trains run from Nuoro to Macomer (€3.10, 1¼ hours, seven daily Monday to Saturday), where you can connect with mainline Trenitalia trains to Cagliari (from Macomer €10.15, 2¼ hours, nine daily).

Getting Around

Local **ATP** (☏0784 3 51 95; www.atpnuoro.it, in Italian) buses 2 and 3 can be useful for the train station and the ARST bus station, and bus 8 from Via Manzoni for heading up to Monte Ortobene (€1.50). Tickets for city routes cost €1 and are valid for 90 minutes.

You can call for a **taxi** (☎0784 20 33 76) or try to grab one along Via Lamarmora.

NORTH OF NUORO

North of Nuoro, the forgotten and lonely countryside harbours a couple of wonderful archaeological sites. They're not easy to get to – even with a car you'll be wondering where on earth you're heading – but persevere and you'll be amply rewarded. Few people make it out here and there are no better places to experience the mystery and isolation of Sardinia's silent interior.

Fonte Sacra Su Tempiesu

Set in dramatic hill country near the dusty town of Orune, the **Fonte Sacra Su Tempiesu** (☎328 756 5148; adult/child €3/2; ☺9am-7pm summer, to 5pm winter) is a sophisticated nuraghic well temple. Curiously, its name has nothing to do with the temple's prehistoric origins but is a reference to a farmer from Tempio who came across it in 1953.

The temple displays a strange keyhole-shaped entrance with stairs leading down to the well bottom, and it's oriented in such a way that on the day of the summer solstice sunlight shines directly down the well shaft. Water brims to the top of the stairs and trickles down a runnel to another small well, part of the original, more primitive temple that was built around 1600 BC. The newer temple, dating to about 1000 BC, is a (partially restored) masterpiece. Above the well and stairs rises an A-frame structure of carefully carved interlocking stones of basalt and trachyte (sealed watertight with lead). The stone was transported from as far away as Dorgali. No other such structure has been found in Sardinia, and this one (excavation only began in 1981) was for centuries hidden by a landslide that had buried it back in the Iron Age.

Getting here is a problem if you don't have your own transport. Head for Orune, 18km northeast of Nuoro (turn off the SS-131DCN highway at the Ponte Marreri exit for the 11km climb to the town). From Orune it is a 5km drive southeast down a sometimes precarious dirt track (signposted). Buses run only as far as Orune. From the ticket office you walk 800m downhill to the temple. You may be accompanied by a guide (in Italian).

Bitti & Complesso Nuragico Romanzesu

From Orune the SS389 continues 12km on to the pastoral town of **Bitti**, made famous in recent years by its singing quartet, the Tenores de Bitti. This male-only vocal group is the most famous exponent of the island's traditional form of harmonic singing. To learn more, stop off at the **Museo Multimediale del Canto a Tenore** (☎0784 41 43 14; Via Mameli 57; adult/reduced €2.60/2.10; ☺9.30am-12.30pm & 3-6pm Tue-Sun), where you can listen to recordings of various groups in action.

About 13km beyond Bitti – follow the road towards Budduso – is the **Complesso Nuragico Romanzesu** (☎0784 41 43 14; admission €3.10, incl the Museo Multimediale del Canto a Tenore €3.60; ☺9am-1pm & 3-7pm Mon-Sat, 9.30am-1pm & 2.30-7pm Sun). Spread over a 7-hectare site in a thick cork and oak wood, this 17th-century BC nuraghic sanctuary comprises several religious buildings and circular village huts. The highlight is the sacred well temple, covered by a typical *tholos* and connected to a semi-elliptic amphitheatre. To make sense of the ruins there are up to six daily guided tours; most are in Italian but tours in English and German are also offered.

Shortly before the site, there's a turn-off signposted for the **Agriturismo Romanzesu** (☎0784 41 57 16; Località Romanzesu). You can't stay overnight here, but you can eat like a king. You'll need to book, but do so and you'll soon be sitting down to a feast of genuine home-produced country cooking – the farmer-host produces all his own pasta, salami, *porceddu* (suckling pig) and lamb. All for the princely sum of €28.

SUPRAMONTE

Southeast of Nuoro rises the great limestone massif of the Supramonte, its sheer walls like an iron curtain just beyond Oliena. Despite its intimidating aspect, it's actually not as high as it seems – its peak, Monte Corrasi, only reaches 1463m – but it is impressively wild, the bare limestone plateau pitted with ravines and ragged defiles. It makes for a raw, uncompromising landscape, made all the more thrilling by its one-time notoriety as the heart of Sardinia's bandit country.

The Supramonte provides some magnificent hiking. But as much of the walking is over limestone, there are often few discernible tracks to follow, and in spring and autumn you should carefully check the weather conditions. You can engage a local guide at one of the cooperatives in Oliena or Dorgali.

Oliena

POP 7440

Few images in Sardinia are as arresting as the magnificent peak of Monte Corrasi (1463m) when the dusky light makes its limestone summit glow. From Nuoro you can see Oliena's multicoloured rooftops cupped in the mountain's palm. The village itself is an unassuming place with a greystone centre, and is a handy base for exploring the Supramonte.

Oliena was probably founded in Roman times, although its name is a reference to the Ilienses people, descendants of a group of Trojans who supposedly escaped Troy and settled in the area. The arrival of the Jesuits in the 17th century was better documented and set the seeds for the village's modern fame. The eager fathers helped promote the local silk industry and encouraged farmers to cultivate the surrounding slopes. The lessons were learnt well, and now Oliena is famous for its beautiful silk embroidery and its blood-red Cannonau wine, Nepente di Oliena. Oliena is also the home town of Gianfranco Zola, English football's favourite Sardinian import, who was born here in 1966.

◉ Sights

Piazza Santa Maria is the village's focal point and the site of the Saturday market, as well as the 13th-century **Chiesa di Santa Maria**. Close by is the blessedly simple 14th-century **Chiesa di San Lussorio** (Via Cavour). Once you've seen these and walked around the steep grey streets you've pretty much covered all of the village's sights. As you wander look out for murals, including one of a notorious bandit and local lad, Giovanni Corbeddu Sali (1844-98) and, on a pink house near Via Cavour, one of an old lady dressed in black and bearing a rifle, symbolising the Easter *S'Incontru* celebrations.

🏃 Activities

The countryside surrounding Oliena provides some awesome trekking for enthusiasts. Just 4km south of town in the woods of Maccione you can find a track that leads right up to the highest peaks of the Supramonte. It's a hair-raising trail of vertigo-defying switchbacks called the **Scala 'e Pradu** (Steps of the Plateau) that culminates at the summit of **Punta sos Nidos** (Nests' Peak).

To reach the trail, head for the trekking centre **Cooperativa Enis** (☏0784 28 83 63; www.coopenis.it; Località Monte Maccione), which can arrange guided treks and 4WD excursions in the Supramonte.

Sardegna Nascosta (☏0784 28 85 50; www.sardegnanascosta.it, in Italian) and **Barbagia Insolita** (☏0784 28 60 05; Corso Vittoria

---

SAFE & RESPONSIBLE TREKKING

Before embarking on a walking trip, consider the following points to ensure a safe and enjoyable experience, and help preserve the ecology and beauty of Sardinia.

» Pay any fees and possess any permits required by local authorities.

» Obtain reliable information about physical and environmental conditions along your intended route (eg from park authorities).

» Be aware of local laws, regulations and etiquette about wildlife and the environment.

» Walk only in regions, and on trails, within your realm of experience.

» Hillsides and mountain slopes, especially at high altitudes, are prone to erosion. Stick to existing trails and avoid shortcuts.

» Where there is no toilet, bury your waste. Dig a small hole 15cm (6in) deep and at least 100m (320ft) from any watercourse.

» Carry out all your rubbish. You can reduce waste by taking minimal packaging.

» Always seek permission from landowners to camp.

» Be aware that weather conditions and terrain vary significantly from one region, or even from one trail, to another.

VALLE DI LANAITTU

Immerse yourself in the karst wilderness of the Supramonte by hiking, cycling or driving through this enchanting 7km valley, signposted off the Oliena–Dorgali road. Towering limestone mountains, cliffs and caves lord it over the narrow valley, scattered with natural and archaeological wonders. Rosemary and mastic, grapes and olives flourish in the valley, which attracts wildlife such as martens, birds of prey, wild boar and goats.

Archaeology buffs will be in their element discovering sites that have been inhabited since the Middle Neolithic period. Skeletons and funerary objects including pots and bone tools were discovered in the **Grotta Rifugio**, used by the Bonu Ighinu people (4700 to 4000 BC) as a burial ground. During excavations in the 1970s, two female pagan deities, ceramics and cooking utensils were discovered in the **Grotta del Guano** occupied by the Neolithic Ozieri people (3800 to 2900 BC).

Close to the *rifugio* (mountain hut) are the must-see **Grotta Sa Oche & Su Ventu** (admission €2; ⊘9am-6pm Apr-Sep), two caves linked by a natural siphon. The former is a wild and enchanting cave named 'Cave of the Voice' after the water that gurgles in its secret underground caverns; the latter has some wonderful stalactites and stalagmites, and was a hideout for notorious Sardinian bandit Corbeddu in the late 19th century.

Three hundred metres north of the *rifugio* is the 5-hectare site of **Sa Sedda 'e Sos Carros** (adult/reduced €5/3; ⊘9am-6pm Apr-Sep), with the remains of some 150 *nuraghe* huts. But the most interesting ruin is the circular **Temple of the Sacred Well**, surrounded by stone spouts that would have fed spring water into a huge central basin.

Emanuele 48) both organise a range of excursions, including trekking, canoeing and abseiling, climbing and riding.

✯ Festivals & Events

Settimana Santa   CULTURAL
The village is a hive of festive activity during Easter week. The culmination of the weeklong celebrations is the *S'Incontru* (The Meeting), a boisterous procession on Easter Sunday in which bearers carry a statue of Christ to meet a statue of the Virgin Mary in Piazza Santa Maria.

Autunno in Barbagia   CULTURAL
From September to December, 27 mountain villages in Barbagia take it in turn to host a weekend of events, from cheese-making workshops to exhibitions and craft demonstrations. Residents open their doors to visitors and put on a feast of local fare. It's a great opportunity to buy local produce.

✗ Eating

Find Su Gologone and Agriturismo Guthiddai by heading towards Dorgali and taking the turning on the right towards Valle di Lanaittu (follow the signs).

TOP CHOICE **Su Gologone**   SARDINIAN €€€
(☎0784 28 75 12; www.sugologone.it; Località Su Gologone; meals around €55; ⊘Mar-Nov) Nestled

at the foot of mountains, this rural retreat is a delight, with a bougainvillea-draped terrace for balmy evenings and *porceddu* roasting to crackling perfection on a big open fire. The local Cannonau red goes well with the Sardinian classics on the menu.

Agriturismo Guthiddai   AGRITURISMO €€
(☎0784 28 60 17; www.agriturismoguthiddai.com; Località Guthiddai; meals €30; ⊘Easter–mid-Nov; ✻) Guests are welcomed like family members at this whitewashed *agriturismo*, romantically set between vineyards and olive groves. Home-grown wine, olive oil and vegies appear on the dinner table, and the house speciality is flavoursome *pecora in cappotto* (ewe stew).

Ristorante Masiloghi   SARDINIAN €€
(☎0784 28 56 96; Via Galiani 68; meals around €30; ⊘daily) Housed in a sunny Mediterranean villa on the main road into town, this smart restaurant showcases local art in its rustic dining hall. Go for house specialities like homemade pasta, local lamb and boar stew. There's a verandah for alfresco dining.

❶ Getting There & Away

BUS ARST runs frequent buses from Via Roma to Nuoro (€1.50, 20 minutes, up to 12 Monday to Saturday, six on Sunday).

BARBAGIA

Sardinia's geographic and spiritual heartland is a tough, mountainous area known as the Barbagia. The name derives from the Latin term 'Barbaria' (itself derived from the Greek word *barbaros* (foreign person, barbarian), which the Romans gave the area after repeatedly failing to subdue it. The dramatic topography and tough-as-hobnail-boots locals kept the legionnaires out, just as they have since kept the outside world at arm's length with their fierce sense of inward-looking pride. Sardinian dialects are widely spoken in the Barbagia villages, and traditional festivities are celebrated with fervour. It's still common to see older women walking down the street wearing traditional black vestments.

At the region's heart are the bald, windswept peaks of the Gennargentu massif, the highest points on the island – ranging from around 1000m to 1834m (Punta La Marmora) – and the centre of the Parco Nazionale del Golfo di Orosei e del Gennargentu, Sardinia's largest national park.

Barbagia Ollolai

ORGOSOLO
POP 4440

High in the brooding mountains, Orgosolo is Sardinia's most notorious town, its name long a byword for the banditry and violence that plighted this part of the island for so long. The violence has now largely dried up and the town is attempting, with some success, to reinvent itself as an alternative tourist attraction. Nowadays, it's not unusual to see visitors walking down the main strip photographing the vibrant graffiti-style murals that adorn the village's buildings. But once the day-trippers have gone, the villagers come out to reclaim their streets – the old boys to sit staring at anyone they don't recognise and the lads with crewcuts to race up and down in their mud-splattered cars.

◉ Sights & Activities

You'll find it all in Orgosolo: WWII, the creation of the atomic bomb, the miners strikes of the Iglesiente, the evils of capitalism, women's liberation – the town is a giant canvas for emotionally-charged graffiti. The majority of **murals** line the main thoroughfare, **Corso Repubblica**, initiated by Professor Francesco del Casino in 1975 as a school project to celebrate the 30th anniversary of the Liberation of Italy. There are now some 200 murals, many of them executed by Casino. Other notable artists include Pasquale Buesca and Vincenzo Floris.

The styles vary wildly according to artist: some are naturalistic, others are like cartoons, and some, such as those on the Fotostudio Kikinu, are wonderfully reminiscent of Picasso. Like satirical caricatures, they depict all the big political events of the 20th and 21st centuries and vividly document the struggle of the underdog in the face of a powerful, and sometimes corrupt, establishment. Italy's own political failings are writ large, including the corruption of the Cassa del Mezzogiorno and Prime Minister Giulio Andreotti's trials for collusion with the Mafia, where speech bubbles mock his court refrain of 'I don't remember'. Even more interesting are the murals depicting recent events. On the corner of Via Monni there are portrayals of the destruction of the two World Trade Center towers (dated 28 September 2001) and the fall of Baghdad (dated 17 April 2003).

Stroll north along Corso Repubblica and you hit Via Gramsci, festooned with colourful depictions of revolutionary fighter Che Guevara, and fathers of Communism Marx, Engels and Lenin.

Five kilometres to the south of the town, the SP48 local road heads up to the Montes

---

ⓘ GET YOUR BEARINGS

Dozens of distinct village communities dot the Barbagia region, which is divided into districts around the Gennargentu. To the north is **Barbagia Ollolai**, to the west **Mandrolisai**, to the southwest the **Barbagia di Belvi**, and in the south there's the **Barbagia di Seulo**. It's a sparsely populated area and travel routes between the towns are usually limited to a single twisty road. Public transport is limited, so it's definitely worth hiring a car if you want to tour the area with any freedom.

The best sources of information are the tourist offices in Nuoro, Oliena and Dorgali. Useful maps include Belletti Editore's *Parco del Gennargentu* (1:100,000; €6) and *Nuoro* (1:200,000; €6.50), a map of the province of Nuoro published by Litografia Artistica Cartografica.

Orgosolo's history makes chilling reading. Between 1901 and 1950 the village was averaging a murder every two months as rival families feuded over a disputed inheritance. In her book *Colombi e sparvieri* (Doves and Hawks), Grazia Deledda describes an effort to defuse the enmities that saw the virtual extermination of these two families. In the postwar years, sheep rustling gave way to more lucrative kidnapping, led by the village's most infamous son, **Graziano Mesina**, otherwise known as the Scarlet Rose. He spent much of the 1960s earning himself a Robin Hood reputation by stealing from the rich and giving to the poor. Although captured in 1968 and imprisoned on the mainland, he had to be flown back to Sardinia in 1992 to help negotiate the release of eight-year-old Saudi Farouk Kassam, who had been abducted from the Costa Smeralda and was being held on Monte Albo, near Siniscola.

heights. Another 13km south is the **Funtana Bona**, the spring at the source of the Cedrino river. On the way you pass through the tall holm oaks of the **Foresta de Montes**.

✨ Festivals & Events

You'll catch Orgosolo at its best during the **Festa dell'Assunta** (Feast of the Assumption) on 15 August, when folk from all around the Barbagia converge on the town for one of the region's most colourful processions.

✖ Eating

Corso Repubblica has a few inexpensive cafe–bars and pizzerias, as well as the **Cortile del Formaggio** (Corso Repubblica 216; ⊘10am-1pm & 3-8pm Mon-Fri Apr-Oct), a tiny courtyard house where you can buy fresh, smoked and roasted varieties of *fiore sardo* – Sardinian pecorino made from raw ewe's milk and matured for a minimum of three months.

Il Portico   PIZZERIA €
(☎0784 40 29 29; Via Giovanni XXIII; pizza €3.50-6, meals €15-20; ⊘daily) An excellent pizzeria-cum-restaurant serving fulsome, woody pizzas and superb local vegetables and meats. The airy dining room and friendly, smiley service add to the pleasure.

A Dommo   TRATTORIA €
(☎0784 40 29 29; Corso Repubblica 206; meals €10-12; ⊘lunch Apr-Oct) Black-and-white photos of Orgosolo line the walls of this modern trattoria. It's a decent lunch stop, with local antipasti, homemade bread and carnivorous faves (such as wild boar ragù) on the menu.

❶ Getting There & Away

BUS Regular buses make the run to/from Nuoro (€2, 35 minutes, six Monday to Saturday, three on Sunday).

MAMOIADA
POP 2590

Just 14km south of Nuoro, the undistinguished village of Mamoiada stages Sardinia's most compelling carnival celebrations. These kick off with the **Festa di Sant'Antonio** on 16 and 17 January. According to myth, Sant'Antonio stole fire from hell to give to man, and to commemorate the fact bonfires are lit across the village. But more than the fireworks, it's the appearance of the *mamuthones,* the costumed characters for which the village is famous, that gives the festival its sinister edge. These monstrous figures re-emerge on Shrove Tuesday and the preceding Sunday, for the main **Carnevale** celebrations. Up to 200 men don shaggy brown sheepskins and primitive wooden masks to take on the form of the *mamuthones*. Weighed down by up to 30kg of *campanacci* (cowbells), they make a frightening spectacle. Anthropologists believe that the *mamuthones* embodied all the untold horrors that rural man feared, and that the ritual parade is an attempt to exorcise these demons before the new spring. The *mamuthones* are walked on a long leash held by the *issokadores,* dressed in the guise of outmoded gendarmes, whose job it is to drive them out of town.

If you can't be here for Carnevale, you can get an idea of what it's all about at the **Museo delle Maschere Mediterranee** (☎0784 56 90 18; www.museodellemaschere.it; Piazza Europa 15; adult/reduced €4/2.60; ⊘9am-1pm & 3-7pm Tue-Sun). The exhibit includes a multimedia presentation and garbed mannequins wearing their famous shaggy sheepskins.

There are a couple of shops in the village selling the wooden masks worn by the *mamuthones*. Don't expect to pay less than €100 for a good one.

For a bite to eat, try **La Campagnola** (☑0784 5 63 96; Via Satta 2; pizzas €4.50-6, meals around €25; ☺Tue-Sun), a sunny eatery with pizza and pasta on the menu.

Infrequent ARST buses connect with Nuoro (€2, 20 minutes, five Monday to Saturday, one Sunday).

ORANI & OTTANA

The main reason to make a stop in the grey, sleepy village of Orani is the **Museo Nivola** (☑0784 73 00 63; www.museonivola.it; Via Gonare 2; adult/reduced €1/free; ☺9am-1pm & 4-9pm summer, 9am-1pm & 4-8pm winter). This museum celebrates the original sculpture and sand-casting techniques of Costantino Nivola, the son of a local stonemason, who fled Sardinia under Fascist persecution in 1938 and subsequently spent most of his life working in America. Part of the museum was closed for renovation at the time of writing.

Five kilometres south of Orani, the village of Sarule sits at the foot of the 1083m Monte Gonare. The village itself doesn't really warrant a stop but a narrow side road to the east leads up to the 17th-century **Santuario di Nostra Signora di Gonare**, a grey buttressed church sitting atop a lone conical hill. It's an important pilgrimage site, and every year between 5 and 8 September villagers celebrate the Madonna di Gonare with horse races, singing and dancing.

More dramatic by far are the carnival celebrations that are held on Shrove Tuesday at **Ottana**, an otherwise lacklustre village considered to be the dead centre of Sardinia. Said to rival those of Mamoiada, festivities culminate in a parade of costumed *boes* (men masked as cattle) herded down the streets by their masters, the *merdules* (masked men symbolising our prehistoric ancestors).

GAVOI
POP 2820

Famous for its *fiore sardo* (Sardinian pecorino cheese) and literature festival, Gavoi is one of Barbagia's prettier villages. It has a pristine historic centre, with a small web of narrow lanes hemmed in by attractive stone houses. Three kilometres to the south, **Lago di Gusana** shimmers amid thick woods of cork, ilex and oak trees.

Up in the village centre, the **Chiesa di San Gavino** was built in the 16th century to a Gothic-Catalan design, as evidenced by the plain red trachyte facade and splendid rose window. From the piazza outside the church, cobbled alleyways lead up through the medieval *borgo* (village).

A popular fishing spot, the lake and surrounding countryside provide plenty of sporting opportunities. **Barbagia No Limits** (☑0784 182 0373; www.barbagianolimits.it; Via Cagliari 186) is a local operator that can organise a whole range of outdoor activities, including trekking, kayaking, canyoning, caving and jeep tours.

Up in the village proper, the rustic **Ristorante Sante Rughe** (☑0784 5 37 74; Via Carlo Felice 2; meals around €30; ☺Mon-Sat) serves fine local cooking. Speciality of the house is *lu su erbuzzu*, a heart-warming soup of bacon, sausage, cheese and beans flavoured with wild herbs. The cheese selection is a further treat and the pizzas (evenings only) are excellent.

By bus, there are four weekday ARST connections from Nuoro (€3, one hour 10 minutes) and one on Sunday.

FONNI & DESULO

At 1000m Fonni is the highest town in Sardinia and has a sizeable rural community. It's also a popular base for hikers, who come to explore Sardinia's highest peaks – the Bruncu Spina (1829m) and the Punta La Marmora (1834m).

DON'T MISS

BOOKS IN THE BARBAGIA

The small Barbagia village of Gavoi is the most unlikely place to bump into the likes of Jonathan Coe, Nick Hornby and Zadie Smith. But these best-selling British authors are just some of the big-name literary stars who have descended on the village for its annual literary festival.

A rare success story, **L'Isola delle Storie** has gone from strength to strength since it was inaugurated in 2003. For four days in early July, the village is transformed into an outdoor stage, hosting readings, concerts, theatrical performances, screenings and seminars. For more information check out the festival's website, www.isoladellestorie.it (in Italian).

PEAK BAGGER

It's relatively easy to reach Sardinia's two highest peaks from either Fonni or Desulo. You'll find the turn-off for the **Bruncu Spina** trailhead 5km out of Fonni, on the road to Desulo. From here a 10km road winds through treeless territory to the base of a ski lift. One kilometre before the lift you'll see a steep dirt trail to the right, from where a 3km track leads right to the summit (1829m). From here you have broad, sweeping views across the island in all directions. If you're here in winter, there's some modest skiing on these slopes, and a daily lift pass and ski hire costs around €30. For details, see www .bruncuspina.com (in Italian).

For a view from 5m higher you need to march about 1½ hours south to **Punta La Marmora** (1834m). Although it looks easy enough from Bruncu Spina, you need a good walking map or a guide, as well as sufficient water in summer.

At the highest point of the village, just off Piazza Europa, is the imposing 17th-century **Basilica della Madonna dei Martiri**, one of the most important baroque churches in the Barbagia region. Surrounded by *cumbessias* (pilgrims' huts), it's famous for a revered image of the Madonna that's said to be made from the crushed bones of martyrs. In June it is the focus of Fonni's two main feast days, the Festa della Madonna dei Martiri on the Monday after the first Sunday in June and the Festa di San Giovanni on 24 June.

Outside the church a couple of trees have been curiously transformed by sculptors into religious scenes, notably one showing the crucified Christ and the two thieves.

From Fonni, a scenic country road (SP7) wriggles south through parkland and oak forests, with grandiose views of limestone peaks rising out of deeply folded valleys. After 25km you hit **Desulo**, a long string of a town that was once three separate villages. There's nothing much to see but, like Fonni, it provides a good base for hikers, given its proximity to the Gennargentu.

✕ Eating

Ristorante Albergo Il Cinghialetto   SARDINIAN €€
(⏹0784 5 76 60; Via Grazia Deledda 193; meals €25-30; ⊗closed Wed) Down in the modern part of the village is this simple, friendly pick, dishing up meaty Sardinian fare and pizza. An open fire keeps things toasty in winter.

❶ Getting There & Away

BUS From Nuoro, there are ARST buses to both Fonni (€3, 40 minutes, eight Monday to Saturday, two Sunday) and Desulo (€4.50, one hour 20 minutes, one Monday to Saturday).

Barbagia di Belvi

ARITZO
POP 1390

A vivacious mountain resort, Aritzo has been attracting visitors since the 19th century. Its cool climate and alpine character (its elevation is 796m) caught the imagination of the Piedmontese nobility, who came here to hunt boar in its forests.

But long before tourism took off, the village was flourishing, thanks to the lucrative business of snow gathering. For some five centuries the village held a monopoly on snow collection and supplied the whole of Sardinia with ice. Snow farmers, known as *niargios,* collected the white stuff from **Punta di Funtana Cungiada** (1458m) and stored it in straw-lined wooden chests before sending it off to the high tables of Cagliari.

You can see some of the chests in the **Museo Etnografico** (⏹0784 62 98 01; Via Guglielmo Marconi; admission incl Sa Bovida Prigione Spagnola adult/reduced €2.50/2; ⊗10am-1pm & 3-6pm Tue-Sun), a small museum in the village elementary school. The museum also has a motley collection of traditional costumes and masks, as well as various farm implements and household objects.

The same ticket gets you into **Sa Bovida Prigione Spagnola** (Via Scale Carceri; ⊗same as Museo), a 16th-century prison just off the main drag. Built of dark grey schist stone, this chilling jail was used as a maximum-security facility right up until the 1940s.

A short hop away, the **Chiesa di San Michele Arcangelo** retains little of its early Gothic origins. Inside, you'll find an 18th-century *pietà* and a 17th-century portrait of San Cristoforo. Across the road from the church is a viewpoint from where you can

SORGONO

As much for the getting there as the being there, Sorgono rewards a detour. Deep in the heart of the Mandrolisai, the remote hilly area to the west of the Gennargentu, the village is surrounded by huge tracts of forest, full of ilex, cork, chestnut and hazel trees. In the vicinity, the **Biru 'e Concas** archaeological site boasts one of the largest collections of menhirs in Sardinia, while, in town, the **Cantina del Mandrolisai** (☎0784 6 01 13; www .mandrolisai.com; Corso IV Novembre 20) is one of the area's most important wine producers, famous for its beefy reds.

By train you can reach Sorgono on the *trenino verde*. If you're driving it's a 25km twisty drive from Aritzo on the SS295.

see the fortresslike limestone peak **Monte Texile**, now a protected natural monument.

There are plenty of marked walking trails around the village, most of which are fine to go alone.

Aritzo also holds two good foodie festivals. In mid-August at the **Festa de San Carapigna** you can try the village's famous lemon sorbet. On the last Sunday of October, people crowd the streets in search of chestnuts at the **Sagra delle Castagne**.

Barbagia di Seulo

To the south and east of Aritzo, the Barbagia di Seulo sidles up to the rocky heights of the Gennargentu national park. It's a lonesome area of small towns and snaking mountain roads.

From Aritzo the road southeast winds through the small towns of **Seulo** and **Seui**, the latter of which has a few traditional houses with wrought-iron balconies. Continue upwards towards Ussassai until after about 9km you come to a fork in the road at Cantoniera Arcueri. Follow for Montarbu and after another 9km or so you'll see Sardinia's largest *nuraghe*, the **Nuraghe Ardasai**, on your left. Built on a rocky outcrop dominating the deep Flumendosa River valley, it's worth a stop for the views. Six kilometres further on is a turn-off for the dense **Foresta di Montarbu**, towered over by the 1304m mountain of the same name. Several kilometres beyond this is the even more impressive **Monte Perda Liana**, at 1293m.

From here the road descends, leading eventually to the southern bank of the **Lago Alto della Flumendosa**. The main road skirts the lake eastward for about 10km before crossing over the *trenino verde* tourist train line a couple of times and reaching the main Nuoro–Lanusei road.

SARCIDANO

Southwest of Aritzo the rugged mountains flatten out to the broad Sarcidano plain, littered with *nuraghi* and other mysterious prehistoric sites.

Laconi
POP 2090

Straddling the SS128 as it twists south, Laconi is a charismatic mountain town, with a blissfully slow pace of life and bucolic views of green, rolling countryside. Its cobbled lanes hide some genuine attractions, including an intriguing archaeological museum, the house where Sardinia's only saint was born, and a castle-topped woodland park.

◎ Sights & Activities

Museo delle Statue Menhir   MUSEUM
(☎0782 69 32 38; Via Amsicora; adult/reduced €5/3; ◎10am-1pm & 3-6pm Tue-Sun) Occupying an elegant 19th-century palazzo, this delightful museum exhibits a collection of 40 menhirs. Taken from sites across the surrounding area, these stark anthropomorphic slabs are strangely compelling. Little is known of their function, but it's thought that they were connected with prehistoric funerary rites. In the backlit gloom they appear all the more mysterious, the shadows emphasising the faded sculptural relief that suggests whether they are 'male' or 'female'. If you find this interesting you may want to detour to Pranu Mutteddu further south, where you can see them in situ.

FREE **Casa Natale di Sant'Ignazio**   NOTABLE BUILDING
(Via Sant'Ignazio 58) Tucked down a cobbled lane, this simple two-roomed house is where St Ignatius is said to have been born (he died

in 1781). The back room, with its low wood ceiling and stone walls, is a good example of what a poor village house must have looked like in the 18th century. Here a simple shrine to St Ignatius is illuminated by candlelight. There are no official hours for visitors but the house is almost always open; if it's not, ask at the tourist office.

Parco Laconi   PARK
(☺8am-7pm summer, to 4pm winter) Continue past the saint's house on Via Sant'Ignazio and take the first left to reach this smashing 22-hectare park. Among the exotic trees (including an impressive cedar of Lebanon and several eucalyptuses), springs, lakes and grottoes, you'll find the remains of an 11th-century castle, the **Castello Aymerich**. From here you have wonderful views across the park and the greenery surrounding Laconi.

✗ Eating

Albergo Ristorante Sardegna   SARDINIAN €€
(☑0782 86 90 33; www.albergosardegna.it; meals €25-30; ☺daily) By the northern entrance to the village, this family-run restaurant serves good old-fashioned Sardinian cooking. Try the delicious handmade *culurgiones* (ravioli) and local organic beef, or go for seasonal specialities, such as pasta with *cinghiale* (wild boar) *ragù*.

❶ Information

Laconi is also one of the few towns in this area with a **tourist office** (☑0782 86 70 13; Piazza Marconi; ☺9am-1pm Mon-Fri). It's over the road from the neoclassical Municipio (Town Hall) on the central piazza.

❶ Getting There & Away

BUS Bus services to Laconi are fairly limited. There are connections with Isili (€2, 35 minutes one daily), Aritzo (€2.50, 40 minutes, three Monday to Saturday) and Barumini (€2.50, 35 minutes, two Monday to Saturday), but most run very early in the morning or in the late afternoon.
TRAIN The *trenino verde* (€11, 1¼ hours, one Tue) calls in here on its way north from Mandas. The station is about 1km west of the town centre.

South of Laconi

About 20km south of Laconi, by the sports centre in Isili, the **Nuraghe Is Paras** (☑0782 80 26 41; adult/reduced €3/2; ☺10am-1pm & 4-7pm summer, 10am-1pm & 3-5pm winter, closed Mon) is notable for its striking *tholos* (cone)

which, at 11.8m, is the highest in Sardinia. Famous for its crags and overhangs, Isili is also a magnet for serious rock climbers, with 250 single-pitch sports routes ranging from 5a to 8b.

Around 15km or so further up the road, beyond the small village of Serri, the **Santuario Santa Vittoria** (☑388 049 2451; adult/reduced €4/2, incl Nuraghe Arrubiu & Prano Mutteddu €9/4.50; ☺9am-7pm daily summer, to 5pm winter) is one of the most important nuraghic settlements in Sardinia. At the end of a scenic road (on one side you look over the Giara de Gesturi, on the other the land rises up towards the Gennargentu), the site was first studied in 1907 and later excavated in 1962. Still, only four of about 22 hectares have been fully uncovered.

What you see today is divided roughly into three zones. The central area, the **Recinto delle Riunioni** (Meeting Area), is a unique enclave thought to have been the seat of civil power. A grand oval space is ringed by a wall within which are towers and various rooms.

Beyond it is the religious area, which includes a **Tempietto a Pozzo** (Well Temple), a second temple, a structure thought to have been the **Capanna del Sacerdote** (Priest's Hut), defensive trenches, and a much later addition, the **Chiesa di Santa Vittoria**, a little country church after which the whole site is now named. Separated from both areas is the **Casa del Capo** (Chief's House), so-called perhaps because it is the most intact habitation, with walls still up to 3m high. Finally, a separate area, made up of several circular dwellings, is thought to have been the main residential quarter.

Nuraghe Arrubiu

Rising out of the Sarcidano plain, about 10km south of Orroli, is the **Nuraghe Arrubiu** (☑0782 84 72 69; adult/reduced €4/2, incl Santuario Santa Vittoria & Prano Mutteddu €9/4.50; ☺9.30am-1pm & 3-7.30pm daily summer, to 5pm winter), which takes its Sardinian name (meaning red) from the curious colour of the trachyte stone. It is an impressive structure, centred on a robust tower, now about 16m high, which is thought to have reached 30m. Surrounding this is a five-tower defensive perimeter and, beyond that, the remains of an outer wall and settlement. The artefacts found on the site indicate that the Romans made good use of it.

Pranu Mutteddu

Near the village of Goni, **Pranu Mutteddu** (⏹0782 84 72 69; adult/reduced €4/2, incl Nuraghe Arrubiu & Santuario Santa Vittoria €9/4.50; ⏲9.30am-1pm & 3-7.30pm daily summer, to 5pm winter) is a unique funerary site dating to the neolithic Ozieri culture (between the 3rd and 4th millennia BC). The site is dominated by a series of *domus de janas* (literally 'fairy houses'; tombs cut into rock) and some 50 menhirs, 20 of them lined up east to west, presumably in symbolic reflection of the sun's trajectory. The scene is reminiscent of similar sites in Corsica and is quite unique in Sardinia.

To get here from the Nuraghe Arrubiu, follow the road south 11.5km to Escalaplano and from there 8km towards Ballao. Take the first turn west to Goni, which you hit after 9km. A few kilometres further on and you reach the site, just north of the road.

GOLFO DI OROSEI

For sheer stop-dead-in-your-tracks beauty, there's no place like this gulf, forming the seaward section of the **Parco Nazionale del Golfo di Orosei e del Gennargentu** (www .parcogennargentu.it, in Italian), Sardinia's largest national park, which takes in the Supramonte plateau and the Golfo di Orosei. Here the high mountains of the Gennargentu abruptly meet the sea, forming a crescent of dramatic cliffs riven by false inlets, scattered with horseshoe-shaped bays and lapped by exquisitely aquamarine waters. Beach space is at a premium in summer, but there's room for everyone, especially in the rugged, elemental hinterland.

Orosei

POP 6790

Scenically positioned at the gulf's northernmost point and surrounded by marble quarries and fruit orchards, Orosei is an unsung treasure. Over centuries the silting of the Rio Cedrino (Cedrino river), Spanish neglect, malaria and pirate raids took their toll on the town, once an important Pisan port. Today the atmospheric historic centre is laced with cobbled lanes that twist to pretty stone-built houses, medieval churches and leafy piazzas for kicking back and watching the world go slowly by.

◎ Sights & Activities

Presiding over Piazza del Popolo is the **Chiesa di San Giacomo**, a Spanish-style church with an imposing neoclassical facade and a series of tiled domes. Its terrace commands views of the mountains rising above a jumble of terracotta rooftops. Across the square, the baroque ochre-hued **Chiesa del Rosario**, with its trio of wooden crosses, wouldn't look out of place in a spaghetti western. The lane leading up from its left-hand side takes you to Piazza Sas Animas and the stone church of the same name, with a vaguely Iberian feel about it. Opposite rises the 15m-high hulk of the **Prigione Vecchia**, also known as the Castello, a tower left over from a medieval castle. The most appealing of all Orosei's churches, though, is the humble yet highly atmospheric 8th-century **Chiesa di San Sebastiano** on Piazza San Sebastiano, with a trio of stone arches and a reed-woven ceiling.

On the fringes of the historic centre, the **Chiesa di Sant'Antonio** dates largely from the 15th century. The broad, uneven courtyard surrounding the church is lined with squat *cumbessias* and has a solitary Pisan watchtower.

✕ Eating & Drinking

Enoteca Osteria Il Portico   OSTERIA €
(⏹0784 99 93 56; Via A de Gasperi 11; meals €20-25; ⏲daily summer, closed Sun winter) Gathered around a walled garden, this brick-vaulted *osteria* does great grilled fish and meat. Or match wines with antipasti for two (€12) – the *crostini* with homemade pâté is delicious. Out front the *enoteca* does a fine line in local wines and preserves.

La Taverna   SARDINIAN €€
(⏹0784 99 83 30; Piazza G Marconi 6; meals €25-30; ⏲daily May-Oct) Tuck into fresh gulf fish and earthy meat dishes such as wild boar at this authentic taverna. It spills out onto a tree-shaded square just off Piazza Sas Animas.

Yesterday Bar   BAR
(Via Nazionale 48) Troubles indeed seem far away at this arty Beatles-themed bar, set around a pocket-sized courtyard. It's a chilled spot for a snack, cold beer or cocktail.

❶ Information

Once in town, follow signs for the *centro* to wind up in Piazza del Popolo, where you'll find the local **tourist office** (☎0784 99 83 67; Piazza del Popolo 13; ⊗10am-12.30pm daily).

❶ Getting There & Away

BUS Several daily buses run to Orosei from Nuoro (€3, about one hour, five daily services Monday to Saturday, three services Sunday) and Dorgali (€2, 25 minutes, two Monday to Saturday, one Sunday).

Around Orosei

OROSEI BEACHES

Orosei's beachfront satellite, **Marina di Orosei**, is 2.5km east of the town proper. The beach marks the northern end of the Golfo di Orosei; from here you can see the gulf arched in all its magnificence to the south. The Marina di Orosei beach is closed off to the north by the Rio Cedrino and behind the beaches stretch the **Stagni di Cedrino** lagoons.

A strip of pale-golden sand fringed by topaz waters runs 5km south and undergoes several name changes along the way: **Spiaggia Su Barone**, **Spiaggia Isporoddai** and **Spiaggia Osalla**. All are equally tempting and are mostly backed by pine stands, giving you the option of retreating to the shade for a picnic or even a barbecue (facilities are scattered about the pines). Past a big breakwater you can wander from Spiaggia Osalla around to **Caletta di Osalla**, the second stretch of sand after the main beach.

More fabulous beaches necklace the coast to the north of Marina di Orosei, including pine-backed **Cala Liberotto** and **Cala Ginepro**, which appeals to families with its shallow water and campground. Further north still is **Bidderosa**, which forms part of a nature reserve and never gets too busy because visitor numbers are restricted. A 4km trail leads down to the beach, a dreamy vision of sugar-white sand, flanked by lush pines, eucalypts and juniper, and lapped by cobalt-blue waters. The northern stretch sidles up to another fine beach, **Berchida**.

GALTELLI
POP 2480
Crouched at the foot of Monte Tuttavista and hemmed in by olive groves, vineyards and sheep-nibbled pastures, Galtelli is quite the village idyll. Its tiny medieval centre is a joy to wander, with narrow lanes twisting to old stone houses and sun-dappled piazzas. If you fancy tiptoeing off the map for a while, this is the place.

Information is available from the **tourist office** (☎0784 9 01 50; www.galtelli.com; Via Sassari 12; ⊗9am-noon & 4-7pm summer, 10am-noon Tue-Sun winter) up in the old town.

The town's main claim to fame is its mention in Grazia Deledda's most famous novel *Canne al Vento* (Reeds in the Wind). The tourist office can advise on Grazia Deledda itineraries which take in the **Chiesa di San Pietro**, a Romanesque-Pisan church near the town cemetery, and the 17th-century **Casa delle Dame Pintor**, the fictional home of the Pintor sisters in Deledda's novel *Reeds in the Wind*, a passionate tale about the demise of a family of aristocratic landowners.

Housed in an 18th-century noble villa, the **Museo Etnografico Sa Domo 'e sos Marras** (☎0784 9 04 72; Via Garibaldi 12; adult/reduced €3/2.50; ⊗9am-1pm & 4-8pm Tue-Sun summer, 10am-noon & 4-6pm winter) contains a fascinating collection of rural paraphernalia. There's a loom made out of juniper wood, a donkey-drawn millstone and a small display of children's toys. Upstairs, rooms have been decorated in their original 18th-century style.

Up to five daily buses connect Galtelli and Orosei (€1.20, 10 minutes).

Dorgali
POP 8520
Dorgali is a down-to-earth town with a grandiose backdrop, nestled at the foot of Monte Bardia and framed by vineyards and olive groves. Limestone peaks rear above the centre's pastel-coloured houses and steep, narrow streets, luring hikers and climbers to their summits.

For more outdoor escapades, the dramatic Golfo di Orosei and spectacularly rugged Supramonte are within easy striking distance.

◉ Sights & Activities

In town, you can browse the shops selling local craftwork – Dorgali is famous for its leathergoods, ceramics, carpets and filigree jewellery. Once you've done that you've pretty much exhausted Dorgali's opportunities and can turn your attention to the area's great limestone wilderness. There are several outfits in Dorgali that organise 4WD excursions, hikes and caving expeditions.

Museo Archeologico　　　　　　MUSEUM
(☎349 442 55 52; Via Vittorio Emanuele; adult/reduced €3/1.50; ⊗9am-1pm & 3.30-6pm, to 7pm

ROAD TRIPPING

It's well worth getting behind the wheel for the sheer pleasure of driving the 60km of road snaking from Dorgali to Santa Maria Navarrese. The serpentine, and at times hair raising, SS125 threads through the mountaintops and the scenery is distractingly lovely: to the right the ragged limestone peaks of the Supramonte rear above the woods, and gorges carve up the broad valley; to the left the mountains tumble down to the bright-blue sea. The views are tremendous as you crest the vertiginous **Genna 'e Silana** pass at 1017m. Shortly afterwards, near the turn-off for Urzulei, you'll spot **Formaggi Gruthas** (☑0782 64 80 08; Località Giustizieri) where you can stop to buy farm-fresh pecorino. The buttress-like peak of 647m Monte Scoine marks the approach to Santa Maria Navarrese. For a great detour on the return trip, follow signs from Lotzorai towards Talana, then Urzulei. The road twists through an otherworldly canyon-like valley, shadowing a river and passing reddish granite outcrops, vineyards and cactus-dotted slopes, before looping back up to the SS125 at Urzulei.

The drive is perhaps most beautiful in spring when wildflowers cloak the hills and broom adds a splash of gold to the landscape. Aside from the odd hell-for-leather Fiat, traffic is sparse, but you should take care at dusk when wild pigs, goats, sheep and cows rule the road and bring down loose rocks from the heights.

Jul & Aug) This modest archaeology museum spells out the region's past in artefacts, from pre-nuraghic to medieval times.

Cooperativa Ghivine   WALKING TOURS
(☑0784 9 67 21; www.ghivine.com; Via Lamarmora 69e) This one-stop action shop organises a huge array of activities, from boat tours to free climbing and archaeology expeditions. Trekking highlights include Gola Su Gorropu (€40) and Tiscali (€40).

Atlantikà   GUIDED TOURS
(☑328 972 97 19; www.atlantika.it, in Italian; Via Lamarmora 195) To better explore the rocky hinterland and coast, check out this consortium of local guides. It can arrange excursions to Gola Su Gorropu and Tiscali (both €35), as well as any number of canoeing, biking, caving, diving and canyoning activities.

✖️ Eating

Inexpensive snack bars, pizzerias and patisseries dot the main drag, Via Lamarmora.

Ristorante Colibrì   SARDINIAN €€
(☑0784 9 60 54; Via Gramsci 14; meals around €30; ☺Mon-Sat) Squirreled away in an incongruous residential area (follow the numerous signs), this lemon-walled restaurant is the real McCoy for meat eaters. Stars of the menu include *cinghiale al rosmarino* (wild boar with rosemary), *capra alla selvatiza* (goat with thyme) and *porceddu*.

❶ Information

The local **tourist office** (☑0784 9 62 43; www .dorgali.it, in Italian; Via Lamarmora 108b; ☺10am-1pm & 4-8pm Mon-Fri, also Sat in Jul & Aug) can provide information on Dorgali and Cala Gonone, including contact details for local trekking outfits and accommodation lists.

❶ Getting There & Away

BUS ARST buses serve Nuoro (€3, 50 minutes, eight Monday to Saturday, four Sunday) and Olbia (€7, two hours 50 minutes, two Monday to Saturday, one Sunday). Up to seven (four on Sundays) shuttle back and forth between Dorgali and Cala Gonone (€1.50, 20 minutes). You can pick up buses at several stops along Via Lamarmora. Buy tickets at the bar at the junction of Via Lamarmora and Corso Umberto.

North of Dorgali

GROTTA DI ISPINIGOLI

A short drive north of Dorgali, the fairytale-like **Grotta di Ispinigoli** (adult/reduced €7.50/3.50; ☺tours on the hr 9am-8pm summer, 9am-noon & 3-5pm winter) cave is a veritable forest of glittering rock formations, including the world's second-tallest stalagmite (the highest is in Mexico and stands at 40m)

Unlike most caves of this type, which you enter from the side, here you descend 60m inside a giant 'well'– at its centre stands the magnificent 38m-high stalagmite. You can admire the tremendous rock formations, many of them sprouting from the walls like giant mushrooms and broccoli, but forget the souvenir snapshots – photography is forbidden.

Discovered by a shepherd in 1950, the caves weren't explored in earnest until the 1960s. A deep network of 15km of caves with eight subterranean rivers has since been found. Cavers can book tours of up to 8km through one of the various tour organisers in Dorgali or Cala Gonone. *Nuraghe* artefacts were discovered on the floor of the main well, and Phoenician jewellery on the floor of the second main 'well', another 40m below. On the standard tour you can just peer into the hole that leads into this second cavity, known also as the **Abbisso delle Vergini** (Abyss of the Virgins). The ancient jewellery found has led some to believe that the Phoenicians launched young girls into the pit in rites of human sacrifice.

Linger for dinner and panoramic sunset views at the **Ristorante Ispinigoli** (0784 9 52 68; www.hotelispinigoli.com, in Italian; meals around €30; ☻closed Sat & Sun in low season), just below the entrance to the cave. Located in Hotel Ispinigoli, the well-known restaurant rolls out local delights such as *fregola con arselle* (Sardinian pasta and clam soup), herb-infused roast kid and a waistline-expanding selection of *formaggi*.

S'ABBA FRISCA

Around 5km from Grotta di Ispinigoli, on the country road towards Cala Gonone, **S'Abba Frisca** (335 656 9072 www.sabbafris ca.com, in Italian; adult/reduced €7/4; ☻9am-noon & 3-7pm summer, by appointment winter) is a veritable trove of ethnographic treasures. It's worth a visit for the gardens alone, bristling with centuries-old olive trees, fragrant *macchia* and medicinal plants. Other displays bringing Sardinia's cultural heritage to life include a shepherd's hut built from basalt and juniper, old olive and wine presses, and a traditional *pane carasau* bread oven.

SERRA ORRIOS & S'ENA 'E THOMES

Eleven kilometres northwest of Dorgali (and 3km off the Dorgali-Oliena road) you'll find the ruins of **Serra Orrios** (adult/reduced €5/2.50; ☻hourly tours 9am-1pm & 3-6pm, shorter hr winter), a nuraghic village inhabited between 1500 and 250 BC. Nestled among olive groves, the remains comprise a cluster of 70 or so horseshoe-shaped huts grouped around two basalt-hewn temples: Tempietto A, thought to be used by visiting pilgrims, and Tempietto B, for the villagers. A third

temple has also been discovered, leading experts to surmise that this may have been a significant religious centre. There's a diagram near the entrance, which helps you to understand the site, as the guided tours are in Italian only.

From here you could continue north to see a fine example of a *tomba di gigante* (literally 'giant's tomb'; ancient mass grave) built at the height of the nuraghic period. Continue 3km north of the crossroads on the Nuoro–Orosei route and **S'Ena 'e Thomes** (admission free; ☻dawn-dusk) is signposted to the right. A narrow path winds through marshy farmland to the central, oval-shaped stone stele (3.65m tall and 2.10m wide) which closes off the ancient burial chamber.

South of Dorgali

GOLA SU GORROPU

Hailed the Grand Canyon of Europe, the **Gola Su Gorropu** (328 897 65 63; www.gor ropu.info; adult/reduced €5/3; ☻tours 10.30am-3.30pm daily) is a spectacular gorge flanked by towering limestone walls of up to 400m in height. The endemic *Aquilegia nuragica* plant only grows here, and at quieter times it's possible to spot mouflon and golden eagles. From the Rio Flumineddu riverbed you can wander about 1km into the boulder-strewn ravine without climbing gear; stick to the right and follow the cairns. After 500m you reach the narrowest point, just 4m wide, and the formidable **Hotel Supramonte**, a tough 8b multipitch climb up a vertical 400m rock face.

To hike into the gorge you'll need sturdy shoes and sufficient water. There are two main routes. The most dramatic begins from the car park opposite Hotel Silana at the **Genna 'e Silana** pass on the SS125 at kilometre 183. The 1¼-hour trail is signposted and fairly easygoing, particularly on the descent, weaving past holm oak woods, boulder-strewn slopes and cave-riddled cliffs. For a bird's-eye perspective of the gorge, you could take the 1¼-hour ridge trail from the car park to 888m **Punta Cucuttos**.

The second and slightly easier route to Gorropu is via the **Sa Barva bridge**, about 15km from Dorgali. To get to the bridge, take the SS125 and look for the sign on the right for the Gola Su Gorropu and Tiscali between kilometre 200 and 201. Take this and continue until the asphalt finishes after about 20 minutes. Park here and cross the Sa Barva

TREKKING TO TISCALI

The hike to Tiscali is pure drama, striking into the heart of the limestone Supramonte. The trailhead is at the **Sa Barva bridge** over the green Rio Flumineddu, the same starting point as the route to Gola Su Gorropu. You'll need sturdy footwear for some easy rock hopping, but most of the path – marked with red arrows – is easygoing, and canopies of juniper and cork oaks afford shady respite. The trail is signposted and takes between 1½ and two hours; allow five hours for the return hike, breaks and visit to Tiscali. Time permitting, you can visit the **Domus de Jana Biduai** (admission free; ⊘dawn-dusk) on the road back to Dorgali. Stepping stones cross the river to this ancient nuraghic tomb.

There are many companies in Oliena, Dorgali and Cala Gonone offering guided tours to Tiscali. Typically these cost around €40 per person and sometimes include lunch.

bridge, after which you'll see the trail for the Gola signposted off to the left. From here it's a scenic two-hour hike along the Rio Flumineddu to the mouth of the gorge.

If you'd prefer to go with a guide, Sandra and Franco at the **Cooperativa Gorropu** (⌧0782 64 92 82, 333 850 71 57; www.gorropu.com; Via Sa Preda Lada 2, Urzulei) arrange all sorts of excursions and activities, from trekking and canyoning to caving and cookery courses; see their website for prices. Their base is in Urzulei, but they also run a small info centre at Genna 'e Silana pass.

TISCALI

Hidden in a mountain-top cave high above the Valle di Lanaittu, the mysterious nuraghic village of **Tiscali** (admission adult/reduced €5/2; ⊘9am-7pm summer, to 5pm winter) is one of Sardinia's archaeological highlights. Dating to the 6th century BC and populated until Roman times, the village was discovered at the end of the 19th century. At the time it was relatively intact, but since then grave robbers have looted the place, stripping the conical stone and mud huts (originally capped by juniper-wood roofs) down to the skeletal remains that you see today. It's an eerie sight: jumbled ruins amid holm-oak and turpentine trees huddled in the twilight of the limestone overhang. The inhabitants of Sa Sedda 'e Sos Carros used it as a hiding place, and its inaccessibility ensured that the Sards were able to hold out here until well into the 2nd century BC.

Cala Gonone

POP 1280

Climbers, divers, sea kayakers, beachcombers and hikers all find their thrill in Cala Gonone. Why? Just look around you:

imperious limestone peaks frame grandstand views of the Golfo di Orosei, sheer cliffs dip into the brilliant-blue sea, trails wriggle through emerald-green ravines to pearly-white beaches. It is quite magnificent. Even getting here is an adventure, with each hairpin bend bringing you ever closer to a sea that spreads out before you like a giant liquid mirror.

Gathered along a pine-shaded promenade, the seaside resort still has the low-key, family-friendly vibe of the small fishing village it once was. August aside, the beaches tend to be uncrowded and the room rates affordable. Bear in mind that the resort slumbers in winter, closing from October until Easter.

◉ Sights & Activities

Cala Gonone is the perfect launchpad for exploring the gulf's most alluring bays, which are scattered like horseshoes along the coast. The fact that the best beaches and grottoes can only be reached by hiking or dropping anchor gives them added castaway appeal.

Cala Gonone Beaches　　　BEACH
In town the small shingle **Spiaggia Centrale** is good for a quick dip, but the finest beaches lie further south. Further along the waterfront is the narrow sandy strip **Spiaggia Palmasera**, interrupted by rocky stretches (watch out for sea urchins). Better for splashing around in the aquamarine sea is **Spiaggia Sos Dorroles**, 1km south, backed by a striking yellow-orange rock wall.

Cala Fuili　　　BEACH
About 3.5km south of town (follow Via Bue Marino), is this captivating rocky inlet backed by a deep green valley. From here you can hike over the cliff tops to **Cala**

Luna, about two hours (4km) away on foot. The trail cuts a scenic path through juniper and mastic trees and is easy to navigate, with triangle-circle symbols marking handy rocks. The coastal views are breathtaking as you approach Cala Luna.

Cala Luna
BEACH

A favourite with rock climbers, this crescent-shaped bay is wildly beautiful, backed by a lush ravine, framed by cave-pitted cliffs and pummelled by exquisite turquoise waters. Linger after the boats have gone and you'll pretty much have the bay to yourself. If your navigation skills are good, you could continue along a tough, unmarked trail to the striking **Arco Lupiru** rock arch (around 1½ hours) or **Cala Sisine** (four hours). Wild camping on the beaches is not permitted, but the authorities have been known to turn a blind eye to discreet campers.

Cala Cartoe
BEACH

Tucked away to the north of town, this is another gorgeous beach, a silky strip of fine white sand bordered by emerald waters and dense woodland. It gets predictably busy in August, but visit out of season and it will probably be all yours. To get there, and you'll need a car, take Via Marco Polo from behind the port and follow it to a T-junction; the cove is signposted to the right (north).

Nuraghe Mannu
ARCHAEOLOGICAL SITE

(adult/reduced €3/2; ☉9am-noon & 3-6pm winter, to 7pm summer) To get an eagle-eye view over the whole coast, follow the signs off the Cala Gonone–Dorgali road to reach this *nuraghe*. After 3km the rocky track peters out at a wild headland where you can see nearly the entire curve of the gulf. The location is terribly romantic, set above a lush gorge and with silver-grey blocks strewn beneath the olive trees. First inhabited around 1600 BC, the tower is a modest ruin, but you can still see niches in its central chamber. The Romans took a shine to the *nuraghe* and, looking at the traces of former dwellings, you can contrast their geometric forms with the elliptical shapes of their predecessors.

Grotta del Bue Marino
GROTTO

(adult/reduced €8/4; ☉tours on the hr 9am-1pm & 3-5pm daily summer) It's a scenic 40-minute hike from Cala Fuili, or a speedy boat ride from Cala Gonone, to this enchanting grotto. It was the last island refuge of the rare monk seal (*'bue marino'* or 'sea ox' as it was known by local fishermen). The watery gallery is impressive, with shimmering light playing on the strange shapes and Neolithic petroglyphs within the cave. Guided visits take place up to seven times a day. In peak season you may need to book.

Acquario di Cala Gonone
AQUARIUM

(☎0784 9 30 47; www.acquariocalagonone.it; Via La Favorita; adult/reduced €10/6; ☉9.30am-7.30pm daily; ➍) Check out the local marine life before taking the plunge at this shiny new aquarium, designed by architects Peter Chermayeff and Sebastiano Gaias. The 25 tanks bubble with seahorses, jellyfish, rays and – moving into more tropical waters – clownfish and anemones.

TOP FIVE CLIMBS

» **Cala Fuili** Easily accessible bay and good for beginners, with 117 routes from 5a to 8b+, including cliffs above the beach and scores of overhangs in the gorge for all tastes and exposures.

» **La Poltrona** A massive limestone amphitheatre close to central Cala Gonone, with compact rock, 75 bolted routes from grades 4 to 8a and a maximum height of 175m. Mornings get too hot here in summer, so wait until late afternoon.

» **Cala Luna** Fabulous climbing above a beautiful bay, accessed on foot or by boat. The 56 routes ranging from 5c and 8b+ include some tricky single-pitches in caves with overhangs.

» **S'atta Ruia** A Dorgali favourite, consisting of a long limestone cliff with vertical walls and overhangs. There are 81 routes from grades 5a to 7b. Climb in the morning for shade.

» **Biddiriscottai** Just before the bay of Cartoe, Biddiriscottai has a stunning mountain setting with dramatic sea views. The sea cliffs and crags rise above a cave. Technical climbing on 50 well-bolted routes ranging from 5b to 8a+.

☞ Tours

A huge fleet of boats, from large high-speed dinghies to small cruisers and graceful sailing vessels, is on hand at Cala Gonone to whisk you along the beautiful coastline. Boats operate from March until about October – dates depend a lot on demand. Prices vary according to season with 'very high season' being around 11 to 25 August. You can get information at agencies around town or at the booths at the port.

Prima Sardegna   HIKING, 4WD
(☑0784 9 33 67; www.primasardegna.com; Via Lungomare Palmasera 32; ☻9am-12pm & 4-7pm) This is the go-to place for climbing information, assistance and equipment rental (from €5 per piece). It also arranges guided excursions to Tiscali and Gorropu (€40), as well as hikes and 4WD tours in the Supramonte. Daily bike/scooter/single kayak/double kayak rental costs €24/48/30/55 respectively.

Nuovo Consorzio Trasporti Marittimi   BOAT
(☑0784 9 33 05; www.calagononecrociere.it, in Italian; Via Millelire 14) This outfit offers tours including return trips to Cala Luna (€12), Cala Sisine (€18), Cala Mariolu (€26) and Cala Gabbiani (€26). A trip to the Grotta Bue Marino costs €16.50, including entry to the cave. All tours are around €5 more in July and August. See the website for timetables.

Argonauta   DIVING
(☑0784 9 30 46, 349 473 86 52; www.argonauta .it; Via dei Lecci 10) PADI-accredited, Argonauta offers a range of water-based activities, including snorkelling tours (€25, €15 for kids), introductory diving courses (€90), cavern and wreck dives (€45) and canyoning excursions (€40).

Cielomar   BOAT
(☑0784 92 00 14; Località Palmasera) This outfit runs daylong tours along the gulf, costing from €40 per person, as well as hiring out *gommone* (motorised dinghies) for €80 to €120 per day, excluding petrol which usually costs an extra €25 or so.

Dolmen   4WD
(☑0784 932 60; www.sardegnadascoprire.it; Via Vasco da Gama 18) Another reliable operator is Dolmen, running 4WD tours into the Supramonte and canyoning excursions to the Gorropu. Bikes, scooters and dinghies are also available for hire. Call ahead for times and prices.

✖ Eating & Drinking

Besides the listings below, there are plenty of snack bars, gelaterias and pizzerias on or near the waterfront. Most places close from November to March.

TOP
CHOICE Agriturismo Nuraghe
Mannu   SARDINIAN €
(☑0784 9 32 64; www.agriturismonuraghemannu. com; off the SP26 Dorgali-Cala Gonone road; meals €25; ☻dinner) Scenically perched above the gulf and nestled amid silvery olive groves, this *agriturismo* puts on a mouth-watering

---

DON'T MISS

THE BLUE CRESCENT

If you do nothing else in Sardinia, you should try to make an excursion along the 20km southern stretch of the Golfo di Orosei by boat. Intimidating limestone cliffs plunge headlong into the sea, scalloped by pretty beaches, coves and grottoes. With an ever-changing palette of sand, rocks, pebbles, seashells and crystal-clear water, the unfathomable forces of nature have conspired to create a sublime taste of paradise. The colours are at their best until about 3pm, when the sun starts to drop behind the higher cliffs.

From the port of Cala Gonone you head south to the **Grotta del Bue Marino**. The first beach after the cave is **Cala Luna**, a crescent-shaped strand closed off by high cliffs to the south. **Cala Sisine** is the next beach of any size, also a mix of sand and pebbles and backed by a deep, verdant valley. **Cala Biriola** quickly follows, and then several enchanting spots where you can bob below the soaring cliffs – look out for the patches of celestial-blue water.

Cala Mariolu is arguably one of the most sublime spots on the coast. Split in two by a cluster of bright limestone rocks, it has virtually no sand. Don't let the smooth white pebbles put you off, though. The water that laps these beaches ranges from a kind of transparent white at water's edge through every shade of light and sky blue and on to a deep purplish hue.

For trekking and climbing maps and guides, check out **Namaste** (☑0784 937 23; Via Colombo di Gometz 11; ☺9am-1pm & 3-7pm daily). It stocks Maurizio Oviglia's *Pietra di Luna* (€30), a comprehensive rock-climbing guide covering the Cala Gonone, Jerzu and Baunei areas; Corrado Conca's *Il Sentiero Selvaggio Blu* (€16), covering the stunning seven-day Selvaggio Blu hike; and *La Sardegna in Bicicletta* (€13.90) detailing 1000km of cycling routes. You can also pick up walking maps and travel guides here.

spread. Loosen a belt notch for a feast of home-produced pecorino, salami, olives and wine, followed by handmade pasta, succulent roast kid or lamb and (phew!) Sardinian sweets.

Il Pescatore SEAFOOD €€
(☑0784 9 31 74; Via Acqua Dolce 7; meals €25-35; ☺daily) Fresh seafood is what this authentic place is about. Sit on the terrace for sea breezes and fishy delights, such as pasta with *ricci* and spaghetti with clams and *bottarga* (mullet roe), all washed down with half a litre of the crisp house white (€5).

Road House Blues ITALIAN €€
(☑0784 9 31 87; Lungomare Palmasera 28; meals €20-30; ☺daily) For a swift beer or a bite to eat, this relaxed haunt on the seafront *lungomare* is just the ticket. Dig into pizzas named after rock bands – think Parma ham, Pearl Jam – and Sardinian dishes such as homemade pasta with chard and pecorino. House wine is a snip at €8 a litre.

Ristorante Acquarius PIZZERIA, SARDINIAN €€
(☑0784 9 34 28; Lungomare Palmasera 34; pizza €6-8, meals around €30; ☺daily) There's always a good buzz at this cheery *lungomare* contender. The pizzas done in a wood-fired oven are spot-on, as is the *porceddu* (suckling pig) served with rosemary potatoes. Refresh your palate with a tangy myrtle sorbet.

Hotel Bue Marino ITALIAN €€
(☑0784 92 00 78; www.hotelbuemarino.it; Via Vespucci 8; meals around €30; ☺daily) The fashionable seafront bar of this smart hotel attracts a good-looking early-evening crowd, and its 4th-floor restaurant highlights locally sourced food. Try fish fresh from the Orosei Gulf and flavoursome Dorgali cheeses.

❶ Information

You can find information at the very helpful **tourist office** (☑0784 9 36 96; www.calagonone. com; Viale Bue Marino 1a; ☺9am-1pm & 3-7pm

summer, to 9pm Jul & Aug, 9.30-11.30am Fri-Wed winter) in the small park off to the right as you enter town.

There's an ATM down at the port, and you can check your email and use Skype at **Internet Point** (Piazza Da Verrazzano 3; internet/wi-fi per hr €5/4; ☺8.30-12.30pm & 4-7.30pm Mon-Sat).

❶ Getting There & Away

BUS Buses run to Cala Gonone from Dorgali (€1.50, 20 minutes, seven Monday to Saturday, four Sunday) and Nuoro (€3.50, 70 minutes, six Monday to Saturday, three Sunday). Buy tickets at **Bar La Pineta** (Viale C Colombo).

OGLIASTRA

Wedged in between Nuoro and Cagliari, the much smaller province of Ogliastra boasts some of the island's most spectacular scenery. Inland, it's a vertical land of unspoilt valleys, silent woods and windswept rock faces, while the coastal stretches become increasingly dramatic the nearer you get to the Golfo di Orosei.

Getting around the area is fairly slow, particularly inland. Distances are not great, but the mountainous landscape means roads are steep and often very twisty. You can travel by bus, but it would be better to hire a car if you want to get to the more out-of-the-way corners.

Tortolì & Arbatax

POP 10,800

Your impressions of Tortolì, Ogliastra's bustling provincial capital, depend on where you've arrived from. If you've just disembarked from the mainland you might be disappointed with the town's mundane, modern appearance. But if you've just emerged from the heavy silences of the interior you might find the cheery souvenir shops and large roadside hotels a welcome change.

KAYAKING IN CARDEDU

There's surely no better way to explore Ogliastra's coves, grottoes and striking rock formations than in a kayak, your paddle slicing rhythmically through the turquoise waters. In Cardedu, 16km south of Tortolì, you'll find **Cardedu Kayak** (☑0782 75185; www.cardedu-kayak.com; Località Perda Rubia), where kayak guru Francesco Muntoni shares his passion for the deep blue with kayakers of all levels. His courses cost €150 for five two-hour lessons and, if you would prefer to go it alone, daily kayak rental starts at €25 per person. Be sure to bring your swimming gear in summer. Francesco can also help arrange longer tours and 'nautical camping' if you fancy fishing from the kayak and sleeping on the secluded beaches.

Ferries from Cagliari arrive at Arbatax port, about 4km away down Viale Monsignor Virgilio, and you can also arrange boat tours up the coast to the Golfo di Orosei from here. In summer you can catch the *trenino verde* from the station in Arbatax.

◉ Sights & Activities

Tortolì and Arbatax are resort towns and sights are few and far between. At the port you can arrange boat excursions up the coast to the beaches and grottoes of the Golfo di Orosei. Costs vary but are typically around €40 to €50 per person.

Arbatax Beaches BEACH
You can hit the beach on either side of Arbatax. You'll find the fine sandy bays and crystal waters of **Spiaggia Orri**, **Spiaggia Musculedda** and **Spiaggia Is Scogliu Arrubius** about 4km south of hotel-dotted Porto Frailis. Or continue even further south to the pristine cliff-flanked cove of **Spiaggia Cala Francese** at **Marina di Gairo**.

Rocce Rosse LANDMARK
If you have a moment in Arbatax, head across the road from the port and behind the petrol station to the Rocce Rosse (red rocks). Like the ruins of some fairy-tale castle, these bizarre, weather-beaten rock formations dropping into the sea are well worth a camera shot or two, framed in the distance by the imperious cliffs of the southern Ogliastra and Golfo di Orosei.

✖ Eating

You'll find a handful of so-so pizzerias and snack bars by the port in Arbatax; nearly all are closed from November to March.

Ittiturismo La Peschiera SEAFOOD €€
(☑0782 66 44 15; Spiaggia della Cartiera; meals around €30; ⊙daily) What swims in the Med in the morning lands on plates by lunchtime at this Ittiturismo, run by Tortolì's fishing cooperative. The humble shack may be in the back of beyond, but it's worth going the extra mile for fish this fresh. Follow the signs as you enter town and walk five minutes along a reed-fringed river bank..

La Bitta ITALIAN €€€
(☑0782 66 70 80; Località Porto Frailis; meals €40-55; ⊙daily) For fine dining in Porto Frailis, you can't beat La Bitta. Dress dandy for exquisitely prepared food – think handmade pasta with skate and dill pesto and macaroni with artichokes, ricotta and *bottarga* (mullet roe).

ℹ Information

At Arbatax you can get information from the **tourist office** (☑0782 66 76 90; Via Lungomare 21; ⊙summer only) by the *trenino verde* terminus.

On the main strip in Tortolì, **Frailis Viaggi** (☑0782 62 00 21; www.frailisviaggi.it; Via Roma 12; ⊙9am-1pm & 4.30-8pm Mon-Fri) is a useful travel agency where you can book ferry and plane tickets, as well as organise boat excursions (€50 per person) and hire a car (€70 per day).

ℹ Getting There & Away

AIR The tiny Arbatax-Tortolì **airstrip** (☑0782 62 43 00; www.aeroportoTortoliarbatax.it) is about 1.5km south of Tortolì. It's served by summer-only charter flights from mainland Italian destinations including Rome and Albenga (in Liguria). Most arrivals come on a package with transport arranged.

BOAT The main ferry company serving Arbatax is **Tirrenia** (☑892 123; www.tirrenia.it). Ferries sail to/from Genoa (€59, 18 hours, twice weekly), Civitavecchia (€49, 10½ hours, twice weekly) and, from late July to August, Fiumicino (€63, 4½ hours, twice weekly). There are also connections with Cagliari (€33, 5¼ hours, twice weekly) and Olbia (€31.50, 4½ hours, twice weekly). You can get tickets and information from Tirrenia's ticket agency, **Torchiani & Co** (☑0782 66 78 41; Via Venezia 10), which is located at the port.

BUS ARST buses connect Tortolì with Santa Maria Navarrese (€1.20, 15 minutes, 11 daily Monday to Saturday, two Sunday), Dorgali (€5, one hour 50 minutes, one daily Monday to Saturday), and Nuoro (€7, 2½ to three hours, four daily Monday to Saturday), as well as many inland villages. Local buses 1 and 2 run from Arbatax to Tortolì and, in the case of the latter service, to the beach and hotels at nearby Porto Frailis.

TRAIN Near the port, you'll find the terminus for the **trenino verde** (☑070 58 02 46; www .treninoverde.com), a scenic train that runs between Arbatax and Mandas (€19, five hours) twice daily, except Tuesday, from mid-June to mid-September. Stops include Lanusei, Arzana, Ussassai and Seui. The route between Arbatax and Mandas is the most scenic on the island, chugging along a gravity-defying track through some of Sardinia's least accessible mountain terrain.

LOTZORAI
POP 2190

Located about 6km north of Tortolì, Lotzorai is not of enormous interest in itself but it sits behind some glorious pine-backed beaches, such as **Spiaggia delle Rose**. To find the beach, follow the signs to the three camping grounds that are clustered just behind it.

On the country road towards Talana, 4km from Lotzorai, you'll find the farm-style **Ristorante Sant'Efisio** (☑0782 64 69 21; www.hotel-santefisio.com; Località Sant'Efisio; meals €25-30; ☺lunch & dinner daily; ⚬). Choose between the rustic dining room and flowery terrace to relax and enjoy classic regional dishes. Try handmade *culurgiones* (ravioli) filled with fresh cheese and mint, spit-roasted wild boar and *tacculas* (quails wrapped in myrtle) with a local Cannonau red.

LOCAL KNOWLEDGE

PETER AND ANNE, OUTDOOR EXPERTS

Owners of the Lemon House (p213) in Lotzorai, Peter and Anne have been exploring Ogliastra's wilderness since the 1990s. Peter has bolted some of the 800 climbs in the area, is the co-founder of Mountain Bike Ogliastra (www.mountainbikeogliastra.it), and has covered 25 mountain-bike routes for the new Versante Sud guide. See www.peteranne.it for tips, route itineraries and videos.

Climbing

For deep water soloists, there's superb granite at the easily accessible **Vascone** south of Cala 'e Luas. The **Aguglia** pinnacle at Cala Goloritzè is an awesome multipitch climb; the toughest bit is the overhang where the hardest move is a 6b+.

Sea Kayaking

The red granite rocks at the **Spiaggetta** near Baunei are stunning. Or paddle in and out of the rocks and caves from **Cardedu** to **Cala e' Luas**, stopping to swim on the beach. More experienced kayakers can head north to **Goloritzè** via the magnificent Pedra Longa sea stack and 300m-high cliffs where the Eleonora's falcon can sometimes be spotted.

Hiking

A great half-day hike that is even accessible for families is from Golgo to **Cala Goloritzè**. There are spectacular views of the turquoise sea and the Aguglia pinnacle. By far the best multiday hike is the coastal **Selvaggio Blu**.

Mountain Biking

The 50km ride from Golgo plateau along an old mule trail to **Cala Sisine** and back up to the Codula is fantastic – and all the better for being natural! It's a technically interesting single track involving 1000m of vertical descent to the sea. Another challenging favourite is the two-hour freeride from **Locorbu** to Santa Maria Navarrese.

SANTA MARIA NAVARRESE

At the southern end of the Golfo di Orosei sits the unpretentious and attractive beach resort of Santa Maria Navarrese. Shipwrecked Basque sailors built a small church here in 1052, and then dedicated it to Santa Maria di Navarra on the orders of the Princess of Navarre, who happened to be one of the shipwreck's survivors. The church was set in the shade of a grand olive tree that is still standing – some say it's nearly 2000 years old.

◎ Sights & Activities

Lofty pines and eucalyptus trees back the lovely beach lapped by transparent water (with more sandy stretches to the south). Offshore are several islets, including the **Isolotto di Ogliastra**, a giant hunk of pink porphyritic rock rising 47m out of the water. The leafy northern end of the beach is topped by a watchtower built to look out for raiding Saracens.

About 500m further north is the small pleasure port, where various operators run cruises up the increasingly wild coastline. The **Consorzio Marittimo Ogliastra** (☑0782 61 51 73; www.mareogliastra.com) charges between €30 and €35 per person for tours that take in sea caves and several stunning swimming spots, such as Cala Goloritzè, Cala Mariolu, and Cala Sisine. If you prefer to dive into the blue stuff, **Nautica Centro Sub** (☑0782 61 55 22) next door organises dives (from €35) to some wonderful underwater spots.

Rearing above the landscape like a bishop's mitre, the crag of **Monte Scoine** attracts climbers to its bolted routes (4b to 6b), especially in summer when it stays shady until midafternoon.

✖ Eating & Drinking

You'll find a handful of bars and pizzerias in town and down by the seafront, including **Bar L'Olivastro** (☑0782 61 55 13; Via Lungomare Montesanto 1; ⊗8am-1am daily) set up on shady terraces below the weird and wonderful branches of the town's famous olive tree.

❶ Getting There & Around

BUS A handful of ARST buses link Santa Maria Navarrese with Tortolì (€1.20, 15 minutes, 11 daily Monday to Saturday, two Sunday), Dorgali (€4, 1½ hours, two daily), Nuoro (€7, 2½ hours, four daily Monday to Saturday, two on Sunday) and Cagliari (€9.50, four hours, four daily Monday to Saturday).

Baunei & the Altopiano del Golgo

POP 3780

Continuing north along the coast, after about 9km you hit the shepherd's town of Baunei. There's little reason to stop off here, but what is seriously worth your while is the 10km detour up to the Altopiano del Golgo, a strange, other-worldly plateau where goats, pigs and donkeys graze in the *macchia* (Mediterranean scrub) and woodland. From here a road snakes down to the rock spike of **Pedra Longa**, a natural monument and also the starting point for Sardinia's star coastal trek, the Selvaggio Blu.

◎ Sights & Activities

TOP
CHOICE Cala Goloritzè   BEACH
The last beachette of the gulf, Cala Goloritzè rivals the best. At the southern end, bizarre limestone figures soar away from the cliffside. Among them is jaw-dropping Monte Caroddi or the Aguglia, a 148m-high needle of rock beloved of climbers. Follow the signs from the Cooperativa Goloritzè at the Golgo plateau and it's a gentle hour's walk down (and slightly tougher 1½ hours back) to Cala Goloritzè. Suitable for families, the easygoing hike along an old mule trail takes you through a beautiful limestone canyon shaded by juniper and holm oaks, passing cliffs honeycombed with caves, dramatic rock arches, overhangs and pinnacles en route.

After you've been walking for around 15 minutes you'll get your first tantalising glimpses of the bay and a sea so blue it will make you gasp. Keep an eye out for a traditional sheepfold and the idiosyncratic spike of the Aguglia as you approach the bay. Steps lead down to the half-moon of bone-white pebbles; this is a perfect picnic spot. Bring along your bathers for a dip in the deliciously warm, astonishingly blue waters.

Il Golgo   NATURAL MONUMENT
From the town a signpost sends you up a 2km climb of impossibly steep switchbacks to the plateau. Head north and, after 8km, follow the Su Sterru (Il Golgo) sign (for less than 1km), leave your vehicle and head for this remarkable feat of nature – a 270m abyss just 40m wide at its base. Its funnel-like opening is now fenced off but,

knowing the size of the drop, just peering into the dark opening is enough to bring on the vertigo.

Chiesa di San Pietro
CHURCH

Just beyond Locanda Il Rifugio's stables is this late-16th-century church, a humble construction flanked to one side by *cumbessias* – rough, largely open stone affairs which are not at all comfortable for the passing pilgrims who traditionally sleep here to celebrate the saint's day.

Cooperativa Goloritzè
WALKING TOURS

(☑0782 61 05 99; Località Golgo; www.coopgolori tze.com, in Italian) Based at Locanda Il Rifugio, this highly regarded cooperative arranges excursions ranging from trekking to 4WD jeep trips. Many treks involve a descent from the plateau through canyons, such as the Codula di Luna or the Codula de Sisine, to the Golfo di Orosei's dreamy beaches. Staff at the refuge also organise guides and logistical support for walkers attempting Sardinia's once-in-a-lifetime Selvaggio Blu trek. If you're interested, make sure to plan well in advance. Prices for the excursions vary depending on the itinerary – which you can agree on beforehand – and how many people are in the group.

Cooperativa Turistica Golgo
WALKING TOURS

(☑0782 61 06 75; www.golgotrekking.com; Località Golgo) This is a similar set up to Cooperativa Goloritzè, organising treks to bays and grottoes along the coast.

Eating & Drinking

Ristorante Golgo
SARDINIAN €€

(☑337 81 18 28; Località Golgo; meals €25-30; ☺daily Apr-Sep). Set among olive trees and commanding magical views over the countryside, this quaint stone restaurant rustles up tasty spit-roasted meats. Follow the signpost opposite the turn-off for Su Sterru.

Locanda Il Rifugio
SARDINIAN €€

(☑0782 61 05 99; Località Golgo; www.coopgolori tze.com, in Italian; meals around €30; ☺daily Apr-Oct) Managed by the Cooperativa Goloritzè, this beautifully converted farmstead puts on a generous spread of regional fare such as *ludeddos* (potato gnocchi) and spit-roasted kid, washed down with local Cannonau red.

Inland Ogliastra

JERZU
POP 3240

Known as the *Citta del Vino* (Wine Town), Jerzu is famous for its full-bodied Cannonau red wine. The town is set precariously on a mountainside, its steeply stacked buildings surrounded by imposing limestone towers, known as *tacchi* (heels), and some 800 hectares of vineyards. Each year about 50,000 quintals of grapes are harvested to make two million bottles of wine at the **Antichi Poderi di Jerzu** (☑0782 7 00 28; www .jerzuantichipoderi.it; Via Umberto 1; ☺8.30am-1pm & 2-5pm Mon-Fri), the town's modern cantina.

SELVAGGIO BLU

For serious hikers, the Selvaggio Blu is the stuff of myth: an epic seven-day, 45km trek along the Golfo di Orosei's wild and imperious coastline, traversing thickly wooded ravines and taking in bizarre limestone formations, caves and staggeringly sheer cliffs. Both the scenery and the walking are breathtaking (in every sense of the word!) on what is often hailed as Italy's toughest trek.

The trail follows the starkly eroded – and often invisible – trails of goatherds and charcoal burners, teetering around cliffs that plunge into the dazzlingly blue sea. Because of its challenging terrain, the trek requires a good level of fitness and some climbing experience for the short climbs and abseiling involved. The seven-day duration is based on the assumption that you will walk six to eight hours a day. You'll also need to come prepared with a bivi bag or an ultralight tent, climbing gear (including two 45m ropes), a roll mat, sturdy boots, a compass, map and ample food.

A guide is recommended as the trail is not well signposted and there's no water en route (guides can arrange for it to be dropped off by boat). The website www.selvaggio-blu.it (in Italian) will give you itchy feet

The author of *Arrampicare a Cala Gonone* (€18) and *Il Sentiero Selvaggio Blu* (€16), **Corrado Conca** (☑347 2 90 31 01; corrado@segnavia.it) is Sardinia's hiking and climbing guru, and a brilliant guide for the trek. Bank on paying around €500 per person. Corrado is often up in the hills climbing, so give him plenty of notice.

ULASSAI & OSINI
POP 1550

Heading north from Jerzu you're in for some scenic treats as the road licks a tortuous path around the titanic mountains to Ulassai, dwarfed by the rocky pinnacles of Bruncu Pranedda and Bruncu Matzei. Although nothing special in itself, this small village is surrounded by some of Sardinia's most thrilling and impenetrable countryside, a vast natural playground for outdoor enthusiasts, with superb rock climbing and trekking.

Climbers in particular will have a high time of it. The sheer rock faces of the Bruncu Pranedda canyon and the Lecori cliffs provide some 80 routes, including a number of pretty tough ascents. Trekkers can walk the canyon or head 7km southwest to view the dramatic Cascata Lequarci waterfall before picnicking in the idyllic environs of the Santuario di Santa Barbara. The www .ulassai.net site is a useful resource.

Housed in the old railway station, the outstanding Stazione dell'Arte Maria Lai (☑0782 78 70 55; www.stazionedellarte.it; adult/ reduced €5/3; ☉9am-9pm daily summer; to 7pm Wed-Sun winter) showcases the emotive artworks of Maria Lai. Born in Ulassai in 1919 (and still working at the age of 92 at the time of writing!), Maria is one of Sardinia's most important contemporary artists.

For rugs, towels, curtains and bedspreads bearing Maria's naturalistic designs, head to the Su Marmuri Cooperative Tessile Artigiana (☑0782 7 90 76 Via Funtana Seri; ☉8am-noon & 2-7pm Mon-Sat summer, 8am-noon & 2-6pm Mon-Fri winter). Here you'll find a group of dedicated ladies keeping alive traditional hand-looming techniques and you can see the noisy looms in action. Prices start at around €20 for a hand towel.

High above Ulassai, the mammoth Grotta di Su Marmuri (☑0782 7 98 59; adult/ reduced €10/6; ☉tours 11am, 2pm, 4pm, 6pm summer, 11am, 2.30pm & 5pm winter) is a 35m-high cave complex. Visits are by guided tour only (minimum of four people), which take you on a one-hour, 1km walk through an underground wonderland festooned with stalactites and stalagmites. By the car park at the cave ticket office is a fine trattoria, the Su Bullicciu (☑0782 7 98 59), where you can lunch on delicious roast meats for about €20 per person.

A short way to the north, and accessible from the village of Osini, is the Scala di San Giorgio. This vertical gully takes its name from the 12th-century saint who is said to have divided the rock as he walked through the area proselytising in 1117. From the top you get vast views over the valley to the abandoned villages of Osini Vecchio and Gairo Vecchio, both destroyed by landslides in 1951.

Also worth visiting are the extensive ruins of the Complesso Nuragico di Serbissi, a complex site with an unusual underground cave once used to store foodstuffs. You can explore the area on your own, but with a guide you'll learn far more. Operating out of the nearby village of Osini, Archeo Taccu (☑329 764 33 43; Via Eleonora D'Arborea) is a small local cooperative running guided tours.

Accommodation

Best Places to Sleep

» Il Cagliarese (p199)

» Mandra Edera (p205)

» Villa Las Tronas (p206)

» The Lemon House (p213)

Best B&Bs

» B&B Lu Pastruccialeddu (p209)

» La Babbajola B&B (p201)

» Silvia e Paolo (p211)

Best Boutique Hotels

» Hotel Panorama (p207)

» Corte Fiorita (p205)

» Hotel Lucrezia (p204)

» Hotel Su Gologone (p211)

Where to Stay

So what's it to be? A B&B housed in a restored palazzo in Nuoro, a chic apartment in Cagliari's medieval Castello district, or a back-to-nature *agriturismo* (farm-stay accommodation) hidden in Gallura's oak forests? With so many atmospheric choices, deciding where to stay in Sardinia is more than just choosing a bed for the night.

If you are here for the beaches, the island's your oyster: whether it's to be the serene Costa Verde in the southwest, the silky sands of the Costa del Sud in the south, or the glamour of the Costa Smeralda in the northeast. Up for an adventure? Base yourself in laid-back Cala Gonone, Dorgali or Santa Maria Navarrese in the east for rock climbing, high-altitude hiking, water sports and sensational coastal walks.

With a little careful planning, accommodation need not be eye-wateringly expensive, either. Outside of high season (mid-June to August), rates invariably drop, often by as much as 50%. Generally, the further you are from the sea, the cheaper it gets. Note that most hotels close from mid-October to Easter.

In this chapter we have tried to feature well-located, independent accommodation options that offer charm, good value and a heartfelt Sardinian welcome. The reviews are listed in order of author preference.

Pricing

The price indicators in this book refer to the cost of a double room with private bathroom – and including breakfast unless otherwise noted. Where half board (breakfast and dinner) and full board (breakfast, lunch and dinner) is included, this is mentioned in the price.

CATEGORY	COST
€ budget	< €100
€€ midrange	€100–200
€€€ top end	> €200

Agriturismi

Bracing country hikes, sundowners under the olive trees and waking to the sound of braying donkeys – if the thought of this appeals, you'll feel at home in an *agriturismo*. Often immersed in greenery at the end of long dirt tracks, these family-friendly working farms are for those who value peace and quiet over creature comforts.

Housed in a traditional *stazzo* (farmstead) or stone cottage, rooms are simple and snug – expect to pay between €70 and €100 for a double – and breakfasts are copious. Many *agriturismi* give you the choice of half board (€60 to €80 per person) and dinner tends to be a jolly communal affair, with a feast of farm-fresh vegies, cheese, meat and wine. The only catch is that you'll almost certainly need your own wheels.

To search for your country escape by region, visit www.agriturismodisardegna.it, www.agriturismo.it and www.tuttoagriturismo.net (in Italian).

B&Bs

Like *agriturismi*, B&Bs often offer good value for money, particularly when compared with the prices of local hotels. There is no island-wide umbrella group for B&Bs, but tourist offices can usually provide contact details. In Cagliari, **Domus Karalitanae** (www.domuskaralitanae.it) offers a comprehensive listing of the city's B&Bs. Online listings are available at www.bed-and-breakfast.it.

On average, budget for about €25 to €45 per person per night in a B&B.

Camping

Campers are well catered for in Sardinia, with most campgrounds scenically located on the coast and offering top-notch facilities like swimming pools, restaurants, supermarkets and kids' clubs. If inflatable mattresses are not your thing, many campgrounds have well-equipped bungalows. Prices can be surprisingly high in July and August, when advance bookings are recommended. Expect to pay between €30 and €40 for a site for two people, a car and a tent, and extra for showers and electricity. Campgrounds usually open from Easter to mid-October.

So you can picture yourself waking up on that secluded beach, huh? Wild camping is officially not permitted, but out of the main season and away from the resorts, you can often get away with it, providing you keep the noise down and don't light fires. Always get permission to camp on private property.

You can get lists of camping grounds from local tourist offices or online at www.campeggi.com or www.camping.it.

Hostels

Sardinia's six youth hostels are run by the **Italian Youth Hostel Association** (Associazione Italiana Alberghi per la Gioventù; ☏06 487 11 52; www.aighostels.com), which is affiliated with **Hostelling International** (HI; www.hihostels.com). You'll need to have a HI card (€18) to stay at these hostels. Dorm rates range from €15 to €25, including breakfast. All the hostels also have beds in private rooms, typically costing around €20 per person.

Hotels

Hotels in Sardinia (and their rates) vary wildly, from small, family-run *pensioni* (guesthouses) with just a couple of no-frills rooms to the mammoth resort-style villages on the coast with private beaches, tennis courts, spas, the works. Quality varies enormously and the official star system should be taken with a pinch of salt.

For guaranteed character and boutique style look out for Charme e Relax (www.charmerelax.it). This Italian association specialises in small to mid-sized hotels, usually in unique buildings (monasteries, castles, old inns and so on) or special locations.

Tourist offices have booklets listing all local accommodation, including prices.

CAGLIARI & THE SARRABUS

Cagliari

For charm, value and a good old-fashioned welcome, Cagliari's B&Bs outshine its so-so hotels. Stay central in the Marina and Il Castello districts, or bag a bargain by going the extra mile to Villanova.

TOP CHOICE **Il Cagliarese** B&B €
(Map p38; ☑070 81 03 46; www.ilcagliarese.com; Via Vittorio Porcile 19; s €40-70, d €60-90; ❄️🛜) Bang in the heart of Marina district, this snug B&B is a find. Mauro bends over backwards to please and his sister, Titziana, plays the cake fairy at breakfast with her scrumptious pastries and tiramisu. The immaculate rooms sport homey touches such as embroidered fabrics and carved wooden furnishings.

Hostel Marina HOSTEL €
(Map p38; ☑070 67 08 18; Scalette San Sepolcro; dm/s/d €22/40/60; ❄️🖥️) Housed in a beautifully converted 800-year-old former monastery, this hostel has oodles of historic charm and original features such as vaulting and beams. Many of the spacious, well-kept dorms overlook the city. Help yourself to fresh bread, fruit and coffee at breakfast. Bike hire, sailing courses and Italian classes can be arranged – just ask.

La Peonia B&B €
(☑070 51 31 64; www.lapeonia.com; Via Riva Villasanta 77; s €50-60, d €72-88; ❄️🛜) Antonello and Vanna are your kindly hosts at this romantic

neo-Gothic abode. Turn-of-the-century interiors with polished wood furnishings are a striking contrast to the sleek, monochrome bathrooms. Bus M from Piazza Matteotti pulls up in front of the B&B, 2.5km northeast of town.

T Hotel HOTEL €€
(☑070 4 74 00; www.thotel.it; Via dei Giudicati; s/d/ste/f €139/159/199/249; 🅿️❄️🛜🖥️♿) This hard-to-miss steel-and-glass tower adds a dash of contemporary design to the cityscape. The rooms reveal a linear, modish look, and the spa invites relaxation with its hydrotherapy pool, jets and treatments. From Piazza Matteotti, take bus M to Via Baracedda and walk 200m.

Residenza Kastrum B&B €
(Map p38; ☑070 66 23 04; www.kastrum.eu; Via Canelles 78; d €70-90, tr €90-120, q €120-160; ❄️🛜♿) This cosy, characterful B&B has marvellous views over the city rooftops to the gulf from its hilltop Castello perch. The simple, spotless rooms are geared up for families (cots are available). Linger over breakfast and memorable sunsets on the terrace.

APARTMENT & VILLA RENTALS

If you plan to stay in one place for a week or more, self-catering accommodation can be excellent value. For a two- to four-bed apartment, rates are typically between €350 and €600 per week in low season, €500 to €900 in high season. You'll pay double that for a more luxurious villa with a swimming pool and sea views. Be sure to read the small print for additional charges such as electricity, water, bed linen and final cleaning.

Apartments are generally well located and equipped with kitchenettes and terraces or balconies. Seven nights is usually the minimum stay and some apartments have fixed change-over days. You may be required to pay a deposit of around 30% by credit card or bank transfer when you book, and some places require the balance to be settled before arrival.

Pick up lists of apartments and villas for rent at local tourist offices, or find one to suit your style on the following websites:

» **Costa Smeralda Holidays** (www.costasmeralda-holidays.com) Offers villas on the Costa Smeralda with luxury trimmings from tennis courts to pools, lemon orchards to private beaches.

» **Holiday Lettings** (www.holidaylettings.co.uk) Great selection of good-value apartments across the island, all searchable by region.

» **HomeAway** (www.holiday-rentals.co.uk) Features around 1500 self-catering options, from country retreats near Alghero to townhouses in Olbia.

» **Owners Direct** (www.ownersdirect.co.uk) An easy-to-navigate website with a wide array of apartments and villas to suit all budgets.

» **Rent Sardinia** (www.rent-sardinia.com) A good selection of 1000 villas and apartments scattered across the island, searchable by location and other criteria.

» **Sardegne.com** (www.sardegne.com/residence) Lists apartment rentals alongside B&Bs, *agriturismi* and hotels.

La Ghirlanda
B&B €

(Map p38; ☑070 20 40 610; www.laghirlan dacagliari.it; Via Baylle 7; s €48-60, d €75-90, tr €100-120; ❋⊕) Antiques and frescoes whisk you back in time at this handsome 18th-century townhouse in the Marina district. The bright, high-ceilinged rooms are tastefully done out in pastel colours and wooden floors. Breakfast at a nearby bar is included in the price.

Suite Sul Corso
B&B €€

(Map p38; ☑349 446 9789; www.lesuitesulcorso.it; Corso Vittorio Emanuele 8; s €70-90, d €90-120, tr €130-160, ste €130-170; ❋⊕) Sleep in style at this boutique B&B just off Piazza Yenne. Exposed stone, floaty fabrics and glass mosaics lend warmth to the minimalist-chic rooms, all with flat-screen TVs and kettles. The triple even has its own whirlpool. The owner's quirky photography jazzes up the corridors.

Il Girasole
B&B €

(Map p38; ☑070 81 03 46; www.ilgirasole.sardegna. it; Vico Barcellona 6; d €70-85; ❋⊕) As bright and cheery as a *girasole* (sunflower), this boho-flavoured B&B is crammed with ethnic knick-knacks and African art. Luca is a happy-go-lucky soul and puts on a decent spread at breakfast. You're welcome to use the kitchen and unwind in the living room or on the terrace.

Hotel Due Colonne
HOTEL €€

(Map p38; ☑070 65 87 10; www.hotel2colonne .it; Via Sardegna 4; s €68-85, d €110-140, tr €145; ❋⊕) This boutique-style hotel is located on one of the Marina district's liveliest streets. Satin sheets add a dash of class to the rooms, and bathrooms positively gleam. When you're hungry, there are plenty of restaurants and cafes right on your doorstep.

B&B La Marina
B&B €

(Map p38; ☑070 67 00 65; www.la-marina.it; Via Porcile 23; d €70-75; ❋⊕) This is a good-value B&B in the atmospheric Marina district. The elderly couple who run the place keep a tight ship and the four wood-beamed rooms are pristine. There are a couple of communal breakfast rooms with fridges available for guest use.

La Terrazza sul Porto
B&B €

(Map p38; ☑070 65 89 97; www.laterrazzasul porto.com; Largo Carlo Felice 36; s €50-60, d €70-100; ❋⊕) Owner Franco has transformed his 19th-century top-floor flat into this wonderfully eccentric, gay-friendly B&B. The high-ceilinged rooms are bursting with original flair, and there's a fully equipped kitchen and a sunny rooftop terrace. Bonus: you can eat breakfast as late as you like.

TOP TEN AGRITURISMI

The best way to experience real authentic Sardinian food is to eat at an *agriturismo* (farm-stay accommodation). There are hundreds dotted around the island, but these are our faves:

» **Agriturismo Ca' La Somara** (p209) This laid-back farm has beautiful gardens, home-grown vegetarian fare and friendly donkeys.

» **Su Pranu** (p204) A genuine working farm on the wild, peaceful Sinis Peninsula. Vegetables and fruit are home-grown.

» **Porticciolo** (p206) A friendly 24-hectare farm near Alghero, with 100 pigs.

» **Rena** (p209) Escape the Costa Smeralda hordes at this rural spot, which produces its own cheese, meat and wine.

» **Agriturismo Su Boschettu** (p204) A blissfully relaxed farmstead nestled amid olive and fruit trees.

» **Bio Agriturismo Bainas** (p205) A simple, no-frills farmstead, surround by olive and orange orchards.

» **Guthiddai** (p211) A delightful whitewashed retreat in the granite Supramonte.

» **Nuraghe Mannu** (p213) Look over the spectacular Orosei coast at this terraced jewel.

» **Li Licci** (p210) Hidden among oak trees in Gallura's green heartland.

» **Agriturismo L'Aquila** (p202) A comfortable and rustic working farm, dishing up a feast of home-grown fare.

Il Profumo del Mare
B&B €

(☎338 1 44 82 75; Viale Poetto 196; d €55-80; P❋) Ignore the nondescript facade – this is a terrific budget pick, just a pebble's throw away from Poetto Beach. The breezy rooms are done out in sky blues, and the terrace has cracking sea views. Antonio is happy to share his tips on Cagliari. Take bus PF or PQ from Piazza Matteotti.

Villasimius

Hotel Mariposas
HOTEL €€

(☎070 79 00 84; www.hotelmariposas.it; Viale Matteotti; s €74-167, d €96-216, f €129-291; P❋🛜🐾♨) A short hop from the beach, this low-slung hotel is set in glorious flower-strewn gardens. The spacious rooms all have their own terrace or balcony, and there's an attractive pool for whiling away an afternoon.

Stella Maris
HOTEL €€€

(☎070 79 71 00; www.stella-maris.com; Località Campulongu; half-board per person €155-255; P❋🛜🐾♨) On the road to the Porto Turistico, this is a beautiful resort hotel set in its own pine wood on a frost-white beach. Rooms are stylish, decorated with Sardinian fabrics and tasteful furniture, and the gardens and split-level pool are perfect for some R&R.

Spiaggia del Riso
CAMPGROUND €

(☎070 79 10 52; www.villaggiospiaggiadelriso.it; Località Campulongu; 2 people, car & tent €21-40, 4-person bungalows €80-160; P) Set in a pine grove near the Porto Turistico, this big beachside campsite has tent pitches, bungalows, a supermarket and a children's play area. Booking is absolutely essential in summer.

Costa Rei

Albaruja Hotel
HOTEL €€

(☎070 99 15 57; www.albaruja.it; Via Colombo; d €98-198, half-board per person €65-119; P❋🐾♨) The Albaruja is a cut above most of the hotels on the Costa Rei, with attractive villa-style residences nestled in flowery gardens, a kids playground and a palm-rimmed pool. It's just a two-minute walk from the beach.

Camping Capo Ferrato
CAMPGROUND €

(☎070 99 10 12; www.campingcapoferrato.it; Costa Rei; 2 people, car & tent €16-37.50, 4-person bungalow €59-124; ♨) Pitch a tent under the eucalyptus and mimosa trees at this beach-

---

BAG A BARGAIN

Surf the following websites for great deals on last-minute accommodation in Sardinia:

» www.alpharooms.com
» www.lastminute.com
» www.laterooms.com
» www.priceline.com
» www.travelsupermarket.com

front campground by the southern entrance to the resort. There's a mini club (summer only) and playground for kids.

IGLESIAS & THE SOUTHWEST

Iglesias

[TOP CHOICE] La Babbajola B&B
B&B €

(Map p58; ☎347 614 46 21; www.lababbajola.com; Via Giordano 13; per person €27-30; ♨) A laid-back, homey B&B in a gorgeous old mansion inside the *centro storico*, La Babbajola (ladybird) is run by the friendly Carla Cani and her mother. Accommodation is in a mini-apartment or one of three big double rooms, each of which features patterned old floor tiles, bold colours and tasteful furniture. There's a kitchen and TV room for guest use. Two of the three double rooms share a bathroom.

Eurohotel
HOTEL €€

(Map p58; ☎078 12 26 43; www.eurohoteliglesias.it, in Italian; Via Fratelli Bandieri 34; s €60-80, d €85-110; P❋) A kitsch rendition of a Pompeian villa, the Eurohotel is difficult to miss. With its pompous porticoed entrance and curling balconies, it hardly matches the workaday buildings that surround it. Inside, the theme carries on as rooms reveal a mix of faux-gilt chairs, Murano-style chandeliers and sombre oil paintings.

The Iglesiente

Hotel Golfo del Leone
HOTEL €

(☎0781 5 49 52; www.golfodelleone.it; Localita Caburu de Figu; s €48-58, d €63-90) This cheery pink hotel boasts bright sea-facing rooms about 1km back from Portixeddu beach. Service is friendly, and the helpful staff can organise horse-riding excursions. The adjacent restaurant serves up decent local food for about €25 per head.

Ostello Su Mannau
HOTEL €

(☎347 009 53 67; www.ostellosumannau.com; Grotta de Su Mannau; r €50-70) On the unnamed road to Grotta de Su Mannau, this is a tranquil three-star place about 200m from the cave car park. Rooms are bright and clean and the location is idyllic, submerged in silent woods and surrounded by greenery.

Costa Verde

Agriturismo L'Aquila
FARMSTAY €

(☎347 822 24 26; www.aglaquila.com; Localita Is Gennas Arbus, Montevecchio; r per person €30, half-board per person €42-55; ✦) A great place to try out local cuisine and stay on a working farm. The rooms are simple, comfortable and rustic, and pretty much frill free. The main draw is the homemade food, sourced from the farm itself. To get here take the signposted exit off the SP65 and follow the dirt track for about 2.5km.

Verdemare
B&B €€

(☎070 97 72 72; www.verdemare.com; Via Colombo, Torre dei Corsari; s €46-68, d €70-104; ☺Easter-Nov; ✱) Immersed in lush gardens, Verdemare has a large terrace with distant sea views and bright, cool rooms. Air-con costs an extra €3 but you can also bed down inside the mosquito net.

Hotel Caletta
HOTEL €

(☎070 97 71 33; www.lacaletta.it; Torre dei Corsari; half board per person €58-98; ☺end Apr-Sep; P✱✱☀) A big three-star hotel on a rocky point overlooking the sea. Rooms have all mod-cons, there's a boomerang-shaped swimming pool, and a small disco. There's a minimum two-week stay over the Ferragosto (15 August) period.

Carbonia & Around

La Ghinghetta
HOTEL €€

(☎078 150 81 43; www.laghinghetta.com; Via Cavour 26, Portoscuso; s €130-135, d €130-140, half board €130-175; ☺May-Oct; ✦) This is a lovely seaside hotel that skilfully combines charm, comfort and cuisine. Overlooking the beach, it has attractive, nautically

themed rooms set in a whitewashed fisherman's house, and a highly regarded restaurant that specialises in seafood – set menus start at €65.

Narcao

Agriturismo Santa Croce
FARMSTAY €

(☎349 879 11 39; Localita Santa Croce; s €22-35, d €42-60) If you want to stay overnight in Narcao, head just outside the town, where a pink roadside bungalow has modest rooms and an excellent restaurant (set menus €10 to €22; dinner by reservation only). Hearty local fare, including home-reared lamb and pork are your best bet.

Southwest Islands

ISOLA DI SAN PIETRO

TOP CHOICE Hotel Riviera
HOTEL €€

(☎0781 85 41 01; www.hotelriviera-carloforte.com, in Italian; Corso Battellieri 26, Carloforte; s €75-120, d €120-190, ste €250-370;✱) Right on the seafront, this swank but relaxed four-star hotel exudes urban chic. The tiled rooms are cool and startlingly modern, with four-poster beds, cream-coloured furniture, and lavish marble-clad bathrooms. Some also have sea views and balconies, although these can cost up to €30 extra.

Hotel Hieracon
HOTEL €€€

(☎0781 85 40 28; www.hotelhieracon.com; Corso Cavour 63, Carloforte; d with view €150-250, without view €100-170;✱) Restored to its art nouveau best, this seafront mansion is a stunning place to stay. Period furniture and original oil paintings adorn rooms, and there's a tranquil garden where you can snooze under the palm trees. To eat at the hotel restaurant, budget for at least €30.

Hotel California
PENSIONE €

(☎078 185 44 70; www.hotelcaliforniacarloforte .com; Via Cavallera 15, Carloforte; s €35-50, d €45-100; ✦) This superfriendly family-run *pensione* is situated in a residential street a few blocks back from the *lungomare* (seafront promenade). It's a modest place but its spacious, sun-filled rooms are more than adequate and the location ensures a good night's sleep.

Hotel La Valle
HOTEL €€

(☎078 185 70 01; www.hotellavalle.com; Localita Commende, Carloforte; s €60-100, d €120-200; P✱✱✦) Signposted off the road to Capo

Sandalo, and at the end of a long dirt track, the salmon-pink hotel is a lovely rural complex in the midst of thick bush. With its tennis court, swimming pool and bright rooms, it's a wonderful place to escape the world.

ISOLA DI SANT'ANTIOCO

SANT'ANTIOCO

Hotel del Corso   HOTEL €
(☎0781 80 02 65; www.hoteldelcorso.it; Corso Vittorio Emanuele 32; s €44-60, d €69-100;❋) In the heart of the action, this polished three-star hotel sits on top of the Cafè del Corso, one of the smartest and most popular drinking spots. Rooms are well-appointed, if rather characterless.

Hotel L'Eden   HOTEL €
(☎078 184 07 68; www.ledenhotel.com; Piazza Parrocchia 15; s €45, d €65; ❋) A hotel with its own catacomb – now there's something to write home about. Ask the friendly owner to take you downstairs for a look and he will happily oblige, proudly pointing out where you can see skulls and crossbones resting in the dank grottoes. The hotel is homey rather than elegant, and the rooms, which can be small, are a little tired round the edges.

AROUND THE ISLAND

Hotel Luci del Faro   HOTEL €€
(☎0781 81 00 89; www.hotelucidelfaro.com; Localita Mangiabarche; s €50-109, d €100-218; P❋@❋) Only a few kilometres outside Calasetta, the well-signposted Luci del Faro stands in glorious solitude on an exposed plain near Spiaggia Grande, the island's best-known beach. Popular with cyclists, it's an excellent, family-friendly place with simple, sunny rooms, sweeping views and a relaxed atmosphere.

Campeggio Tonnara   CAMPGROUND €
(☎078 180 90 58; www.campingtonnara.it; Localita Cala Saboni; 2 people, tent & car €50-110; ☺Apr-Sep) Before you reach the beach you'll pass this well-equipped and wonderfully remote camping ground, ideal for relaxing in natural surrounds.

South Coast

PORTO BOTTE TO PORTO DI TEULADA

Camping Sardegna   CAMPGROUND €
(☎/fax 0781 96 70 13; 2 people, tent & car €35, 4-person bungalows €50-65; ☺mid-May-Sep; ❋)

Just off the main road into Porto Pino, this place has basic camping facilities in a pine grove on the beach.

Hotel Cala dei Pini   HOTEL €
(☎0781 50 87; www.cortehotels.com; Localita Porto Pino; B&B per person €40-50, full-board per person per week €400-990; P❋❋) This is a big, modern hotel favoured by tour operators. It's not a bad option in the low season, but from June to September there's a minimum seven-night stay.

CHIA TO SANTA MARGHERITA DI PULA

TOP CHOICE❯ B&B S'Olivariu   B&B €
(☎339 367 40 88; www.solivariu.it; SS195, km 33, Santa Margherita di Pula; per person €30-50;❋❋) An unpretentious farm B&B with three cool rooms and four colourful mini-apartments. Set amid fruit orchards – in winter you can have oranges fresh from the trees – 500m back from the beach, it offers few frills, just a genuine Sardinian welcome and hearty farm breakfasts (think pecorino cheese and fruit).

Forte Village   HOTEL €€€
(☎070 92 15 16; www.fortevillage.com; s €290-1910, d €380-2158, half board per person €220-1110; Santa Margherita di Pula; P❋@❋) It's here, in a wooded grove off the SS195, that you'll find the extraordinary: the godfather of all southern Sardinian resorts. Closed off to the world behind high security gates, this 250-sq km site is an unapologetic bastion of luxury with seven hotels, 10 swimming pools, shopping malls, bowling alleys, discos and up to 1km of beach frontage.

Camping Flumendosa   CAMPGROUND €
(☎070 920 83 64; www.campingflumendosa.it; SS195km 33, Santa Margherita di Pula; per person/ tent/car €8.50/8.50/2.50; ❋) Decent camping facilities are available at this handy campsite, about 50m or so from the beach.

PULA

TOP CHOICE❯ Hotel Baia di Nora   HOTEL €€
(☎070 924 55 51; www.hotelbaiadinora.com; Localita Su Guventeddu; half board per person €95-205; ☺Apr-Oct; P❋❋) A swish four-star hotel with all the trimmings, this is the sort of place you won't want to leave. OK, there's a chance you might manage to stumble across the perfectly tended garden to the swimming pool bar, or even to the private beach.

La Marmilla

VILLANOVAFORRU & NURAGHE GENNA MARIA

TOP CHOICE **Agriturismo Su Boschettu** FARMSTAY €

(📞070 93 96 95, 3334797401; www.suboschettu. it; Localita Pranu Laccu; B&B per person €35, meals around €20-25; 🏠) This is a charming farmstay nestled amid olive groves and fruit trees. Rooms are modest, but the setting is wonderfully relaxing and the food local and quite delicious.

Hotel Funtana Noa HOTEL €

(📞070 933 10 19; www.residencefuntananoa.it; Via Vittorio Emanuele III 66-68; s/d €45/65, half board per person €55; ❄) Tasteful three-star accommodation is to be relished in a large, airy palazzo just down from the village centre. The style is rustic with plenty of heavy timber, antique-style furniture and brick arches. Enjoy summer evenings with drinks in the beautiful courtyard.

BARUMINI

Albergo Sa Lolla GUESTHOUSE €

(📞070 936 84 19; Via Cavour 49 s €42-47, d €55-65, half board per person €55-60; P❄🏠) Sa Lolla is a tastefully refurbished farmstead with seven decent rooms and a good restaurant (meals €25). Breakfast costs €6. You'll need to book in July and August.

ORISTANO & THE WEST

Oristano

TOP CHOICE **Eleonora B&B** B&B €

(Map p94; 📞0783 7 04 35; www.eleonora-bed -and-breakfast.com; Piazza Eleonora d'Arborea 12; s €35-50, d €60-70, apt €80; ❄📶) Possibly one of the island's most charming B&Bs, the Eleonora is housed in a medieval palazzo on Oristano's central piazza. The rooms are tastefully decorated with antique furniture and the floors are covered in gorgeous old tiles. Wifi is available. There's an elegant, two-bedroom loft apartment, ideal for longer stays.

Duomo Albergo HOTEL €€

(Map p94; 📞0783 77 80 61; www.hotelduomo.net; Via Vittorio Emanuele II 34; s €70-80, d €108-130; ❄📶) Inside and out, Oristano's top hotel is a refined, elegantly understated four-star de-

light. Outside the simple facade is a model of discretion, while inside, guestrooms reveal a quiet, cool decor with white colour schemes, light fabrics and unobtrusive furniture.

B&B L'Arco B&B €

(Map p94; 📞0783 7 28 49; www.arcobedandbreak fast.it; Vico Ammirato 12; s/d without bathroom €40/65) Set inside a couple's home, L'Arco sits hidden away in a quiet cul-de-sac near Piazza Martini. There are only two guest rooms but they are spacious and tastefully decorated with exposed wood beams, terracotta tiles and dark-wood furnishings. Breakfast is served in the family kitchen, and there's a small terrace upstairs.

South of Oristano

ARBOREA

Horse Country Resort HOTEL €€

(📞0783 80 51 73; www.horsecountry.it; Strada a Mare 24; half board per person €71-128; P❄@❄🏠) This resort is the biggest equestrian centre in Sardinia and has 1000 beds, two swimming pools and excellent sporting facilities. Staff can arrange horse-riding lessons as well as day trips to Marceddi, Tharros and the Costa Verde.

Sinis Peninsula

SAN SALVATORE

TOP CHOICE **Agriturismo Su Pranu** FARMSTAY €

(📞0783 39 25 61; www.agriturismosupranu.com; Localita San Salvatore; half board per person €52- 65; ❄🏠) This genuine working farm has six bright guestrooms that are decorated in a simple and neat style. There is a shared terrace outside the rooms that looks onto the garden, perfect for an afternoon *aperitivo*.

Agriturismo Sinis FARMSTAY €

(📞0783 39 25 61; www.agriturismoilsinis.it; Localita San Salvatore; half-board per person €52-65; ❄🏠) Over the road, this farmstay is run by the same family as Agriturismo Su Pranu and has a further lovely six bedrooms. The accommodation is frill-free but clean and airy, and the views of the lush garden can be enjoyed from the chairs on the patio.

RIOLA SARDO

TOP CHOICE **Hotel Lucrezia** HOTEL €€

(📞0783 41 20 78; www.hotellucrezia.it; Via Roma 14a, Riola Sardo; s €75-90, d €120-150; ❄@🏠). Housed in an ancient *cortile* (courtyard house) that belonged to the owner's grandfather, Hotel Lucrezia has rooms surrounding an inner courtyard complete with wisteria-draped pergola, fig and citrus trees. The decor is rustic and lush, with high 18th-century antique beds and mighty wooden furniture. Free bikes are provided, and the welcoming staff regularly organise cooking, painting and wine-tasting courses.

Francesca's House APARTMENT €
(☑0783 41 14 56, 340 501 74 64; www.francesca house.net; Via Marconi 11, 2 people per week €280-350; ❋@⊞) This is a lovely self-contained one bedroom house with a garden, perfect for those who want a base in the area and to self-cater. The little blue house is adjacent to the owner Francesca's wonderful adobe house, both structures restored almost from scratch.

North of Oristano

BOSA

TOP CHOICE **Corte Fiorita** HOTEL €€
(Map p102; ☑0785 37 70 58; www.albergo-diffuso .it; Via Lungo Temo de Gasperi 45; s €45-90, d €65-115; ❋❋@) A so-called *albergo diffuso,* Corte Fiorita has beautiful, spacious rooms in four refurbished palazzi across town: one on the riverfront and three in the historic centre. No two rooms are exactly the same, but the overall look is rustic-chic with plenty of exposed stonework, wooden beams and vaulted ceilings. Reception is at Le Palme, from where the owner will ferry you up to your room in an electric buggy – a good way of seeing the *centro storico.*

Bio Agriturismo Bainas FARMSTAY €
(☑339 209 09 67, 0785 37 31 29; www.agrituris mobainasbosa.com; Via San Pietro; s €30-45, d €60-75, q €118-136, meals €20) Surrounded by fields of artichokes, and olive and orange orchards, this modest *agriturismo* is about 1km outside of town. There are few frills but the guest rooms in the small farmstead are clean and do the job well enough. Outside, there's a verandah with sweeping bucolic views.

La Torre di Alice B&B €
(Map p102; ☑0785 850 404; www.latorredialice.it; Via del Carmine 7; s €30-40, d €50-70;@) Set in a wonderful old house in Bosa's medieval centre, you'll notice La Torre di Alice by its bright colours and wacky signpost outside – the name, Alice, belongs to one half of the friendly couple who run the place.

The rooms are neat and comfortable, with wrought iron beds and relaxing decor, and the downstairs kitchen has a rustic communal table and tons of colourful crockery. A good budget place right in the centre.

Monti Ferru & Lago Omodeo

SANTU LUSSURGIU

TOP CHOICE **Antica Dimora del Gruccione** HOTEL €
(☑0783 55 20 35; www.anticadimora.com; Via Michele Obinu 31; r per person/half board €45/70;❋) Set in a beautifully restored 17th-century palazzo and surrounding historical buildings, this *albergo diffuso* oozes character. Rooms are spread over various sites in the historic centre, but the best are on the first floor of the main mansion where there is a double-flanked staircase, creaking floorboards and stunning stone arches.

NURAGHE LOSA & AROUND

TOP CHOICE **Mandra Edera** HOTEL €
(☑320 151 51 70; www.mandraedera.com; r per person €49-59, ste €59-69, half-board per person €69-89; ☉end Apr-1st week Oct; P❋❋⊞) The welcoming, kid-friendly Mandra Edera is a lovely ranch-style hotel set amidst towering oak trees and fruit orchards. Rooms are in bungalows laid out on neat lawns and there's a smart restaurant (meals around €23).

ALGHERO & THE NORTHWEST

Alghero

TOP CHOICE **Angedras Hotel** HOTEL €€
(Map p114; ☑079 973 50 34; www.angedras.it; Via Frank 2; s €60-140, d €75-150;❋❋@) A model of whitewashed Mediterranean style, the Angedras has cool, airy rooms with big French doors opening onto sunny patios. The chic terrace, where breakfast is served in summer, is a cool place for iced drinks on hot evenings. Guests get 10% discount at the restaurant on Bastioni Marco Polo (see p119).

Camping La Mariposa CAMPGROUND €
(off Map p114; ☑079 95 03 60; www.lamariposa .it; Via Lido 22; 2 people, tent & car €39, 4-person bungalows €50-80; ☉Apr-Oct; @⊞) About

2km north of the town centre, this camping ground is on the beach, set amid pine and eucalyptus trees. It's location, and the excellent facilities, including a windsurfing school and diving centre, make it a popular choice.

Villa Las Tronas
HOTEL €€€

(Map p114; ☑079 98 18 18; www.hotelvillalastronas.it; Via Lungomare Valencia 1; s €150-250, d €190-410; P✳@✻) A 19th-century art nouveau palace once used as a holiday home by Italian royalty, this ravishing hotel is set in its own lush gardens on a private promontory. The rooms are pure fin de siècle with acres of brocade, elegant antiques and moody oil paintings. A beauty centre, complete with indoor pool, hammam-massage facility and gymnasium, adds to the decadence.

Mario & Giovanna's B&B
B&B €

(Map p114; ☑339 890 35 63; www.marioandgiovanna.com; Via Canepa 51; d €55-80) Cheerfully cluttered with ornaments, paintings and Giovanna's lovingly tended collection of English porcelain, this B&B has three sunny rooms and a small courtyard garden. Located in the blander modern part of town, it's about a 15-minute stroll to the *centro storico* (historic centre). Mario also has self-catering apartments to rent.

Hotel San Francesco
HOTEL €€

(Map p116; ☑079 98 03 30; www.sanfrancescohotel.com; Via Ambrogio Machin 2; s €52-63, d €82-101; ✳@🛜) You'll need to book early to get a room at Alghero's only *centro storico* hotel, especially in the summer months. Housed in an ex-convent – the monks still live on the 3rd floor – the rooms are straightforward but comfortable with white walls, pine furniture and brown tiled floors. If available, ask for a room overlooking the medieval cloisters.

Riviera del Corallo

NORTH OF CAPO CACCIA

Agriturismo Porticciolo
FARMSTAY €

(☑079 91 80 00; www.agriturismoporticciolo.it; Localita Porticciolo; B&B per person €30-45, 4-person apt per week €600-1000; ✳🛠) This welcoming place is a 24-hectare working farm with 100 pigs, along with pleasant accommodation inside small apartments. The restaurant, housed in a grand barn with a heavy timber ceiling and huge fireplace, serves delicious home-made food.

Hotel El Faro
HOTEL €€€

(☑079 94 20 30; www.elfarohotel.it; Porto Conte; s €160-420, d €232-920; P✳@✻) Right at the southern tip of the bay, near where the road peters out next to a Catalano-Aragonese tower and lighthouse, you'll find this gorgeous, manicured complex with two pools, a private jetty and coolly stylish rooms. A great place to get away from it all.

The North Coast

Try to avoid spending the night in Porto Torres if you can. If you need to sleep here, you'll find a couple of no frills options by the port.

WEST OF PORTO TORRES

Albergo Silvestrino
HOTEL €€

(☑079 52 34 73; www.hotelsilvestrino.it; Via XXI Aprile 4, Stintino; s €35-67, d €70-150;✳) Difficult to miss at the sea end of the main street, this is a decent three-star. Rooms are summery with cool tiled floors and functional furniture, and the restaurant, the best in Stintino, serves scrumptious seafood (meals €35 to €40).

La Pelosetta Residence Hotel
HOTEL €€

(☑079 52 71 88; www.lapelosetta.it; Capo del Falcone; d half board per person €60-170; ☺May-Sep; 🛠) One of the best places to stay in this area is this gorgeously sited hotel. Its classy seafront restaurant (meals €40) virtually sits on the Spiaggia della Pelosa. There's a mix of rooms (available on a daily basis) and self-catering apartments (rented out by the week), all with uninterrupted sea views. Note that half board is obligatory.

EAST OF PORTO TORRES

Casa Doria
B&B €

(☑349 355 78 82; www.casadoria.it; Via Garibaldi 10, Castelsardo; r €55-80;✳) One of a number of B&Bs in the medieval centre, this has all the trappings of a rustic guest house: period furniture, wrought-iron bedsteads, wooden ceilings. There are three rooms, each simply decorated, and a 3rd-floor breakfast room with fantastic views.

Sassari

Casa Chiara
B&B €

(Map p132; ☑079 200 50 52, 333 695 71 18; www.casachiara.net; Vicolo Bertolinis 7; s/d €35/70;@) In the buzzing uni area, this is a laid-back B&B with a breezy, homey atmosphere.

Resembling a well-kept student flat, it's got three colourful bedrooms, a dining room and a cheerfully cluttered kitchen.

Hotel Vittorio Emanuele　　　　　HOTEL €
(Map p132; ☑079 23 55 38; www.hotelvittorio
emanuele.ss.it, in Italian; Corso Vittorio Emanuele II
100-102; s €50-70, d €70-89; ✳@) Housed in a renovated medieval palazzo, this slick three-star provides corporate comfort at reasonable rates. Rooms are spacious and bright with a sterile colour scheme.

OLBIA, THE COSTA SMERALDA & THE GALLURA

Olbia

☑ Hotel Panorama　　　　　HOTEL €€
(Map p144; ☑0789 2 66 56; www.hotelpanoramaol
bia.it; Via Mazzini 7; s €65-119, d €79-159; P✳@⊚) The name says it all: the roof terrace at this friendly, central hotel has peerless views over the rooftops of Olbia to the sea and Monte Limbara. The rooms are fresh and elegant, with gleaming wooden floors and marble bathrooms, and there's a whirlpool and sauna for quiet moments.

La Locanda del Conte Mameli　　　B&B €€
(Map p144; ☑0789 20 30 40; www.lalocandadel
contemameli.com; Via delle Terme 8; r €80-140, ste €100-180; ✳@) Raising the style stakes is this boutique hotel, housed in an 18th-century *locanda* (inn) built for Count Mameli. A wrought-iron balustrade twists up to chic caramel-cream rooms with Orosei marble bathrooms. An original Roman well is the centrepiece of the vaulted breakfast room.

Ciro's House　　　　　B&B €
(off Map p144; ☑0789 2 40 75; www.bbolbia.com; Via Aspromonte 7; s €25-55, d €50-90; @) Eduardo welcomes you with a smile at this smashing little B&B, 1.5km west of the town centre. Kitted out in a mishmash of styles and sporting colourful tiled bathrooms, the rooms are basic but comfy. Light sleepers may find the street a tad noisy.

B&B Lu Aldareddu　　　　　B&B €€
(☑335 6 85 15 08; www.lualdareddu.com; Località Monte Plebi; r €70-100; ✳) This lovely rustic B&B is housed in an 18th-century farmhouse on the tree-covered slopes of Monte

Hotel L'Oasi, Cala Gonone

Ostello Bellavista, Santa Maria Navarrese

Hotel El Faro, Porto Conte

Hotel Panorama, Olbia

La Villa Giulia, Costa Smeralda

Il Profumo del Mare, Cagliari

Verdemare, Costa Verde

Casa Solotti, Nuoro

Agriturismo Guthiddai, near Oliena

La Pelosetta Residence Hotel, Capo del Falcone

ACCOMMODATION OLBIA

Plebi, a low-lying hill about 10km north of Olbia (off the main SS125 towards Arzachena). There are four rooms decorated in breezy farmhouse style. From here you are within reasonable cycling distance of the Costa Smeralda's finest beaches.

Around Olbia

GOLFO ARANCI

La Lampara　　　　　HOTEL €€
(☑0789 61 51 40; www.lalamparahotel.com; Via Magellano; d €75-130, tr €90-145; ⊙Mar-Oct, ✳@) La Lampara is a delightful family-run hotel just off the main street. Its 10 summery rooms are a blaze of blue and white with cool tiled floors and simple, no-frills furniture.

Hotel Gabbiano Azzurro　　　　　HOTEL €€
(☑0789 4 69 29; www.hotelgabbianoazzurro.com; Via dei Gabbiani; half board per person €93-180; P✳⊠) Overlooking the aquamarine waters of Spiaggia Terzo, the Gabbiano Azzurro is a big, anonymous hotel. But that shouldn't put you off, as the benefits are many: a pool with jetted seats, a sea-view restaurant and a pretty private beach to name a few. Activities, from cookery classes to wine tastings, sport fishing and trekking, can be arranged.

South Coast

Browse for hotels, *agriturismi* and apartments at www.visitsanteodoro.com, or see www.bbsanteodoro.com for a list of 22 B&Bs in the area.

Agriturismo L'Aglientu AGRITURISMO €€
(☎0789 4 10 91; www.turismorurale.org; Via l'Aglientu 1, Porto San Paolo; s €50-75, d €70-100, tr €90-130; P※⊞) Serene and delightfully green, this farmstead is a fine country escape – you can even buy home-grown organic vegies. The rooms are bright and rustic, with colour-scheme themes like lemon, olive and lilac. There's a laid-back vibe in the living room, where you can peruse the books and games.

Hotel L'Esagono HOTEL €€
(☎0784 86 57 83; www.hotelesagono.com; Via Cala d'Ambra 141, San Teodoro; half board per person €50-122; ☎⊞) Down on the beachfront, this is a smart complex with a pool, palm-fringed gardens and a sea-view restaurant. Rooms, housed in low villas nestled in the greenery, are bright and sunny with locally embroidered bedspreads that display a refreshing lack of chintz.

Camping San Teodoro
La Cinta CAMPGROUND €
(☎0784 86 57 77; www.campingsanteodoro.com; Via del Tirreno, San Teodoro; 2 people, car & tent €18.50-35.50, 4-person bungalows €70-118; ☎) About 800m from the town centre, this popular campground is set in a huge tree-filled plot right on the southern end of La Cinta beach.

Costa Smeralda & Around
SOUTH OF PORTO CERVO

TOP CHOICE La Villa Giulia B&B €
(☎348 511 12 69; www.lavillagiulia.it; Monticanaglia; d €65-89) At the top of a tough dirt track, this wonderful B&B has six rooms in a rustic stone villa. The rooms, with their lime-washed walls and jolly-tiled bathrooms, are decorated with flair, and the lovely natural surroundings, warm welcome and spectacular rates make this a real winner. There's also the possibility of renting an apartment complete with kitchenette and fireplace. The villa is about 2km inland from Spiaggia Liscia Ruia and signposted off the main coastal road.

Villaggio Camping
La Cugnana CAMPGROUND €
(☎0789 3 31 84; www.campingcugnana.it; Località Cugnana; 2 people, car & tent €20.50-30, 2-person bungalows per week €190-599; ⊞) This seaside campground is located on the main road just north of Porto Rotondo. There's

plenty to keep the kids amused with a swimming pool, a playground and organised activities. A free shuttle bus can whisk you to some of the better Costa Smeralda beaches.

Hotel Capriccioli HOTEL €€
(☎0789 9 60 04; www.hotelcapriccioli.it; Località Capriccioli; half board per person €90-170; P※⊞) In an area dominated by luxury hotel chains, it's a real pleasure to find a welcoming family-run place like Hotel Capriccioli. Right on the Capriccioli beach, it offers bright rooms furnished in typical Sardinian style with wrought-iron beds and classical island fabrics.

PORTO CERVO & AROUND
Prices are hardly bargain basement, but you'll certainly get more for your euro if you stay slightly outside of megabucks Porto Cervo.

TOP CHOICE B&B Costa Smeralda B&B €€
(☎0789 9 98 11; www.bbcostasmeralda.com; Lu Cumitoni; d €80-130; ※☎) Tucked in the hills above the fjordlike harbour of Poltu Quatu, 3km north of Porto Cervo, this is an especially charming B&B. Sunlight streams into rooms which are a blaze of blue and white. There are tantalising sea views from the verandah, where you can enjoy some of Luciana's freshly made breads and pastries at breakfast.

Hotel Le Ginestre HOTEL €€€
(☎0789 9 20 30; www.leginestrehotel.com; Località Porto Cervo; half board per person €115-250; P※☎⊞) In typical Costa style, this hotel has rooms in low-lying ochre buildings interwoven with perfect lawns, palms and bougainvillea. Uniformed staff provide impeccable service, rooms are light and elegant, and there's a pool and beauty centre for R&R. It's 1km south of Porto Cervo.

La Murichessa HOTEL €
(☎339 5 31 65 32; www.lamurichessa.it; Località Vaddimala; d €50-100, tr €70-130; P☎) Planning a peaceful escape? This bucolic country house delivers with views of mountains, centuries-old olive trees and the glinting sea. The big, sunny rooms bear artistic touches like shell-shaped lights. Anna Lisa is a great cook – be sure to try her homemade marmalade at breakfast. To find La Murichessa take the SP59 Porto Cervo–Arzachena road and look carefully for the wooden sign.

La Rocca Resort & Spa HOTEL €€€
(☎0789 93 31 31; www.laroccaresort.com; Località Pulicino, Baia Sardinia; half board per person €125-240; P✳✳) A postcard ensemble of pastel pink villas, green lawns and flower-lined walkways, La Rocca is a plush retreat with cool, summery rooms and excellent facilities. The pool has a natural rocky fountain, and there's a free shuttle bus to take you to the private beach at Cala di Ginepre, 800m away.

Inland from the Costa Smeralda

SAN PANTALEO

TOP CHOICE Agriturismo Ca' La Somara AGRITURISMO €€
(☎0789 9 89 69; www.calasomara.it; r €58-116, half board per person extra €20; P✳) Donkeys guide the way to this welcoming *agriturismo*, 1km along the road to Arzachena. A relaxed, ramshackle farm, it offers 12 simple guest rooms, and is full of quiet nooks where you can swing in a hammock, stroll in gardens and enjoy back-to-nature spa treatments. Vegetarian dishes prepared with home-grown produce are served in the rustic dining room. Credit cards (and kids) are not accepted.

Hotel Sant'Andrea HOTEL €€
(☎0789 6 52 98; www.giagonigroup.com, in Italian; Via Zara 43; s €72-105, d €120-180, half board per person extra €30-50; P✳✳) Located near the entrance to the village, this tranquil pick has bright, well-kept rooms and a bougainvillea-framed pool. The same family manages the highly regarded Ristorante Giagoni (p152), so breakfast is predictably good and includes homemade cakes and pastries.

Hotel Arathena HOTEL €€
(☎0789 6 54 51; www.arathena.it; Via Pompei; d €120-256; P✳@✳) Knotted, gnarled wood beams and ochre-tinted stone walls set the tone at this attractive hotel, while rooms are furnished with terracotta tiles, wood and natural fabrics. Outside, an infinity pool shimmers against a sublime backdrop of green peaks.

ARZACHENA & AROUND

To get to the first two accommodation options, turn right (if exiting Arzachena) just after the Galmarket supermarket at the northern edge of town.

TOP CHOICE **B&B Lu Pastruccialeddu** B&B €€
(☎0789 8 17 77; www.pastruccialeddu.com; Località Lu Pastruccialeddu, Arzachena; s €50-100, d €75-120; P✳✳) This is the real McCoy, a smashing B&B housed in a typical stone farmstead, with pristine rooms, a beautiful pool and two resident donkeys. It's run by the ultra-hospitable Caterina Ruzittu, who prepares the sumptuous breakfasts – a vast spread of biscuits, yoghurt, freshly baked cakes, salami, cheese and cereals.

Agriturismo Rena AGRITURISMO €
(☎0789 8 25 32; www.agriturismorena.it; Località Rena; half board per person €45-60; P✳) It's half board only at this hilltop *agriturismo*, but consider that no great sacrifice as the farmhouse food is a delight – cheese, honey, meat and wine are all home produced. Rooms have a rural look, with heavy wooden furniture and beams holding up 100-year-old ceilings.

Hotel del Porto HOTEL €€
(☎0789 89 20 55; www.hoteldelporto.com, in Italian; Via Nazionale 94, Cannigione; d €90-206, half board per person €59-123; ✳@) Overlooking the marina in Cannigione, this is a good central choice. The breezy rooms are simply decorated with traditional Sardinian fabrics and polished tiles.

North Coast

SANTA TERESA DI GALLURA

B&B Domus de Janas B&B €€
(Map p156; ☎338 4 99 02 21; www.bbdomusdejanas .it; Via Carlo Felice 20a; d €60-120, tr €80-140; ✳) Daria and Simon are your affable hosts at this sweet B&B in the centre of town. There are cracking sea views from the terrace and the rooms are cheery, scattered with art and knick-knacks.

Hotel Moderno HOTEL €€
(Map p156; ☎0789 75 42 33, 0789 75 51 08; www .modernohotel.eu; Via Umberto 39; s €50-80, d €65-140; ✳) This is a homey, family-run pick near the piazza. Rooms are bright and airy with little overt decor but traditional blue-and-white Gallurese bedspreads and tiny balconies.

Camping La Liccia CAMPGROUND €
(☎0789 75 51 90; www.campinglaliccia.com; SP for Castelsardo km59; 2 people, car & tent €18-35, 2-person bungalow €50-96; ✳✳) This

eco-friendly campground, 5km west of town on the road towards Castelsardo, has fab facilities including a playground and sports area.

Hotel Marinaro
HOTEL €€

(Map p156; ☑0789 75 41 12; www.hotelmarinaro.com; Via Angioi 48; s €40-110, d €60-140; ❄@♿) Fresh, unfussy rooms, including connecting rooms for families, make this evergreen hotel a popular choice. Staff are friendly and the location, a quick hop from the main square, makes it a good choice if you want to stay near the action.

PALAU

L'Orso e Il Mare
B&B €

(☑331 22 22 000; www.orsoeilmare.com; Vicolo Diaz 1, Palau; d €60-100, tr €70-120; ❄) Pietro gives his guests a genuinely warm welcome at this B&B, just steps from Piazza Fresi. The spacious rooms sport cool blue-and-white colour schemes. Breakfast is a fine spread of cakes, biscuits and fresh fruit salad.

Camping Baia Sardegna
CAMPGROUND €

(☑0789 70 94 03; www.baiasaraceno.com; Località Punta Nera, Palau; 2 people, tent & car €16-37, 2-person bungalows €90-174) Beautifully located on Palau's beach and shaded by pine trees, this campground has an on-site pizzeria, playground and dive centre.

Hotel La Roccia
HOTEL €€

(☑0789 70 95 28; www.hotellaroccia.com; Via dei Mille 15, Palau; s €50-90, d €80-150; P❄) A very friendly three-star, La Roccia offers bright, spacious rooms and excellent value for money. The blue-and-white boating decor lends a Mediterranean feel and the balconies provide the bonus of some fantastic views.

Parco Nazionale Dell'arcipelago di La Maddalena

TOP CHOICE B&B Petite Maison
B&B €€

(Map p160; ☑0789 73 84 32; www.lapetitmaison.net; Via Livenza 7, La Maddalena; d €70-110) Liberally sprinkled with paintings and art deco furnishings, this B&B is a five-minute amble from the main square. Miriam's artistically presented breakfasts, with fresh homemade goodies, are served in a bougainvillea-draped garden. Credit cards (and kids) are not accepted.

Camping Abbatoggia
CAMPGROUND €

(Map p160; ☑0789 73 91 73; www.campingabbatoggia.it, in Italian; two people, car & tent €17.50-23) The facilities at this spartan campground might not be the most luxurious but the location, close to a couple of excellent beaches, more than makes up for this. You can arrange the hire of canoes and windsurfing equipment on site.

The Interior

TOP CHOICE Li Licci
AGRITURISMO €€

(☑079 66 51 14; www.lilicci.com; Località Valentino; d €90-100, half board per person €65-75; ♿) To really appreciate the empty silence that lies so heavily over this area, book a night or two at Li Licci, one of the region's best *agriturismi*. Set deep within an oak forest, it's a gorgeous stone farmhouse with simple rooms and a highly regarded restaurant (see p165). The cordial English owner, Jane Ridd, will happily organise excursions for you and advise on walking, horse riding and rock climbing in the area. Li Licci is signposted off the SP38 between Olbia and Sant'Antonio di Gallura.

Agriturismo Muto di Gallura
AGRITURISMO €

(☑079 62 05 59; www.mutodigallura.com; Località Fraiga, Aggius; d €96, half board per person €84; P⬜♿) Free-roaming donkeys, cows, goats, sheep and hens, beautiful stone cottages nestled in cork oak woods, bucolic views, a quiet pool – what more could you want from an *agriturismo*? Nothing, except, perhaps, the delicious home-produced organic cheese, meat, vegies and wine that land on the dinner table. You can also organise horse riding, 4WD excursions and donkey trekking here.

Tenuta Lochiri
AGRITURISMO €

(☑339 1 19 72 66; www.tenutalochiri.com; r per person €40-45, apt per week €600-700; P) A delightful *agriturismo* with sweeping views over Monte Acuto, Tenuta Lochiri is at the end of a 3km dirt track off the Berchidda–Oschiri road. The farm produces its own olive oil, wine, honey and liqueur, which you can sample in the panoramic restaurant (meals €35 to €40).

Il Gallo di Gallura
B&B €

(☑079 481 21 67; www.ilgallodigallura.com; Corso Matteotti 28, Tempio Pausania; d €60-80; P❄@)

Sitting pretty in Tempio Pausania's historic centre is this family-run B&B housed in an early 19th-century palazzo. The rooms are sweet and sunny, done out in lemons and blues and typical Sardinian fabrics. Breakfast is an appealing spread of fresh juice, pastries and preserves. Look for the cockerel sign.

NUORO & THE EAST

Nuoro

TOP CHOICE **Silvia e Paolo** B&B €
(Map p172; ✆0784 312 80; www.silviaepaolo.it, Corso Garibaldi 58; s €30-35, d €50-60, tr €70; ❄@) Silvia and Paolo run this sweet B&B. Family treasures from dolls to old leather trunks make you feel right at home in the bright, spacious rooms. There's a roof terrace for observing the action on Corso Garibaldi by day and star-gazing by night, as well as a tasteful living room with films, books and maps of Sardinia.

Casa Solotti B&B €
(✆0784 3 39 54; www.casasolotti.it; per person €26-35; P❄🤶) Surrounded by lush oak woods and walking trails, this welcoming B&B sits in a rambling garden near the top of Monte Ortobene. It's a relaxed place with rustic rooms decorated with stone and beams – some with their own fireplace. Horse riding, packed lunches and guided hikes in the Supramonte can be arranged. To reach the B&B by public transport, take local bus 8 from Via A Manzoni. It's 7km east of Nuoro.

Nuraghe Oro B&B €
(Map p172; ✆0784 182 32 55; www.nugheoro.it; Via Matteotti 14; s €30-45, d €50-70, tr €85-95;❄🤶🐾) On the 6th floor of an elegant townhouse, this B&B has light, spacious and well-kept rooms, as well as fine city views from the verandah. Your friendly hosts, Max and Clara, put on a good spread at breakfast, with local fruit, cakes and dairy products. Cots are available.

Agriturismo Testone AGRITURISMO €
(✆0784 23 05 39; www.agriturismotestone.com, in Italian; Via Giuseppe Verdi; r €76-90, half board per person €55-65; P) About 20km from Nuoro, deep in a cork oak forest, is this rustic farmstay, with exposed walls, heavy wooden furniture and hanging pots and pans. To get here from the SS131DCN take the SS389 exit towards Bitti and follow for about 10km until the fork for Benetutti; go left and after a further 3km turn right and follow the signs.

Supramonte

OLIENA

TOP CHOICE **Agriturismo Guthiddai** AGRITURISMO €€
(✆0784 28 60 17; www.agriturismoguthiddai.com; Nuoro-Dorgali bivio Su Gologone; half-board per person €60-75; 🤶) On the road to Su Gologone, this bucolic, whitewashed farmstead sits at the foot of rugged mountains, surrounded by fig, olive and fruit trees. Olive oil, Cannonau wine and fruit and veg are all home produced. The rooms are exquisitely tiled in pale greens and cobalt blues.

Hotel Su Gologone HOTEL €€€
(✆0784 28 75 12; www.hotelsugologone.com; s €105-160, d €140-240, ste €340-440; P❄❄) Treat yourself to a spot of rural luxury at Su Gologone, nestled in glorious countryside 7km east of Oliena. Rooms are decorated with original artworks and handicrafts, and the facilities are top notch – there's a pool, a wine cellar and a restaurant (meals around €55), which is considered one of Sardinia's best.

Hotel Monte Maccione HOTEL €
(✆0784 28 83 63; www.coopenis.it; s €39-49, d €66-80; P) Run by the Cooperativa Enis, this place offers simple, rustic rooms and fine views from its hilltop location, 4km above Oliena.

Hotel Cikappa HOTEL €
(✆0784 28 80 24; www.cikappa.com; Corso Martin Luther King 2-4; s/d/tr €40/70/85; ❄🤶) Good, modest digs above a popular restaurant in central Oliena (meals €25 to €45). The best rooms have balconies overlooking the surrounding mountains.

Barbagia

BARBAGIA OLLOLAI

Hotel Sa Orte HOTEL €
(✆0784 5 80 20; www.hotelsaorte.it; Via Roma 14; s €35-40, d €60-80, tr €85-110; ❄) Housed in an attractively restored palazzo in the historic centre, this is one of Fonni's best hotels. The granite facade opens onto a vibrant modern interior decorated with tangerine walls, parquet floors and blanched wood furniture.

Hotel Sa Valasa
HOTEL €

(☑0784 5 34 23; http://hotelsavalasa.com; Località Sa Valasa; s/d €25/60, half board per person €40-45; P) This is a big, rambling two-star hotel set in its own lakeside grounds. The simple pine-furnished rooms and surrounding silence ensure a good night's sleep and the downstairs pizzeria/restaurant makes an attractive, laid-back dining option.

BARBAGIA DI BELVI

Sa Muvara
HOTEL €€

(☑0784 62 93 36; www.samuvarahotel.com; Aritzo; s/d/f €85/130/200, half board per person €90-150; ☒🖫) Tucked away in the mountains, this is the perfect getaway for hikers and cyclists, with large, airy rooms dressed with carved wood furniture. The spring-water pool, lush gardens and mini spa invite relaxation, and the restaurant serves up a feast of local fare (meals around €40).

Hotel La Capannina
HOTEL €

(☑0784 62 91 21; www.hotelcapannina.net; Via A Maxia 36, Aritzo; s/d €50/70, half board per person €60) A smart chalet-style affair with unfussy rooms bathed in white light. It's a couple of kilometres from the village centre.

SARCIDANO

Antico Borgo
B&B €

(☑0782 86 90 47; www.anticoborgoweb.it; Via Sant'Ambrogio 5, Laconi; s/d €45/70; ☒) You'll receive a heartfelt welcome from Peppe and Tomasina at this B&B, housed in a restored 18th-century palazzo opposite the parish church. The place oozes warmth and character, with an open fire, period furnishings and cosy rooms. Breakfast is a treat, with fresh fruit, juice, bread and homemade sweets.

Golfo di Orosei

OROSEI & AROUND

🔺TOP CHOICE Albergo Diffuso Mannois
B&B €€

(☑0784 99 10 40; www.mannois.it; Via G Angioy 32; s €40-85, d €70-140; ☒🖢) Spread across three lovingly restored buildings in the medieval centre of Orosei, Albergo Diffuso Mannois is very special. Each of the light-filled, pastel-hued rooms is individually decorated, with lovely touches such as exposed stone, Sardinian fabrics and juniper-wood beams. Various excursions, including horse riding and diving, can be arranged here.

Anticos Palathos
HOTEL €€

(☑0784 9 86 04; www.anticospalathos.com; Via Nazionale 51; s €85-135, d €120-180; ☒) Centred on a beautiful courtyard, this stone townhouse keeps it rustic with a vaulted breakfast room and characterful rooms featuring wrought-iron bedsteads and ornamental fireplaces. Freshly baked bread and pastries are served at breakfast.

Antico Borgo
HOTEL €

(☑0784 9 02 88; www.borgodigaltelli.it; Via Sassari, Galtelli; s/d €35/70, half board per person €65; ☒) Hidden down a tranquil lane in the cute-as-a-button village of Galtelli, this family-run hotel is gathered around a courtyard. The tasteful rooms are decked out with wooden ceilings, brick floors and wrought-iron beds.

DORGALI

To find a place to stay in Dorgali, try contacting **Cala 'e Luna Bookings** (☑0784 92 80 87; www.calaeluna.com; Via Lamarmora 4), a local accommodation booking service.

📋 Hotel Il Querceto
HOTEL €€

(☑0784 9 65 09; www.ilquerceto.com; Via Lamarmora 4; s €43-124, d €67-140, half board per person extra €19; P☒🖢) An eco-friendly hotel using solar and geothermal energy, Il Querceto boasts nicely low-key rooms with lashings of cream linen and honey-coloured tiles. The pools and oak-shaded garden invite relaxation, while the restaurant emphasises seasonal cuisine. It's just southwest of town.

Sa Corte Antica
B&B €

(☑0784 9 43 17; www.sacorteantica.it, in Italian; Via Mannu 17; d €50-60, tr €65-75; ☒) Gathered around an old stone courtyard, this B&B housed in an 18th-century townhouse oozes charm from every brick and beam. The rooms are traditional and peaceful, with reed ceilings and wrought-iron bedsteads. Enjoy homemade bread and biscotti at breakfast.

Hotel S'Adde
HOTEL €€

(☑0784 9 44 12; Via Concordia 38; s €40-70, d €70-110, half board per person €60-80; P☒🖢) Only a short, signposted walk up from the main thoroughfare, this welcoming chalet has pine-clad rooms with terraces and green views. The restaurant–pizzeria (meals €25 to €30) opens onto a 1st-floor terrace. Breakfast costs an extra €5.

CALA GONONE

TOP CHOICE **Hotel L'Oasi** B&B €€

(☎0784 9 31 11; www.loasihotel.it; Via Garcia Lorca 13; s €53-79, d €68-136; [P][❄][@][✈]) Perched on the cliffs above Cala Gonone and nestling in flowery gardens, this B&B offers enticing sea views from many of its breezy rooms. It's worth paying an extra €15 or so for half board, as the three-course dinners are prepared with fresh local produce. The friendly Carlesso family can advise on activities from climbing to diving. L'Oasi is a 700m uphill walk from the harbour.

Agriturismo Nuraghe Mannu AGRITURISMO €

(☎0784 9 32 64; www.agriturismonuraghemannu.com; off the SP26 Dorgali-Cala Gonone road; d €54-68, half-board per person €43-48; [❄]) Immersed in greenery and with blissful sea views, this is an authentic, eco-friendly working farm with four simple rooms, a restaurant open to all, and home-produced bread, milk, ricotta and sweets at breakfast. For campers, there are also five tent pitches available for €9 to €12 per person.

Hotel Villa Gustui Maris HOTEL €€

(☎0784 92 00 76; www.villagustuimaris.it; Via Marco Polo 57; s €80-160, d €98-188, tr €180-305; [❄][@][✈][❄]) Wake up to sweeping views of the Golfo di Orosei at this Mediterranean villa-style hotel, a stiff 800m uphill walk from the resort centre. Rooms are bright and spacious, with tiled floors, lashings of cream and terracotta, and balconies or terraces. The pool is great for a scenic swim.

Hotel Costa Dorada HOTEL €€

(☎0784 9 33 32; www.hotelcostadorada.it; Lungomare Palmasera 45; s €74-120, d €108-190; [❄][✈]) The vine-clad Costa Dorada offers dreamy sea views and tasteful rooms decorated with pastel colours, painted wood furnishings and local handicrafts. It's at the southern end of the *lungomare,* just across the road from the beach. The flowery garden is full of twittering birds and turtles.

Hotel Nettuno B&B €

(☎0784 9 33 10; www.nettuno-hotel.it; Via Vasco de Gama 26; s €40-75, d €55-100, tr €75-140, q €80-155; [❄][✈][❄]) This family-run B&B is a super-central choice, a minute's walk from the beach. The simple tiled rooms are kept spick and span; a balcony will set you back an extra €10 per night. There's a shady garden for relaxing over a cool drink.

Hotel Miramare HOTEL €€

(☎0784 931 40; www.htlmiramare.it; Piazza Giardini 12; s €40-75, d €60-140; [❄][@]) This spruce white hotel near the harbour is Cala Gonone's oldest (it opened in 1955). Sea breezes cool the simple, tiled-floor rooms; the best have terraces overlooking the Med, while cheaper rooms face the church and mountains. Snag a lounger on the rooftop terrace to kick back and enjoy the view.

Camping Cala Gonone CAMPGROUND €

(☎0784 9 31 65; www.campingcalagonone.it; Via Collodi; 2 people, car & tent €30-39, 2-bed bungalow €51-105; [✈][❄]) By the entrance to town on the main road from Dorgali, this pine-tree-shaded campsite has excellent facilities including a tennis court, barbecue area, mini market, pizzeria and swimming pool.

Ogliastra

TORTOLI & ARBATAX

For beachside, resort-style hotels, head for Porto Frailis, near Arbatax.

La Bitta HOTEL €€€

(☎0782 66 70 80; www.hotellabitta.it; Località Porto Frailis; half board per person €59-178; [P][❄][❄][✈]) Right on the beach in Porto Frailis, this is a luxurious affair with palatial, vaulted rooms (sea views cost extra), a seafront pool and beauty treatments ranging from shiatsu to lymph drainage. Have a drink at the swish new lounge bar while admiring close-ups of local marine life splashing around in an enormous aquarium.

La Vecchia Marina HOTEL €€

(☎0782 66 70 20; www.hotellavecchiamarina.com; Via Praga 1, Località Porto Frailis; d €70-140; [P][❄][✈]) Beams, terracotta floors and palm-dotted gardens give this low-rise, white-washed hotel an almost colonial feel. The big, light rooms sport handcrafted furnishings. It's in a quiet area five minutes' stroll from the beach.

NORTH OF TORTOLI & ARBATAX

TOP CHOICE **The Lemon House** B&B €

(☎0782 66 95 07; www.peteranne.it; Via Dante 10, Lotzorai; per person €30-42; [✈]) Peter and Anne run this lime-hued B&B, a terrific base for outdoor escapades, with a bouldering wall for limbering up and a relaxing roof terrace for winding down. The sports-loving duo can arrange bike hire and pick-ups, lend you a GPS and give you invaluable tips on hiking, climbing, mountain biking and kayaking. Be sure to try the homemade lemon marmalade at breakfast.

Ostello Bellavista   HOTEL €
(☑0782 61 40 39; www.ostelloinogliastra.com; Via Pedra Longa, Santa Maria Navarrese; s €35-65, d €50-100; ✳️🛜) More a hotel than a hostel, this cheery hilltop place has a 'beautiful view', just as its name promises. Its plainly decorated rooms, some with balconies, are in a series of buildings rising up the hill, so the higher you go the better the view you will get.

Albergo Santa Maria   HOTEL €€
(☑0782 61 53 15; www.albergosantamaria.it; Via Plammas 30, Santa Maria Navarrese; half board per person €64-95; P✳️🛜) It's just a short amble from the beach to this low-rise, whitewashed

hotel, where a warm welcome extends to all. The colourful rooms open onto balconies overlooking the courtyard or flower-dotted gardens. Substantial breakfasts and a gym (to work them off) are other pluses.

ULASSAI

TOP CHOICE **Hotel Su Marmuri**   HOTEL €
(☑0782 7 90 03; www.hotelsumarmuri.com; Corso Vittorio Emanuele 20; s €30-50, d €60-80, tr €75-95) Accommodation in Ulassai is provided by the irrepressible Tonino Lai and his wife at this well-known village institution. It offers simple, neat rooms and stupendous views. Tonino can offer you all the advice you need about the surrounding area, and delights in showing visitors its hidden corners – from nearby caves to scenic picnic spots.

Understand
Sardinia

> ❯

Sardinia Today

Left to Right

Sardinian regional elections in 2009 ousted the centre-left governor Renato Soru and brought in Ugo Cappellacci of Berlusconi's centre-right People of Freedom (PDL) party. Cappellacci was the lesser known of the two candidates, and his 51.9% majority vote was a hard blow to the PD, Sardinia's opposing Democratic Party.

The election ushered in a new political era. While some were sorry to see Soru go, others were tired of his 'Robin Hood' approach to politics. Soru introduced the controversial 'salvacoste' law, severely restricting development along Sardinia's coastline. The WWF called it one of the first 'long-sighted policies' of conservation in Italy, but developers were unimpressed. Despite Cappellacci's pledge to relax restrictions, the disputes remain, and so far there has been no significant boom in construction.

In response to soaring ferry prices, which caused a 30% fall in tourism in summer 2011, Cappellacci launched 'la flotta sarda', a Sardinian ferry company to compete with private operators. The Berlusconi government tried to persuade Cappellacci to withdraw the fleet, but he didn't back down. Tensions with the Berlusconi government have escalated recently following disputes over tax remittances, and Cappellacci has publicly given back his PDL membership card in protest, together with some 20 other PDL Sardinian politicians. It seems the central government will have to make concessions to avoid the PDL 'losing' the island.

Economic Strife

Despite Ugo Cappellacci's aim to reduce unemployment, the economic outlook remains bleak for Sardinia. In 2010, inflation reached a record 2.4%, unemployment hovered at a worrying 13.6% and prospects for young people entering the labour market looked dismal.

» Population: 1.67 million

» Area: 24,090 sq km

» GDP per capita: €15.895

» GDP growth: 1.3%

» Inflation: 2.4%

» Unemployment: 13.6%

Dos & Don'ts

» Do accept offers of hospitality (eg a glass of wine, beer or *mirto* – a spirit) when offered.

» Do find out about Sardinia, for instance that Grazia Deledda was a Nobel Prize winner and that ex-Chelsea-manager Gianfranco Zola is Sard – locals like this!

» Don't expect everyone to speak English (many don't); a little Italian goes a long way.

» Don't go around scantily-clad in mountain areas where people are quite conservative.

» Don't say Sardo is a dialect of Italian; it's a separate language.

Top Films

Padre Padrone (Father and Master; 1977) The true story of Gavino Ledda's harsh life as a shepherd.

Ballu a Tre Passi (Three-Step Dance; 2003) Four snapshots of life in Sardinia, with some beautiful shots of the Costa del Sud.

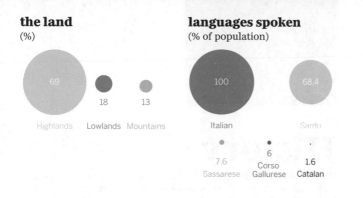

the land
(%)

languages spoken
(% of population)

217

69
18   13

Highlands Lowlands Mountains

100   68.4

Italian   Sardu

7.6
Sassarese

6
Corso
Gallurese

1.6
Catalan

The chemical industry around Porto Torres is in crisis. Workers occupied the abandoned high-security prison on Asinara in February 2010, but their protest went largely unnoticed. Sheep farming, meanwhile, is on the brink of collapse, with sheep's milk prices below costs. Crippled by debt, their livelihood on the line, farmers have recently protested at ferry terminals and in Rome against imported livestock. Most vocal of all were the Movimento Pastori Sardi (MPS; Sardinian Farmers' Movement).

It seems that the cause of the sheep's milk crisis is not an intrinsic lack of competitiveness, but a lack of structural reform and modernisation of the sector, with small, inefficient producers being supported by government assistance for years. Other agricultural sectors, such as wine, bread and cow's milk, are performing better, and the hope is that sheep farming will soon follow suit.

The Future's Green

On the positive side, the tourism industry remains fairly stable. In a bid to make tourism sustainable, Sardinia is starting to promote itself as a year-round destination, not just for the Costa Smeralda's beaches in summer. The developments currently underway to create a joint Italian-French marine park, the Parco Marino Internazionale delle Bocche di Bonifacio, should further help to protect the fragile ecosystem of Sardinia's most beautiful archipelago, La Maddalena.

In a referendum in May 2011, 98% of Sardinians voted against nuclear power, dashing Berlusconi's grand plans for nuclear construction. The news in 2011 that Enel received the go-ahead to build a 90 MW wind farm at Portoscuso was also music to environmentalists' ears. The wind farm will be the biggest of its kind in Italy, capable of generating 185 million kWh annually, enough to power some 70,000 households.

Of Italy's 20 regions, five have autonomous powers: Sardinia, Sicily, and the Alpine regions of Valle d'Aosta, Trentino-Alto Adige, and Friuli-Venezia Giulia.

Top Websites

La Destinazione (The Destination; 2003) The story of a young Italian *carabinieri* (police officer) sent to a remote Sardinian village in Barbagia to investigate the murder of a shepherd.

Get Around Sardinia (www. getaroundsardinia.com) Handy tips for exploring Sardinia by public transport.
Sardegne.com (www.sardegne. com) The lowdown on accommodation, restaurants, transport and weather in Sardinia.

Sardegna Turismo (www. sardegnaturismo.it) Comprehensive and easy-to-navigate official tourism site.

History

If world history were a library, Sardinia would be one of the most gripping reads in the 'Mediterranean island' department. Sitting between Europe and Africa, the island's strategic position and rich mineral reserves have brought tidal waves of power-hungry invaders to its shores; while its rugged, impenetrable mountains have attracted everyone from Stone Age man to 19th-century bandits in hiding. Thanks to a certain inward-looking pride and nostalgic spirit, the Sards have not allowed time and the elements to erase their story. Travellers can easily dip into the chapters of the island's past by exploring tombs and towers, forts and churches.

Flicking back to the beginning brings you to the neolithic Ozieri culture, their menhirs and ancient rock tombs still standing today. A millennia or so later came the nuraghic people, whose 7000 *nuraghi* (Bronze Age towers and fortified settlements) scatter the island like pieces of a hard-to-solve puzzle. Next up were the enterprising, sea-faring Phoenicians, followed by the Carthaginians and the Romans, who built roads and developed cities. When the Empire crumbled, the Vandals were quick to invade. Medieval Sardinia is a mixed tale of prosperity under Pisan and Genoese rule, and poverty under the Catalan-Aragonese. The island ping-ponged between Spain and Austria in the early 18th century, before finally landing in the court of the Duchy of Savoy. Banditry, malaria and two world wars brought death and misery in the early 20th century. In more recent times, the rise of tourism, EU investment and eco awareness signal a bright future for Sardinia.

In his book *Le Colonne d'Ercole. Un' inchiesta* (The Pillars of Hercules. An investigation), Sergio Frau stakes a claim for Sardinia as the lost civilisation of Atlantis. The debate is reflective of an island whose origins lie beyond the reach of traditional history.

Mysteries of the Ancients

Palaeolithic & Neolithic Ages

When the first islanders arrived and where they came from are questions that have been puzzling researchers for centuries. The most likely

TIMELINE	350,000 BC	4000–2700 BC	1800–1500 BC
	Fragments of basic flint tools indicate the first traces of human culture on the island.	Thriving Copper Age communities formed around the town of Ozieri. Copper was smelted into ingots and traded, and the first *domus de janas* (rock tombs) appear.	The nuraghic period: most of the stone ruins that litter Sardinia date back to this time. Some 30,000 fortified stone towers were built.

hypothesis is that they landed on Sardinia's northern shores sometime during the lower Palaeolithic period (Old Stone Age). When flint tools were found at Perfugas in 1979, archaeologists muttered excitedly about primitive humans crossing from mainland Italy as far back as 350,000 BC. It's thought they came from Tuscany, although it's possible that other waves arrived from North Africa and the Iberian Peninsula via the Balearic Islands. Geneticists have attempted to solve the riddle by researching the island's curious genetic make-up – in certain parts of the interior a particular gene mutation is found in concentrations only otherwise present in Scandinavia, Bosnia & Hercegovina and Croatia. However, in spite of this research, the geneticists seem just as puzzled as the rest of us.

Wherever the early settlers came from, they were apparently happy with what they found, for by the neolithic period (8000 BC to 3000 BC), Sardinia was home to several thriving tribal communities. The island would have been a perfect home for the average neolithic family – it was covered with dense forests that were full of animals, there were caves for shelter, and land suitable for grazing and cultivation. Underlying everything were rich veins of obsidian, a volcanic black stone that was used for making tools and arrow tips. This black gold became the Mediterranean's most coveted commodity, and was traded across the area – shards of Sardinian obsidian have been found as far away as France.

Most of what we know of this period, known as the Ozieri (or San Michele) culture, comes from findings unearthed in caves around Ozieri and in the Valle Lanaittu. Fragments of ceramics, tools and copper ingots attest to knowledge of smelting techniques and artistic awareness, while early *domus de janas* (literally 'fairy houses'; tombs cut into rock) tell of complex funerary rituals.

The funerary site of Pranu Muttedu on the central Sarcidano plain offers a deeper insight into Sardinia's neolithic Ozieri culture, strewn with *domus de janas* and around 50 menhirs. Another megalithic wonder is Biru 'e Concas in the Mandrolisai, one of Sardinia's largest collections of menhirs, with some 200 standing stones in situ. Around 30 of them are lined up east to west, presumably as a symbolic representation of the sun's trajectory.

Nuraghic Civilisation

Sardinia is scattered with stone towers – *nuraghi* – most built between 1800 and 500 BC. These Bronze Age fortified settlements were used as watchtowers, sacred areas for religious rites, and meeting places, and provide some of the few insights into nuraghic civilisation. For more on *nuraghi,* see the boxed text (p81).

Five Neolithic Wonders

» Pranu Muttedu, Goni

» Museo delle Statue Menhir, Laconi

» Caves in the Valle Lanaittu, Nuoro province

» Museo Archeologico, Ozieri

» Dolmen Sa Coveccada, Mores

HISTORY MYSTERIES OF THE ANCIENTS

Some historians argue that the nuraghic populace of Sardinia were the Shardana, a piratical seafaring people who appear in early Egyptian inscriptions.

1500 BC	1100 BC
Sardinia's most important *nuraghe*, Nuraghe Su Nuraxi, is built near Barumini.	The Phoenicians establish the town of Nora on the southwest coast, one of a series of important trading posts along with Karalis (Cagliari) and Tharros.

» Tower at Nora

THE LAST LAUGH

When Homer wrote about hero Odysseus smiling 'sardonically' when being attacked by one of his wife's former suitors, he was surely alluding to a grin in the face of danger. Yet the word sardonic, from the Greek root *sardánios*, has come to mean simply 'scornful' or 'mocking' in today's usage.

If recent scientific findings are anything to go by, Homer may have been on the right track with his hint at danger. Studies carried out by scientists at the University of Eastern Piedmont in 2009 identified hemlock water dropwort *(Oenanthe crocata)* as being responsible for the sardonic smile from, of course, Sardinia. It seems that in pre-Roman times, ritual killings were carried out using the toxic perennial (known locally as 'water celery'). The elderly, infirm and indeed anyone who had become a burden to society were intoxicated with the poisonous brew, which made their facial muscles contract into a maniacal sardonic grin, then finished off by being pushed from a steep rock or savagely beaten.

Regardless of whether the word sardonic refers to this sinister prehistoric malpractice, it seems that the findings could have positive implications in the field of medicine. The head of Cagliari University Botany Department, Mauro Ballero, believes that the molecule in hemlock water dropwort could be modified by pharmaceutical companies to have the opposite effect, working as a muscle relaxant to help people to recover from facial paralysis.

Best Nuraghic Sites

» Nuraghe Su Nuraxi

» Tiscali

» Nuraghe Losa

» Santuario Santa Vittoria

» Nuraghe di Palmavera

» S'Ena 'e Thomes and Serra Orrios

The discovery of Mycenaean ceramics in Sardinia and nuraghic pottery in Crete suggest an early trade in tableware and contact with other cultures. Evidence of pagan religious practices are provided by *pozzi sacri* (well temples). Built from around 1000 BC, these were often constructed so as to capture light at the yearly equinoxes, hinting at a naturalistic religion. The well temple at Santa Cristina is a prime example.

But perhaps the most revealing insights into nuraghic culture come from the *bronzetti* (bronze figurines) that populate many of Sardinia's archaeological museums, most notably those in Cagliari and Sassari. Scholars reckon that these primitive depictions of shepherd kings, warriors, farmers and sailors were used as decorative offerings in nuraghic temples.

One thing is certain: Sardinia's mysterious, unfathomable *nuraghi* reveal a highly cultured civilisation. The nuraghic people were sophisticated builders, constructing their temples with precisely cut stones and no mortar; they travelled and exchanged (as revealed by the discovery of seal remains and mussel shells inland); and they had the time, skills and resources to stop and build villages, and to dedicate to arts such as ceramics and jewellery.

1000 BC	650 BC	227 BC	216 BC
The nuraghic people begin to build elaborate *pozzi sacri* (sacred wells or well temples).	Phoenicians build their first inland fortress on Monte Sirai following clashes with Sardinians.	More than a decade after victory in the First Punic War (264–241 BC), Sardinia becomes a Roman province.	The Carthaginians are defeated. The Romans build roads and develop centres at Karalis (Cagliari), Nora, Sulcis, Tharros, Olbia and Turris Libisonis (Porto Torres).

The Phoenicians

Sardinia's strategic position and its rich natural resources (silver and lead reserves) and fertile arable land have long made the island a victim of the Mediterranean's big powers.

The first foreigners on the scene were the Phoenicians (from modern-day Lebanon). The master mariners of their day, they were primarily interested in Sardinia as a staging post – they had colonies on Sicily, Malta, Cyprus and Corsica – so Sardinia was an obvious addition. The exact date of their arrival is unclear, although Semitic inscriptions suggest that Spain-based Phoenicians may have set up at Nora, on the south coast of Sardinia, as early as 1100 BC.

In the early days the Phoenicians lived in relative harmony with the local nuraghic people, who seemed happy enough to leave the newcomers to their coastal settlements – Karalis (Cagliari), Bithia (near modern Chia), Sulci (modern Sant'Antioco), Tharros and Bosa. However, when the outsiders ventured inland and took over the lucrative silver and lead mines in the southwest, the locals took umbrage. Clashes ensued and the Phoenicians built their first inland fortress on Monte Sirai in 650 BC. This proved wise, as disgruntled Sardinians attacked several Phoenician bases in 509 BC.

Against the ropes, the Phoenicians appealed to Carthage for aid. The Carthaginians were happy to oblige and joined Phoenician forces in conquering most of the island. Most, though, not all. As the Carthaginians found out to their cost and the Romans would discover to theirs, the tough, mountainous area now known as the Barbagia didn't take kindly to foreign intrusion.

Set against the backdrop of the glittering Mediterranean, the archaeological remains of the mighty Phoenician port Tharros, founded in 730 BC, are one of Sardinia's most stunning sights. More tangible vestiges of the Phoenicians are visible in Sant'Antioco's historic centre, littered with necropolises and with an intact *tophet,* a sanctuary where the Phoenicians and Carthaginians buried their stillborn babies. Monti Sirai near Carbonia also offers a glimpse into the island's past with its ruined Phoenician fort built in 650 BC.

Phoenician & Roman Must-Sees

» Tharros, Sinis Peninsula
» Nora, Pula
» Villa di Tigellio, Cagliari
» Sant'Antioco, Isola di Sant'Antioco
» Monte Sirai, Carbonia
» Anfiteatro Romano, Cagliari

Carthaginians & Romans

It was the Carthaginians, rather than the Phoenicians, who first dragged Sardinia into the Mediterranean's territorial disputes. By the 6th century BC, Greek dominion over the Mediterranean was being challenged by the North African Carthaginians. So when the Greeks established a base on Corsica, the Carthaginians were happy to accept Phoenician invitations

177 BC	AD 456	456–534	600
Some 12,000 Sardinians die under Roman rule, and some 50,000 are sent to Rome as slaves.	In the wake of the fall of the Roman Empire, the Vandals land on Sardinia.	Byzantine chroniclers, not the most objective, record the almost 80 years of Vandal rule as a time of misery for islanders.	Christianity is finally imposed on the Barbagia region, the last to succumb to Byzantine proselytising.

MALARIA

Sardinia has endured millennia of invasion and foreign control, but until 1946 the island's single-most dangerous enemy was malaria.

Although scientists reckon that the disease was probably present in prehistoric times – some maintain that *nuraghi* were built as defence against weak-flying mosquitoes – it became a serious problem with the arrival of the Carthaginians in the 5th century BC. Keen to exploit the island's agricultural potential, the colonists cut down swathes of lowland forest to free land for wheat cultivation. One of the effects of this was to increase flooding and create areas of free-standing water, perfect mosquito breeding grounds. The problem was exacerbated by the arrival of imported soldiers from North Africa, many of whom were infected.

By the time the Romans took control of the island in the 3rd century BC, Sardinia was a malarial hothouse, its *mal aria* (bad air) thought to bring certain death. Despite this the Romans followed the Carthaginian lead and continued to exploit the island's fertile terrain. The Campidano plain became, along with Sicily and occupied North Africa, the granary of the entire Roman Empire.

Most of Nora's Punic-Roman ruins are submerged in the sea. For total historic immersion, hook up with a local diving company to explore them.

to help them subdue the by-now rebellious islanders. It was the foot in the door that the Carthaginians needed to take control of the island and boost their defences against the growing threat from Rome.

The ambitious Roman Republic faced two main challenges to their desire to control the southern Mediterranean: the Greeks and the Carthaginians. The Romans saw off the Greeks first, and then, in 241 BC, turned their attention to Carthaginian-controlled Sardinia.

The Romans arrived in Sardinia buoyed by victory over Carthage in the First Punic War (264–241 BC). But if the legionnaires thought they were in for an easy ride, they were in for a shock. The new team of the Sards and their former enemies, the Carthaginians, were in no mood for warm welcomes. The Romans found themselves frequently battling insurgents, especially in the mountainous Gennargentu area, which they dubbed Barbaria in reluctant homage to the sheer bloody-minded courage of the region's shepherd inhabitants.

In 215 BC Sardinian tribesmen, under their chieftain Ampsicora, joined the Carthaginians in the Second Punic War and revolted against their Roman masters. But it was a short-lived rebellion, and the following year the rebels were crushed at the second battle of Cornus.

Once they had Sardinia in their hands, the Romans set about shaping it to suit their own needs. Despite endemic malaria and frequent harassment from locals, they expanded the Carthaginian cities, built a road network to facilitate communications and organised a hugely efficient

1000–1400

Sardinia is divided into four *giudicati* (provinces), the most famous being the Giudicato d'Arborea, centred on Oristano. The *giudicati* are eventually incorporated into Pisan and Genoese spheres.

» Oristano

1015

Pisa and Genoa begin their long struggle for control of the island. By the late 13th century, the mainlanders control three-quarters of the island.

1297

In the face of Catalan pressure, Pope Boniface VIII creates the Regnum Sardiniae et Corsicae (Kingdom of Sardinia and Corsica) and declares Jaume II of Aragon its king.

agricultural system. The Romans also severely decreased the island's population – in 177 BC around 12,000 Sardinians died and as many as 50,000 were sent to Rome as slaves. Many noble families managed to survive and gain Roman-citizen status and came to speak Latin, but on the whole, the island remained an underdeveloped and overexploited subject territory.

Sun, Sea & Sex Scandals

The Rise of Tourism

Until malaria was eradicated in the mid-20th century, visitors (at least those with peaceful intent) were few and far between. DH Lawrence famously grumped his way round the island in 1921, and his words paint a fairly depressing picture of poverty and isolation. Were he to return today, he'd find a very different island. Poverty still exists, particularly in the rural interior, and unemployment remains a serious issue (in 2010 it stood at 13.6%), but the island has changed almost beyond recognition.

Before the Aga Khan 'discovered' the Costa Smeralda in the late 1950s and developed it together with a consortium of international high rollers in the 1960s, Gallura's northeastern coast was a rocky backwater, barely capable of supporting the few shepherds who lived there. Now the Costa Smeralda (Emerald Coast) is one of the world's glitziest destinations, its beaches a playground for Russian oligarchs, bling-laden football players and VIPs, including former Formula One racing manager Flavio Briatore.

Berlusconi's Island Idyll

Sardinia became caught up in the scandal surrounding Italian Prime Minister Silvio Berlusconi thanks to the location on the Costa Smeralda of Villa Certosa, Berlusconi's extravagant €450 million holiday home – identified in November 2010 by 28-year-old escort Nadia Macri as one of the

In 1921 DH Lawrence spent six days travelling from Cagliari to Olbia. The result was *Sea and Sardinia*, his celebrated travelogue full of amusing and grumpy musings.

SO LONG, SORU

Dubbed the Sardinian Bill Gates, self-made billionaire Renato Soru has been central to tourism in the island's recent past. He founded the internet company Tiscali in 1998, entered politics in 2003 and was voted regional president a year later, a position he held until February 2009. But away from the controversial 'luxury tax' and *salvacoste* (save the coast) ban on coastal development, what will Soru be remembered for? Certainly, one of his most lasting achievements was to oversee the withdrawal of US atomic naval forces from the environmentally sensitive Arcipelago di La Maddalena after 35 years. This divided local opinion, with environmentalists and Soru fans applauding the move, and business owners mourning the loss of free-spending American sailors.

1323	1392	1400–1500	1478
The Aragonese invade the southwest coast and take actual possession of the island.	Sardinia's great heroine and ruler of the Giudicato d'Arborea, Eleonora d'Arborea, publishes the Carta de Logu, the island's first code of common law.	Under Catalan-Aragonese control, absentee landlords impose devastating taxes and leave the rural population to struggle against famine and plagues, which claim 50% of the island's population.	On 19 May Sardinian resistance to Aragonese control is crushed at the Battle of Macomer. Led by the Marquis of Oristano, Leonardo de Alagon, Sard forces prove no match for the Iberian army.

locations of the prime minister's alleged 'bunga bunga' sex parties. Much covered in the media, these parties are a major focus of the trial in which Berlusconi faces charges of under-age prostitution and abuse of power in relation to Karima el-Mahroug – a belly dancer more widely known by her stage name, Ruby Rubacuori, or Heart Stealer. The trial was underway at the time of press. A guilty verdict would see Berlusconi face a maximum combined sentence of 15 years. Berlusconi maintains his innocence.

In July 2011, Berlusconi's holding company Fininvest was ordered to pay €560 million in damages to rival media company CIR over bribing a judge during a battle with CIR for control of Montadori, Italy's biggest publishing house. Berlusconi maintains he is innocent of any wrong-doing, insisting he is the victim of persecution by the Italian judiciary.

In 2009 Villa Certosa attracted attention for a different reason. The prime minister was reported to have told an escort that there were Phoenician tombs below the artificial lake in the villa's grounds. This would be a major archeological find for the region. Villa Certosa was put on the market in August 2011.

Raids & Resistance: Medieval Sardinia

Pisa vs Genoa

By the 9th century, the Arabs had emerged as a major force in the Mediterranean. They had conquered much of Spain, North Africa and Sicily, and were intent on further expansion. Sardinia, with its rich natural resources and absentee Byzantine rulers, made for an inviting target and the island was repeatedly raided in the 9th and 10th centuries. But as Arab power began to wane in the early 11th century, so Christian ambition flourished, and in 1015 Pope Benedict VIII asked the republics of Pisa and Genoa to lend Sardinia a hand against the common Islamic enemy. The ambitious princes of Pisa and Genoa were quick to sniff an opportunity and gladly acquiesced to the pope's requests.

At the time Sardinia was split into four self-governing *giudicati* (provinces), but for much of the 300-year period between the 11th and 14th centuries, the island was fought over by the rival mainlanders. Initially the Pisans had the upper hand in the north of the island, while the Genoese carried favour in the south, particularly around Cagliari. But Genoese influence was also strong in Porto Torres, and the *giudicati* swapped allegiances at the drop of a hat. Against this background of intrigue and rivalry, the period was strangely prosperous. The island absorbed the cultural mores of medieval Europe, and powerful monasteries ensured that islanders received the message of Roman Christianity loud and clear. The Pisan-Romanesque basalt churches of the Logudoro in the northwest remain a striking legacy of the period.

Medieval Marvels

» Torre dell'Elefante, Cagliari

» Basilica della Santissima Trinità di Saccargia, Logudoro

» Chiesa di San Simplicio, Olbia

» Castello Malaspina, Bosa

» *Centro storico*, Iglesias

» Torre Porta a Terra, Alghero

1700	1708	1720	1795–99
The death of heirless Habsburg ruler Carlos II puts Sardinia up for grabs once again.	English and Austrian forces seize Sardinia from King Felipe V of Spain during the War of the Spanish Succession, a European-wide scramble for the spoils of the rudderless Habsburg Empire.	Duke Vittorio Amedeo II of Savoy becomes King of Piedmont and Sardinia after the island is yo-yoed between competing powers: Austria, then Spain, Austria again, Spain for a second time and finally the Savoys.	After Piedmontese authorities deny requests for greater self-rule, angry mobs take to the streets of Cagliari, killing senior Savoy administrators. By 1799 the revolutionary flame has burnt itself out.

Fighting Spirit & Spanish Conquerors

Described as Sardinia's Boudicca or Joan of Arc, Eleonora d'Arborea (1340–1404) was the talismanic figure of Sardinia's medieval history and embodies the islanders' deep-rooted fighting soul. As the island's most inspirational ruler, she is remembered for her wisdom, moderation and enlightened humanity.

Queen of the Giudicato d'Arborea, one of four *giudicati* – the others were Cagliari, Logudoro (or Torres) in the northwest and Gallura in the northeast – into which the island had been divided, she became a symbol of Sardinian resistance for her unyielding opposition to the Pisans, Genoese and Catalan-Aragonese.

By the end of the 13th century, Arborea was the only *giudicato* not in the hands of the Pisans and Genoese. The Arboreans, however, toughed it out and actually increased their sphere of influence. At its height under King Marianus IV (1329–76) and Eleonora, the kingdom encompassed all of the modern-day provinces of Oristano and Medio Campidano, as well as much of the Barbagia mountain country.

Initially Arborea had supported the Catalan-Aragonese in their conquering of Cagliari and Iglesias, but when they realised that their allies were bent on controlling the whole island, their support for the foreigners quickly dried up. Eleonora became Giudicessa of Arborea in 1383, when her venal brother, Hugo III, was murdered along with his daughter. Surrounded by enemies within and without (her husband was imprisoned in Aragon), she silenced the rebels and for the next 20 years worked to maintain Arborea's independence in an uncertain world.

ELEONORA'S CARTA DE LOGU

Eleonora d'Arborea's greatest legacy was the Carta de Logu, which she published in 1392. This progressive code, based on Roman law, was far ahead of the social legislation of the period. The code was drafted by her father, Mariano, but Eleonora revised and completed it. To the delight of the islanders, it was published in Sardinian, thus forming the cornerstone of a nascent national consciousness. For the first time the big issues of land use and the right to appeal were codified, and women were granted a whole raft of rights, including the right to refuse marriage and – significantly in a rural society – property rights. Alfonso V was so impressed that he extended its laws throughout the island in 1421, and this remained so until 1871.

Eleonora never saw how influential her Carta de Logu became. She died of the plague in 1404, and the Aragonese took control of Arborea only 16 years after her death. Eleonora remains the most respected historical figure on the island.

1823	1840	1847	1861
Intended to promote land ownership among the rural poor, the Enclosures Act sees the sale of centuries-old communal land and the abolition of communal rights. It's not popular and riots result.	Legislation is introduced giving the state (the ruling Savoys) control of underground resources and starts a mining boom.	Requests that the Kingdom of Sardinia, up to this point a separate entity ruled by a viceroy, be merged with the Kingdom of Piedmont are granted. From this point on, Sardinia is governed from Turin.	In a series of military campaigns led by Giuseppe Garibaldi, King Carlo Emanuele annexes the Italian mainland to create the united Kingdom of Italy.

Log onto www.
sardegnaturismo.
it for historic
itineraries of the
island, taking you
in the footsteps
of the nuraghic
people, Phoeni-
cians, Romans
and the *giudicati*.

From 1383 to 1404, Eleonora bitterly opposed the Catalan-Aragonese. But Eleonora couldn't live forever and her death in 1404 paved the way for defeat. In 1409 the Sardinians were defeated at the Battle of Sanluri, in 1410 Oristano fell, and in 1420 the *giudicato*'s exhausted Arborean rulers finally gave in to the inevitable and sold their provinces to the Catalans.

Spain & the Savoys

Aragonese Invaders

Sardinia's Spanish chapter makes for some grim reading. Spanish involvement in Sardinia dates back as far as the early 14th century. In 1297 Pope Boniface VIII created the Regnum Sardiniae e Corsicae (Kingdom of Sardinia and Corsica) and granted it to the Catalan-Aragonese as an inducement to the Spaniards to relinquish their claims on Sicily. Unfortunately, however, the kingdom only existed on paper and the Aragonese were forced to wrench control of Sardinia from the hands of its stubborn islanders. In 1323 the Aragonese invaded the southwest coast, and this was the first act in a chapter that was to last some 400 years.

Under the Catalan-Aragonese and Spanish, the desperately poor Sardinian population was largely abandoned to itself – albeit on the crippling condition that it pay its taxes – and the island remained underdeveloped. But Spanish power faded in the latter half of the 17th century and the death of the heirless Habsburg ruler Carlos II in 1700 once again put Sardinia up for grabs.

Habsburgs & Piedmontese

The death of Carlos II triggered the War of the Spanish Succession, which set pro-Habsburg Austrian forces against pro-Bourbon French factions in a battle for the spoils of the Habsburg empire. In 1708 Austrian forces backed by English warships occupied Sardinia. There followed a period of intense politicking as the island was repeatedly passed back and forth between the Austrians and the Spanish, before ending up in the hands of the Duchy of Savoy.

Piedmontese rule (from 1720, until Italian unification in 1861) was no bed of roses, either, but in contrast to their Spanish predecessors the Savoy authorities did actually visit the areas they were governing. The island was ruled by a viceroy who, by and large, managed to maintain control.

In 1847 the island's status as a separate entity ruled through a viceroy came to an end. Tempted by reforms that had been introduced in the Savoys' mainland territories, a delegation requested the 'perfect

1915	1921	1928–38	1943
The Brigata Sassari (Sassari Brigade) is founded and sent into WWI action in the northeastern Alps. Its Sardinian soldiers earn a reputation for valour and suffer heavy losses – 2164 deaths, 12,858 wounded or lost.	The Partito Sardo d'Azione (PSd'Az; Sardinian Action Party) is formed by veterans of the Brigata Sassari. It aims to pursue regional autonomy and politicise the Sardinian public.	As part of Mussolini's plans to make Italy economically self-sufficient, Sardinia is given a makeover. Large-scale irrigation, infrastructure and land-reclamation projects begin and new towns are established.	Allied bombing raids destroy three-quarters of Cagliari.

union' of the Kingdom of Sardinia with Piedmont, in the hope of acquiring more equitable rule. The request was granted. At the same time, events were moving quickly elsewhere on the Italian peninsula. In a series of daring military campaigns that were led by Giuseppe Garibaldi and encouraged by King Carlo Emanuele, Sardinia managed to annex the Italian mainland to create the united Kingdom of Italy in 1861.

Nowhere is the Spanish influence more palpable than in Alghero, which fell to Spanish invaders in 1353 after 30 years of resistance. Even today Catalan is still spoken and street signs and menus are often in both languages.

Buried Treasures

Boom Years

Although all but extinct, Sardinia's mining industry has played a significant role in the island's history. Southwest Sardinia is riddled with empty mine shafts and abandoned mine works, hollow reminders of a once-booming sector.

Sardinia's rich mineral reserves were being tapped as far back as the 6th millennium BC. Obsidian was a major earner for early Ozieri communities and a much sought-after commodity. Later, the Romans and Pisans tapped into rich veins of lead and silver in the Iglesias and Sarrabus areas.

The history of Sardinian mining really took off in the mid-19th century. In 1840 legislation was introduced that gave the state (the ruling Savoys) control of underground resources, while allowing surface land to remain in private hands. This, combined with an increased demand for raw materials fuelled by European industrial expansion, started a mining boom on the island.

By the late 1860s there were 467 lead, iron and zinc mines in Sardinia, and at its peak the island was producing up to 10% of the world's zinc.

Inward investment had spillover effects. The birth of new towns, the introduction of electricity, construction of schools and hospitals – these were all made possible thanks to mining money.

But however much material conditions improved, the life of a miner was still desperately hard, and labour unrest was not uncommon – strikes were recorded in southwest Sardinia at Montevecchio in 1903, and a year later at Buggerru. The burgeoning post-WW1 socialist movement attempted to further politicise Sardinia's mine workers, but without any great success.

GIUSEPPE GARIBALDI

Italy's revolutionary hero, Giuseppe Garibaldi, died on 2 June 1882 on the Isola Caprera, his private island in the Arcipelago di La Maddalena. Today you can visit his home, the Compendio Garibaldino, for an insight into the man who succeeded in uniting Italy.

ANDY CHRISTIANI / LONELY PLANET IMAGES ©

» The city of Cagliari

1948	1946–51
Sardinia becomes a semiautonomous region with a regional assembly, the Giunta Consultativa Sarda, that has control over agriculture, forestry, town planning, tourism and the police.	The sinister-sounding Sardinia Project finally rids the island of malaria. The US Army sprays 10,000 tonnes of DDT over the countryside. The effects are still being researched.

Iglesiente miners only went on strike in September, when the wild prickly pear came into fruit. This meant their families would have something to eat while the miners weren't earning a wage.

Fascism & Failure

Following the worldwide recession sparked off by the 1929 Wall Street Crash, the Sardinian mining industry enjoyed something of a boom under the Fascists. Production was increased at Montevecchio, and the Sulcis coalmines were set to maximum output. In 1938 the town of Carbonia in southwest Sardinia was built to house workers from the Sirai-Serbariu coalfield.

Mining output remained high throughout Italy's post-WWII boom years, but demand started to decline rapidly in the years that followed. Regular injections of public money couldn't stop the rot, which was further exacerbated by high production costs, the poor quality of the minerals and falling metal prices. One by one the mines were closed and, as of 2008, Sardinia's only operative mine was Nuraxi Figus, near Carbonia.

Bravery, Banditry & Identity

WWI Heroes

Sardinia's martial spirit found recognition on a wider stage in the early 20th century. The island's contributions to Italy's campaigns in WWI are legendary. In 1915 the Brigata Sassari was formed and immediately dispatched to the northeastern Alps. The regiment was manned entirely by Sards, who quickly distinguished themselves in the merciless slaughter of the trenches. It is reckoned that Sardinia lost more young men per capita on the front than any other Italian region, and the regiment was decorated with four gold medals.

Kidnap Country

A less salubrious chapter is the island's tradition of banditry, which had reached epidemic proportions by the late 19th and early 20th centuries. In May 1899 the New York Times reported: 'The Italian Government is at last realizing that the increase of brigandage in certain parts of Sardinia, and especially in the Province of Sassari, is becoming serious, and steps are being taken by the authorities to bring the bandits to justice.' It was a crusade the government was destined to lose as poverty and an inhospitable environment fuelled banditry throughout the 20th century.

Vittorio de Seta's 1961 classic film, *Banditi a Orgosolo* (Bandits of Orgosolo), brilliantly captures the harsh realities of rural life in mid-20th-century Sardinia.

The town of Orgosolo, deep in Barbagia hill country, earned a reputation as a hotbed of lawlessness, and as recently as the 1990s gangs of kidnappers were still operating in its impenetrable countryside. Between 1960 and 1992, 621 people were kidnapped in Italy, 178 of them in Sardinia.

1950–70	1962	1985	1999
Sardinia benefits from the Cassa per il Mezzogiorno, a development fund for southern Italy. But improvements in agriculture, education, industry, transport and banking cannot prevent widespread emigration.	The Aga Khan forms the Consorzio della Costa Smeralda to develop a short stretch of northeastern coast. The resulting Emerald Coast kick-starts tourism on the island.	Sassari-born Francesco Cossiga is elected President of the Republic of Italy. He was Minister of the Interior when the Red Brigade (extreme-left terrorists) kidnapped and killed ex-PM Aldo Moro in 1978.	The EU identifies Sardinia as one of a handful of places in Europe in dire need of investment for 'development and structural upgrading'.

WWII left Sardinia shattered. The island was never actually invaded, but Allied bombing raids in 1943 destroyed three-quarters of Cagliari. Worse still, war isolated the island. The ferry between the mainland and Olbia was knocked out of action and did not return to daily operation until 1947. As a result of the political upheavals that rocked Italy in the aftermath of the war – in a 1946 referendum the nation voted to dump the monarchy and create a parliamentary republic – Sardinia was granted autonomy in 1948.

A Political Awakening

WWI was a watershed for Sardinia. Not only in terms of lives lost and horrors endured, but also as a political awakening. When Sardinian soldiers returned from the fighting in 1918, they were changed men. They had departed as illiterate farmers and returned as a politically conscious force. Many joined the new Partito Sardo d'Azione (PSd'Az; Sardinian Action Party), founded in Oristano in 1921 by Emilio Lussu and fellow veterans of the Brigata Sassari (the Sardinian regiment that served in WWI).

The party's central policy was administrative autonomy on the island, embracing the burgeoning sense of regional identity that was spreading throughout the island. This led many to start viewing Sardinia as a region with its own distinct culture, aspirations and identity.

But a call for autonomy was just one of the cornerstones of the party's political manifesto. Combining socialist themes (a call for social justice and development of agricultural cooperatives) with free-market ideology (the need for economic liberalism and the removal of state protectionism), it created a distinct brand of Sardinian social-democratic thought. Some 90 years on, the party is still active. It stood independently in the 2009 regional election, winning 4.3% of the Sardinian vote.

HISTORY BRAVERY, BANDITRY & IDENTITY

2004	**2008**	**2009**	**2011**
Self-made billionaire Renato Soru is elected president of Sardinia. He sets the cat among the pigeons by banning building within 2km of the coast and taxing holiday homes and mega-yachts.	After 36 years, the US Navy withdraws from the Arcipelago di La Maddalena. It had long divided opinion: friends pointed to the money it brought; critics highlighted the risks of hosting atomic submarines.	Renato Soru is defeated in the February regional election by centre-right candidate Ugo Cappellacci.	In a May referendum, 98% of Sardinians vote against nuclear power. Enel gets the green light to build a 90 megawatt wind farm at Portoscuso.

The Sardinian Way of Life

When DH Lawrence described Sardinia as 'lost between Europe and Africa, and belonging to nowhere' he was missing the point. Sardinia belongs to the Sardinians. History might suggest otherwise, but centuries of colonial oppression have done little to dent the islanders' fierce natural pride and their patient, melancholic resolve. On the surface, Sardinians display none of the exuberance usually associated with mainland Italians, nor their malleability or lightness of heart. They come across as friendly and hospitable, but modest and quietly reserved. Unlike other islanders, they don't look outwards, longing for escape and opportunity; instead they appear becalmed in the past, gripped by an inward-looking intensity.

A strong sense of fraternity, respect for tradition and passion for a good *festa* – these are what unite Sardinians. But to speak of a regional identity is to overlook the island's geography.

Isolation & Introspection

'We never knew the sea, even if it was only about 150km away by the roads of those days,' says Maria Antonietta Goddi, a Cagliaritana by adoption who spent her early childhood in Bitti, a dusty inland town north of Nuoro. By modern roads, Bitti is only about 50km from the sea, but until relatively recently it was a world unto itself, cut off from the rest of the island by inhospitable mountains and a lack of infrastructure.

The same could be said of any one of hundreds of inland communities, left to fend for themselves by island authorities unable or unwilling to reach them. Such isolation nurtured introspection and a diffidence towards outsiders, while also preserving local traditions – many towns speak their own dialects, cook their own recipes and celebrate their own festivals that have been developed without any outside interference. It also exacerbated the ever-increasing divide between coast and interior. The advent of tourism and industrial development has had a far greater impact on coastal towns than on the island's hinterland, and there's a world of difference between the modern-minded cities of Alghero, Sassari, Olbia and Cagliari and the traditional lifestyles of inland villages.

Yet for all the hardship isolation has inflicted on the islanders, it has left Sardinia with some unique qualities. In recent years, researchers have been falling over themselves to study the island's uncontaminated gene pool, and musicologists have long appreciated the island's strange and unique musical traditions.

Life in the Slow Lane

Perhaps another reason for the Sardinians' celebrated longevity is the island's laid-back, unhurried approach to life. After all, who cares if you

Sardinia is an island of shepherds, counting around four million sheep (around 2.5 per capita).

In 2007 Italy's oldest woman, Rafaella Monni, died in Arzana in the province of Ogliastra, at 109. Five years earlier the then oldest man in the world, 112-year-old Antonio Todde, had died in Tiana, province of Nuoro.

are a little late in the grand scheme of things? There are far more important matters in life, such as friends and family, enjoying your free time, and stopping to chat with the baker, the newsagent, the neighbour and his dog, and just about anyone else who crosses your path. Friendliness is paramount.

This go-slow approach comes naturally to Sardinians. Never mind if Massimo is waffling on about the economy for the umpteenth time that day, while the queue snakes to the back of his grocery store – you know he always has a big smile for you. Or that Silvia is deeply embroiled in conversation at the post office counter – everyone knows that she could talk the hind leg off a donkey. Or that the tourist in front of you on the SS125 is driving at only 30km/h, braking on every bend and has now – *incredibile!* – stopped to take photos of a passing shepherd and his flock; this is frustrating, but you won't beep your horn, only an Italian would do that. And besides, patience is a Sardinian virtue.

La Famiglia

'My 32-year-old son is too fat. Should I put him on a diet?' It's the typical agony-aunt conundrum in the problem pages of Sardinia's magazines and newspapers. Paolo may be 32, but he will always be a boy in the eyes of his doting *mamma*. Like Italy, Sardinia can come across as something of a matriarchal society at times, with around 25% of men staying at home well into their 30s, and a smaller percentage of women following suit. While their decision to fly the nest late, typically not until they marry, is the subject of much ridicule, it is often an economic decision – many young people, particularly with unemployment at around 13.6%, simply can't afford to leave home.

Whichever way you look at it, the family is central to life in Sardinia, and so it comes as something of a surprise that the average rate of fertility is an incredibly low 1.1% (the EU average is 1.6%). The latest figures show that Sardinians are also waiting longer to have a family, with 32.5 being the average age for a woman to have her first baby.

The Island of the Ancients, by Ben Hills, features interviews with Sardinia's most extraordinary centenarians and reveals their life elixir.

GENE GENIES

A kent'annos, may you live to be 100. This traditional greeting may sound like wishful thinking but, then again, maybe not – the odds are good in Sardinia. Forget super foods macrobiotic diets and 10-years-younger supplements, this island holds the secret to longevity, apparently, with some 150 centenarians out of a population of 1.67 million, about twice the normal level. Of these, five live in the tiny village of Ovadda (population 1700). Ask Sardinians why and you'll get a different answer every time – the air, the outdoor living, eating and drinking well, God.

Previous studies have highlighted environmental and lifestyle factors (local Cannonau wines are rich in procyanidins, chemicals that contribute to red wine's heart-protecting qualities) as the main reasons for this longevity, but researchers from the University of Sassari remain convinced that there's a fundamental genetic element. The inhabitants of the mountainous province of Ogliastra have long been undisturbed by the outside world. As a result intermarriage has produced a remarkably pure gene pool, a veritable goldmine of genetic raw material.

A research team, led by Professor Luca Deiana, spoke on the findings of the A Kent'Annos (AKeA) study at a conference in Pavia and Bareggio in May 2011. As well as revealing that some (but not all) of Sardinia's centenarians share genetic characteristics, Deiana brought to light other similarities: most 100 year olds are well-balanced optimists with good social and family networks and a strong sense of identity, and nearly all appear to have a diet rich in antioxidants.

MOTHER TONGUE

Sardo (or Sardu), Sardinia's first language, is the largest minority language in Italy. Originally derived from the Latin brought over by the Romans in the 3rd century BC, it has four main dialects: Logudorese (in the northwest), Campidanese (in the south), Gallurese (in the northeast) and Sassarese (in the Sassari area). These dialects are further complicated by the incorporation of distinct local influences, so in Alghero residents speak a variation of Catalan, and on the Isola di San Pietro locals converse in a 16th-century version of Genoese. The Gallura and Sassari dialects also reflect the proximity of Corsica.

Recent studies on the usage of Sardo brought to light some humorous facts: apparently 60.2% use the mother tongue when they're angry and 64% when they want to be funny, but only 26.5% to discuss politics and a mere 16.5% to speak about the kids.

La Donna

Il Corpo Delle Donne is on TV and barely dressed women are cavorting on the stage as the crowd cheers, lights flash and the music throbs; outside, a woman wearing traditional black vestments walks up the hill. Two women – one *molto sexy,* the other the respect-demanding mother, wife, nurturer. Of course, these are both extremes and to a degree stereotypes, but they nevertheless embody the dual attitude of men towards women in Sardinia, which largely resembles that of their Italian neighbours.

Attitudes are changing, but many families still live according to the classic model, with women staying at home and men going out to earn. These gender roles were originally dictated by the practical division of labour – with the men away from home pasturing their flocks, women were left running the house and raising the children; although nowadays they're as much about tradition and convention as practical necessity.

'It's nothing like in the past when girls weren't allowed to be out on the street past 8pm,' says Maria Angela Tosciri from Baunei. 'Today men and women are in many respects equal, as Sardinia opens up to tourism and new media.' According to Maria Antoinetta Goddi, in the interior there's a lot less chauvinism than in the rest of Sardinia; inland women impose themselves and make other people value them.

Faith & La Festa

Conservative and for much of the year politely reserved, Sardinians let go with a bang during their great festivals. These boisterous and spectacular occasions reveal much about the islanders' long-held beliefs, mixing myth with faith and folklore.

Religious belief has deep roots in Sardinia. The presence of *sacri pozzi* (well temples) in nuraghic settlements attests to naturalistic religious practices dating to the 2nd millennium BC. Christianity arrived in the 6th century and quickly established itself. Today Sardinian faith finds form in street parties as much as church services, and many of the island's biggest festivities are dedicated to much-loved saints. The greatest of them all, St Ephisius, an early Christian martyr and Sardinia's patron saint, is the star of Cagliari's huge May Day carnival.

Elsewhere in the island, you'll find a number of *chiese novenari,* small countryside chapels that are only opened for several days of the year to host saints' day celebrations. These churches are often surrounded by *cumbessias* (also known as *muristenes*), simple lodgings to house the pilgrims who come to venerate the saint honoured in the church.

Easter is an important event in Sardinia, marked by island-wide celebrations, many of which reflect Spanish influence. Castelsardo, Iglesias and Tempio Pausania all put on night processions featuring hooded members of religious brotherhoods more readily associated with Spain.

The Arts

Music

Shielded from outside influences, the island's musical traditions sound like nothing else on the planet and they fuel a contemporary fusion scene of vibrant beauty.

Canto a Tenore

If ever music could encapsulate the spirit of Sardinia's rugged mountains and pastoral landscapes, it is *canto a tenore*. This traditional male harmony singing is one of the oldest known forms of vocal polyphony. It is performed by a four-part male choir, the *tenores,* made up of *sa oghe,* the soloist and lead voice, *su bassu* (bass), *sa contra* (contralto) and *sa mesu oghe* (countertenor). Little is known of the *canto's* origins but it's thought that the voices were originally inspired by the sounds of nature – the *contra* based on a sheep's bleat, the *bassu* on a cow's moo and the *mesu oghe* on the sound of the wind. The *canto* is performed in a tight circle, with the soloist singing a poem to choral accompaniment.

Canto a tenore is most popular in the centre and north of the island, with the best-known groups coming from the Barbagia region. The most famous is the Tenores di Bitti (p175), which has recorded on Peter Gabriel's Real World record label and performed at Womad festivals. Other well-known choirs hail from Oniferi, Orune and Orgosolo.

A similar style, although more liturgical in nature, is the *canto a cuncordu,* again performed by four-part male groups. To hear this head for Castelsardo, Orosei and Santu Lussurgiu.

Launeddas

The *launeddas* is Sardinia's trademark musical instrument. A rudimentary wind instrument made of three reed canes and played using circular breathing, it is particularly popular at village festivals in the south. If you can't attend a festival, buy the legendary recordings *Launeddas,* by Efisio Melis and Antonio Lara. Other names to look out for on the *launeddas* circuit are Franco Melis, Luigi Lai, Andria Pisu and Franco Orlando Mascia.

For an interesting insight into Sardinian music, visit the Sardegna Cultura website, www.sardegnacultura.it (in Italian), which has recordings of traditional island music.

Poetry

Like many of the island's art forms, Sardinian poetry is not, and never has been, the preserve of the chattering classes. It is a much-felt part of local culture, which in the 19th century gave rise to an early form of rap duelling, the so-called *gare poetiche* (poetry duels). At village festivals, villagers would gather to watch two verbal adversaries improvise rhyming repartee that was sarcastic, ironic or simply insulting. The audience

Read up about Sardinia's best-known traditional group and listen to them in action at www.tenores dibitti.com.

Sardinia has produced some fine female vocalists, most notably Maria Carta, a 20th-century island legend. The folksy tunes of Elena Ledda are also widely known.

SEA AND SARDINIA

Sardinia's wild, untamed landscapes, sense of space and age-old traditions sparked the fervent imagination of 20th-century literary giant DH Lawrence. The nine days he spent travelling the island with his wife Frieda inspired one of his most impassioned travel books, *Sea and Sardinia*, which Lawrence himself hailed a 'marvel of veracity'.

Travelling on the Trenino Verde, the Lawrences visited Cagliari, Mandas, Sorgono and Nuoro before taking a boat back to Sicily, where DH Lawrence dashed off the book entirely from memory in just six weeks. His rapturous prose beautifully captures the spirit of the island he described as 'left outside time and history; a place that is like "freedom itself"'. If you're planning a slow journey through Sardinia by narrow-gauge train, the book is the perfect travel companion. To follow in the Lawrences' footsteps, visit the itineraries page of www.sardegnaturismo.it.

loved it and would chime in with their own improvised shots! Little of this was ever written down, but you can find CDs featuring a classic duo from the mid-20th century, Remundo Piras and Peppe Sozu.

Bardic contests still take place in the mountain villages and there are two important poetry competitions, Ozieri's Premio di Ozieri (p138) and the Settembre dei Poeti in Seneghe (p105).

In the 1930s the Fascists banned the Sardinian *cantadores* (poets), whose attacks on church and state they deemed dangerous and subversive.

Sardinia's most famous poet is Sebastiano Satta (1867–1914), who celebrated the wild beauty of the island in his poetry *Versi Ribelli* and *Canti Barbaricini*.

Dance & Festivals

Ballo Sardo

No Sardinian festival or celebration would be complete without folk dancing, referred to as *ballo sardo* (Sardinian dance) or *su ballu tundu* (dancing in the round), which is interpreted slightly differently from region to region. It generally involves a group of dancers or couples in a line or open circle, who hold hands or link arms and move gracefully across the floor with agile steps, twists and turns. Their movements often become sprightlier as the music quickens.

Launeddas is often performed during the dance, while a *canto a tenore* might accompany slower pieces. Like the *launeddas,* it is thought that *ballo sardo* dates back to nuraghic times. There has been much speculation on the connections between *ballo sardo* and the similar *sardana* (circular folk dance) of Catalonia in northeastern Spain.

The Art of Celebration

The Art-Culture section of www.marenostrum.it details up-and-coming cultural events and festivals, including art retrospectives and cinema events.

Sardinians find expression for their heritage, history, faith and identity through folk music, dance and intricately embroidered costumes at their rich and varied festivals. Many festivals have a religious base, such as the numerous holy or feast days, the solemn Easter processions, and pilgrimages like the Festa di Sant'Efisio in Cagliari and the Festa del Redentore in Nuoro. As an agricultural island, seasonal products from cherries to asparagus, chestnuts, wine and tuna are another cause for celebration (and indulgence).

In the west, horse races and parades bring historic triumphs to life, from Sassari's spirited Cavalcata Sarda marking victory over the Saracens in AD 1000 to the fiery S'Ardia horse race in Sedilo trumpeting the victory of Roman Emperor Constantine over Maxentius in AD 312.

For more detail on festivals, see p19.

Literature

Sardinia's rural society had no great literary tradition, but the early 20th century marked a watershed. Grazia Deledda (1871–1936) won the 1926 Nobel Prize and a series of talented scribes began to emerge from the shadows. Their work provides an unsentimental picture of island life, as well as a fascinating insight into how the islanders see themselves.

Taking inspiration from the petty jealousies and harsh realities of the Nuoro society in which she grew up, Grazia Deledda towers above the world of Sardinian literature. Her best-known novel is *Canne al vento* (Reeds in the Wind), which recounts the slide into poverty of the aristocratic Pintor family, but all her works share a strong local flavour.

Also Nuoro born, Salvatore Satta (1902–75) is best known for *Il giorno del giudizio* (The Day of Judgement), a biting portrayal of small-town life, which is often compared to Giuseppe di Lampedusa's Sicilian classic *Il gattopardo* (The Leopard).

A contemporary of Satta, Giuseppe Dessì (1909–77) found fame with *Il disertore*, the story of a shepherd who deserts his WWI army unit and returns to his native Sardinia where he finds himself caught between a sense of duty and his own moral code.

One of the most famous works to have emerged from postwar Sardinia is *Padre Padrone*, Gavino Ledda's bleak autobiographical depiction of his early life as a shepherd. Later made into a critically acclaimed but unpopular film by the Taviani brothers, it paints a harrowing picture of the relentlessness of poverty and the hardships it provokes.

The intractability of political and social life in postwar Italy is the central theme of *Il figlio di Bakunin* (Bakunin's Son), the one translated work of Sergio Atzeni (1952–95). One of the giants of Sardinia's recent literary past, Atzeni, like Deledda before him, depicts a society that resists the simple reductions of comfortable moral and political assumptions.

In recent times Sardinia has produced a good crop of noir writers, including Flavio Soriga (b 1975), whose *Diavoli di Nuraio* (The Devil from Nuraio) won the Premio Italo Calvino prize in 2000.

Each of the 370 villages and towns on the island has its own traditional costume.

THE ARTS LITERATURE

Get the lowdown on Sardinia's top literary event, Gavoi's Festa Letterario di Sardegna, at www.isoladellestoric.it.

SARDINIAN HANDICRAFTS

» **Filigree jewellery** Cagliari, Alghero and Dorgali are the best places to purchase exquisitely crafted gold and silver *filigrana* (filigree work).

» **Red coral** Top-quality coral is harvested off Alghero's Riviera del Corallo (Coral Riviera). In many cases coral is combined with filigree work.

» **Ceramics** Oristano, Sassari and Assemini (north of Cagliari) are famous for their ceramics, glazed in blue or white or yellow and green, and embellished with naturalistic motifs such as birds and flowers.

» **Wool carpets** Aggius and Tempio Pausania have a strong cottage industry in wool carpets, decorated with traditional geometric designs.

» **Basketry** In the north, around Castelsardo and in Oristano, women still make traditional baskets from asphodel, rush, willow and dwarf palm leaves.

» **Festival masks** The festival masks handcrafted in the Nuoro region are real works of art. Look out for Mamoiada's *mamuthones* and Ottana's *boes* and *merdules* masks.

» **Textiles** Traditional hand-looming techniques are used in Ulassai to make one-of-a-kind towels, curtains and bedspreads.

» **Cork** In Gallura, cork wood is used to make everything from decorative bowls to stools and chopping boards.

» **Pocket knives** Handmade pocket knives with horn-carved handles are produced in Pattada and Arbus by a handful of remaining master craftsmen.

Traditional Crafts

As befits an agricultural island, Sardinia has a long tradition of handicrafts, many of which make the most of local materials from cork wood to coral. But where objects were originally made for practical, everyday use, they are now largely made for decoration. Local ironworkers around Santu Lussurgiu, for example, have adapted to the modern market by replacing agricultural tools, the mainstay of their traditional income, with decorative lamps, gates and bedsteads.

Quality still remains high, however, and you can find some excellent buys. To be sure of reasonable prices and quality, head for the local Istituto Sardo Organizzazione Lavoro Artigiano (ISOLA) shop, which authenticates each piece it sells.

The Sardinian Kitchen

Groves of olives and lemons ripening in the sun, wild thyme, rosemary, juniper and myrtle perfuming coastal breezes, shepherds guiding their flocks home from the pastures to make ricotta, fishermen reeling in mullet and lobster from the Med at daybreak...this isn't romance, it's reality. Nowhere does slow food like Sardinia.

The real beauty of Sardinian cuisine is its freshness and simplicity. After all, what could be better than *pane carasau* still warm from a wood oven drizzled with extra-virgin olive oil, the clean, bright flavours of home-made antipasti, or suckling pig roasted on a spit until beautifully crisp? Throw in views of mountains and sea, some fine home-produced Cannonau or Vermentino wine and you are looking at a great culinary experience – simple but great.

Ah yes, the Sardinians might say, but Sardinian cuisine is not as simple as it seems: the devil is in the detail. Indeed, nowhere else in Italy will you find such a smorgasbord of bread (some of it incredibly artistic) and pecorino (sheep's milk cheese; including the maggot-riddled *casu marzu*). And just when you think you've got it sussed, Sardinia introduces idiosyncrasies to the stove. Those ricotta-filled pasta pockets you are eating are not ravioli but *culurgiones*. The shell-shaped dumplings swimming in herby tomato sauce you're enjoying are not gnocchi but *malloreddus*. Oh, and by the way, your nutty, granular pasta studded with plump clams: it's not couscous, it's *fregola*. Got it? Bravo. *Buon appetito!*

For a three-course meal, including house wine
» € Under €25
» €€ €25 to €45
» €€€ Over €45

A Day at Sardinia's Table

Like most Italians, Sardinians rarely eat a sit-down *colazione* (breakfast), preferring a cappuccino and *cornetto* (croissant) standing at a bar. Out in the wilds, shepherds would start the day with a handful of bread and a slice of hard cheese.

WHEN IN...TRY...

» **Cagliari** *Burrida,* dogfish marinated in walnuts, garlic, vinegar and spices.

» **Gallura** *Zuppa cuata* or *zuppa gallurese,* a heart-warming casserole comprising layers of bread, cheese and meat ragu, drenched in broth and baked to a crispy crust.

» **Olbia** *Zuppa di cozze e vongole* (garlicky clam and mussel soup), *ricci* (sea urchins) and *ortidas* (fried sea anemones).

» **Barbagia** *Pecora in capoto,* a hearty, flavoursome ewe stew.

» **Alghero** *Aragosta alla catalana,* lobster with tomato and onion.

» **Cabras** *Muggini* (mullet) and *bottarga* (mullet roe).

» **Nuoro & Ogliastra** *Fioro sardo pecorino,* suckling lamb and pig, and wild boar.

Pranzo (lunch) remains a ritual observed by many Sardinians. Workers can't always get home, but across the island shops and businesses close for three to four hours to ensure lunch is properly taken and digested. A full meal will consist of an *antipasto* (starter) followed by a *primo* – usually a thick soup, pasta or risotto – and a *secondo* of meat or fish. Inlanders will invariably prefer meat, often served roasted or in thick stews. To finish *alla sarda* (in Sardinian style) go for cheese and a *digestivo*, perhaps a shot of grappa, although it is now usual to wind up with dessert and coffee.

Cena (the evening meal) was traditionally a simpler affair, but as work habits change and fewer people lunch at home, it increasingly becomes the main meal of the day.

Sardinian Cuisine

Daily Bread

Few experiences in Sardinia beat walking into a neighbourhood *panetteria* in the morning, breathing in the yeasty aromas and feasting your eyes on the loaves of freshly baked bread. The Sardinians hold the humble loaf in high esteem and have come up with literally hundreds of types of bread, each one particular to its region and town. Traditional bakeries pride themselves on using durum wheat of the best quality and age-old kneading techniques.

Originally from the Campidano region, the commonly seen *civraxiu* is a thick, circular loaf with a crispy crust and a soft white interior. Another common bread is the *spianata* or *spianada*, which is a little like Middle Eastern pitta. In Sassari snack bars you'll discover *fainè*, the chickpea-flour *farinata* flat bread imported centuries ago by Ligurians from north-western Italy. The Spaniards contributed *panadas*, scrumptious little pies that can be filled with anything from minced lamb or pork to eel.

For special occasions such as weddings and religious feast days, bread is elevated to an art form called *su coccoi*, with intricate floral wreaths, hearts and animals that are impossibly delicate and almost too pretty to eat.

Antipasti

A tasty Italian import, antipasti appear on almost every menu as a lead to *primi* (first courses). *Antipasti di terra* ('of the land') is often a mouth-watering assortment of home-made bread, cured ham, tangy Sardinian salami, olives and a range of cooked, raw and marinated vegetables such as artichokes and eggplant. There is also *frittelle di zucchine,* an omelette stuffed with zucchini (courgettes), breadcrumbs and cheese. Along the coast you'll find *antipasti di mare* ('of the sea'), such as thinly sliced bottarga (mullet or tuna roe), the best of which comes from the lagoon town of Cabras. Cagliari is famous for its *burrida* (marinated dogfish).

Top Sardinian Cookbooks

» *The Foods of Sicily & Sardinia,* by Giuliano Bugialli

» *Sweet Myrtle & Bitter Honey: The Mediterranean Flavours of Sardinia,* by Efisio Farris

» *Gastronomia in Sardegna,* by Gian Paolo Caredda

Civraxiu takes its name from *cibaria,* the word for 'flour' during the Roman occupation when Sardinia was one of the major grain suppliers to the Empire.

MUSIC PAPER

As crisp as a cracker, as light as a wafer and thin enough for the sun to shine through, *pane carasau,* also known as *carta da musica* (music paper), is the star of Sardinia's bread basket. It is most ubiquitous in the rural interior, particularly in the Gallura, Logudoro and Nuoro regions, where it is still made by hand using the simplest of ingredients – durum wheat, water and a pinch of salt – and twice baked in a wood-fired oven to achieve its distinctive crispness. For centuries this long-lasting bread has been ideal for shepherds out in the pasture.

Brushed with olive oil and sprinkled with salt, *pane carasau* becomes a moreish snack known as *pane guttiau.* A fancier version often served as a first course is *pane frattau,* where *pane carasau* is topped with tomato sauce, grated pecorino and a soft-boiled egg.

Ask Sardinians about the island's infamous *casu marzu*, 'rotten cheese' alive with maggots, and watch them raise a knowing eyebrow, snigger at hilarious memories of trying to eat the stuff, or else swiftly change the subject. Everyone, it seems, has a story or an opinion about the *formaggio che salta* (cheese that jumps). It's creamier and tastier than anything you've ever tried, say some; it makes your skin crawl and festers in the gut, warn others.

If you were a horror movie scriptwriter with a passion for pecorino you couldn't make it up: pecorino deliberately infested with the larvae of the *piophila casei* cheese fly, whose digestive acids break down the cheese fats, advancing fermentation and rapidly leading to decomposition. The pungent liquid that oozes out of the cheese is called the *lagrima* (tear). When eating the cheese, locals cover it with one hand to stop the sprightly little larvae from jumping into their face – they can leap up to 15cm, apparently. Others prefer to remove the maggots by placing the cheese into a paper bag and letting them starve of oxygen.

Tempted? Well, even if you are, you would have to be pretty determined to find the cheese. Though considered a 'traditional food' exempt from EU health regulations, it is still illegal to sell and serve *casu marzu*, and most is produced for private consumption. Its elusiveness adds to its mystery: ask those same Sardinians where to find *casu marzu* and they will probably make a wide, sweeping gesture and tell you in the mountains... maybe. Head to the lonesome Barbagia in summer and with a little luck and one very strong stomach, you might just find a farmer willing to reveal his secret stash.

Cheese, Glorious Cheese

Sardinia is an island of shepherds, so it's hardly surprising that cheese making is a fine art here. Cheese has been produced here for nearly 5000 years, and Sardinia makes about 80% of Italy's pecorino. Gourmands will delight in flavours and textures, from tangy *pecorino sardo* to smoked varieties, creamy goat's cheeses (such as *ircano* and *caprino*), ricottas and speciality cheeses like *canestrati*, with peppercorns and herbs.

Fiore sardo, a centuries-old cheese recipe, is eaten fresh, smoked or roasted and packs a fair punch. It is traditionally made from ewe's milk, but varieties such as *fresa* and *peretta* are made from cow's milk. The most popular goat's cheese is *caprino*, and the soft *crema del Gerrei* is a combination of goat's milk and ricotta.

Only the bravest connoisseurs will want to sample *formaggio marcio* or *casu marzu*, quite literally a 'rotten cheese' alive with maggots!

Sardinian Pasta

Sardinia generally has an individual way of doing things, and the island's pasta is no different.

Malloreddus, dense shell-shaped pasta made of semolina and flavoured with saffron, is usually served with *salsa alla campidanese* (sausage and tomato sauce) and is sometimes called *gnocchetti sardi*. Another uniquely Sardinian creation is *fregola*, a granular pasta similar to couscous, which is often served in soups and broths.

Culurgiones (spelt in various ways) is a ravioli-like pasta that appears on many menus. Typically it has a ricotta or pecorino filling and is coated in a tomato and herb sauce. *Culurgiones de l'Ogliastra*, made in Nuoro province, is stuffed with potato purée and sometimes meat and onions. A little pecorino, olive oil, garlic and mint are added, and a tomato sauce is the usual accompaniment.

Maccarones furriaos are strips of pasta folded and topped with a sauce (often tomato based) and melted cheese. *Maccarones de busa*, or just plain *busa*, is shaped by wrapping the pasta around knitting needles.

Top Five Dining Experiences

» **La Botteghina**, Alghero

» **Su Gologone**, near Oliena

» **Peschiera Pontis**, Cabras

» **Pintadera**, Iglesias

» **Ristorante Gallura**, Olbia

Other pastas you may come across are *pillus,* a small ribbon pasta, and *filindeu,* a threadlike noodle usually served in soups.

On the Spit

Sardinia's carnivorous heart beats to its own unique drum. Three specialities stand out: *porceddu* (suckling pig), *agnello* (lamb) and *capretto* (kid). These dishes are flavoured with Mediterranean herbs and spit-roasted.

The most famous of this culinary triumvirate is the *porceddu* (also spelt *porcheddu*), which is slow roasted until the skin crackles and the meat is meltingly tender, then left to stand on a bed of myrtle leaves.

Agnello is particularly popular around December, although it's served year-round. *Capretto* is harder to find on menus, but it gets more common up in the mountains, where it is flavoured with thyme.

A country classic – and a rarity – is *su carraxiu* (literally 'of the buried') – the meat is compressed between two layers of hot stones, covered in myrtle and left to cook slowly in a hole dug in the ground.

Sards also have a penchant for game birds, rabbit and wild boar. A wonderful local sauce for any meat dish is *al mirto* – made with red myrtle, it is a tangy addition.

To hide evidence of their crime, bandits would slow roast stolen pigs in underground holes under bonfires. The technique is known as *su carraxiu.*

Fish & Seafood

Sardinians point out that they are by tradition *pastori, non pescatori* (shepherds, not fishermen). There is some tradition of seafood in Cagliari, Alghero, Cabras and other coastal towns, but elsewhere the phenomenon has arrived from beyond Sardinia.

At the top end of the scale, lobster (legally in season from March to August) is *the* local speciality, particularly in Alghero, where it's served as *aragosta alla catalana* with tomato and onion. *Muggine* (mullet) is popular on the Oristano coast, and *tonno* (tuna) dishes abound around the Isola di San Pietro. *Cassola* is a tasty fish soup, while *zuppa alla castellanese,* a Castelsardo speciality, is similar but with a distinct tomato edge.

Cagliari also has a long tradition of seafood recipes that run the gamut from sea bream to bass, although the most famous is based on the local *gattucio di mare* (dogfish). Clams, cockles, octopus and crab also feature, as do eels around the marshes of Cabras. For something more adventurous, try *orziadas* (deep-fried sea anemones) and *ricci* (sea urchins).

Room for Dessert

Sardinia's sweet trolley has always been constrained by the natural flavours of the island. Take the recipe for *amarettes* (almond biscuits): there

---

WE DARE YOU TO TRY...

» *Casu marzu* – Rotten pecorino alive with maggots, if you can find it.

» *Cordula* – Lamb tripe grilled, fried or stewed with peas.

» *Granelle* – Calf's testicles sliced, covered in batter and lightly fried.

» *Salsiccia* or *salame di cavallo/d'asino* – Horsemeat or donkey sausages.

» *Tataliu* or *trattalia* – A mix of kidney, liver and intestines stewed or grilled on skewers. The dish is made with veal, lamb, kid or suckling pig.

» *Zimino russo* – A selection of roasted offal, usually from a calf, including the heart, diaphragm, liver, kidney and other red innards.

» *Zurrette* – A black pudding made of sheep's blood cooked, like haggis, in a sheep's stomach with herbs and fennel.

Sweets, tarts, cakes and biscuits – Sardinia's dessert menu is rich and varied. Alongside the island staples, there's a never-ending list of local specialities.

'Every town has its own recipes,' explains Maria Antonietta Goddi, one of four sisters who along with their mother, the formidable Signora Maurizia, run Durke, a traditional sweet shop in Cagliari's Marina district.

'For example, there's a *dolce* (sweet) called *papassino* (from papassa, which means raisin) that's made all over Sardinia, but there are lots of local variations. So you have variations from Torralba, Benetutti, Bitti and Selargius in the province of Cagliari. The version from Selargius uses cinnamon and *vino cotto* (mulled wine).'

Such variations often reflect an area's history, incorporating foreign influences into traditional recipes. 'In the centre and the south of Sardinia, the Arab influence is very strong – orange blossom, cinnamon and vanilla are used a lot. In the north they use a lot of *vino cotto* and *vino selvatico* (wine from wild plants). In the centre they also use pecorino to make *casatinas,* which have a much stronger taste. Here in Cagliari we use a lot of ricotta, often with saffron.

'Then there's *torrone* (nougat), a *dolce* that is made in Sicily as well, but is made in Sardinia without the addition of sugar, so with honey, egg whites, almonds and walnuts.' For more info on Durke, see p48.

are just three ingredients – almonds, sugar and eggs – but the biscuits are delightfully fluffy and moist.

Though traditionally an Easter recipe, you might spot *pardulas* (also known as *casadinas* and *formagelle*) in cake shops at other times of the year. These delectable mini cheesecakes are made from ricotta or pecorino, flavoured with saffron and baked in a crisp shell.

Other sweets and biscuits are strictly seasonal. *Ossus de mortu* (dead men's bones) biscuits, infused with cinnamon and studded with almonds, are served on All Saints' Day in November. After the grape harvest you'll start to see *papassinos de Vitzi* (almond and sultana biscuits) and *pabassinas cun saba,* mixed with almonds, honey, candied and grape must. At festivities you may well come across *sospiri di Ozieri,* rich patties of minced almonds, sugar, honey and lemon glazed with icing, and *coffettura,* tiny baskets of finely shaved orange peel and almonds drenched in honey.

The island's most famous dessert, however, is the *seadas* (or *sebadas*), a deliciously light pastry (vaguely like a turnover) stuffed with bran, orange peel and ricotta or sour cheese and then drenched in *miele amaro* (bitter honey).

Sardinian Drinks

Coffee

The espresso is the standard coffee drink in Sardinia and is what you get if you ask for *un caffè. Doppio espresso* is a double shot and a *caffè americano* is a watered-down version. If you prefer your coffee with milk, there are various options. A *caffè latte,* regarded by locals as a breakfast drink, is coffee with a reasonable amount of milk. A *caffè macchiato* is an espresso with a dash of hot milk, and a *latte macchiato* is a glass of hot milk with a dash of coffee. The cappuccino is a frothy version of the *caffè latte.*

Wine

Sardinian wines might not be as venerated as those from Italy, but times are changing, as vintners push for a higher profile and quality gets better and better. Contemporary producers have started taming the mighty alcoholic content of their traditional blends and are now producing some light, dry whites and more sophisticated reds.

The best winegrowing regions for visitors are the Gallura for Vermentino whites, the Ogliastra, Baronia, Barbagia and Mandrolisai for Cannonau reds, and Sulcis in southwest Sardinia for Carignano reds and rosés.

On the whole Sardinian wine is very reasonably priced, with quality labels often available from around €10 to €15 per bottle. You can buy wine directly from the producer or from a *cantina sociale* (wineproducers' cooperative). Lots of these organisations offer a *degustazione* (tasting). Many *agriturismi* (farm-stay accommodation) also produce their own wine, much of which is surprisingly good value.

WINE ON THE WEB

Dry and authoritative, www.winecountry. it provides technical details for all of Sardinia's major wines.

Vermentino Whites

Introduced to Sardinia in the 18th century, the Vermentino grape flourishes on the sandy granite-based soil in the northeast. The area's best wine is the Vermentino di Gallura, Sardinia's only DOCG. A crisp aromatic white with a slightly bitter almond aftertaste, it's best drunk young as an aperitif or with fish. But Vermentino is not confined to the Gallura DOCG area, although the Vermentino di Sardegna produced elsewhere only carries the DOC rating

Cannonau Reds

The island's best-known red wines are made from the Cannonau vine. This is cultivated across the island, although it's particularly widespread on the mountains around Oliena and Jerzu. Especially good paired with roasted meats, Cannonau reds are a rich, heavy drop that has been sustaining locals for centuries. Research has revealed that Cannonau wines are particularly rich in procyanidins, one of the chemicals that

---

WINE TASTING

You can buy and drink Sardinian wines at any *enoteca* (wine bar), but you'll get far more out of a proper tasting. Here is our pick of the best wineries and cellars that open their doors for tastings.

» **Sella e Mosca** (p123) Sardinia's top wine producer has free guided tours of its museum. Sample wines such as pale, crisp Vermentinos and ruby red Cannonaus with a hint of oak.

» **Cantine Surrau** (see the boxed text, p151) A strikingly contemporary winery near Arzachena, with guided tours, art exhibitions and tastings. Be sure to try the intense, fruity Cannonau reds and the mineral-rich Vermentino whites.

» **Cantina del Vermentino** (p166) Pass through the arch to descend to this winery, where you can taste and buy some of the finest Vermentino whites to be found in the Gallura.

» **Antichi Poderi di Jerzu** (p195) Sip beefy Cannonau red wines in the town nicknamed the Citta del Vino (Wine Town), surrounded by fabulous scenery.

» **Cantina del Mandrolisai** (see the boxed text, p182) In the heart of the hilly Mandrolisa, this *cantina* is famous for its beefy reds.

» **Cantine Argiolas** (see the boxed text, p51) Just a short detour north from Cagliari brings you to this award-winning winery in vine-strewn Serdiana. Stop by for a guided tour and tasting.

» **Cantina Santadi** (p71) The biggest winery in the southwest whose reds include the highly rated Roccia Rubia and Grotta Rossa. Note that booking a visit can be done online.

is reputed to give red wine its heart-protecting qualities, which may go some way to explaining the exceptional longevity of people in the Nuoro province.

Vernaccia & Malvasia

Produced since Roman times on the alluvial plains around Oristano, Vernaccia is one of Sardinia's most famous wines. It's best known as an amber sherry-like drop usually taken as an aperitif or to accompany pastries like *mustazzolus*. However, there are nine Vernaccia wines, ranging from dry still whites to aged fortified wines.

Another excellent tipple, Malvasia (Malmsey) is produced in the Planaragia hills near Bosa, but it's also made around Cagliari (Malvasia di Cagliari). The Malvasia di Bosa, a delicious honey-coloured dessert wine, is widely available in the Bosa area.

Spirits

Mirto is Sardinia's national drink, a smooth, powerful liqueur distilled from the fragrant purple fruit of the myrtle bush. In its most common form it's a purplish berry-red, although a less common white version is also made.

But *mirto* is just the tip of the iceberg for Sardinian spirits. Islanders have developed a range of local firewaters made using easily found ingredients, such as *corbezzolo* (an autumnal plant that is similar to wild strawberry), prickly pears and basil. There's even a local form of *limoncello*, a sweet lemon-based tipple, similar to the better known Amalfi Coast drink.

The strangely named *filu e ferru* (the iron wire) provides quite a kick. Similar to grappa, it is made from a distillate of grape skins and positively roars down the throat – the alcohol content hovers around 40%, with some home brews reaching an eye-watering 60%.

Zedda Piras is a reliable brand of *mirto* and *filu e ferru*.

Eating Out in Sardinia

The most basic sit-down eatery in Sardinia is called a *tavola calda* (literally 'hot table'), which generally offers canteen-style food. For a full meal you'll want to go to a trattoria or a *ristorante*. Traditionally, trattorias were family-run places that served a basic menu of local dishes at affordable prices and, thankfully, a few still do this. *Ristoranti* offer more choice, often with a more extensive wine list and smarter service. House wine is nearly always available and is the most inexpensive choice at between €5 and €10 for a litre. It generally comes in quarter, half and full litre carafes. Some, but not all, restaurants will provide *acqua di rubinetto* (tap water) if you ask for it, but locals tend to order a bottle of *acqua frizzante* (sparkling mineral water) to drink with their meal. All eating establishments in Sardinia are officially non-smoking.

On a restaurant/trattoria bill you can expect to be charged for *pane e coperto* (bread and a cover charge). This is standard and is added even if you don't ask for or eat the bread. Typically it ranges from €1 to €4. *Servizio* (service charge) of 10% to 15% may or may not be included in the bill; if it's not, tourists are expected to round up the bill or leave a 10% tip.

Vegetarians & Vegans

Vegetarians will have a tough time of it in Sardinia, a robustly meat-eating island. The good news is that vegetables are of a universally high standard and appear in many antipasti and *contorni* (side dishes).

Italian Wines, published by Gambero Rosso and Slow Food Editore, is the definitive annual guide to Italian wines. Producers and their labels are reviewed in encyclopaedic detail.

To avoid taxes Sardinians hid their home made *acquavita*. They'd mark the hideout with an iron wire (the *filu e ferru*), from which the drink derives its name.

A SARDINIAN WOULD NEVER...

» Split the bill. It isn't the done thing – the person who invites pays.
» Drink cappuccino after a meal; after noon it's espresso only.
» Eat on the hoof (unless it's gelato).
» Season their food without trying it first.
» Finish the bread before the food arrives; it's for mopping up delicious sauces.

However, note that even apparently meat-free food such as risotto or soup is often prepared with meat stock. Vegans will find it even harder as so many dishes feature some sort of animal product, be it dairy, eggs or animal stock.

Cookery Classes

To discover the nuances of Sardinian cuisine, consult www.sarnow. com and www. sardegnaturismo. it, which give a great overview of the specialities of each region.

Sardinia is not as well served with cooking schools as many Italian regions, but there are a handful of places where you can get behind the stove. These include the Cooperativa Gorropu (p187), based in the highlands around Dorgali; Hotel Gabbiano Azzurro (p207), a seafront resort hotel in Golfo Aranci; and Hotel Lucrezia (p204), in the flatlands north of Oristano. At Cantine Argiolas (see the boxed text, p51) you can learn to cook Sardinian specialities like *fregola* and enjoy them with Argiolas wines.

There are a number of specialist operators selling cooking holidays to Sardinia. One such is **Ciao Laura** (www.ciaolaura.com), an American outfit that arranges culinary stays in Orosei (p184), on the east coast. A four-day course costs €625, including accommodation.

Seasonal Food & Wine Festivals

A history of rural isolation has led to a fierce pride in local traditions, many of which find form in extravagant celebrations and food-based *sagre* (festivals dedicated to a particular food). Traditionally these were based on the farming calendar and provided a rare occasion for villagers to meet up, show off their most splendid costumes and prepare their finest recipes. Here's our pick of the best:

Sagra del Bogamarì (p118) In Alghero, an ode to the humble *ricci* (sea urchin), held on several weekends in March.

Sagra degli Agrumi (p53) Muravera's folksy Citrus Fair, held on the second or third weekend in April.

Sagra del Torrone (p178) Located in Tonara in the Barbagia di Belvi, a sweet tribute to nougat; held on Easter Monday.

Girotonno (p72) In Carloforte, this is a four-day festival celebrating the island's famous *mattanza* (tuna catch) in early June.

Sagra delle Castagne (p181) An autumnal feast of chestnuts in the mountain town of the Aritzo, held on the last Sunday of October.

Rassegna del Vino Novello (p105) In Milis, one of Sardinia's top wine festivals, where new wine is sniffed, tasted and sold; held in mid-November.

Survival Guide

Directory A–Z

Business Hours

» In many of the touristy areas, shops stay open later in summer, sometimes till 11pm. The midday break can range from three hours to five.

» In big towns, major department stores and some supermarkets are open from 9am (sometimes 10am) to 7.30pm Monday to Saturday.

» Food shops are often closed Thursday afternoons; some other shops are shut on Monday mornings.

» All post offices close at least two hours earlier than normal on the last business day of each month (not including Saturday).

» *Farmacie* (pharmacies), when closed, are required to post a list of places open in the vicinity.

» Bars and cafes with live or DJ music stay open until about 1am during the week and 2am Friday and Saturday.

» In summer (June to September) most restaurants open seven days for lunch and dinner. Many restaurants in coastal resorts close for several months in low season. Those that stay open usually close one day a week.

» The following business hours apply to all reviews, unless otherwise indicated.

BUSINESS	OPENING HOURS
Bank	8.30am-1.30pm & 2.45-4.30pm Mon-Fri
Bar	7pm-1am Mon-Sat
Cafe	7am or 8am-10pm or 11pm Mon-Sat
Club	10pm-3am, 4am or 5am Thu-Sat
Pharmacy	9am-1pm & 4-7.30pm Mon-Fri, 9am-1pm Sat
Post office	8am-6.50pm Mon-Fri, 8am-1.15pm Sat
Restaurant	lunch noon-2.30pm or 3pm, dinner 7-10pm or 11pm
Shop	9am-1pm & 4-8pm Mon-Sat

Customs Regulations

» Entering Italy from another EU country you can bring, duty-free: 10L spirits, 90L wine and 800 cigarettes.

» Arriving from a non-EU country, the limits are 1L spirits, 2L wine, 50mL perfume, 250mL eau de toilette, 200 cigarettes and other goods up to a total of €175.50; anything over this must be declared on arrival and duty paid.

» On leaving the EU, non-EU citizens can reclaim any value-added tax on expensive purchases (for details, see www.globalrefund.com).

» You can bring up to €10,000 cash into Italy.

Discount Cards

» Discount cards yield fantastic benefits and easily pay for themselves.

» As well as the card fee, you'll often need a passport-sized photo and some form of ID with proof of age (eg passport or birth certificate).

» People over 60 or 65 years are entitled to discounts on museum admission fees and some public transport.

» An **International Student Identity Card** (ISIC; www.isic.org; €12) entitles you to various shopping, accommodation and museum discounts in Cagliari, Sassari and Nuoro. A similar card is available to teachers, the **International Teacher Identity Card** (ITIC; www.isic.org; €12), and to non-students under 26 years, the **International Youth Travel Card** (IYTC; www.isic.org; €12).

» There is also a **European Youth Card** (Euro<26 card; www.euro26.org), which offers a wide range of discounts across Europe. Card-holders do not need to be European citizens

» Student cards are issued by student unions, hostelling organisations and some youth travel agencies. In Cagliari, the **Centro Turistico Studentesco e Giovanile** (www.cts.it, in Italian) youth travel agency can issue ISIC and ITIC cards and the European Youth Card (Euro<26 card).

Climate

Cagliari

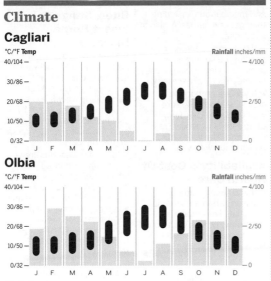

Olbia

Oristano

Ireland (☎06 697 91 21; www.
ambasciata-irlanda.it; Piazza
Campitelli 3, Rome)

Netherlands (☎070 30 38
73; www.olanda.it; Viale Diaz 76,
Cagliari)

New Zealand (☎06 853 75
01; www.nzembassy.com; Via
Clitunno 44, Rome)

Spain (☎06 684 04 01; www.
mae.es/embajadas/roma/es/
home; Palazzo Borghese, Largo
Fontanella Borghese 19, Rome)

UK (☎070 82 86 28; www.
britishembassy.gov.uk/italy;
Viale Colombo 160, Quartu
Sant'Elena, Cagliari)

USA (☎06 4 67 41; www.usis.
it; Via Vittorio Veneto 119a,
Rome)

Food

Throughout this book we
have used the following price
ranges for a three-course
meal, including wine:

€	under €25
€€	€25 to €45
€€€	over €45

For information on eating in
Sardinia, see The Sardinian
Kitchen (p237).

Gay & Lesbian Travellers

Discretion is the key. Although homosexuality is
legal, Sardinian attitudes
remain largely conservative.
There is practically no open
gay scene on the island and
overt displays of affection
could attract unpleasant
attention, especially in the
rural interior. The only places
where attitudes towards
homosexuality are really
changing are the island's two
largest cities, Sassari and
Cagliari.

The island's most high-
profile gay activist organisation is the Sassari-based
**Movimento Omosessuale
Sardo** (☎079 21 90 24; www.
movimentomosessualesardo.
org, in Italian; Via Rockfeller
16c). In Cagliari the main
organisation is the **Associazione Arc** (Via Leopardi 3).

Electricity

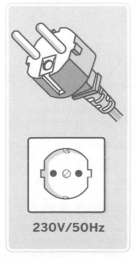

230V/50Hz

Embassies & Consulates

Most countries have an embassy in Rome, and several
also maintain an honorary
consulate in Cagliari. Passport inquiries should be ad-
dressed to the Rome-based
offices:

Australia (☎06 85 27 21,
emergencies 800 87 77 90;
www.italy.embassy.gov.au; Via
Antonio Bosio 5, Rome)

Canada (☎06 85 44 41; www.
international.gc.ca/canada-
europa/italy; Via Salaria 243,
Rome)

France (☎06 68 60 11; www.
ambafrance-it.org; Piazza
Farnese 67, Rome)

Germany (☎070 30 72 29;
www.rom.diplo.de; Via Rafa
Garzia 9, Cagliari)

The national gay organisation **Arcigay** (www.arcigay. it/Sardegna) is also a useful point of reference.

Online, www.gayfriendly italy.com is an excellent resource with background information on gay life in Italy, links, and listings of gay-friendly B&Bs and beaches in Sardinia.

Health

Excellent health care is readily available throughout Sardinia, but standards can vary. As well as selling over-the-counter medication for minor illnesses, pharmacists can give you valuable advice. Pharmacists are also able to advise when more specialised help is required and point you in the right direction.

Before You Go

» A little planning before departure, particularly for pre-existing illnesses, will save trouble later.

» Bring medications in their original, clearly labelled containers.

» A signed and dated letter from your physician describing your medical conditions and medications, including their generic names, is also a good idea.

» If carrying syringes or needles, be sure to have a physician's letter documenting their medical necessity.

» If you are embarking on a long trip, make sure your teeth are OK (dental treatment is expensive in Italy) and take your optical prescription with you.

Availability & Cost Of Health Care

» If you need an ambulance anywhere in Sardinia call ☑118. For emergency treatment, go straight to the *pronto soccorso* (casualty) section of a public hospital, where you can also get emergency dental treatment.

» The Guardia Medica is an on-call medical service that offers assistance throughout the night (8pm to 8am) on weekends and on public holidays. It does not provide emergency care (for that go to the *pronto soccorso* department at the nearest hospital), although it will make home visits when absolutely necessary. The service is available in most major towns.

Bites, Stings & Insect-Borne Diseases

» Mosquitoes are a real problem around low-lying marshy areas such as Cabras and Olbia; you should be particularly wary if you are considering camping. If travelling in summer, you should pack mosquito repellent as a matter of course.

» Sardinian beaches are occasionally inundated with jellyfish. Their stings are painful but not dangerous. Dousing in vinegar will deactivate any stingers that have not fired. Calamine lotion, antihistamines and analgesics may reduce the reaction and relieve pain.

» On dry land, you'll be much safer as Sardinia has absolutely no poisonous snakes.

Insurance

» Getting comprehensive travel insurance to cover theft, loss and medical problems is highly recommended.

» Some policies specifically exclude dangerous activities such as scuba diving, motorcycling, skiing and even trekking, so read the fine print.

PRACTICALITIES

» Sardinia uses the metric system for weights and measures.

» Buy or watch DVDs on the PAL system.

» The most common electric plugs (Type F, pictured p247) have two round pins; the current is 230V, 50Hz. Sardinia also has Type C and Type L plugs (three pins). Converters are readily available.

» The two main newspapers are Cagliari's *L'Unione Sarda* and Sassari's *La Nuova Sardegna*; a third is *Il Sardegna*. These papers tend to focus on island affairs and pay scant attention to national and international news. You can get English-language newspapers in most tourist centres, in summer only, and usually a day or two late.

» Radio Sardegna and Radiolina are popular local radio stations. National stations RAI-1, RAI-2 and RAI-3 play a mix of phone-ins, sport, news and music. Frequencies change depending on where you are. The BBC World Service is on medium wave at 648kHz and long wave at 198kHz.

» Local TV, such as Videolina and Sardegna 1, is usually pretty dire, pumping out news, football and traditional costumed dancing. You can also watch Italy's commercial stations Canale 5, Italia 1, Rete 4 and La7, and the state-run RAI-1, RAI-2 and RAI-3. Reception is not always the best, however, particularly for RAI-2 in the southwest.

EUROPEAN HEALTH INSURANCE CARD

Citizens of the EU, Switzerland, Iceland, Norway or Liechtenstein receive free or reduced-cost state-provided health-care cover with the European Health Insurance Card (EHIC) for medical treatment that becomes necessary while in Sardinia or other parts of Italy. (The EHIC replaced the E111 in 2006.) Each family member will need a separate card. In the UK, get application forms from post offices, or download them from the Department of Health website (www.dh.gov.uk), which has comprehensive information about the card's coverage.

The EHIC does not cover private health care, so make sure that you are treated by a state health-care provider. You will need to pay directly and fill in a treatment form; keep the form to claim any refunds. In general, you can claim back around 70% of the standard treatment cost.

Citizens from other countries need to check if there is a reciprocal arrangement for free medical care between their country and Italy. Australia, for instance, has such an agreement. If you do need health insurance, make sure you get a policy that covers you for the worst possible scenario, such as an accident requiring an emergency flight home. Find out in advance if your insurance plan will make payments directly to providers or reimburse you later for overseas health expenditures.

» Check that the policy covers ambulances or an emergency flight home.

» Find out in advance if your insurance plan will make payments directly to providers or reimburse you later for overseas health expenditures.

» If you have to claim later, make sure you keep all documentation.

» Paying for your airline ticket with a credit card often provides limited travel accident insurance – ask your credit-card company what it is prepared to cover.

» Worldwide travel insurance is available at www.lonelyplanet.com/travel_services. You can buy, extend and claim online anytime – even if you are already on the road.

Internet Access

» Throughout this guide, only accommodation providers that have an actual computer that guests can use to access the internet are flagged with a computer icon (@); the (🛜) icon indicates anywhere with wifi access. The easiest way to access the internet is at an internet cafe, which you'll find in all the major holiday centres and dotted sporadically around the island (and listed in this book).

» You can't rely on finding an internet cafe in small towns and villages. Access is expensive, typically costing around €5 an hour.

» Note also that whenever you use an internet cafe you're legally obliged to show an ID card or passport.

» Many hotels offer internet access, and an increasing number are providing wifi.

» Italy's phone companies **Telecom Italia** (www.tim.it, in Italian) and **Wind** (www.wind.it, in Italian) both offer wireless connection packages that allow you to connect through the mobile phone network. They're not especially cheap though, costing about €25 per month with a 12-month minimum.

Legal Matters

The police is divided into three main bodies – the *polizia*, who wear navy-blue jackets; the *carabinieri*, in a black uniform with a red stripe; and the grey-clad *guardia di finanza*, responsible for fighting tax evasion and drug smuggling. If you run into trouble, you're most likely to end up dealing with the *polizia* or *carabinieri*. That is, unless you're on the receiving end of a parking ticket, in which case you'll be cursing the *vigili urbani*, the local traffic police.

If you are detained for any alleged offence, you should be given verbal and written notice of the charges laid against you within 24 hours. You have no right to a phone call upon arrest, but you can choose not to respond to questions without the presence of a lawyer. For serious crimes, it is possible to be held without trial for up to two years.

In February 2006 the Italian parliament approved tough antidrug laws that abolished the distinction between hard and soft drugs, effectively putting cannabis on the same legal footing as cocaine, heroin and ecstasy. If caught with what the police deem to be a dealable quantity, you risk fines of up to €260,000 or prison sentences of between six and 20 years.

The legal limit for a driver's blood-alcohol reading is 0.05%. Following a spate of road fatalities in 2007, authorities stamp down hard on drink-driving.

Money

» Sardinia's unit of currency is the euro (€), which is divided into 100 cents.

» Coin denominations are one, two, five, 10, 20 and 50 cents and €1 and €2. The seven euro notes come in denominations of €5, €10, €20, €50, €100, €200 and €500.

» For exchange rates and costs, see p14.

» Money can be exchanged in banks, post offices and exchange offices.

» Banks generally offer the best rates, but shop around, as rates tend to fluctuate considerably.

ATMs

» ATMs (known in Italian as *bancomat*) are widely available in Sardinia and are undoubtedly the simplest (and safest) way to access your money while travelling. Most will accept cards tied into the Visa, MasterCard, Cirrus or Maestro systems. As a precaution, though, check that the appropriate logo is displayed on the ATM before inserting your card. The daily limit for cash withdrawal is €250.

» When you withdraw money from an ATM, the amounts are converted and dispensed in euros. However, there will be fees. Typically, you'll be charged a withdrawal fee (usually around 1.5%) as well as a conversion charge; if you're using a credit card, you might also be hit by interest on the cash withdrawn.

Cash

» Cash is readily available from ATMs, so there's little point in bringing large quantities with you.

» When travelling around the island, you'll need cash for many day-to-day transactions, as credit cards are not always accepted, especially in many B&Bs and cheap trattorias.

Credit Cards

» Carrying plastic is the simplest way to organise your holiday funds. You don't have large amounts of cash to lose, you can get money after hours and the exchange rate is often better.

» Major cards such as Visa, MasterCard, Eurocard, Cirrus and Eurocheque are accepted in Sardinia. Check charges with your bank, but most banks now build a fee of around 3% into every foreign transaction, as well as a charge of around 1.5% for ATM withdrawals.

» If your card is lost, stolen or swallowed by an ATM, telephone one of the following toll-free numbers to block it:
Amex (☑800 914 912)
MasterCard (☑800 870 866)
Visa (☑800 81 90 14)

Tipping

» You're not expected to tip on top of restaurant service charges, but if you think the service warrants it, feel free to round up the bill or leave a little extra – 10% is fine.

» In bars, Italians often leave small change (€0.10/0.20) as a tip.

» Tipping taxi drivers is not common practice, but you should tip the porter at top-end hotels.

WHERE	CUSTOMARY TIP
bar	round to nearest euro
hotel cleaning staff	€1 per day
hotel porter	€1 to €1.50 per bag
restaurant	not customary, but 10% if you like
taxi	not customary

National Parks

Besides three national parks, Sardinia harbours two regional parks and numerous marine reserves. Visit www. parks.it for more details.

Parco Nazionale del Golfo di Orosei e del Gennargentu (p184) Sardinia's largest national park, in the Nuoro province, encompasses the coastlines of the Golfo di Orosei and parts of Barbagia and the Supramonte.

Parco Nazionale dell'Arcipelago di La Maddalena (p159) This park covers all the islands of this northwestern archipelago. Isola Caprera, joined to Isola Maddalena by a narrow causeway, has its own status as a natural reserve.

Parco Nazionale dell'Asinara (p129) This remarkable coastal wilderness off the northwest tip of the island is named after its unique *asino bianco* (albino donkey).

Post

» Italy's, and by association Sardinia's, postal system **Poste** (☑80 31 60; www.poste. it) is not the world's most efficient, although it has improved in recent years. Unfortunately, Sardinia's distance from the mainland doesn't help matters.

» Stamps (*francobolli*) are available at post offices and tobacconists (*tabacchi*) – look for the official sign, a big white 'T' against a black background. Since letters often need to be weighed, what you get at the tobacconist's for international airmail will occasionally be an approximation of the proper rate.

Public Holidays

Most Italians take their annual holiday in August, deserting the cities for the coast or cool mountain resorts. And with Sardinia ranked as one of the Mediterranean's top beach destinations, the island gets pretty busy.

Over July and August, hundreds of thousands of Italians and foreigners flock to the island, while city-dwelling Sardinians head out to holiday homes on the coast. As a consequence, many city businesses and shops close for a couple of weeks, typically in the period around Ferragosto (Feast of the Assumption) on 15 August. Settimana Santa (Easter Week) is another busy holiday time for Italians.

National holidays include the following:

Capodanno (New Year's Day) 1 January

Epifania (Epiphany) 6 January

Pasqua (Easter Sunday) March/April

Pasquetta (Easter Monday) March/April

Giorno della Liberazione (Liberation Day) 25 April

Festa del Lavoro (Labour Day) 1 May

Festa della Repubblica (Republic Day) 2 June

Ferragosto (Feast of the Assumption) 15 August

Ognissanti (All Saints' Day) 1 November

Immacolata Concezione (Feast of the Immaculate Conception) 8 December

Natale (Christmas Day) 25 December

Festa di Santo Stefano (Boxing Day) 26 December

Safe Travel

Despite past notoriety as a centre of banditry and kidnapping, Sardinia is a peaceful island, and you will seldom be subject to the more unsavoury cons or petty crime that are prevalent in many mainland Italian cities. Muggings, moped-assisted bag-snatching and over-charging in hotels are almost unheard of, and your stay should be trouble free.

Theft

Although theft is not a big problem in Sardinia, you should still use your common sense.

» A money belt with your essentials (passport, cash, credit cards) is a good idea. However, to avoid delving into it in public, carry a wallet with a day's cash.

» If you're carrying a bag or camera, wear the strap across your body and away from the road.

» Be careful when you sit down at a street-side table – never drape your bag over an empty chair by the road or put it where you can't see it.

» Don't leave valuables lying around your hotel room.

» And *never* leave valuables visible in your car – in fact, try not to leave anything in the car and certainly not overnight. It's worth paying extra to leave your car in supervised car parks.

» In case of theft or loss, always report the incident at the *questura* (municipal police station) within 24 hours and ask for a statement, otherwise your travel insurance company won't pay out.

» Emergency numbers are listed throughout this book.

Traffic

On the whole, driving in Sardinia isn't nearly as intimidating as it is in the rest of Italy, and islanders generally observe the road rules.

» In July and August traffic on minor roads can be a pain, as can parking.

» In the bigger towns you'll need to keep a keen eye on what's going on around you, especially when slowing down to check street names or to look for a parking spot.

» As a pedestrian you'd still be advised to keep your wits about you.

Women Travellers

Women will find it more difficult to travel alone than men, especially in the interior. There's no particular danger – in fact, you'll invariably be treated with duty-bound courtesy – but local attitudes are largely based on old-fashioned norms of gender division. In practical terms, this means that you won't see many local women in bars and cafes in rural areas, and that lone women travellers will often attract stares that may make them uncomfortable. Fortunately, though, it usually stops there, and unpleasant comments and heavy harassment are rare.

Telephone

Mobile Phones

» Phones operate on the GSM 900/1800 network, which is compatible with the rest of Europe and Australia but not with the North American GSM 1900 or the Japanese system (although some GSM 1900/900 phones do work here).

» If you have a GSM, dual- or tri-band phone that you can unlock (check with your service provider), you can activate a *prepagato* (prepaid) SIM card in Italy.

» **TIM** (www.tim.it), **Wind** (www.wind.it) and **Vodafone** (www.vodafone.it) all offer SIM cards and all have retail outlets in locations across the island.

» To recharge a card, simply pop into the nearest outlet or buy a *ricarica* (charge card) from a *tabacchi*.

» Call rates vary according to the call plan you activate but are typically around €0.20 per minute to Italian fixed phones and €0.50 to €3 per minute to Europe and the US.

» When you buy a card, make sure you have your passport with you.

Phone Codes

Direct international calls can easily be made from public telephones or cut-price call centres.

Calling Italy from abroad First dial your country's international access code, then ⊠39 (Italy's country code), then the local number. Note that area codes are an integral part of all Italian phone numbers, meaning that you must always dial the full number, even when you are calling locally.

Calling internationally from Italy Dial ⊠00 (the international access code), the country code, the area code (without the initial zero if there is one) and the local number.

Mobile phone numbers These begin with a three-digit prefix such as 330 or 339.

Toll-free (free-phone) numbers Known as *numeri verdi,* free-phone numbers usually start with 800.

National call rate numbers Start with 848 or 199.

Directory inquiries ⊠1254.

Emergency numbers Can be dialled from public phones without a phonecard. See inside the front cover.

International directory inquiries For numbers outside Italy, dial ⊠11 87 00.

Time

» Sardinian time is one hour ahead of GMT/UTC. Daylight-saving time, when clocks are moved forward one hour, commences on the last Sunday in March. Clocks are put back an hour on the last Sunday in October.

» Italy operates on a 24-hour clock, so 6pm is written as 18.00.

» The following times do not take daylight-saving time into account.

CITY	NOON IN CAGLIARI
Auckland	11pm
Berlin	noon
Cape Town	noon
London	11am
New York	6am
San Francisco	3am
Sydney	9pm
Tokyo	8pm

Tourist Information

Tourist information is widely available in Sardinia, although the quality varies enormously. On the whole, offices in important tourist centres such as Alghero, Cala Gonone, Santa Teresa di Gallura and Villasimius are efficient and helpful with English-speaking staff.

Alongside the 'official' tourist offices there are a plethora of private agencies advertising tourist information, alongside tours and accommodation. In some cases, these places are more useful than the official sources. Where this is the case we've listed them in this book.

On the ground you may come across an Azienda Autonoma di Soggiorno e Turismo (AAST) office with town-specific information on things like bus routes and museum opening times, or an office of the Azienda di Promozione Turistica (APT) or Ente Provinciale per il Turismo (EPT), which can provide information on the town you're in and the surrounding province.

» In small towns and villages the only tourist office is usually the Pro Loco, which is run by the local council and has limited local information.

» Tourist offices are generally open 9am to 12.30pm or 1pm and then from 4pm to 6pm Monday to Friday.

However, hours are usually extended in summer, when some offices also open on Saturday and Sunday.

» Most offices will respond to written and telephone requests for information. Useful websites:

Sardegna Turismo (www.sardegnaturismo.it) Excellent source of information on Sardinia.

Italian State Tourist Board (ENIT; www.enit.it) Another good place to inform yourself on Sardinia.

Travellers With Disabilities

Sardinia has little infrastructure to ease the way for disabled travellers, and few museums and monuments have wheelchair access. A notable exception is Cagliari's Museo Archeologico Nazionale.

Under European law, airports are obliged to provide assistance to passengers with disabilities, so if you need help en route to Sardinia, or on arrival, tell your airline when you book your ticket and they should inform the airport. Information on services available at Rome's two airports is available online at www.adrassistance.it.

If you need assistance travelling by train, Trenitalia runs a dedicated telephone line on ⊠199 30 30 60. It's active daily between 7am and 9pm.

The Italian State Tourist Office in your country may be able to provide advice on Italian associations for the disabled and information on what help is available in the country.

Some useful organisations include the following:

Accessible Italy (⊠378 94 11 11; www.accessibleitaly.com) A San Marino-based company that specialises in holiday services for the disabled, including tours and the hiring of adapted transport.

Associazione Italiana Assistenza Spastici (☎070 37 9101; www.aiasnazionale. it, in Italian; Viale Poetto 312, Cagliari) The Italian Spastics Assistance Association has a branch in Cagliari.

Disability World (www.disa bilityworld.com) A UK website with hotel listings across the world. At the time of research it had three hotels in Sardinia.

Holiday Care Service (☎in the UK 0845 124 99 71; www. holidaycare.org.uk) Produces an information pack on Italy (£3.50) for the physically disabled and others with special needs. The website also has a useful FAQs section.

Lonely Planet (www. lonelyplanet.com) The Thorn Tree forum has a section dedicated to travellers with disabilities.

Royal Association for Disability & Rehabilitation (RADAR; ☎in the UK 020 7250 32 22; www.radar.org.uk) A British-based organisation that can advise on all aspects of travelling.

Visas

Visa Requirements

» EU nationals and citizens of Iceland, Norway and Switzerland need only a passport or a national identity card in order to enter Italy and stay in the country, even for stays of over 90 days. However, citizens of new EU member states may be subject to various limitations on living and working in Italy.

» Citizens of Australia, the USA, Canada, Israel, Hong Kong, Japan, Malaysia, New Zealand, Singapore, South Korea and many Latin American countries do not need visas to visit Italy as tourists for up to 90 days. For long stays of over 90 days, contact your nearest Italian embassy or consulate and begin your application well in advance as it can take months.

» Other people wishing to come to Italy as tourists have to apply for a Schengen Visa, named after the agreements that abolished passport controls between 15 European countries. It allows unlimited travel throughout the entire zone for a 90-day period. Application should be made to the consulate of the country you are entering first, or that will be your main destination. The visa is not renewable inside Italy. Among other things for visa renewal, you will need travel and repatriation insurance and be able to show that you have sufficient funds to support yourself.

» For further information on Schengen visas and to download an application form, go to www.schengen visa.cc.

» Tourist visas cannot be changed into student visas after arrival. However, there are short-term visas available for students sitting university-entrance exams in Italy.

» Technically all foreign visitors to Sardinia are supposed to register with the local police within eight days of their arrival. However, if you are staying in a hotel, you don't need to bother, as the hotel does this for you – this is the reason why they always take your passport details.

» Up-to-date visa information is available on www. lonelyplanet.com – follow links through to the Italy destination guide.

Permesso di Soggiorno

» A *permesso di soggiorno* (permit to stay) is required by all non-EU nationals who stay in Sardinia longer than three months. You should apply for one within eight days of arriving in Italy but few people do.

» EU citizens don't require a *permesso di soggiorno*.

» To get one you'll need a valid passport, containing a stamp with your date of entry into Italy (ask for this as it's not automatic); a photocopy of your passport; a study visa if necessary; four passport-style photographs; proof of your ability to support yourself financially (ideally a letter from an employer or school/university); and a €14.92 official stamp (known as a *marca da bollo*).

» Up-to-date information is available on the website of the **Polizia di Stato** (www. poiziadistato.it, in Italian).

» Kits containing application forms are available from main post offices.

Study Visas

» Non-EU citizens who want to study in Sardinia must have a study visa. These can be obtained at your nearest Italian embassy or consulate.

» You will normally require confirmation of your enrolment, proof of payment of fees and proof that you can support yourself financially.

» The visa covers only the period of the enrolment.

» This type of visa is renewable within Italy but, again, only with confirmation of ongoing enrolment and that you are still financially self-supporting (bank statements are preferred).

Work Visas

» To work in Italy all non-EU citizens require a work visa. Apply to your nearest Italian embassy or consulate.

» You'll need a valid passport, proof of health insurance and a *permesso di lavoro* (work permit).

» If your employer is an Italian company, they will obtain the *permesso* in Italy and then forward it to you prior to your visa application.

» In other cases, you'll have to organise it yourself through the Italian consulate in your country.

Volunteering

Websites like www.volunteerabroad.com and www.transitionsabroad.com throw up a limited but interesting selection of volunteering opportunities in Sardinia, such as helping prevent bird poaching.

Other interesting volunteering opportunities:

World Wide Opportunities on Organic Farms (WWOOF; www.wwoof.org or www.wwoof.it) Work on a small farm or other organic venture (harvesting olives, helping with beehives, tending vegetable patches, help with milking and cheese making etc.).

Volunteers for Peace (www.vfp.org) A US-based nonprofit organisation. Can link you up with a voluntary service project dealing with social work, the environment, education or the arts.

Women Travellers

» Sardinians are almost universally polite to women, and it is unlikely that you will suffer the sort of harassment that you might in parts of mainland Italy.

» If you do find yourself the recipient of unwanted male attention, it's best to ignore it. If that doesn't work, politely tell your would-be companion that you are waiting for your *marito* (husband) or *fidanzato* (boyfriend) and, if necessary, walk away.

» Avoid becoming aggressive as this may result in a confrontation. If all else fails, approach the nearest member of the police or *carabinieri*.

» It is wise – and polite – to dress modestly in inland Sardinia. Communities here are very conservative, and you will still see older women wearing the traditional long, pleated skirts and shawls. Take your cue from Sardinian women.

Work

» EU nationals have an automatic right to work in Italy, though few EU nationals come to work in Sardinia.

» Pretty much anyone else who'd like an Italian job will need a hard-to-get work permit, issued at the request of your employer, who will have to show that no one in Italy – or the entire European Economic Area – can do your job.

» Exceptions may be made for artists, computer engineers and translation specialists.

» Working 'on the black' (that is, without documents) is difficult and risky for non-EU nationals.

» The only instance in which the government turns a blind eye to workers without documents is during fruit and wine harvests.

Finding Work

EU nationals with the right to work in Italy can find seasonal and casual work in restaurants, bars and hotels. Teaching English is another option, either for a company or through private lessons. Useful websites for finding your dream job include the following:

Natives (www.natives.co.uk) Good for winter and summer jobs.

Season Workers (www.seasonworkers.com) Search for summer and winter jobs.

Aeroporto Olbia Costa Smeralda (OLB; ☑0789 56 34 44; www.geasar.it) In Olbia, in the northeast.

255

Arbatax-Tortoli airstrip (☑0782 62 43 00; www. aeroportotortoliarbatax.it, in Italian) On the southern Nuoro coast, 1.5km south of Tortoli. It's tiny and opens in summer only for specialist charter flights.

AIRLINES FLYING TO/FROM SARDINIA

The number of airlines flying into Sardinia has risen, and you can now easily pick up flights across Europe, including Amsterdam, Barcelona, Brussels, Birmingham, Dublin, Hamburg, London, Madrid, Manchester, Paris, Prague, Stuttgart and Vienna.

International and national airlines flying to/from Sardinia include the following:

Air Berlin (AB; ☑199 400737; www.airberlin.com)

Air Dolomiti (EN; ☑045 288 61 40; www.airdolomiti.it)

Air One (AP; ☑199 207080; www.flyairone.it)

Alitalia (AZ; ☑06 22 22; www.alitalia.it)

Austrian Airlines (OS; ☑02 896 34 296; www.aua.com)

British Airways (BA; ☑199 712266; www.britishairways.com)

easyJet (U2; ☑899 234589; www.easyjet.com)

Iberia (IB; ☑199 101191; www.iberia.com)

Lufthansa (LH; ☑199 400044; www.lufthansa.com)

Meridiana (IG; ☑892928; www.meridiana.it)

MyAir (8I; ☑848 868120; www.myair.com)

Ryanair (FR; ☑899 678910; www.ryanair.com)

Transavia (HV;☑899 009901; www.transavia.com)

TUIfly (X3; ☑199 192692; www.tuifly.com)

Tickets

» The best place to buy airline tickets for Sardinia is on the web with one of the (low-cost) airlines we have just listed.

Transport

GETTING THERE & AWAY

Flights, tours and rail tickets can be booked online at www.lonelyplanet.com/travel services.

Entering The Region

The easiest and fastest way to get to Sardinia is by air. The boom in budget air travel has done much to open up Sardinia's skies, and if you are coming from elsewhere in Europe you should have no problem finding a direct flight.

» If you're travelling from outside Europe, you will have to fly to Italy and pick up a connecting flight on the mainland.

» There are flights to Sardinia from most Italian airports but most frequently from Rome and Milan. All customs and immigration formalities will take place there, and the Sardinian leg of your journey will be considered an internal flight.

» A slower, cheaper alternative to flying is to catch a ferry from Genoa, Livorno, Civitavecchia or Naples.

» Boarding a ferry to Sardinia is as easy as getting on a bus. Book your passage if you're travelling in high season.

» You don't need to show your passport on these internal routes, but it's a good idea to keep some ID handy.

» Citizens of EU member states can travel to Italy with their national identity cards. People from countries that do not issue ID cards must carry a valid passport. All non-EU nationals must have a full valid passport.

Air

High season in Sardinia is June to September. Holidays such as Easter also see a huge jump in prices.

Airports & Airlines

Flights from Italian and European cities serve Sardinia's three main airports. Flight schedules are available on the websites of all three airports.

Elmas (CAG; ☑070 21 12 11; www.sogaer.it) In Cagliari.

Fertilia (AHO; ☑079 93 52 82; www.algheroairport.it) Near Alghero, in the northwest.

» Students and people aged under 26 years (under 30 in some countries) coming from outside Europe have access to discounted fares with valid ID such as an International Student Identity Card (ISIC; for details, see p246). Discounted tickets are also released to selected travel agents and specialist discount agencies.

» The alternative to booking direct with a low-cost airline on the internet is to surf online agents.

AUSTRALIA

Flights from Australia to mainland Italy generally go via Southeast Asian capitals. From Sydney you'll be looking at airfares upwards of A$2200. Flights from Perth are generally a few hundred dollars cheaper.

Qantas (www.qantas.com. au) Along with Alitalia offers the only direct flights from Melbourne and Sydney to Rome.

Also try:

Malaysian Airlines (www. malaysianairlines.com)

Star Alliance (www.staralli ance.com)

Thai Airways International (www.thaiair.com)

Singapore Airlines (www. singapore.com)

Air China (www.airchina.com)

CANADA

For airfares from the Canadian east/west coast, reckon on around C$750/820.

Alitalia has flights to Rome from Toronto.

Air Transat (www.airtransat. com) Flies nonstop from Montreal to Rome in summer.

Air Canada (www.aircanada. com) Flies daily from Toronto to Rome direct and via Montreal and Frankfurt, and to Milan via Frankfurt, Munich or Zurich.

CONTINENTAL EUROPE

There are plenty of flights from continental Europe direct to Sardinia, although

services drop off considerably in winter, particularly to Alghero and Olbia.

» In Spain, Ryanair operates flights to Cagliari from Barcelona, Girona and Madrid, and to Alghero from Madrid. In addition, Iberia runs seasonal flights to Olbia from Madrid and Barcelona.

» From Paris, Meridiana operates flights to Cagliari and, in summer, to Olbia.

» If you're travelling from Germany, you shouldn't find it difficult to pick up a flight to Sardinia. TUIfly flies to Cagliari from Stuttgart, Cologne and Munich, and to Olbia from Hamburg. In summer Ryanair operates flights to Alghero from Dusseldorf and Frankfurt, and easyJet flies to Olbia from Berlin.

» If you want to travel via the Italian mainland, all national European carriers fly to Italy. The largest of these, Air France, Iberia, Lufthansa and KLM, have representatives in all major European cities.

ITALY

Domestic flights from the Italian mainland are operated by a number of international companies, including Ryanair and easyJet, and Italy's big three domestic airlines: Alitalia, Meridiana and Air One.

» For the internal leg of the journey, return fares cost approximately €70 to €160 from Rome and €130 to €180 from Milan.

» You can also pick up flights to Sardinia from Bergamo, Bologna, Brescia, Florence, Naples, Palermo, Parma, Perugia, Pisa, Rimini, Trieste, Turin, Venice and Verona.

NEW ZEALAND

Singapore Airlines flies from Auckland via Singapore to Rome's Fiumicino airport, sometimes with more than one stop.

Alternatively Air New Zealand (www.airnewzealand. com) flies to Rome from

Auckland via Hong Kong or Los Angeles and then London. Otherwise, Qantas or Alitalia flights from Australia are the most direct way to get to Italy and then Sardinia.

UK & IRELAND

From the UK you're looking at around £70 for a direct flight to Sardinia with a low-cost airline such as Ryanair or easyJet.

» Between the end of March and the end of October Ryanair flies twice weekly to Alghero from London Stansted and Dublin.

» From mid-April there are two weekly flights from London Stansted to Alghero.

» EasyJet operates daily flights to Cagliari from London Stansted and, between June and October, twice-weekly flights to Olbia from London Gatwick.

» Over spring and summer, British Airways gets in on the act with weekly flights between April and October from Gatwick to Cagliari.

» Alitalia and Aer Lingus (www.aerlingus.com) both have regular daily flights from Dublin to Rome.

USA

The North Atlantic is the world's busiest long-haul air corridor and the flight options are bewildering. There are no direct flights from the USA to Sardinia, so you'll have to fly via Rome or Milan.

From the US east/west coast fares start at about US$600/750. Standby fares are often sold at 60% of the normal price for one-way tickets.

» Delta Airlines (www.delta. com) and American Airlines (www.aa.com) and Alitalia have regular flights from New York's JFK to Malpensa in Milan and Rome's Fiumicino airport. The latter also flies from Chicago O'Hare to Rome.

» Continental Airlines (www.continental.com) operates from Newark to Rome and Milan, while **United Airlines** (www.united.com) has a service from Washington to Rome. Standard fares can be expensive, but you can usually find something cheaper if you shop around.

» **Airhitch** (www.airhitch.org) is an online specialist. You give a general idea of where and when you need to go, and a few days before your departure you will be presented with a choice of two or three flights.

» **Courier Travel** (☑303 5707586; www.couriertravel.org) is a comprehensive search engine for courier and standby flights. You can also check out the **International Association of Air Travel Couriers** (IAATC; ☑308 6323273; www.courier.org).

Land

Sardinia is the most isolated island in the Mediterranean, some 200km from the nearest land mass, so any overland trip will include a ferry leg; for details, see p258.

» The shortest ferry route is from Civitavecchia, north of Rome, to Olbia on the northeast coast of Sardinia, although there are various alternatives.

» The other main points of departure are Genoa, Livorno and Naples.

» In summer there are a couple of ferries from Marseille in France.

» Travelling to Sardinia this way can either be an enormous drain on your time and money (ferry tickets are not cheap) or, if you have plenty of time to spare, a bit of a European adventure.

» If you are travelling by bus, train or car to Italy, check whether you require visas to the countries you intend to pass through.

Bicycle

» Transporting your bike to Sardinia poses no special problems.

» Different airlines apply different rules, but most will require your bike packed in a bike bag or box, pedals and handlebars turned flush with the frame, and tyres deflated.

» There'll then be an additional charge, typically €25 to €40.

» You can also carry bikes with you on ferries to Sardinia for a small fee, usually €3 to €10.

Bus

» **Eurolines** (☑055 35 70 59; www.eurolines.com) is a consortium of 32 European coach companies operating across Europe with offices in all major European cities.

» Italy-bound buses head to Ancona, Florence, Rome, Siena and Venice.

» Its multilanguage website gives details of prices, passes and travel agencies where you can book tickets.

Car & Motorcycle

Most people travelling overland to Sardinia will be bringing their own wheels.

» For many, the most convenient port to travel from will be Genoa, although you could add a few hours' driving time and continue down as far as Livorno, from where the sea crossing is shorter.

» Drivers coming from the UK, Spain or France may prefer to time their trip with vessels leaving from Marseille. For breakdown assistance and comprehensive cover in Europe, try:

» **AA** (☑0870 600 03 71; www.theaa.co.uk)

» **RAC** (☑0870 010 63 82; www.rac.co.uk)

Online resources:
Practical information on driving in Europe (www.ideamerge.com) Click on the Moto Europa Guidebook link in the left-hand column.
Route Planning (www.viamichelin.com) Provides printable maps and driving directions.

For road rules and more information on driving in Sardinia, see p261.

Train

» The simplest way to take the train to Sardinia is to travel to Marseille to get a summer ferry to Porto Torres.

» You can also get a train from Genoa, via Paris and Milan or via Paris and Nice.

TRAVELLING OVERLAND INTO ITALY

The main points of entry into Italy are the Mt Blanc tunnel from France at Chamonix, which connects with the A5 for Turin and Milan; the Grand St Bernard tunnel from Switzerland (SS27), which also connects with the A5; the Gotthard tunnel, also from Switzerland; the Swiss Lötschberg Base tunnel that connects with the century-old Simplon tunnel into Italy; and the Brenner Pass from Austria (A13), which links up with the A22 to Bologna. All are open year-round.

Mountain passes in the Alps are often closed in winter and sometimes even in autumn and spring, making the tunnels a less scenic but more reliable option. Make sure you have snow chains in winter.

For more details on getting to Italy overland, see www.lonelyplanet.com/italy/transport/getting-there-away.

From Genoa you can pick up ferries to Olbia, Arbatax and Porto Torres.

» For the latest fare information on journeys to Italy, including Eurostar, contact the **Rail Europe Travel Centre** (☎08448 484 064; www.raileurope.co.uk) or **Rail Choice** (☎0870 165 73 00; www.railchoice.com).

» For advice, information and handy rail tips check out the encyclopaedic **Seat 61** (www.seat61.com). There is almost nothing this website can't tell you about travelling in Europe, or indeed the entire world, by train.

Sea

» The island is accessible by ferry from the Italian ports of Genoa, Savona, La Spezia, Livorno, Piombino, Civitavecchia, Fiumicino and Naples, and from Palermo and Trapani in Sicily.

» Ferries also run from Bonifacio and Porto Vecchio in Corsica.

» French ferries running from Marseilles and Toulon sometimes call in at the Corsican ports of Ajaccio and Propriano en route to Sardinia.

» The arrival points in Sardinia are Olbia, Golfo Aranci, Palau, Santa Teresa di Gallura and Porto Torres in the north; Arbatax on the east coast; and Cagliari in the south.

» Numerous ferry companies ply these routes, and services are most frequent from mid-June to mid-September, when it is advisable to book well ahead.

» Ferry prices are determined by the season and are at their highest between June and September.

» You can book tickets at travel agents throughout Italy or directly on the internet.

FERRIES TO SARDINIA

The following is a rundown of the main ferry routes to Sardinia, the companies that operate them and the route details. Prices quoted are high-season fares for a 2nd-class *poltrona* (reclinable seat). Children aged four to 12 generally pay around half-price; children under four years go free.

FROM	TO	COMPANY	FARE	CAR	DURATION (HR)	FREQUENCY
Civitavecchia	Arbatax	Tirrenia	€49	€100	10½	2 weekly
Civitavecchia	Cagliari	Tirrenia	€61	€106	14½	daily
Civitavecchia	Olbia	Moby	€63	€115	4½-10	4 weekly mid-Mar–May, daily Jun-Sep
Civitavecchia	Olbia	SNAV	€59	€119	7½	daily
Civitavecchia	Olbia	Tirrenia	€45	€103	7	daily
Civitavecchia	Golfo Aranci	Sardinia F	€54	incl	6¾	3 weekly mid-Mar–May, daily Jun-Sep
Civitavecchia	Golfo Aranci+	Sardinia F	€79	€135	3½	3 weekly mid-Mar–May, daily Jun-Sep
Fiumicino	Arbatax+	Tirrenia	€63	€109	4½	2 weekly late Jul-Aug
Fiumicino	Golfo Aranci+	Tirrenia	€63	€110	4	daily late Jul-Aug
Genoa	Arbatax	Tirrenia	€59	€107	18	2 weekly
Genoa	Olbia	GNV	€95	€156	8-10	daily mid-May–mid-Sep
Genoa	Olbia	Moby	€88	€135	10	daily mid-May–mid-Oct
Genoa	Olbia	Tirrenia	€62	€109	13¼	3 weekly, 5 weekly Jul-Aug
Genoa	Palau	Enermar	€73	€121	11	5 weekly Jun-Sep

Useful online booking services:

Traghetti Web (www.traghettiweb.it) Covering all the ferry companies in the Mediterranean.

Traghetti Online (www.traghettionline.com) Lists all the routes into Sardinia and has links to the ferry companies operating them.

Corsica

There are links between Santa Teresa di Gallura and Bonifacio, in Corsica.

Saremar (☑892123; www.saremar.it) Run by Tirrenia, has three daily departures each way (two on weekends between October and mid-March). A one-way adult fare in high season is €10 and a small car costs up to €37. Taxes add another €8 to the price. The trip takes one hour.

Moby Lines (☑199 303040; www.mobylines.it) Operates four daily crossings between the end of March and late September. Adult tickets cost €9 to €13.50 plus €4.20 tax; a car costs €22 to €63 plus €2.80 tax.

Sardinia Ferries (☑199 400500; www.sardiniaferries.com) Sails three times daily between April and September, less often throughout rest of year. Adults pay €10 plus €4.10 tax; to transport a car costs €37 plus €2.50 tax.

SNCM (☑France 08 91 70 18 01, in Sardinia☑079 51 44 77; www.sncm.fr) Ferries between Porto Torres and the French mainland call at Propriano or, less frequently, Ajaccio en route to Marseille and Toulon. The adult one-way fare for Propriano is €32.30 or €73.90 with a small car; for Ajaccio costs €33.70 per adult, €79 with a car.

FROM	TO	COMPANY	FARE	CAR	DURATION (HR)	FREQUENCY
Genoa	Porto Torres	GNV	€92	€155	11	4 weekly, daily mid-May–mid-Sep
Genoa	Porto Torres	Moby	€86	€132	10	6 weekly mid-May–Sep
Genoa	Porto Torres+	Tirrenia	€107	€183	10	daily
Livorno	Golfo Aranci	Sardinia F	€53	incl	10	daily Mar-Oct
Livorno	Golfo Aranci+	Sardinia F	€76	€133	6	daily Mar-Oct
Livorno	Olbia	Moby	€68	€124	7-9	daily
Naples	Cagliari	Tirrenia	€54	€94	16¼	1 weekly, 2 Aug
Palermo	Cagliari	Tirrenia	€53	€93	14½	1 weekly
Piombino	Olbia	Moby	€65	€118	6½	6 weekly, daily mid-May–Sep
Trapani	Cagliari	Tirrenia	€52	€94	11	1 weekly

+ indicates a high-speed service

Ferry Operators

Enermar (☑899 200001; www.enermar.it) To Palau from Genoa.

Grandi Navi Veloci (☑010 209 45 91; www.gnv.it) To Olbia and Porto Torres from Genoa.

Moby Lines (☑199 303040; www.mobylines.it) To Olbia from Civitavecchia, Genoa, Livorno and Piombino; to Porto Torres from Genoa.

Sardinia Ferries (☑199 400500; www.sardiniaferries.com) To Golfo Aranci from Civitavecchia and Livorno.

SNAV (☑081 428 55 55; www.snav.it) To Olbia from Civitavecchia.

Tirrenia (☑892123; www.tirrenia.it) To Cagliari from Civitavecchia, Naples, Palermo and Trapani; to Olbia from Civitavecchia and Genoa; to Arbatax from Civitavecchia, Fiumicino and Genoa; to Golfo Aranci from Fiumicino; and to Porto Torres from Genoa.

France

Both **SNCM** (☑France 0825 88 80 88; www.sncm.fr) and **CMN La Méridionale** (☑France 0810 20 13 20; www.cmn.fr) operate ferries from Marseille to Porto Torres (via Corsica). There are two to four sailings weekly, but in July and August some leave from Toulon instead. Crossing time is 15 to 17 hours (12½ hours from Toulon). A reclinable seat costs €78 and a small car €148.

For tickets and information in Porto Torres, contact: **Agenzia Paglietti** (☑079 51 44 77; fax 079 51 40 63; Corso Vittorio Emanuele 19)

Italy

Several companies run ferries of varying types and speeds from a number of Italian ports to Sardinia.

» For route and operator details, see the boxed text, p258.

» The prices quoted in the table are for standard high-season one-way fares in a *poltrona* (reclinable seat) for adults – children aged four to 12 generally pay around half price; those under four years go free – and small cars.

» Depending on the service you take, you can also get cabins, the price of which varies according to the number of occupants (generally one to four) and position (with or without window).

» Most companies offer discounts on return trips and other deals – it's always worth asking.

» You might want to consider taking a sleeping berth for overnight trips, which will cost as much as double.

GETTING AROUND

If at all possible it is preferable to have your own car in Sardinia. Getting around the island on public transport is difficult and time-consuming but not impossible. In most cases buses are preferable to trains, which are nearly always slower and often involve lengthy changes.

The website www.get aroundsardinia.com has some useful advice about navigating the island without a car.

Air

Sardinia is so small that you don't really need internal flights. If you do need to fly, Italian airline **Meridiana** (☑892928; www.meridiana.it) operates a daily flight between Cagliari and Olbia. The flight takes 35 minutes and costs €30 to €90.

Bicycle

» Sardinia lends itself well to cycling but keep in mind it can be pretty tough going and the hilly (sometimes mountainous) terrain will take it out of you and your bike.

» The roads are rarely busy outside of high summer, the scenery is magnificent and it doesn't rain much.

» Bikes are available for hire in most major towns and resorts, including Alghero, Santa Teresa di Gallura, La Maddalena, Palau and Olbia.

» Rates range from around €10 per day to as much as €25 for mountain bikes. See Getting Around under the relevant cities in this book for more information.

» You cannot cycle on the highway.

» If cycling in summer, make sure you have plenty of water and sunblock as the heat can be exhausting.

» Bikes can be taken on almost all trains. They are put in a separate wagon and the cost (€5) is the same regardless of destination.

» In the UK, **Cyclists' Touring Club** (☑0844 736 84 50; www.ctc.org.uk) can help you plan your own bike tour or organise guided tours. Membership costs £35.

Boat

Services are cut back considerably over the winter months so always check ahead. If taking a car in summer, try to arrive in good time as boats fill up quickly.

» In summer it is possible to join boat tours from various points around the coast. This is an excellent way to see Sardinia's more inaccessible highlights.

» The most popular tours include trips out of Cala Gonone and Santa Maria Navarrese along the majestic Golfo di Orosei. Close behind is a trip around the islands of the Maddalena archipelago.

» Boats frequently head out of Porto San Paolo (p147), south of Olbia, for trips around Isola Tavolara and the nearby coast. Others sail out of Alghero and from the Sinis Peninsula.

» Most trips are by motorboats or small tour ferries, but a handful of sailing vessels are also on hand.

» For more information, see the relevant destination chapters.

» **Enermar** (☑899 200001; www.enermar.it) and **Saremar** (☑892123; www.saremar. it) connect Palau with the Isola di La Maddalena. In summer services run every 15 minutes and cost €5 for the 20-minute crossing. A car fare is €13.

» **Saremar** (☑892123; www. saremar.it) has up to 17 sailings daily from Portovesme to Carloforte on the Isola di San Pietro. Saremar also links Carloforte with Calasetta on Isola di Sant'Antioco. In summer there are nine daily crossings between 7.35am and 8.20pm.

» **Delcomar** (☑0781 85 71 23; www.delcomar.it) operates nightly crossings from Portovesme to Carloforte on the Isola di San Pietro, as well as between Carloforte and Calasetta on Isola di Sant'Antioco.

Bus

Bus services within Sardinia are provided mainly by **Azienda Regionale Sarda Trasporti** (ARST; ☎800 865042; www.arst.sardegna.it, in Italian), which runs the majority of local and long-distance services. ARST also operates a limited network of private narrow-gauge railways, most notably the Trenino Verde (see p263).

» All of the island's big towns have an ARST bus station, usually centrally located.

» In smaller towns and villages there will simply be a *fermata* stop for intercity buses, not always in an immediately apparent location.

» Bus tickets must be bought prior to boarding at stations or designated bars, *tabacchi* (tobacconists) and newsstands near the stop.

» Timetables are sometimes posted next to the stop, but don't hold your breath.

» Tourist offices in bigger towns can usually provide timetables for their area.

» In smaller locations you may need to ask where you can buy tickets.

» Note that services might be frequent on weekdays but are cut back drastically on Sundays and holidays – runs between smaller towns often fall to one or none.

» Keep this in mind if you depend on buses, as it is easy to get stuck in smaller places, especially on weekends.

Car & Motorcycle

Driving in Sardinia is fairly stress free. Away from the main towns (Cagliari, Sassari and Olbia) and outside of high summer, traffic is rarely a problem and local drivers are courteous. The main hazards are flocks of sheep and the stunning scenery.

Main roads are generally good, although to really explore the island, you'll need to use the system of provincial roads (*strade provinciali*), marked as P or SP on maps. These are sometimes little more than country lanes, but they provide access to some of the more beautiful scenery and the many small towns and villages.

» Many of the more spectacular beaches are only accessible by dirt tracks.

» Motorcycle fever has not yet made it out to Sardinia, although the island is very popular with German and Austrian bikers who enjoy racing around the island's scenic roads and hairpin bends.

» Crash helmets are compulsory.

» Unless you're touring it's probably easier to rent a bike once you are in Sardinia.

Automobile Associations

Italy's motoring organisation, **Automobile Club d'Italia** (ACI; www.aci.it), is an excellent source of information and provides 24-hour roadside assistance – call ☎803116 or ☎800 116800 if calling from a non-Italian mobile phone. Foreigners do not have to join but instead pay a fee in case of breakdown assistance (€100 to €120, 20% more on weekends and holidays).

AA (☎0870 600 03 71; www.theaa.co.uk) and the **RAC** (☎0870 010 63 82; www.rac.co.uk) offer breakdown cover in Europe.

Bring Your Own Vehicle

Cars entering Italy from abroad need a valid national licence plate and an accompanying registration card. You should always carry proof of ownership of a private vehicle. A warning triangle is compulsory in Italy, as is a fluorescent orange or yellow safety vest to be worn if you have to get out of your car in the event of a breakdown. A first-aid kit, a spare-bulb kit and a fire extinguisher are also recommended.

Driving Licence

All EU driving licences are recognised in Sardinia. Holders of non-EU licences must get an International Driving Permit (IDP) to accompany their national licence. Your national automobile association can issue this, and it is valid for 12 months.

Fuel

Fuel is pretty expensive in Sardinia and you'll pay around €1.15 per litre for *benzina senza piombo* (unleaded petrol) and around €1 per litre for *gasolio* (diesel). There are plenty of fuel stations in and around towns and on the main road networks.

Hire

It is *always* better to arrange car hire before you arrive. Major car-hire outlets have offices at the airports, where you usually pick up your car and deposit it at the end of your stay.

The most competitive national and multinational car-hire agencies.

Avis (☎06 452 10 83 91; www.avis.com)

Budget (☎800 283438; www.budgetautonoleggio.it)

Europcar (☎199 307030; www.europcar.com)

Hertz (☎199 112211; www.hertz.com)

Italy by Car (☎091 639 31 20; www.italybycar.it)

Maggiore (☎199 151120; www.maggiore.com)

» If you only want to hire a car for a couple of days, or decide to hire one after you have arrived, you'll find hire outfits in most coastal resorts, although the big international companies only have offices in a handful of big cities.

» Age restrictions vary from agency to agency but generally you'll need to be aged 21 or over.

» If you're under 25, you'll probably have to pay a young-driver's supplement on top of the usual rates.

» You'll need a credit card.

» In tourist hot spots (like Santa Teresa di Gallura and Alghero) you'll usually find a few rental outlets offering motorcycles and scooters.

» Most agencies will not hire out motorcycles to people aged under 18.

» Note that many places require a sizeable deposit and that you could be responsible for reimbursing part of the cost of the bike if it is stolen.

Insurance

» Third-party motor insurance is a minimum requirement in Italy.

» To drive your own vehicle in Sardinia you'll also need to carry an International Insurance Certificate, known as a Carta Verde (Green Card), from your car insurer.

» While you're at it ask your insurer for a European Accident Statement form, which can simplify matters in the event of an accident.

» Similarly, a European breakdown-assistance policy will make your life a whole lot easier if you break down.

Road Conditions

Sardinia's road network is dictated by its geography. Much of the mountainous interior is untarnished by tarmac, and it's generally easier to travel north–south (or vice versa) than east–west.

» The island's principal artery, the mostly dual-carriageway SS131 Carlo Felice Hwy, runs from Cagliari to Sassari (and on to Porto Torres) via Oristano and Macomer. Branching off it at Abbasanta, the SS131 runs up to Olbia via Nuoro.

» Another strip, the SS130, runs west from Cagliari to Iglesias, and dual-carriageway stretches reach from Sassari part of the way to Alghero, and from Porto Torres to the SS291 Sassari–Alghero road.

» Along the north coast, the SS200 bypasses Castelsardo en route from Porto Torres to Santa Teresa di Gallura. From nearby Palau, the SS125, or Orientale Sarda, is another key artery, running down the eastern side of the island to Cagliari in the south.

» These and many roads in the more touristy coastal areas are well maintained but can be narrow and curvy.

» In summer, when the island fills with visitors, it is virtually impossible not to get caught in traffic jams along many roads. The area between Olbia and Santa Teresa di Gallura is particularly bad.

» Inland, the quality of roads is uneven. Main roads are mostly good but narrow and winding, while many secondary routes are in poor shape.

» Getting into and out of the cities, notably Cagliari and Sassari, can be a test of nerves as traffic chokes approaches and exits.

» You will also be surprised by the number of unpaved roads on the island – a cause of worry in that expensive rental car. Still, you'll find many a good *agriturismo* (farm-stay accommodation), prehistoric site or fine country restaurant at the end of a dirt track.

Road Rules

» In Sardinia, as in the rest of continental Europe, drive on the right-hand side of the road and overtake on the left.

» Unless otherwise indicated, you must always give way to cars entering an intersection from the right.

» It is compulsory to wear front seat belts, as well as rear seat belts if the car is fitted with them. If you are caught not wearing a seatbelt, you will be required to pay an on-the-spot fine.

» Random breath tests take place. If you're involved in an accident while under the influence of alcohol, the penalties can be severe. The blood-alcohol limit is 0.05%.

» Speed limits on main highways (there are no *autostrade* in Sardinia) are 110km/h, on secondary highways 90km/h and in built-up areas 50km/h.

» Speeding fines follow EU standards and are proportionate with the number of kilometres that you are driving over the speed limit, reaching up to €1433 with possible suspension of your licence.

» Since 2002 drivers are obliged to keep headlights switched on day and night on all dual carriageways.

» You don't need a licence to ride a moped under 50cc, but you should be aged 14 or over and you can't carry passengers or ride on highways. The speed limit for a moped is 40km/h. To ride a motorcycle or scooter up to 125cc, you must be 16 or over and have a licence (a car driving licence will do). For motorcycles over 125cc you will need a motorcycle licence. Helmets are compulsory in all cases.

» On a motorcycle you will be able to enter restricted traffic areas in cities and towns without any problems, and traffic police generally turn a blind eye to motorcycles or scooters parked on footpaths. There is no daytime lights-on requirement for motorcycles.

» Note that it is illegal for nonresidents to drive in Alghero's old town (see p122).

Hitching

» Hitching is never entirely safe in any country, and we don't recommend it.

» Travellers who decide to hitch should understand that they are taking a small but potentially serious risk.

» Hitchhiking is extremely uncommon in Sardinia.

» Sardinians can be wary of picking up strangers, which makes travelling this way a frustrating business.

» Never hitch where drivers can't stop in good time or without causing an obstruction.

» Look presentable, carry as little luggage as possible and

hold a sign in Italian indicating your destination.

» Do not use the normal thumbs-up signal, as this can offend (in these parts it means 'up yours'!).

» Women travelling on their own would be extremely ill-advised to hitch.

Local Transport

Bus and train travel are the main options for getting around locally in Sardinia.

» All the major towns have a reasonable local bus service.

» Generally, you won't need them, as the towns are compact, with sights, hotels, and bus/train stations all within walking distance of each other.

» Bus tickets (around €1) must be purchased from newspaper stands or *tabacchi* outlets and stamped on the bus.

» All three airports are linked by local bus services to their respective town centres.

Tours

Throughout the island local operators offer all manner of guided excursions and tours. These include the following:

Archeo Tours (☎329 7643343; Via Eleanora D'Arborea, Osini) This small association leads archaeological and nature tours through the countryside around Osini and Ulassai.

Atlantikà (☎328 9729719; www.atlantika.it; Via Lamarmora 195, Dorgali) A consortium of guides in Dorgali, offering everything from hiking day trips to canyoning and kayaking in the Gennargentu.

Barbagia No Limits (☎0784 5 29 06; www.barbagianolimits.it; Via Cagliari 85, Gavoi) This adventure sports outfit organises all sorts of outdoor activities, including caving trips, jeep tours and survival courses.

Esedra Sardegna (☎0785 37 42 58; www.esedrasardegna.it; Corso Vittorio Emanuele 64, Bosa) Arranges excursions in and around Bosa, and across the whole island.

Gallura Viaggi Avventura (☎079 63 12 73; c/o Pro Loco Tourist Office, Piazza Gallura 2, Tempio Pausania) A small local group organising biking and hiking tours of Monte Limbara.

Mare e Natura (☎393 9850435; www.marenatura.it; Via Sassari 77, Stintino) Organises tours of the Parco Nazionale dell'Asinara.

Sardinia Hike & Bike (☎070 924 32 329; www.sardiniahikeandbike.com; Loc Pixina Manna, Pula) Based on the south coast, this outfit runs hiking and cycling tours for all levels.

» As well as these specialist organisations, you'll find hundreds of outfits running boat trips along Sardinia's coastal waters.

» Popular spots include Alghero, Cala Gonone, Stintino, Santa Maria Navarrese and Porto San Paolo.

Train

» Travelling by train in Sardinia may be slow, but it's straightforward and cheap.

» You will find the *orario* (timetable) posted on station noticeboards.

» *Partenze* (departures) and *arrivi* (arrivals) are clearly indicated.

» Note, however, that there are all sorts of permutations on schedules, with services much reduced on Sundays.

» Handy indicators to look out for are *feriale* (Monday to Saturday) and *festivo* (Sunday and holidays only).

» There is only one class of service in Sardinia, the basic *regionale*. Most of these trains are chuggers that stop at every village on the way, so you won't get anywhere fast by train.

» Some trains offer 1st and 2nd class, but you won't find there's a big difference between them, other than few people opt to pay extra for 1st class.

» It is not worth buying a Eurail or InterRail pass if you are only travelling in Sardinia.

» The following train services operate within Sardinia:

Trenitalia (☎892021; www.trenitalia.com) The state train system that runs the bulk of the limited network in Sardinia. Sardinia's main Trenitalia line runs from Cagliari to Oristano and on to Chilivano-Ozieri, where it divides into two branches. One line heads northwest to Sassari and Porto Torres; the other goes northeast to Olbia and Golfo Aranci. Macomer is another important hub with connections to Nuoro.

Azienda Regionale Sarda Trasporti; (ARST;☎800 865042; www.arst.sardegna.it, in Italian) ARST operates a limited network of private narrow-gauge railways (*servizi ferroviari*), and the Trenino Verde.

Trenino Verde (☎800 460220; www.treninoverde.com, in Italian) Between mid-June and early September, ARST operates this tourist train. Trenino Verde operates four lines: Arbatax to Mandas (which connects with the Mandas–Cagliari rail/metro service); Isili to Sorgono; Bosa Marina to Macomer (which links with the Macomer–Nuoro line); and Palau to Nulvi (where you can connect with a regular service to Sassari) via Tempio Pausania. As a means of public transport the Trenino Verde is of limited use – it's extremely slow and covers few likely destinations – but it's an excellent way of experiencing the island's most dramatic and inaccessible countryside that you might otherwise never see. The Mandas–Arbatax route is particularly impressive.

Language

WANT MORE?
For in-depth language information and handy phrases, check out Lonely Planet's *Italian Phrasebook*. You'll find it at **shop .lonelyplanet.com**, or you can buy Lonely Planet's iPhone phrasebooks at the Apple App Store.

In Italy, regional dialects are an important part of identity in many parts of the country, but you'll have no trouble being understood anywhere if you stick to standard Italian and this also holds true for Sardinia. Many Sardinians are bilingual, switching from Sardinian, the island tongue, to Italian with equal ease. Their pronunciation of Italian is refreshingly clear and easy to understand, even if you have only a limited command of the language.

The sounds used in spoken Italian can all be found in English. If you read our coloured pronunciation guides as if they were English, you'll be understood. The stressed syllables are indicated with italics. Note that ai is pronounced as in 'aisle', ay as in 'say', ow as in 'how', dz as the 'ds' in 'lids', and that r is a strong and rolled sound. Keep in mind that Italian consonants can have a stronger, emphatic pronunciation – if the consonant is written as a double letter, it should be pronounced a little stronger, eg *sonno son*·no (sleep) versus *sono so*·no (I am).

BASICS

Italian has two words for 'you' – use the polite form *Lei* lay if you're talking to strangers, officials or people older than you. With people familiar to you or younger than you, you can use the informal form *tu* too.

In Italian, all nouns and adjectives are either masculine or feminine, and so are the articles *il/la* eel/la (the) and *un/una* oon/oo·na (a) that go with the nouns.

In this chapter the polite/informal and masculine/feminine options are included where necessary, separated with a slash and indicated with 'pol/inf' and 'm/f'.

Hello.	Buongiorno.	bwon·*jor*·no
Goodbye.	Arrivederci.	a·ree·ve·*der*·chee
Yes./No.	Sì./No.	see/no
Excuse me.	Mi scusi. (pol)	mee *skoo*·zee
	Scusami. (inf)	*skoo*·za·mee
Sorry.	Mi dispiace.	mee dees·*pya*·che
Please.	Per favore.	per fa·*vo*·re
Thank you.	Grazie.	*gra*·tsye
You're welcome.	Prego.	*pre*·go

How are you?
Come sta/stai? (pol/inf) ko·me sta/stai

Fine. And you?
Bene. E Lei/tu? (pol/inf) be·ne e lay/too

What's your name?
Come si chiama? pol ko·me see *kya*·ma

My name is ...
Mi chiamo ... mee *kya*·mo ...

Do you speak English?
Parla/Parli *par*·la/*par*·lee
inglese? (pol/inf) een·*gle*·ze

I don't understand.
Non capisco. non ka·*pee*·sko

ACCOMMODATION

Do you have a ... room?	Avete una camera ...?	a·*ve*·te *oo*·na *ka*·me·ra ...
double	doppia con letto matrimoniale	*do*·pya kon *le*·to ma·tree·mo·*nya*·le
single	singola	*seen*·go·la

How much is it per ...?	Quanto costa per ...?	kwan·to kos·ta per ...
night	una notte	oo·na no·te
person	persona	per·so·na

Is breakfast included?
La colazione è compresa? — la ko·la·tsyo·ne e kom·pre·sa

air-con	aria condizionata	a·rya kon·dee·tsyo·na·ta
bathroom	bagno	ba·nyo
campsite	campeggio	kam·pe·jo
guesthouse	pensione	pen·syo·ne
hotel	albergo	al·ber·go
youth hostel	ostello della gioventù	os·te·lo de·la jo·ven·too
window	finestra	fee·nes·tra

DIRECTIONS

Where's ...?
Dov'è ...? — do·ve ...

What's the address?
Qual è l'indirizzo? — kwa·le leen·dee·ree·tso

Could you please write it down?
Può scriverlo, per favore? — pwo skree·ver·lo per fa·vo·re

Can you show me (on the map)?
Può mostrarmi (sulla pianta)? — pwo mos·trar·mee (soo·la pyan·ta)

at the corner	all'angolo	a·lan·go·lo
at the traffic lights	al semaforo	al se·ma·fo·ro
behind	dietro	dye·tro
far	lontano	lon·ta·no
in front of	davanti a	da·van·tee a
left	a sinistra	a see·nee·stra
near	vicino	vee·chee·no
next to	accanto a	a·kan·to a
opposite	di fronte a	dee fron·te a
right	a destra	a de·stra
straight ahead	sempre diritto	sem·pre dee·ree·to

EATING & DRINKING

What would you recommend?
Cosa mi consiglia? — ko·za mee kon·see·lya

What's in that dish?
Quali ingredienti ci sono in questo piatto? — kwa·li een·gre·dyen·tee chee so·no een kwe·sto pya·to

To get by in Italian, mix and match these simple patterns with words of your choice:

When's (the next flight)?
A che ora è (il prossimo volo)? — a ke o·ra e (eel pro·see·mo vo·lo)

Where's (the station)?
Dov'è (la stazione)? — do·ve (la sta·tsyo·ne)

I'm looking for (a hotel).
Sto cercando (un albergo). — sto cher·kan·do (oon al·ber·go)

Do you have (a map)?
Ha (una pianta)? — a (oo·na pyan·ta)

Is there (a toilet)?
C'è (un gabinetto)? — che (oon ga·bee·ne·to)

I'd like (a coffee).
Vorrei (un caffè). — vo·ray (oon ka·fe)

I'd like to (hire a car).
Vorrei (noleggiare una macchina). — vo·ray (no·le·ja·re oo·na ma·kee·na)

Can I (enter)?
Posso (entrare)? — po·so (en·tra·re)

Could you please (help me)?
Può (aiutarmi), per favore? — pwo (a·yoo·tar·mee) per fa·vo·re

Do I have to (book a seat)?
Devo (prenotare un posto)? — de·vo (pre·no·ta·re oon po·sto)

What's the local speciality?
Qual è la specialità di questa regione? — kwa·le la spe·cha·lee·ta dee kwe·sta re·jo·ne

That was delicious!
Era squisito! — e·ra skwee·zee·to

Cheers!
Salute! — sa·loo·te

Please bring the bill.
Mi porta il conto, per favore? — mee por·ta eel kon·to per fa·vo·re

I'd like to reserve a table for ...	Vorrei prenotare un tavolo per ...	vo·ray pre·no·ta·re oon ta·vo·lo per ...
(two) people	(due) persone	(doo·e) per·so·ne
(eight) o'clock	le (otto)	le (o·to)

I don't eat ...	Non mangio ...	non man·jo ...
eggs	uova	wo·va
fish	pesce	pe·she
nuts	noci	no·chee
(red) meat	carne (rossa)	kar·ne (ro·sa)

Key Words

bar	locale	lo·ka·le
bottle	bottiglia	bo·tee·lya
breakfast	prima colazione	pree·ma ko·la·tsyo·ne
cafe	bar	bar
cold	freddo	fre·do
dinner	cena	che·na
drink list	lista delle bevande	lee·sta de·le be·van·de
fork	forchetta	for·ke·ta
glass	bicchiere	bee·kye·re
grocery store	alimentari	a·lee·men·ta·ree
hot	caldo	kal·do
knife	coltello	kol·te·lo
lunch	pranzo	pran·dzo
market	mercato	mer·ka·to
menu	menù	me·noo
plate	piatto	pya·to
restaurant	ristorante	ree·sto·ran·te
spicy	piccante	pee·kan·te
spoon	cucchiaio	koo·kya·yo
vegetarian (food)	vegetariano	ve·je·ta·rya·no
with	con	kon
without	senza	sen·tsa

Meat & Fish

beef	manzo	man·dzo
chicken	pollo	po·lo
duck	anatra	a·na·tra
fish	pesce	pe·she
herring	aringa	a·reen·ga
lamb	agnello	a·nye·lo
lobster	aragosta	a·ra·gos·ta

Signs

Entrata/Ingresso	Entrance
Uscita	Exit
Aperto	Open
Chiuso	Closed
Informazioni	Information
Proibito/Vietato	Prohibited
Gabinetti/Servizi	Toilets
Uomini	Men
Donne	Women

meat	carne	kar·ne
mussels	cozze	ko·tse
oysters	ostriche	o·stree·ke
pork	maiale	ma·ya·le
prawn	gambero	gam·be·ro
salmon	salmone	sal·mo·ne
scallops	capasante	ka·pa·san·te
seafood	frutti di mare	froo·tee dee ma·re
shrimp	gambero	gam·be·ro
squid	calamari	ka·la·ma·ree
trout	trota	tro·ta
tuna	tonno	to·no
turkey	tacchino	ta·kee·no
veal	vitello	vee·te·lo

Fruit & Vegetables

apple	mela	me·la
beans	fagioli	fa·jo·lee
cabbage	cavolo	ka·vo·lo
capsicum	peperone	pe·pe·ro·ne
carrot	carota	ka·ro·ta
cauliflower	cavolfiore	ka·vol·fyo·re
cucumber	cetriolo	che·tree·o·lo
fruit	frutta	froo·ta
grapes	uva	oo·va
lemon	limone	lee·mo·ne
lentils	lenticchie	len·tee·kye
mushroom	funghi	foon·gee
nuts	noci	no·chee
onions	cipolle	chee·po·le
orange	arancia	a·ran·cha
peach	pesca	pe·ska
peas	piselli	pee·ze·lee
pineapple	ananas	a·na·nas
plum	prugna	proo·nya
potatoes	patate	pa·ta·te
spinach	spinaci	spee·na·chee
tomatoes	pomodori	po·mo·do·ree
vegetables	verdura	ver·doo·ra

Other

bread	pane	pa·ne
butter	burro	boo·ro
cheese	formaggio	for·ma·jo
eggs	uova	wo·va
honey	miele	mye·le

ice	ghiaccio	gya·cho
jam	marmellata	mar·me·la·ta
noodles	pasta	pas·ta
oil	olio	o·lyo
pepper	pepe	pe·pe
rice	riso	ree·zo
salt	sale	sa·le
soup	minestra	mee·nes·tra
soy sauce	salsa di soia	sal·sa dee so·ya
sugar	zucchero	tsoo·ke·ro
vinegar	aceto	a·che·to

Drinks

beer	birra	bee·ra
coffee	caffè	ka·fe
(orange) juice	succo (d'arancia)	soo·ko (da·ran·cha)
milk	latte	la·te
red wine	vino rosso	vee·no ro·so
soft drink	bibita	bee·bee·ta
tea	tè	te
(mineral) water	acqua (minerale)	a·kwa (mee·ne·ra·le)
white wine	vino bianco	vee·no byan·ko

EMERGENCIES

Help!
Aiuto! a·yoo·to

Leave me alone!
Lasciami in pace! la·sha·mee een pa·che

I'm lost.
Mi sono perso/a. (m/f) mee so·no per·so/a

There's been an accident.
C'è stato un incidente. che sta·to oon een·chee·den·te

Call the police!
Chiami la polizia! kya·mee la po·lee·tsee·a

Call a doctor!
Chiami un medico! kya·mee oon me·dee·ko

Where are the toilets?
Dove sono i gabinetti? do·ve so·no ee ga·bee·ne·tee

Question Words

How?	Come?	ko·me
What?	Che cosa?	ke ko·za
When?	Quando?	kwan·do
Where?	Dove?	do·ve
Who?	Chi?	kee
Why?	Perché?	per·ke

I'm sick.
Mi sento male. mee sen·to ma·le

It hurts here.
Mi fa male qui. mee fa ma·le kwee

I'm allergic to ...
Sono allergico/a a ... (m/f) so·no a·ler·jee·ko/a a ...

SHOPPING & SERVICES

I'd like to buy ...
Vorrei comprare ... vo·ray kom·pra·re ...

I'm just looking.
Sto solo guardando. sto so·lo gwar·dan·do

Can I look at it?
Posso dare un'occhiata? po·so da·re oo·no·kya·ta

How much is this?
Quanto costa questo? kwan·to kos·ta kwe·sto

It's too expensive.
È troppo caro/a. (m/f) e tro·po ka·ro/a

Can you lower the price?
Può farmi lo sconto? pwo far·mee lo skon·to

There's a mistake in the bill.
C'è un errore nel conto. che oo·ne·ro·re nel kon·to

ATM	Bancomat	ban·ko·mat
post office	ufficio postale	oo·fee·cho pos·ta·le
tourist office	ufficio del turismo	oo·fee·cho del too·reez·mo

TIME & DATES

What time is it? Che ora è? ke o·ra e

It's one o'clock. È l'una. e loo·na

It's (two) o'clock. Sono le (due). so·no le (doo·e)

Half past (one). (L'una) e mezza. (loo·na) e me·dza

in the morning	di mattina	dee ma·tee·na
in the afternoon	di pomeriggio	dee po·me·ree·jo
in the evening	di sera	dee se·ra

yesterday	ieri	ye·ree
today	oggi	o·jee
tomorrow	domani	do·ma·nee

Monday	lunedì	loo·ne·dee
Tuesday	martedì	mar·te·dee
Wednesday	mercoledì	mer·ko·le·dee
Thursday	giovedì	jo·ve·dee
Friday	venerdì	ve·ner·dee
Saturday	sabato	sa·ba·to
Sunday	domenica	do·me·nee·ka

Numbers

1	uno	oo·no
2	due	doo·e
3	tre	tre
4	quattro	kwa·tro
5	cinque	cheen·kwe
6	sei	say
7	sette	se·te
8	otto	o·to
9	nove	no·ve
10	dieci	dye·chee
20	venti	ven·tee
30	trenta	tren·ta
40	quaranta	kwa·ran·ta
50	cinquanta	cheen·kwan·ta
60	sessanta	se·san·ta
70	settanta	se·tan·ta
80	ottanta	o·tan·ta
90	novanta	no·van·ta
100	cento	chen·to
1000	mille	mee·le

January	gennaio	je·na·yo
February	febbraio	fe·bra·yo
March	marzo	mar·tso
April	aprile	a·pree·le
May	maggio	ma·jo
June	giugno	joo·nyo
July	luglio	loo·lyo
August	agosto	a·gos·to
September	settembre	se·tem·bre
October	ottobre	o·to·bre
November	novembre	no·vem·bre
December	dicembre	dee·chem·bre

TRANSPORT

Public Transport

At what time does the ... leave/arrive?	A che ora parte/ arriva ...?	a ke o·ra par·te/ a·ree·va ...
boat	la nave	la na·ve
bus	l'autobus	low·to·boos
ferry	il traghetto	eel tra·ge·to
metro	la metropolitana	la me·tropo·lee·ta·na
plane	l'aereo	la·e·re·o
train	il treno	eel tre·no

... ticket	un biglietto ...	oon bee·lye·to
one-way	di sola andata	dee so·la an·da·ta
return	di andata e ritorno	dee an·da·ta e ree·tor·no
bus stop	fermata dell'autobus	fer·ma·ta del ow·to·boos
platform	binario	bee·na·ryo
ticket office	biglietteria	bee·lye·te·ree·a
timetable	orario	o·ra·ryo
train station	stazione ferroviaria	sta·tsyo·ne fe·ro·vyar·ya

Does it stop at ...?
Si ferma a ...?   see fer·ma a ...

Please tell me when we get to ...
Mi dica per favore   mee dee·ka per fa·vo·re
quando arriviamo a ...   kwan·do a·ree·vya·mo a ...

I want to get off here.
Voglio scendere qui.   vo·lyo shen·de·re kwee

Driving & Cycling

I'd like to hire a/an ...	Vorrei noleggiare un/una ... (m/f)	vo·ray no·le·ja·re oon/oo·na ...
4WD	fuoristrada (m)	fwo·ree·stra·da
bicycle	bicicletta (f)	bee·chee·kle·ta
car	macchina (f)	ma·kee·na
motorbike	moto (f)	mo·to
bicycle pump	pompa della bicicletta	pom·pa de·la bee·chee·kle·ta
child seat	seggiolino	se·jo·lee·no
helmet	casco	kas·ko
mechanic	meccanico	me·ka·nee·ko
petrol/gas	benzina	ben·dzee·na
service station	stazione di servizio	sta·tsyo·ne dee ser·vee·tsyo

Is this the road to ...?
Questa strada porta a ...?   kwe·sta stra·da por·ta a ...

(How long) Can I park here?
(Per quanto tempo)   (per kwan·to tem·po)
Posso parcheggiare qui?   po·so par·ke·ja·re kwee

The car/motorbike has broken down (at ...).
La macchina/moto si è   la ma·kee·na/mo·to see e
guastata (a ...).   gwas·ta·ta (a ...)

I have a flat tyre.
Ho una gomma bucata.   o oo·na go·ma boo·ka·ta

I've run out of petrol.
Ho esaurito la   o e·zow·ree·to la
benzina.   ben·dzee·na

AAST – Azienda Autonoma di Soggiorno e Turismo (tourist office)

ACI – Automobile Club d'Italia (Italian automobile club)

acqua – water

agnello – lamb

agriturismo – farm-stay accommodation

albergo – hotel (up to five stars)

albergo diffuso – hotel spread over more than one site, typically in the historic centre of a town

alimentari – food shops

alto – high

anfiteatro – amphitheatre

aperitivo – aperitif

aragosta – lobster

ARST – Azienda Regionale Sarda Trasporti (state bus company)

bancomat – ATM

benzina – petrol

benzina senza piombo – unleaded petrol

borgo – ancient town or village

bottarga – mullet roe

burrida – dogfish with pine nuts, parsley and garlic

calamari – squid

camera – room

campanile – bell tower

cappella – chapel

capretto – kid (goat)

carabinieri – military police (see *polizia*)

carciofi – artichokes

Carnevale – carnival period between Epiphany and Lent

castello – castle

cattedrale – cathedral

cena – evening meal

centro – centre

centro storico – literally 'historical centre'; old town

chiesa – church

colazione – breakfast

comune – equivalent to a municipality or county; town or city council

coperto – cover charge

cornetto – croissant

corso – main street, avenue

cortile – courtyard

cotto/a – cooked

cozze – mussels

CTS – Centro Turistico Studentesco e Giovanile (student/youth travel agency)

culurgiones – ravioli filled with cheese and/or potato

cumbessias – pilgrims' lodgings found in courtyards around churches, traditionally the scene of religious festivities (of up to nine days' duration) in honour of a particular saint

cupola – dome

digestivo – after-dinner liqueur

dolci – sweets

domus de janas – literally 'fairy house'; ancient tomb cut into rock

duomo – cathedral

ENIT – Ente Nazionale Italiano per il Turismo (Italian state tourist office)

enoteca – wine bar or wine shop

farmacia – pharmacy

festa – festival

fiume – (main) river

fontana – fountain

formaggio – cheese

fregola – a large couscous-like grain

fritto/a – fried

frutti di mare – seafood

funghi – mushrooms

gasolio – diesel

gelateria – ice-cream shop

giudicato – province; in medieval times Sardinia was divided into the Giudicato of Cagliari, Giudicato of Logudoro, Giudicato of Gallura and Giudicato of Arborea

golfo – gulf

grotta – cave

guardia medica – emergency call-out doctor service

insalata – salad

isola – island

lago – lake

largo – (small) square

latte – milk

libreria – bookshop

lido – managed section of beach

lungomare – seafront road; promenade

macchia – Mediterranean scrub

malloreddus – semolina dumplings

mare – sea

mattanza – literally 'slaughter'; the annual tuna catch in southwest Sardinia

miele – honey

mirto – myrtle berries; also a liqueur distilled from myrtle berries

monte – mountain, mount

muggine – mullet

municipio – town hall

muristenes – see *cumbessias*

Natale – Christmas

nuraghe – Bronze Age stone towers and fortified settlements

oratorio – oratory

ospedale – hospital

palazzo – palace; a large building of any type, including an apartment block

panadas – savoury pie

pane – bread

panino – bread roll

parco – park

Pasqua – Easter

passeggiata – traditional evening stroll

pasticceria – pastry shop

pensione – small hotel, often with board

piazza – square

pietà – literally 'pity or compassion'; sculpture, drawing or painting of the dead Christ supported by the Madonna

pinacoteca – art gallery

polizia – police

polpo – octopus

poltrona – literally 'armchair'; airline-type chair on a ferry

ponte – bridge

porceddu – suckling pig

porto – port

pronto soccorso – first aid, casualty ward

prosciutto – cured ham

questura – police station

rio – secondary river

riserva naturale – nature reserve

ristorante – restaurant

sagra – festival, usually dedicated to one culinary item, such as funghi (mushrooms), wine etc

saline – saltpans

santuario – sanctuary, often with a country chapel

scalette – 'little stairs' (as in Scalette di Santa Chiara, a steep stairway up into Cagliari's Il Castello district)

sebadas – fried pastry with ricotta

seppia – cuttlefish

servizio – service fee

spiaggia – beach

stagno – lagoon

stazione marittima – ferry terminal

stazzo/u – farmstead in the Gallura region

strada – street, road

tavola calda – canteen-style eatery

teatro – theatre

tempio – temple

terme – thermal baths

tholos – name used to describe the conical tower of a *nuraghe*

tomba di gigante – literally 'giant's tomb'; ancient mass grave

tonnara – tuna-processing plant

tonno – tuna

tophet – sacred Phoenician or Carthaginian burial ground for children and babies

torre – tower

trippa – tripe

via – street, road

viale – avenue

vicolo – alley, alleyway

vino (rosso/bianco) – wine (red/white)

vongole – clams

zucchero – sugar

zuppa – soup or broth

behind the scenes

SEND US YOUR FEEDBACK

We love to hear from travellers – your comments keep us on our toes and help make our books better. Our well-travelled team reads every word on what you loved or loathed about this book. Although we cannot reply individually to postal submissions, we always guarantee that your feedback goes straight to the appropriate authors, in time for the next edition. Each person who sends us information is thanked in the next edition – and the most useful submissions are rewarded with a free book.

Visit **lonelyplanet.com/contact** to submit your updates and suggestions or to ask for help. Our award-winning website also features inspirational travel stories, news and discussions.

Note: We may edit, reproduce and incorporate your comments in Lonely Planet products such as guidebooks, websites and digital products, so let us know if you don't want your comments reproduced or your name acknowledged. For a copy of our privacy policy visit lonelyplanet.com/privacy.

OUR READERS

Many thanks to the travellers who used the last edition and wrote to us with helpful hints, useful advice and interesting anecdotes:
Martin Åberg, Peter and Anne, Michael Bendon, Jan Bryla, Silvana Cao, Deborah Toppan, Iris Elliott, Elisa Guardiani, Kerstin Hartinger, Julienne Ingram, Shamiran Kiriakos, George Laszlo, Debbie Mcneil, Katie Mitchell, Rob Montanari, Kieran O Sullivan, Liz Paxton, Matthias Quaas, Michael Richter, Kees Rietdijk, Yu Sheng Chou, Adriana Thomas, Albert Vila, Jonathan Wickens.

AUTHOR THANKS
Kerry Christiani

Mille grazie to Tonino Tosciri and his sister Maria Angela in Baunei for their friendship and insight. Thanks too to outdoor pros Peter and Anne at The Lemon House in Lotzorai, to climbing expert Corrado Conca for his *arrampicata* tips, and to Maria Antonietta Goddi at Durke, Cagliari, for sweet inspiration. A special thanks also to coauthor Vesna Maric, commissioning editor Joe Bindloss and the in-house Lonely Planet team. Finally, big thanks to my husband and brilliant travel companion, Andy Christiani.

Vesna Maric

My thanks go to Rafael and Frida for coming along, and a *gracias* to Susana. *Velika hvala* to my mother for write-up babysitting. Thanks to Joe Bindloss for giving me the opportunity to work on the guide, and to Kerry Christiani for being a kind and helpful coordinating author. In Sardinia, thank you to all those helpful people who made life easier, namely Francesca Vanoni Pugni and Carla Cani for their kindness. Big thanks to Alessandra and Simone for making it all the way from Sicily and meeting up. In memory of baby Sveva.

ACKNOWLEDGMENTS

Climate map data adapted from Peel MC, Finlayson BL & McMahon TA (2007) 'Updated World Map of the Köppen-Geiger Climate Classification', *Hydrology and Earth System Sciences*, 11, 163344.

Cover photograph: Tourists swimming in waters of Cala Mariolu in the Golfo di Orosei. Dallas Stribley/Lonely Planet Images.

Many of the images in this guide are available for licensing from Lonely Planet Images: www.lonelyplanetimages.com.

THIS BOOK

This 4th edition of Lonely Planet's *Sardinia* guidebook was researched and written by Kerry Christiani and Vesna Maric. The previous three editions of this guidebook were written and researched by Duncan Garwood, Paula Hardy and Damien Simonis. This guidebook was commissioned in Lonely Planet's London office, and produced by the following:

Commissioning Editor Joe Bindloss

Coordinating Editor Kate Whitfield

Coordinating Cartographer Csanad Csutoros

Coordinating Layout Designer Frank Deim

Managing Editor Brigitte Ellemor

Managing Cartographer Mandy Sierp

Managing Layout Designer Chris Girdler

Assisting Editors Karyn Noble, Kristin Odijk, Victoria Harrison, Paul Harding, Jackey Coyle

Assisting Cartographers Jolyon Philcox, Sonya Brooke, Jennifer Johnston

Cover Research Naomi Parker

Internal Image Research Aude Vauconsant

Language Content Annelies Mertens

Thanks to Sasha Baskett, Ryan Evans, Suki Gear, Jocelyn Harewood, Jane Hart, Gina Tsarouhas, Gerard Walker

NOTES

NOTES

NOTES

index

how to use this book

These symbols will help you find the listings you want:

◉ Sights	☞ Tours	⬤ Drinking
🏖 Beaches	✳ Festivals & Events	☆ Entertainment
🏃 Activities	⛱ Sleeping	🛍 Shopping
🎓 Courses	✗ Eating	ⓘ Information/Transport

Look out for these icons:

TOP CHOICE	Our author's recommendation
FREE	No payment required
🌿	A green or sustainable option

Our authors have nominated these places as demonstrating a strong commitment to sustainability – for example by supporting local communities and producers, operating in an environmentally friendly way, or supporting conservation projects.

These symbols give you the vital information for each listing:

☎ Telephone Numbers	⊛ Wi-Fi Access	⊟ Bus
☺ Opening Hours	⊠ Swimming Pool	⊞ Ferry
P Parking	✔ Vegetarian Selection	Ⓜ Metro
⊜ Nonsmoking	⊡ English-Language Menu	Ⓢ Subway
❄ Air-Conditioning	⊞ Family-Friendly	⊖ London Tube
@ Internet Access	⊡ Pet-Friendly	⊟ Tram
		⊟ Train

Reviews are organised by author preference.

Map Legend

Sights
- ◉ Beach
- ⊕ Buddhist
- ⊕ Castle
- ✚ Christian
- ⊕ Hindu
- ◑ Islamic
- ✡ Jewish
- ❶ Monument
- 🏛 Museum/Gallery
- ⊗ Ruin
- ⊕ Winery/Vineyard
- ⊗ Zoo
- ◎ Other Sight

Activities, Courses & Tours
- ⊝ Diving/Snorkelling
- ⊕ Canoeing/Kayaking
- ⊕ Skiing
- ⊕ Surfing
- ⊕ Swimming/Pool
- ⊕ Walking
- ⊕ Windsurfing
- ✚ Other Activity/Course/Tour

Sleeping
- ⊟ Sleeping
- ⊕ Camping

Eating
- ✗ Eating

Drinking
- ⊜ Drinking
- ⊜ Cafe

Entertainment
- ✪ Entertainment

Shopping
- ⊜ Shopping

Information
- ⊠ Post Office
- ⓘ Tourist Information

Transport
- ⊕ Airport
- ⊗ Border Crossing
- ⊟ Bus
- ⊕ Cable Car/Funicular
- ⊕ Cycling
- ⊖ Ferry
- Ⓜ Metro
- ⊟ Monorail
- P Parking
- Ⓢ S-Bahn
- ⊜ Taxi
- ⊟ Train/Railway
- ⊟ Tram
- ⊖ Tube Station
- Ⓤ U-Bahn
- • Other Transport

Routes
- Tollway
- Freeway
- Primary
- Secondary
- Tertiary
- Lane
- Unsealed Road
- Plaza/Mall
- Steps
- ⊹ ☰ Tunnel
- Pedestrian Overpass
- Walking Tour
- Walking Tour Detour
- Path

Boundaries
- International
- State/Province
- Disputed
- Regional/Suburb
- Marine Park
- Cliff
- Wall

Population
- ⊕ Capital (National)
- ◎ Capital (State/Province)
- ⊙ City/Large Town
- ⊙ Town/Village

Geographic
- ⊕ Hut/Shelter
- ⊕ Lighthouse
- ⊕ Lookout
- ▲ Mountain/Volcano
- ⊕ Oasis
- ⊕ Park
-)(Pass
- ⊕ Picnic Area
- ⊕ Waterfall

Hydrography
- River/Creek
- Intermittent River
- Swamp/Mangrove
- Reef
- Canal
- Water
- Dry/Salt/Intermittent Lake
- Glacier

Areas
- Beach/Desert
- + + + Cemetery (Christian)
- × × × Cemetery (Other)
- Park/Forest
- Sportsground
- Sight (Building)
- Top Sight (Building)

OUR STORY

A beat-up old car, a few dollars in the pocket and a sense of adventure. In 1972 that's all Tony and Maureen Wheeler needed for the trip of a lifetime – across Europe and Asia overland to Australia. It took several months, and at the end – broke but inspired – they sat at their kitchen table writing and stapling together their first travel guide, *Across Asia on the Cheap*. Within a week they'd sold 1500 copies. Lonely Planet was born.

Today, Lonely Planet has offices in Melbourne, London and Oakland, with more than 600 staff and writers. We share Tony's belief that 'a great guidebook should do three things: inform, educate and amuse'.

OUR WRITERS

Kerry Christiani

Coordinating Author; Cagliari & the Sarrabus, Olbia, the Costa Smeralda & the Gallura, Nuoro & the East Kerry's relationship with Sardinia began one hazy post-graduation summer when, craving a little *dolce vita,* she embarked on a grand tour of Italy in a 1960s bubble caravan. She's still as taken with the island's gorgeous beaches, high-altitude hiking and culinary oddities today as she was back then. Born in the UK and based in Germany's Black Forest, Kerry is an award-winning travel writer. Her itchy feet have taken her to six continents, inspiring articles for magazines such as *Lonely Planet* and BBC's *Olive*, and some 20 guidebooks, including Lonely Planet guides to Italy, Germany, Austria, Switzerland and France. See her latest work at www.kerrychristiani.com.

Vesna Maric

Iglesias & the Southwest, Oristano & the West, Alghero & the Northwest Vesna's love of Mediterranean islands was enhanced by the spring flowers and tranquil virgin beaches of Sardinia. She researched the island's western half with her partner and one-year-old daughter, and can vouch for the incredible child-friendliness of the Sardinians.

Sardinia.   MAR   2012

Published by Lonely Planet Publications Pty Ltd
ABN 36 005 607 983
4th edition – Jan 2012
ISBN 978 1 74179 586 8
© Lonely Planet 2012   Photographs © as indicated 2012
10 9 8 7 6 5 4 3 2 1
Printed in China